Human Rights in International Relations

David Forsythe's successful textbook provides an authoritative overview of the place of human rights in international politics. A central paradox summarizes the book: while human rights is more firmly established in international law than ever before, the actual protection of human rights faces increased challenges. The book focuses on four central themes: the resilience of the human rights norm, the importance of "soft" law, the key role of non-governmental organizations, and the changing nature of state sovereignty. Human rights standards are examined according to global, regional, and national levels of analysis with a separate chapter dedicated to transnational corporations. This third edition has been updated to reflect recent events, notably the persistence of both militant Islam and tough counterterrorism policies, the growing power of China and other states not entirely sympathetic to many human rights, and various economic difficulties which highlight the costs associated with a serious attention to human rights. Containing chapter-by-chapter guides to further reading and discussion questions, this book will be of interest to undergraduate and graduate students of human rights, and their teachers.

DAVID P. FORSYTHE is Emeritus Professor at the University of Nebraska, Lincoln, where he was Charles J. Mach Distinguished Professor of Political Science. He is the author of numerous International Relations titles, including *The Humanitarians: The International Committee of the Red Cross* (2005). He is the general editor of *Encyclopedia of Human Rights* (2009, five vols.), which won the Dartmouth Medal as the best reference work published in the United States that year.

Themes in International Relations

This new series of textbooks aims to provide students with authoritative surveys of central topics in the study of International Relations. Intended for upper level undergraduates and graduates, the books will be concise, accessible, and comprehensive. Each volume will examine the main theoretical and empirical aspects of the subject concerned, and its relation to wider debates in International Relations, and will also include chapter-by-chapter guides to further reading and discussion questions.

Human Rights in International Relations

Third Edition

David P. Forsythe

CAMBRIDGE
UNIVERSITY PRESS

CAMBRIDGE UNIVERSITY PRESS
Cambridge, New York, Melbourne, Madrid, Cape Town,
Singapore, São Paulo, Delhi, Tokyo, Mexico City

Cambridge University Press
The Edinburgh Building, Cambridge CB2 8RU, UK

Published in the United States of America by Cambridge University Press,
New York

www.cambridge.org
Information on this title: www.cambridge.org/9781107015678

First published 2000
Second edition 2006
Fourth printing 2008

Third edition 2012

A catalog record for this publication is available from the British Library

Library of Congress Cataloging in Publication data
Forsythe, David P., 1941–
Human rights in international relations / David P. Forsythe. – 3rd ed.
    p.   cm. – (Themes in international relations)
Includes index.
1. Human rights.   2. International relations.   I. Title.
K3240.F67   2012
341.4′8 – dc23   2011043833

ISBN 978-1-107-01567-8 hardback
ISBN 978-1-107-62984-4 paperback

Contents

Preface to the third edition

My preface to the first edition explains the objectives of this book, and they have not changed. My preface to the second edition explains the considerations that guide revisions, and they have not changed either. As before, revisions seek both to clarify the presentation and to incorporate recent developments. In particular I have now added some brief case studies to provide more specificity to certain rights in political context. My overall approach, hence the structure of the book, remains unchanged.

From the origins of this work as a gleam in the author's eye, the tension between personal rights and the workings of the state system of world affairs has been highlighted. If anything, the new edition emphasizes this tension even more. It is now even clearer that when states perceive a serious threat to their interests, above all their physical security, it becomes more difficult to get serious attention to human rights, especially the rights of those perceived as enemies. Moreover, when ruling elites elevate perceived challenges to the level of existential threats, sometimes to the nation but often just to the nature of their rule, serious attention to human rights suffers. Complicating analysis is that fact that some non-state actors see the existing situation as so objectionable that unrestricted violence is justified. This then feeds into a downward spiral of animosity and violence that tends to push human rights to the margins of public policy. Pursuit of victory in total war is not a mind set conducive to human rights.

Still, such is the power of the idea of human rights, defined to include humanitarian law, that states continue to profess their commitment to at least some of those standards, even as their record of compliance is often far short of what it should be. And armed non-state actors who attack civilians and kill prisoners face an uphill journey as they try to explain why they should be considered the new legitimate elite with the right to rule. The Arab Spring of 2011, with its demand for more democracy and other human rights, was a rejection of the militancy of Al Qaeda and other Islamist violent actors. Al Qaeda and its allies were not completely spent forces, but they were mostly irrelevant to major developments in Tunisia, Egypt, and many other places.

After the demise of European communism some thought the world had entered a golden age of human rights. Forces such as militant Islam and the globalized but impersonal for-profit corporation, however, showed that the promised land remained distant. But the story is yet to be concluded, and the competing tensions are yet to be fully resolved. This third edition is an attempt to indicate the contemporary synthesis between clashing trends over human rights.

As the cliché has it, one thing is perfectly clear. Not only in the West but around the world the teaching of human rights in schools and universities has increased. There are now more scholarly journals focused on human rights, and more articles are being published on human rights in disciplines such as political science. Even in places such as China and Iran, human rights is now a subject of lively and officially sanctioned discussion. This gives some reason for long-term optimism. In the meantime, I sadly note the passing of some of those educators who led the way in this domain, such as Louis Henkin and Richard P. Claude in the United States, Kevin Boyle in the United Kingdom, and Peter R. Baehr in the Netherlands. Three of the four were affected by their family origins whether in Belarus, Northern Ireland, or Nazified Berlin. The lives of each of these three demonstrated that repression can produce human rights progress over time through personal commitment. Surely it is now evident that it is precisely human wrongs that lead to the demand for more practice of human rights, and that this dynamic has yet to run its course. (This is a good spot to refer the reader to Richard Pierre Claude, "Right to Education and Human Rights Education," in David P. Forsythe, ed., *Encyclopedia of Human Rights* [New York: Oxford University Press, 2009], vol. II, 97–107.)

As with earlier editions I had the help of many persons who called material to my attention or who were kind enough to read passages for accuracy and clarity: Danny Braaten, Jack Donnelly, Kathleen Fallon, Barb Flanagan, John Gruhl, Jorge Heine, Courtney Hillebrecht, Rhoda Howard-Hassmann, Mark Janis, Alice Kang, Bert Lockwood, Peter Malcontent, Jay Ovsiovitch, Scott Pegg, David Rapkin, David Richards, Bill Schabas, Fusun Turkmen, Andy Wedeman, David Weissbrodt, and Jake Wobig.

As before, the production team at Cambridge University Press was efficient and helpful, especially my editor John Haslam.

DAVID P. FORSYTHE
Summer, 2011

Preface to the second edition

In writing the second edition to this work, I have been initially guided by the old axiom: if it's not broke, don't try to fix it. The response by students and faculty to the first edition has been such, including translation into five foreign languages, that I have left unchanged the basic approach and overall structure of the book. The emphasis remains on the transnational policy making process concerned with internationally recognized human rights. The nine chapters remain the same in subject matter content.

At the same time, the world has not stood still since the first edition was written in the late 1990s. So a number of changes have been made within chapters to account for various developments: the creation of the International Criminal Court, including the selection of its first prosecutor; a renewed debate about international humanitarian law (for human rights in armed conflict) and whether it has become *passé* in an "era of terrorism"; an accelerated debate about "humanitarian intervention" and its possible misuse in places like Iraq; further developments about the mainstreaming of human rights in the United Nations system; an updated evaluation of the multifaceted efforts to link human rights with the behavior of transnational corporations; an ongoing debate about the importance of socioeconomic rights compared to civil-political rights; shifts in US foreign policy since September 11, 2001, which affect many things in international relations, given the great power of that state; and so on.

Sometimes I have restructured chapters rather boldly in the hopes of making analysis more systematic and clear. This is the case particularly in Chapter 4 dealing with international criminal justice and the debate about prosecution of those who have done terrible things, versus other means to the progressive development of a rights-protective society. In the same vein I have added a section to the conclusion to make it more reflective of social science research on human rights.

As was true of the first edition, it is a daunting task to try to provide anything approaching a timely and comprehensive introduction to the subject of internationally recognized human rights. When I was an undergraduate student, I took no classes in human rights – because there weren't any. Now there are many human rights classes in law, political science, philosophy, sociology, anthropology, etc. These reflect the growing attention to the subject, accompanied by a great variety of intriguing perspectives. The law on human rights is further developed, the court cases more numerous, the impact on diplomacy more thorough, the very notion of human rights more pervasive in society, the debates broader. I suppose one should not complain if a certain ideational or normative progress makes even a summary introduction exceedingly difficult. One can legitimately complain, however, about the remaining gap between human rights standards on the one hand, and on the other the human wrongs that are so clearly manifest.

In any event, the second edition seeks to refine the first, without changing drastically what I try to accomplish. I still try to give the reader a reasonably succinct overview of the extent to which the idea of internationally recognized human rights does or does not affect behavior around the world. The target audience comprises university students and the general public, not advanced law students. In this quest I have been greatly aided by the students and colleagues at various institutions who have told me what worked and what did not in the first edition, what was clear and what was not, what was omitted and should be added. I am particularly grateful to Barb Rieffer, Mutuma Ruteere, Collin Sullivan, Jordan Milliken, Evian Littrell, Carrie Heaton, Eric Heinze, Peter R. Baehr, Eva Brems, Mark Janis, Rhoda Howard-Hassmann, Jack Donnelly, Robert Johansen, Bill Schabas, and James Patrick Flood. Richard Claude gave support to my earliest efforts and pushed me into needed changes. To all of them I am very grateful, as well as to the editors and staff and Cambridge University Press who have expressed confidence not only in this work but also in another book I wrote for them in 2004–2005 on the International Committee of the Red Cross. I am especially appreciative of John Haslam and his guidance and support at CUP.

DAVID P. FORSYTHE
Lincoln, September 2005

Preface to the first edition

This book is intended for students interested in international relations. Rather than do a third edition of an earlier work of similar scope and purpose, I decided to start again from scratch. The changes in international relations have been so momentous, with the end of the Cold War and the collapse of European communism, that mere revisions seemed inadequate.

My emphasis is on political and diplomatic processes. I seek in general to show *how and why* human rights standards come into being, impact the notion of sovereignty, become secondary or tertiary to other values and goals, are manipulated for reasons other than advancing human dignity and social justice, and sometimes change behavior to improve the human condition. I use particular legal cases and material situations mainly to demonstrate the policy making processes associated with international human rights. I conceive of law and legal cases as derivative from politics and diplomacy, mostly. I make little attempt to summarize the substantive decisions of particular human rights agencies and courts, other than to give an indication of their general importance or irrelevance. My central objective remains that of giving the reader an overview of decision making processes pertaining to human rights in the context of international relations. I intend to give readers a framework of process, within which, or from which, they can plug in whatever changing particulars seem important.

I seek to show two important trends:
(1) the extent of changes in international relations pertaining to human rights over the second half of the twentieth century, and
(2) how difficult it is to mesh personal human rights, based on the liberal tradition, with the state system dominated as it has been by the realist approach to international relations.

Along the way I repeatedly address the distinction between human rights and humanitarian affairs. Legally and traditionally speaking, human rights pertains to fundamental personal rights in peace, and humanitarian affairs pertains to protecting and assisting victims of war and other victims in exceptional situations. International human rights law and international humanitarian law are different bodies of law, with different histories, and supposedly pertaining to different situations. But in the scrum of international relations, legal categories get blurred. Legal categories sometimes entail distinctions without a difference. Was the situation in Bosnia 1992–1995 an international war, an internal war, both, or neither? Did it matter for practical action on the ground? And Somalia 1992–1995? And Kosovo in 1998–1999? What does the United Nations mean by "complex emergency"? The point I stress is the following: the international community, represented by different actors, is taking an increasing interest in persons in dire straits, whether in peace or war or some mixture of the two. If states cannot maintain a humane order, the international community may take a variety of steps, sometimes referring to human rights, and sometimes to humanitarian law and diplomacy. It is thus important not only to understand the law and diplomacy of human rights, but also – to give a few concrete examples – the Geneva Conventions and Protocols for victims of war, and the International Committee of the Red Cross which is the theoretical and practical guardian of that humanitarian tradition. In other words, I take a broad, practical definition of human rights – including human rights in war and political unrest.

The book is organized according to two concepts that are both useful and imperfect: the idea of levels of analysis; and the idea of organizations that act, or may act, for human rights. As for the first, after an introduction I proceed from the global level (the United Nations), through the regional (in Europe and the Western Hemisphere and Africa), through the national (state foreign policy), to the sub-national (private human rights groups and transnational corporations). This means that I take up global actors like the United Nations and associated international criminal courts; regional organizations such as the Council of Europe, European Union, Organization for Security and Co-operation in Europe, Organization of American States, and Organization of African Unity; state foreign policy in comparative perspective (especially that of the United States); private groups active on human rights (e.g., Amnesty International), relief (e.g., the International Committee of the Red Cross), and development (e.g., Oxfam); and transnational corporations like Nike and Royal Dutch Shell. This structure is useful for organizing an ever-growing body of information into an introductory overview.

The structure is also imperfect. There is nothing magical about four levels of analysis. Other authors have used both more and fewer. Also, one level can intrude into others. The United Nations is made up of state representatives as well as personnel not instructed by states. So in discussing UN action for human rights, one has to deal with state foreign policy. Likewise in analyzing the impact of transnational corporations on human rights, especially on labor rights, one has to talk about both states and traditional human rights advocacy groups like the Lawyers Committee for Human Rights.

There are other actors for human rights besides the ones emphasized in this work. One could just as well have a separate chapter on religious organizations, rather than dealing with them briefly as part of human rights movements entailing traditional advocacy groups like Human Rights Watch. One could well envisage a separate chapter on the communications media and human rights.

Yet given the purpose of this book, viz., to provide an overview of the status of human rights in contemporary international relations, and the limitation on length imposed by the publisher, the combination of levels of analysis and actors allows a reasonably accurate survey. This is, after all, an introductory overview. It does not pretend to be the definitive word on international human rights.

I have also tried to pull together in this work much of my thinking on international human rights from the past thirty years. If the reader finds that I cite my own previous publications, it is not because I am thrilled to see my name in the reference notes. Like some other authors who have worked in a field for some time, I have tried to put in one publication, in an integrated way, my cumulative – and sometimes revised – thoughts on the subject.

A number of persons have helped me refine my thinking along the long, unusually tortuous path to publication of this book. None has been more helpful than Jack Donnelly, although some might think he and I have been competitors in writing for university students of human rights. I published the first classroom book on the subject for political science students, he then came out with a similar book that pretty much preempted my second edition, and now I presume this book will at least compete with his recent edition. But he assigned my first work to his students, I praised and assigned his parallel publication to my students, and I am pleased to acknowledge his helpful role in this work. I am glad to say I think of Jack more as a colleague with shared interests than a competitor.

Special thanks should also go to Peter Baehr who invited me to be a Visiting Fellow at the Research School for the Study of Human Rights based at the University of Utrecht in the Netherlands, which allowed me an excellent opportunity to work on this project. Peter also gave me insightful comments on parts of the book. The University of Nebraska–Lincoln, especially my Dean, Brian Foster, was flexible in accommodating my stay in Utrecht. I should also like to thank the Graduate Institute of International Studies of the University of Geneva for inviting me to be a Visiting Professor there, where the final revisions were made. Danny Warner was most helpful in arranging my renewed contacts in a city closely associated with international human rights.

I would like to acknowledge those, in addition to Professors Donnelly and Baehr, who read all or parts of this work in manuscript form and whose comments led to helpful revisions: William P. Avery, David R. Rapkin, Jeffery Spinner-Halev, and Claude Welch.

A special word of thanks goes to Ms. Barbara Ann J. Rieffer, who was my graduate assistant for part of the time this work was in preparation. She helped enormously not only with technical matters but in commenting on substance and thereby helping with the task of revisions.

Ms. Monica Mason was of great assistance in the preparation of final copy.

Mr. John Haslam was a most understanding editor at Cambridge University Press, despite the fact that events beyond my control delayed the publication of the manuscript more than is my custom.

Part I

The foundations

1 Introduction: human rights in international relations

Human rights are widely considered to be those fundamental moral rights of the person that are necessary for a life with human dignity. Human rights are thus means to a greater social end, and it is the legal system that tells us at any given point in time which rights are considered most fundamental in society. Even if human rights are thought to be inalienable, a moral attribute of persons that public authorities should not contravene, rights still have to be identified – that is, constructed – by human beings and codified in the legal system.[1] While human rights have a long history in theory and even in spasmodic practice, it was the American and French revolutions of the eighteenth century that sought to create national polities based on broadly shared human rights. Despite the rhetoric of universality, however, human rights remained essentially a national matter, to be accepted or not, until 1945 when they were recognized in global international law.

This book is about the evolution and status of human rights in international relations at the start of the twenty-first century. Thus this extended essay is about the effort to liberalize international relations – to make international relations conform to the liberal prescription for the good society. In the classical liberal view, the good society is based on respect for the equality and autonomy of individuals, which is assured through the recognition and application of the fundamental legal rights of the person. In this book liberalism is a synonym for attention to personal rights. But in international relations it has been widely believed that the state, not the individual, is the basic unit. And the core principle has been said to be state sovereignty and non-interference in the domestic affairs of states. In this book realism is a synonym for attention to state interests – foremost among which is security – and state power. The subject of international human rights thus projects liberalism into a realist

---

[1] Jack Donnelly, "The Social Construction of International Human Rights," in Tim Dunne and Nicholas J. Wheeler, eds., *Human Rights in Global Politics* (Cambridge: Cambridge University Press, 1999), 71–102.

3

world – a world dominated for several centuries by states and their collective interests.[2]

To paraphrase Charles Dickens, human rights in modern international relations represents both the best of times and the worst of times.[3] During the half-century after World War II, truly revolutionary developments occurred in the legal theory and diplomatic practice of internationally recognized human rights. Human rights language was written into the United Nations Charter, which was not the case with the Covenant of the League of Nations. Member states of the United Nations negotiated an international bill of rights, which was then supplemented by other treaties and declarations codifying that human beings had certain fundamental legal rights that were to be respected. By the first decade of the twenty-first century more than 160 states (United Nations membership was 192 in 2010) had formally adhered to the International Covenant on Civil and Political Rights and the companion International Covenant on Economic, Social, and Cultural Rights. Some regional developments were even more impressive. The Council of Europe (made up of forty-seven states in 2010) manifested not only a regional convention on civil and political rights, widely accepted in that region, but also an international court to adjudicate disputes arising under that treaty. The Western Hemisphere was also characterized by a regional treaty on human rights and a supranational court to give binding judgments. The 1949 Geneva Conventions were formally accepted by all states; they enshrined the view that certain personal protections were to be respected even by parties engaged in armed conflict. In the fall of 1993 the UN General Assembly approved the creation of a High Commissioner for Human Rights. In the mid-1990s the UN Security Council created international criminal courts to try individuals for violations of the laws of war, genocide, and crimes against humanity in the former Yugoslavia and Rwanda, thus rejuvenating international criminal responsibility after the Nuremberg and Tokyo trials of the 1940s. In the summer of 1998 a diplomatic conference in Rome approved the statute for a standing international criminal court with jurisdiction similar to the two *ad hoc* courts. In 2005 a United Nations summit meeting affirmed the principle of the responsibility to protect (R2P). Henceforth, while sovereign states had the primary responsibility for protecting human rights in their jurisdictions, if states

---

[2] For an excellent discussion of varieties of liberalism and realism, see Michael W. Doyle, *Ways of War and Peace* (New York: Norton, 1997), especially 41–48 and 205–213.

[3] Lynn Miller, *World Order: Power and Values in International Politics*, 3rd edn. (Boulder: Westview, 1994), ch. 1.

proved unwilling or unable to prevent gross violations, outside parties had the responsibility to become involved.

Other developments also indicated the central point that human rights was no longer a matter necessarily or always within state domestic jurisdiction. In principle, states were to answer to the international community for their treatment of individuals. International relations regularly entailed not only subjects like war and trade, but also human rights. Human rights had been internationalized, and at least some attention to internationally recognized rights had become routinized. International relations involved aspects of governance in the sense of public management of policy questions.[4] Attention to human rights was part of this international governance. Concerns about the equal value, freedom, and welfare of individuals had long affected many national constitutions and much domestic public policy. From 1945 those same concerns about individual autonomy and respect and welfare also began to affect international relations in important ways – regardless of whether the distribution of power was bipolar, multipolar, or unipolar.[5]

The other side of the coin, however, merits summary attention as well. Perhaps no other situation captures so well the inhumanity that occurs in the world as the famine in China between 1958 and 1962, induced by Mao's regime, that claimed approximately 30 million lives.[6] Not only did the international community not respond, but also many outsiders even denied that a catastrophe of major proportion was occurring or had occurred. If one judges events by number of human lives lost, Mao's famine made him a greater mass murderer than either Hitler or Stalin. The twentieth century, with its record of mass murder and mass misery, was plainly not a good era for the practice of liberal values in many ways. It has been estimated that some 35 million persons were killed in armed conflict during the twentieth century; but perhaps 150–170 million persons were killed by their own governments through political murder or mass misery that could have been ameliorated.[7] The journalist David Rieff was quite perceptive when he wrote that the twentieth century, by

---

[4] James N. Rosenau and Ernst-Otto Czempiel, eds., *Governance Without Government: Order and Change in World Politics* (Cambridge: Cambridge University Press, 1992).

[5] Lea Brilmayer, *American Hegemony: Political Morality in a One-Superpower World* (New Haven: Yale University Press, 1994).

[6] For an introduction, see Andrew Wedeman, "China: The Famine of the 1960s," in David P. Forsythe, ed., *Encyclopedia of Human Rights* (New York: Oxford University Press, 2009), vol. I, 321–328. See further Jasper Becker, *Hungary Ghosts: China's Secret Famine* (London: J. Murray, 1996).

[7] R. J. Rummel, *Death by Government* (Somerset, NJ: Transaction Publishers, 1996).

comparison to those that came before, had the best norms and the worst realities.[8]

Even after the collapse of European communism and the demise of communist economics in other places like China and Vietnam, a number of persons embraced the traditional view that international relations remained a dangerous game, and that those who wanted decisive international action for human rights were naively optimistic.[9] In the post-Cold War world, the rise of Islamic jihadists – or militant Islamists if one prefers – seemed to confirm this dark view of the perpetual human condition. Thus the end of the Cold War did not mean the demise of "realists" who argued that pursuit of human rights in international relations had to take a back seat to the self-interested pursuits of the territorial state. It was ironic but nevertheless true that democratic realists like Henry Kissinger, however much they might be philosophical liberals at home in their support for democracy and human rights, were prepared to sacrifice foreign rights and foreign democracy to advance the interests of their state. Democratic societies surely had a collective right to defend themselves. The rub came in whether a democratic society should sacrifice the human rights of others to advance its own security and prosperity. Even commentators sympathetic to universal human rights agreed that anarchical international relations, without central government, meant that it was not easy to interject human rights considerations into the small policy space left over from intense national competition.[10]

This book, focusing on human rights in international relations since World War II, will present an analysis of competing liberal and realist perspectives. It will also chart the enormous gap between legal theory and political behavior, as public authorities both endorsed human rights standards and systematically violated – or failed to correct violations of – the newly emergent norms. The following pages will explain why legal and diplomatic progress transpired, analyzing both moral and expediential influences. It will also outline major sources of opposition to the consolidation of the legal-diplomatic revolution. The analysis will hence trace the successes and failures of international action for human rights, with the latter being frequently more visible than the former. Along the

---

[8] *A Bed for the Night: Humanitarianism in Crisis* (New York: Simon & Schuster, 2002), 70.

[9] E.g., John Mearsheimer, "Disorder Restored," in Graham Allison and Gregory Treverton, eds., *Rethinking America's Security: Beyond Cold War to New World Order* (New York: Norton, 1992), 213–237.

[10] Stanley Hoffmann, *Duties Beyond Borders: On the Limits and Possibilities of Ethical International Politics* (Syracuse: Syracuse University Press, 1981).

way we will pay attention to critiques of liberalism other than realism, such as some versions of feminism and Marxism.

The long-term vision that emerges from the pages that follow is guardedly optimistic, even if the short-term balance sheet is rather pessimistic. We should keep in mind that contemporary international relations is characterized by much turbulence, with ample evidence of contradictory findings and trends.[11] Nevertheless, for pragmatic liberals such as the author who regard international human rights as good and proper, but whose application must be matched to contextual realities thus leading to difficult policy choices, the twenty-first century holds the promise that it could be better than the twentieth. Like other observers, but for different reasons, I am cautiously optimistic about a liberal world order in the long term.[12] I hold to this view even after the events of September 11, 2001, which supposedly ushered in an era of terrorism, leading to tough counterterrorism policies by many states. I believe that the future of human rights in international relations is not predetermined by structural (meaning fundamental or systemic) factors but depends on policy choice by public authorities. In the light of what social scientists call the agent–structure problematique, I believe that agents have some freedom of choice even while structures cannot be discounted.

In addressing this subject, one has to admit that the topic of human rights in international relations is too big and complex for one macro-thesis – aside from a guardedly optimistic if long-term interpretation about the evolution of liberal ideas. Four smaller themes, however, permeate the pages that follow. The first is that international concern with human rights is here to stay. The second is that one should appreciate human rights as important and pervasive soft law, not just the occasional hard law of court pronouncements. The third is that private parties merit extensive attention, not just public authorities. The fourth is that the notion of state sovereignty is undergoing fundamental change, the "final" form of which is difficult to discern. But, as never before, to be "sovereign" entails the duty to protect human rights.

Human rights as end of history?

There is no reasonable prospect of a return to the international relations of, say, the early nineteenth century. As mentioned above, and as will

---

[11] James N. Rosenau, *Turbulence in World Politics: A Theory of Change and Continuity* (Princeton: Princeton University Press, 1990).

[12] Max Singer and Aaron Wildavsky, *The Real World Order: Zones of Peace, Zones of Turmoil*, 2nd edn. (Chatham, NJ: Chatham House Publishers, 1996).

be shown in some detail in Chapters 2 and 3, human rights standards and basic diplomatic practices have been institutionalized in international relations.[13] The first and most simple explanation for this is that there are now so many treaties, declarations, and agencies dealing with internationally recognized human rights that especially the last fifty years of international interactions cannot be undone. But there are deeper and more interesting explanations, some accepted, some debated.

Second and relatedly, western power has made a difference. Liberal democracies still constitute the most important coalition in international relations. The affluent liberal democracies which comprise the core of the Organization for Economic Cooperation and Development (OECD) constitute not only a caucus or interest group. These states also exercise considerable military, economic, and diplomatic power. They constitute the current motor to a process that has been going on for several centuries: the westernization of international relations.[14] In general, these states and the non-governmental actors based within them have been introducing human rights into world affairs especially since 1945. The globalization of the western version of liberalism has been going on for some time, especially when one understands that globalization pertains to social as well as economic issues.

If the Axis powers had won World War II or if the communist alliance had won the Cold War, international relations would be different than it is today – and much less supportive of human rights. In broader retrospective, if conservative Islamic actors had proved dominant over the past four centuries and not western ones, human rights would not have fared so well. I do not mean that each liberal democracy has been genuinely supportive of every human rights issue that arose in international relations. Clearly that was not the case. France and the United States, the two western states most prone to present themselves to the rest of the world as a universal model for human rights, have compiled a quite mixed record on the practice of human rights in international relations. France actively supported various repressive regimes within its former African colonies, even in the 1990s after the demise of Soviet-led communism. During the Algerian war of 1954–1962 it operated a torture bureau as part of its military structure. The United States, to put it kindly, did not always interest itself in various individual freedoms in Central America during much of the Cold War. In places like Guatemala, Nicaragua,

---

[13] David P. Forsythe, "The United Nations and Human Rights at Fifty: An Incremental but Incomplete Revolution," *Global Governance*, 1, 3 (September 1995), 297–318.

[14] Theodore H. Von Laue, *The World Revolution of Westernization: The Twentieth Century in Global Perspective* (New York: Oxford University Press, 1987).

and El Salvador Washington was indirectly responsible for many political killings and other forms of repression. It is quite clear that during the Cold War, the democratic West, to protect its own human rights, supported the denial of many human rights in many parts of the world many times. It has proved all too possible for liberal democracies at home to manifest less than liberal foreign policies abroad.

But a larger point remains valid. Dominant international norms and central international organizations reflect to a large extent the values of the most powerful members of the international community. The OECD coalition has been the most powerful, and particularly in terms of basic norms and diplomatic practices, OECD states, along with certain other actors, have made a liberal imprint on international relations. At least in this one sense, and for limited purposes, it is correct to view international relations sometimes as a clash of civilizations.[15] For all their domestic imperfections and imperialistic foreign policies, the liberal democracies have advanced the notion of the equal autonomy of and respect for the individual. History does not move in straight lines, but certain ideas do advance. Should an authoritarian China come to dominate international relations, the place of human rights in world affairs would change.

However, the economic and military increase in China's power and the concomitant decline in US economic clout and military effect raise troubling questions about the long-term future of human rights – if China remains authoritarian and if the United States does not make needed adjustments to its power base. Other troubling factors can also be briefly noted – e.g., repressive trends in Russia, the growing power of authoritarian Iran, Pakistan's inability to suppress illiberal Islamist movements, India's colonial experience and hence its distaste for western-inspired review of national policies (not to mention its highly repressive control of Kashmir), and so on. In short, the westernization of international relations may come to an end by 2050 if not before.[16]

Third, there is a more intriguing but debatable explanation for the staying power of human rights in world affairs, beyond these first two and related factors: the weight of international institutions (meaning the cumulative weight of international law and organizations), and the political influence of the most powerful states. This third factor pertains to political theory and personal values. Francis Fukuyama argues that

---

[15] Samuel P. Huntington, "The Clash of Civilizations," *Foreign Affairs*, 72, 3 (Summer 1993), 22–49; Huntington, *The Clash of Civilizations and the Remaking of World Order* (New York: Simon & Schuster, 1996).

[16] See further Gideon Rachman, "American Decline: This Time It's for Real," *Foreign Policy Flashpoints*, January–February 2011, www.foreignpolicy.com/articles/2011/01/02/think_again_american-decline.

all persons have a drive to be respected, and that the ultimate form of personal respect finds satisfaction in the idea of human rights.[17] Stated differently, Fukuyama argues that the process of history drives persons toward acknowledgment of human rights, since the *ideal* of human rights (rather than its imperfect practice) constitutes the most perfect form of contribution to human dignity.

In this Hegelian interpretation of purposeful or teleological world history, liberal democracies have been instrumental to the institutionalization of human rights less because of their military and economic power, and more because they have adopted an ideology of human respect that cannot be improved upon. Or, liberal democracies exert influence for human rights because they reflect an appealing way to legitimate power. Liberal democracies stipulate that power must be exercised in conformity with, primarily, individual civil and political rights. Other states, such as Sukarno's Indonesia or Khomeini's Iran, may temporarily achieve popular goals such as economic growth or conformity with fundamentalist religious principles. But in the long run they suffer a crisis of legitimacy, because they have an inferior way of trying to justify their power. In this third view, accepting human rights is the best way to legitimate power. Thus human rights becomes a hegemonic idea with staying power because of its theoretical or ideational supremacy. We have the "end of history" and have seen the "last political man" because the formal-legal triumph of human rights cannot be improved upon as legitimating ideal. Never mind for now that human practice fails to fully implement the theoretical ideal.

It is true that a number of authoritarian governments especially in the Islamic world and also in Asia criticize the view that Fukuyama personifies. These governments and more broadly many elites in the non-western world see a smug self-satisfaction in his argument. They are inclined to argue that in particular the US model of human rights is overly individualistic, causing great damage to a sense of community and perhaps even to order. This view is sometimes presented in the form of the superiority of certain Asian values.[18] Several western observers are also critical of the extent of individual rights found especially in the United States.[19] Some

---

[17] Francis Fukuyama, *The End of History and the Last Man* (New York: The Free Press, 1992). Fukuyama has not changed his views, except to say that if medical psychology could change the nature of man, his theory would have to be revisited. See Fukuyama, "Second Thoughts: The Last Man in a Bottle," *The National Interest*, 56 (Summer 1999).

[18] See further among many sources Joanne R. Bauer and Daniel A. Bell, eds., *The East Asian Challenge for Human Rights* (New York: Cambridge University Press, 1999).

[19] Michael Hunt writes of those critics of the USA who worried about its "aggressive and asocial individualism," in *Ideology and US Foreign Policy* (New Haven: Yale University

critics argue there is too much western emphasis on civil and political rights, and not enough emphasis on the economic, social, and cultural aspects of human dignity, which after all is the commonly agreed end product. Others argue that Fukuyama's view of human rights is too secular as well as too universal, and thus too demeaning to local cultures and religions that give fundamental meaning to many people.[20] Some observers saw socioeconomic globalization giving rise to a particularistic and fundamentalist backlash that was the antithesis of the triumph of the idea of universal human rights.[21] Even many pragmatic liberals said that human rights is only one means, and not necessarily always the most significant one, for achieving human dignity.[22] There was, for example, considerable attention to the idea of human security, a notion that might or might not be compatible with the human rights discourse.

Still, Fukuyama may be proven correct when he notes that as of the end of the twentieth century liberal democratic state capitalism as grounded in human rights ideas has proved broadly appealing. One sees this appeal in the Arab Spring of 2011 in which broad grassroots activism demanded more democracy and human rights as traditionally understood (in part because they were seen as leading to more economic opportunity). Moreover, one has only to compare the numbers seeking entrance to OECD states with those seeking to enter various illiberal or repressive states. This is not to say that the OECD states do not present problems of material consumption, ecological overload, democratic deficits, mismanagement of economics and finances, and a host of other problems. The perfect society has yet to manifest itself. Nevertheless, liberal democratic state capitalism is associated with a broadly appealing series of human rights centering on civil and political rights, including a right to private property. Most OECD states other than the USA have added the conception of economic and social human rights to their view of the fundamental entitlements of the individual in society. This OECD model has indeed proved broadly attractive even beyond the western world. Many "have nots" in places like Asia, the Arab world, Africa, etc. do indeed accept

---

Press, 1987), 44 and *passim*. Rhoda Howard, *Human Rights and the Search for Community* (Boulder: Westview, 1995), believes that the US version of human rights has undermined a sense of community but suggests that Canada's version has not.

20 Michael J. Perry in *The Idea of Human Rights: Four Inquiries* (New York: Oxford University Press, 1998) argues that religion is a necessary base for human rights.

21 Benjamin R. Barber, *Jihad v. McWorld* (New York: Ballantyne Publishing Group, 1995).

22 See further Herbert C. Kelman, "The Conditions, Criteria, and Dialectics of Human Dignity: A Transnational Perspective," *International Studies Quarterly*, 21, 3 (September 1977), 529–552; and Harold K. Jacobson, "The Global System and the Realization of Human Dignity and Justice," *International Studies Quarterly*, 26, 3 (September 1982), 315–332; and see below, especially Chapter 4.

the superiority of the idea of respect for human rights, and they are active in organizing groups to pursue that goal. Some non-western elites, too, have endorsed the human rights model in places like Japan and South Korea.

Just as the originally western notion of state sovereignty has been widely accepted, so the once western notion of human rights has found broad acceptance especially during the past fifty years of world history. This stems in part from western military and economic achievements. But it also stems in part from an intellectual or ethical hegemony as outlined by Fukuyama. The *idea* of individual human rights has proved broadly appealing. As Michael Ignatieff has noted, human rights can be seen as a form of "idolatry," of worshiping the human being, and naturally enough this vision has proven attractive to lots of human beings.[23] Even those like Stalin, who denied most human rights in practice, wrote liberal constitutions and organized (controlled) elections so as to pretend to recognize human rights.

Is Fukuyama guilty of triumphalism, of overstating the appeal of western-style democracy after NATO's victory in the Cold War? It is difficult to fully separate basic political theory from the net results of the practice associated with theory. If all liberal democracies had compiled the practical record of Weimar Germany, the theory of liberal democracy would be dead today. Probably the greatest challenge to the fundamental ideas of democratic state capitalism (based on human rights) comes from authoritarian capitalism along the lines of China or Singapore. While these two states do not overtly reject the fundamental notion of human rights leading to liberal democracy, their practice indicates that their core political theory is really authoritarian capitalism. (In China's case it is certainly not Marxism-Leninism, and never was for Singapore.)

In the past thirty years China has overcome instability and poverty to grow at an annual average of 9–10 percent. It is the most impressive record of sustained national economic growth in history. In approximately the same period Singapore has moved from being a poor colony in the British Empire to surpassing the British in per capita gross national product. This politically illiberal model of national development is appealing to some. Much remains to be seen as to how attractive the Chinese/Singapore model proves. China in particular has much uneven development and many pockets of discontent. It is not at all clear that China can continue to encourage considerable personal freedom in economic matters but deny significant individual freedom in the political

---

[23] Michael Ignatieff, *Human Rights as Politics and Idolatry* (Princeton: Princeton University Press, 2001).

system. Moreover, in many authoritarian states beyond China and Singapore there is much corruption and much less impressive development. One has only to look at Egypt and Tunisia at the time of writing to conclude that authoritarianism can lead to considerable socioeconomic problems and instability.

It is premature to say that Fukuyama is definitely either correct or incorrect regarding the superiority of legitimating ideologies based on civil-political rights. As Chinese foreign minister Chou En-lai supposedly said to Henry Kissinger in the 1970s with regard to an evaluation of the French revolution of 1789 made in the name of the "rights of man," it is too soon to say. If China disintegrates into renewed instability because of bad decisions made by its authoritarian elite, the human rights promises of the French revolution will look more attractive.[24]

It bears stressing that Fukuyama's argument in support of human rights is mostly about political theory and not about democratic practice. One of the points emphasized in this book is that western states, including the USA, can greatly benefit from a more serious consideration of how internationally recognized human rights might improve their societies.[25] Ultra-nationalists like the late US senator Jesse Helms resist international review of the racist strains and other imperfections in American society, as shown especially in Chapters 4 and 6 of the present volume. A certain intellectual isolationism persists among some US policy makers and voters. They easily accept the notion that because the US Constitution is revered, and because the United States manifests an independent and powerful judicial system, American society has no need of international standards or international review of human rights practices. Their intellectual or cultural isolationism causes them to overlook much pertinent evidence about the utility of international review of democratic violations of human rights.

During the Cold War the Council of Europe was made up of only liberal democracies (excepting Greek and Turkish governments during certain periods). Yet human rights violations by these liberal democracies, under the European Convention on Human Rights, as reviewed by the European Commission on Human Rights and the European Court of Human Rights, were not few. As will be noted in Chapter 5, the case

---

[24] For a short discussion of the power and problems of China with its projected status as the largest economy in the world by 2030, see Rachman, "American Decline: This Time It's for Real."

[25] See further David P. Forsythe, *Global Human Rights and American Exceptionalism* (Lincoln: University of Nebraska, University Professor Distinguished Lecture, 1999); and Forsythe, ed., *The United States and Human Rights: Looking Inward and Outward* (Lincoln: University of Nebraska Press, 1999).

load at the European Court of Human Rights was such that procedures had to be changed to accommodate the large and growing number of cases. Against this background, it is difficult to sustain the view that the US Constitution and Bill of Rights emphasizing the American version of human rights could not benefit from further international review. It is perfectly clear that even well-intentioned democracies violate some human rights, both at home and through their foreign policies.[26] Fukuyama's argument was not that western democracies are perfect or cannot be improved, only that they institutionalize a superior political theory for legitimating power (that they helped transfer to international relations from 1945). This mode of legitimating power is the theory of protecting human rights.

For the immediate future, the international law of human rights exists for whatever reason. Hence the primary issue about human rights in international relations is not whether we should acknowledge them as fundamental norms. Rather, the primary issue is when and how to implement human rights in particular situations. A central dilemma has always been, and remains, how to guarantee personal rights when the community itself, or its major interests, is threatened. Thus, what is the proper protection of human rights when the order or security of the nation-state is at risk, or its major economic interests are challenged?

Human rights as soft law

Hard law is "black letter law," the exact law as specified in court decisions. Soft law comes in two forms. There are legal rules that are not the subject of court decisions, but which nevertheless influence extra-judicial policy making. For example, some influential treaties are never or rarely adjudicated in court. They achieve their impact on policy and behavior by being interpreted by non-judicial bodies such as the legal office of the foreign ministry. Additionally there are norms that do not meet the procedural test of being law, but which nevertheless influence policy making as if they were law. For example, some UN resolutions become accepted as authoritative guidelines even while remaining, legally speaking, non-binding recommendations.

One of the official long-term goals of many actors in international relations is to institute the rule of law on behalf of human rights. This means not only that world affairs would be characterized by human rights

---

[26] Donald W. Jackson, *The United Kingdom Confronts the European Convention on Human Rights* (Gainesville: University Press of Florida, 1997).

standards, but also that these general norms would lead regularly to international and national court cases to protect human rights. Court cases would transform international legal principles into specific rules providing concrete protection. In this vision the international law of human rights would become hard law. This is an admirable goal, already partially realized.

For example, within the Council of Europe, and under the European Convention on Human Rights, we already have hard law. As will be shown primarily in Chapter 5, we have not just legal principles on behalf of civil and political rights. We also have hard or black letter law: we have court cases comprising specific judgments about what is legal and illegal in particular situations. The European states party to this legal system, which created, *inter alia*, a supranational court to issue binding judgments in human rights matters under this multilateral treaty, have thus far largely complied with all judgments of the European Court of Human Rights. There is nothing in the nature of the international law of human rights that prevents it from becoming hard law, even reasonably effective hard law. (The subject of national compliance with international court judgments is complex. For example, some states will pay reparations to wronged individuals as ordered by courts, but fail to make changes in national law so as to prevent future violations. So there is the matter of partial compliance.)

This book, however, is not a case book for law students. While covering considerable traditional legal materials, it stresses the importance, perhaps sometimes even the superiority, of soft law on human rights. The primary form of soft law covered is the attention given to international human rights standards through non-judicial means such as state foreign policy, the action of non-profit non-governmental organizations (NGOs) like Amnesty International, the action of for-profit corporations, and the actions of private individuals. When these actors pursue human rights standards through their various actions, sometimes they can have greater impact than through court cases.

Apartheid was not ended in South Africa by a court case. Communism was not ended in Europe by a court case. Torture was not terminated in the Shah's Iran by a court case. Death squads were not suppressed in El Salvador by a court case. In all these examples, considerable progress was made on human rights through non-judicial action. This book emphasizes the reality of action on human rights through soft law – the implementation of human rights norms via public policy, reflecting the interplay of governments, intergovernmental organizations (IGOs), NGOs, corporations, and even individuals.

Two further examples can be cited to make the same point. If important strides are to be made on the problem of child soldiers, we need not only legal rules backed by court cases prohibiting child soldiers, but also a multifaceted approach to society's structures that lead to the recruitment of child soldiers.[27] Similarly one might recall the Danish cartoon controversy from 2006 in which there was a negative reaction (managed by certain actors leading to violent events with fatalities) to cartoons published in Copenhagen making fun of the prophet Mohamed. Certainly a court case will not resolve the problem. When the practice of freedom of speech and freedom of the press led to charges of defaming a religion, that clash was resolved, to the extent that it was, by diplomacy and cross-cultural communication.[28] Hence on these subjects, as on most others, we need soft law in addition to hard law.

Global international relations would be much improved if it approximated the regional international law of Western Europe with its interlocking human rights standards as specified by the European Court of Human Rights and European Court of Justice – the latter court ruling on certain human rights questions although it is supposedly and primarily a court for economic issues. When US courts have ruled on certain human rights issues affecting foreign relations, at least some symbolic victories have been achieved on such matters as prosecution of alien torturers.[29]

But one can make advances on human rights apart from courts and hard law. Armed conflict is a clear case in point. Since 1864 there have been a number of treaties codifying various legal protections for persons not active in armed conflict. What is now called international humanitarian law, or the law for the protection of victims of war, or the law of human

---

[27] Scott Gates and Simon Reich, eds., *Child Soldiers in the Age of Fractured States* (Pittsburgh: University of Pittsburgh Press, 2010).

[28] For background, see David Keane, "Cartoon Violence and Freedom of Expression," *Human Rights Quarterly*, 30, 4 (November 2008), 845–875. In the UN Human Rights Council during the spring of 2011, a resolution was adopted that dropped language about defaming Islam. This language had been pushed for years by certain Arab and other Islamic actors. It had been strongly resisted by Denmark and other liberal states. Contributing to events was the assassination of Pakistani officials for supposedly defaming Islam. The resolution reaffirmed freedom of speech but opposed incitement to imminent violence. See Patrick Goodenough, "UN Human Rights Council Moves Away from 'Dangerous' Defamation of Religion Concept," March 25, 2011, www.cnsnews.com/news/article/un-human-rights-council-moves-away.

[29] US federal courts have asserted jurisdiction over alien torts that violate the law of nations. Thus certain foreign or alien torturers who enter the United States have been successfully prosecuted for violations of international human rights. Monetary judgments have rarely been collected, but international travel has been restricted for those convicted. See further Henry J. Steiner and Philip Alton, *International Human Rights in Context: Law, Politics, Morals* (New York: Oxford University Press, 1996), 779–810. This subject is updated later in the text.

rights in armed conflict, manifests a rich normative history. Numerous books, and even a few libraries, focus on these legal standards. We do not lack for lawyers in the various national military establishments. However, the number of important or influential national and international court cases adjudicating this international law, and the national laws derived from it, over the past 140 years is minuscule by any means of calculation. The relative paucity of court cases (excepting Germany after World War II) pertaining to the international law of human rights in armed conflict does not mean that the law is irrelevant to armed conflict. Rather, this law is brought to bear (to the extent that it is) mostly by military and political decisions, and by the private efforts of groups like the International Committee of the Red Cross. (This macro-evaluation remains valid even though one can point to the occasional important court case dealing with international humanitarian law, such as the US Supreme Court's Hamdan judgment of 2006 holding that a provision of the 1949 Geneva Conventions applied to the US military prison at Guantanamo Bay on the island of Cuba.)

In the complicated armed conflicts that characterized much of the territory of the former Yugoslavia between 1992 and 1995, eventually it proved possible to reduce the violations of international humanitarian law. This was achieved primarily by political means, chief of which was the negotiation of the 1995 Dayton accords. Systematic rape as a weapon of war, the killing and mistreatment of prisoners, and attacks on – and evictions of – civilians were all reduced over time, but not through court cases. Indeed, Chapter 4 in particular addresses the thorny question of whether attempts at war crimes trials during or immediately after an armed conflict always comprise a preferred course of action. Suffice it to say at this point that the Clinton Administration, with widespread support among European governments, decided not to vigorously pursue certain of those indicted as war criminals circa 1995, making the political judgment that pursuit of peace in former Yugoslavia – and with it the reduction of abuses of civilians and prisoners – overruled pursuit of legal justice at least for certain persons for certain times.[30] This book emphasizes those types of policy decisions in relation to international human rights, rather than hard law emerging from courts. (The creation in 1993 of the International Criminal Tribunal for the former Yugoslavia did not alter the fact that it was US mediation at the Dayton conference in 1995 that greatly reduced atrocities mainly in Bosnia, in the context

---

[30] See Richard Holbrooke, *To End a War* (New York: Random House, 1999), who says that in mediating the Dayton accords his mandate was to obtain peace and not to pursue legal justice.

of broader political and military developments. The first Balkan war of 1991–1995, and its series of atrocities, was not ended by court cases.)

One of the basic functions of all law, international law included, is to educate in an informal sense. To the extent that the international law of human rights informs military training, foreign policy decisions, and the actions of private groups, *inter alia*, it has achieved one of its primary purposes. It is not necessary to have court cases for the law to exert influence – and sometimes broad influence. It is commonplace to have legal obedience or compliance without legal enforcement. Indeed, the optimum situation is for legal standards to be internalized by individuals to such an extent that court cases are unnecessary. Effective law is usually that law which is internalized successfully, with court cases attempting to sanction a few violators. When violations are widespread, they overwhelm the justice system and usually lead to the collapse of the law. The ineffective laws in the USA making alcoholic drinks illegal during the era of prohibition classically demonstrate this point.

A number of lawyers active on human rights issues always argue for more hard law on human rights. From one point of view that is a laudable objective. The OECD states endorse the principle that all individuals are equal before the law. All those who violate the law should be prosecuted without regard to "political" considerations. From another point of view, however, the pursuit of international human rights standards through mostly hard law decisions is not likely to transpire with any regularity in the coming century – nor should it in all situations. The USA tried to arrest one of the more powerful warlords in Somalia during the early 1990s, holding him personally responsible for a number of violations of international law. The result was a firefight in downtown Mogadishu in October of 1993 that killed eighteen US soldiers and many more Somalis, led to the withdrawal of US troops from that failed state, and contributed to the reluctance of the USA to have the UN decisively engage to stop massive genocide in Rwanda during 1994. There is no doubt in retrospect that the pursuit of legal justice in Somalia led to a hell of good intentions, and that it would have been better, for Somalia and for the entire Great Lakes region of Africa, if the USA and other actors had defined their objectives in less criminal terms.

At the end of the Desert Storm campaign in early 1991, the USA and its coalition partners decided not to follow up on all their talk about war crimes committed by the Iraqi leadership. Such a pursuit would have entailed a continuation of the war, as the Allied Coalition would have had to launch a ground attack on Baghdad in order to try to capture Saddam Hussein and his commanders. That attack would have cost many Coalition lives and entailed much "collateral damage" to civilians in Baghdad. It is highly doubtful if American public opinion would have sustained such an operation at that time, based on pursuit of legal justice. To expect the first President Bush and his military staff to ignore such political calculations and look only at human rights violations and other violations of international law is to joust with windmills in the tradition of Don Quixote. Putting human rights violators in the dock is, after all, only one human rights strategy.[31]

After the US invasion of Iraq in 2003, with a prolonged insurgency that cost more than 4,000 US military deaths by 2010, and tens of thousands of Iraqi deaths, mostly civilian, debate grew about the wisdom of decisions by George W. Bush to pursue a radical solution to the problem of Saddam Hussein – especially since weapons of mass destruction were never found. One of the outcomes from the US invasion was the increased power of the Shi'ite government of Iran next door, a government that was brutally repressive and anti-USA. And the trial and execution of Hussein after his overthrow and capture proved not to be a decisive factor in the evolution of Iraqi and regional politics. The decision to remove by force a gross violator of human rights such as Saddam Hussein can be fraught with complexity, especially since the "law of unintended consequences" often comes into play. When it became clear that the Saddam regime had not been a clear and present danger to US society, American opinion turned against the invasion and the Administration that had produced it – especially when the follow-on occupation and transition were badly managed for several years.

In El Salvador by the early 1990s, the USA, the UN, and others decided that human dignity would be best advanced by avoiding the question of legal justice for those on both sides of the civil war who had murdered civilians or engaged in other violations of human rights. Human rights concerns were addressed through various political and administrative steps, but prosecutions of past crimes associated with the political struggle were not attempted. Likewise in the Republic of South Africa after the era of apartheid, the government of Nelson Mandela decided to emphasize a national Truth and Reconciliation Commission that had the authority to pardon those on either side who had violated human rights during the long and brutal conflict over apartheid, provided they were truthful and publicly took full responsibility for their actions.

Whether international courts are created, whether they are supported with adequate political and material resources, and whether national

---

[31] Paul Hunt, *Reclaiming Social Rights: International and Comparative Perspectives* (Aldershot: Dartmouth, 1997), 41.

courts are to be encouraged to take up human rights issues on sensitive foreign policy questions are all considerations that policy makers face. Whether and how far human rights issues should be pushed at the expense of traditional security and economic concerns is a classic dilemma in soft law decisions. This is the clash of liberalism and realism. Foreign policy is inescapably about the management of contradictions.[32] This fact means that policy makers will frequently find it necessary to strike compromises between the advancement of human rights and that of another perceived public good such as physical security and/or economic welfare.

Even after a "third wave" of democratization in the world,[33] many governments remain authoritarian and without serious interest in advancing democratic and other rights. Moreover, public and especially corporate opinion in the liberal democracies does not always or easily endorse national cost in order to advance the rights of foreigners. As one scholar has written, even in the 1990s there were many "structural" constraints faced by those interested in international human rights.[34] Policy makers, including those in the OECD states, operate in this context, in which there can be genuine debate about how best to advance human dignity, and what can be attempted with reasonable prospect of success. This book focuses on those debates and dilemmas in soft law decisions – while not omitting the contributions of hard law to the place of international human rights in the modern world.

This orientation leads to an emphasis on politics in the form of power and policy choice, not just legal judgments. In both national and international societies, it is politics that determines the content of the law. All law is made in a legislative process, and the legislative process always involves policy choice and calculations of power.[35]

With regard to applying the law, even in the OECD states a political decision frequently affects judicial or administrative application of the law. If a federal or state attorney-general in the USA decides to make the prosecution of a certain category of crime – or a particular defendant – a high priority, this is in essence a policy choice; no legal rule tells an attorney-general that he/she must have certain priorities. If the US Environmental Protection Agency or an equivalent agency in one of the states

---

[32] Stanley Hoffmann, "The Hell of Good Intentions," *Foreign Policy*, 29 (1977–1978), 3–26.

[33] Samuel P. Huntington, *The Third Wave: Democratization in the Late Twentieth Century* (Norman: University of Oklahoma Press, 1991).

[34] Jack Donnelly, *International Human Rights*, 2nd edn. (Boulder: Westview, 1997).

[35] See further Werner Levi, *Law and Politics in the International Society* (Beverly Hills: Sage Publications, 1976).

decides to prosecute an entity for violation of environmental laws, as opposed to seeking a negotiated solution outside court, that decision is in essence a policy one, not controlled by a rule of law. Prosecutorial discretion is not tightly regulated by legal rules. So even in the OECD states characterized by the rule of law in general, the law does not make itself or apply itself. Political decisions based on policy choice and calculations of power are intertwined in various ways with decisions mandated by legal rules. Within states, chief executive officers and their legal staff make political decisions all the time about whether and how to apply the law in particular situations. International relations presents this same basic situation, but with much greater emphasis on political decisions in a soft law process, and relatively less emphasis on hard law emerging from judges in adjudication.

Because my approach does not simply ask, "What is the law, and how can we get courts to adjudicate it?," in Chapter 2 I explain the difference between classical liberals (who emphasize hard law for personal rights), pragmatic liberals (who emphasize both hard law and various soft law decisions for personal welfare, not just for rights), and realists (who emphasize national interest and power).

Non-governmental actors

Under the Westphalian system of international relations, in place more or less since the middle of the seventeenth century, it is states that make the basic rules of the game. It is states that are full legal subjects, or have full legal personality, under the international law which is fashioned on the basis of state consent – explicit consent via treaty law, implicit consent via international customary law. As noted above, states can fulfill their duties and exercise their rights through judicial action, but even more so by their extra-judicial foreign policies. But this traditional and somewhat legalistic view of international relations has great difficulty in accommodating the sometimes important role played by various non-governmental actors. This book seeks to expand the usual state-centric focus by paying considerable attention to non-profit and for-profit private actors. Whether or not the state has actually lost control of many important foreign policy decisions to a variety of non-state actors is a matter of considerable debate.[36] It is reasonably clear that on many issues in international relations, including those pertaining to human rights, the

---

[36] See further Robert H. Jackson and Alan James, eds., *States in a Changing World: A Contemporary Analysis* (New York: Oxford University Press, 1993).

state *shares* decisions with important non-state actors – especially from a political rather than strictly legal perspective.

It should be noted here that some observers view human rights NGOs as the real motor to the process of growing attention to international human rights. In this view, it is the relatively well known transnational human rights organizations (e.g., Amnesty International, Human Rights Watch, the International Commission of Jurists, the International Federation for Human Rights, etc.) and their less well known colleagues (e.g., Africa Rights, Lawyer's Committee for International Human Rights, now renamed Human Rights First, etc.) that push states into giving attention to rights issues. Without the sum total of human rights NGOs, it is said, contemporary international relations would be far less supportive of human rights.

A related view is that it is not human rights NGOs *per se* that account for much transnational influence on behalf of human rights, but rather these groups acting in tandem with other actors, the sum total of which is a human rights network.[37] It is said that various human rights actors, the international communications media, the Catholic Church, the Inter-American Commission on Human Rights, etc. all brought effective pressure to bear on certain countries in the Western Hemisphere leading to an improved human rights situation. In this view, state foreign policy was relatively unimportant in improving the human rights situation in places like Mexico, because it was an essentially non-governmental network that generated most of the effective pressure.

It follows from the above that if important for-profit actors such as multinational corporations join this transnational human rights network, or act parallel to it, even more pressure can be generated for human rights – whatever the position taken by states through their official foreign policies. Some believe it was a series of private decisions by for-profit actors that helped convince white supremacists in the Republic of South Africa that apartheid, and with it, minority rule, had to be abandoned. When western investors judged the future of South Africa too risky and otherwise problematical for safe and productive investments, in this view progressive change was accelerated. In other situations for-profit actors have taken clear human rights decisions in fashioning their various market strategies, as will be noted especially in Chapter 8. Pepsico has refused to expand operations into Burma/Myanmar because of military rule there, with related rights violations of various types. Levi Strauss refused to

---

[37] See especially Kathryn Sikkink, "Human Rights, Principled Issue-Networks, and Sovereignty in Latin America," *International Organization*, 47, 3 (Summer 1993), 411–442.

make blue jeans in China between 1993 and 1998 because of certain violations of labor rights.[38] A coalition of sporting goods companies, including Nike and Reebok, will only produce soccer balls in Pakistan and elsewhere if they can certify that child labor is not involved.

At the same time, if important corporations refuse to engage for the advancement of human rights, but rather take the view that profits and not human rights are their proper concern, then that is a factor of considerable importance. In the 1990s there was considerable debate about the role of the Royal Dutch Shell Oil Company in Nigeria, where authoritarian government, human rights violations, and ecological damage led some states to consider various types of sanctions.

The central debate for present purposes concerns the precise role played, and influence generated, by all these non-governmental actors, relative to governments and their intergovernmental organizations. This is a longstanding and complex debate, similar to the debate about national politics and the role and influence of interest groups. Some observers and policy makers are not convinced that governments have been so relatively unimportant in international human rights developments. Two examples suffice to make the point. One author believes that officials in the Truman Administration, not the representatives of private groups (or Latin American states), were primarily responsible for the human rights language that eventually appeared in the UN Charter.[39] Also, Donald Fraser, who organized a series of hearings on human rights and foreign policy when he was a Member of Congress in 1974, and who is generally regarded as having been instrumental in the placing of human rights on the agenda of US foreign policy from that time, indicated that he was not pushed into that action by any human rights NGO.[40] His account is that the basic idea of renewed attention to human rights in US foreign policy was his, and that he then subsequently invited the rights groups to testify in order to support his objectives.

This latter situation typifies the problems for social science analysis in this regard. Private action for human rights is frequently merged, or dovetails, with public action (governmental and intergovernmental), making it extremely difficult to separate the lines of influence that went into a decision or impacted a situation. Was US foreign policy, bilaterally and through NAFTA, really unimportant for rights in Mexico, relative to

[38] Mark Landler, "Levi Strauss Going Back to China Market," *International Herald Tribune*, April 9, 1998, 1.
[39] Cathal Nolan, *Principled Diplomacy: Security and Rights in US Foreign Policy* (Westport: Greenwood, 1993).
[40] David P. Forsythe, *US Foreign Policy and Human Rights: Congress Reconsidered* (Gainesville: University Press of Florida, 1989).

an essentially private and transnational network at play? How can we be sure, since we cannot hold one line of influence constant or even remove it, while we replay history with only the other line of influence at play?

Fortunately we do not need to be so precise about who generated what exact influence in what exact situation. For some questions, it is enough to know that the combined weight of public and private actors for human rights led to definite developments. We know, for example, that both representatives of Amnesty International and the Dutch government, *inter alia*, combined to negotiate the UN Convention against Torture.[41] We know that various public and private actors combined to negotiate the UN Convention on the Rights of the Child.[42]

Because of such cumulative effects of non-governmental *and* governmental actors on human rights matters, we know that there have been considerable changes in international relations.

Changing state sovereignty

This book treats the notion of state sovereignty as a social construct.[43] It is an idea devised by social beings. It can change along with changing circumstances. Like the concept of human rights itself, the idea of state sovereignty is a claim relating to proper exercise of public authority, a claim to be evaluated by the rest of the international community. Thus state sovereignty is not some immutable principle decreed in fixed form once and for all time, but rather an argument about state authority whose meaning and scope are constantly subject to re-evaluation. Just as the nature of "states' rights" can change over time in a federal political-legal system, ebbing and flowing with political tides, so the notion of state sovereignty can change in international relations.

Prior to 1945, the relation between an individual and the state controlling "its" citizens was a matter for that state alone. The state was sovereign in an almost absolute sense, exercising supreme legal authority within its jurisdiction. International law existed primarily to keep states apart, and thus prevent conflicts, by confirming separate national jurisdictions.[44] Prior to 1945 there were four exceptions to the basic rule

---

[41] Peter R. Baehr, "Negotiating the Convention on Torture," in David P. Forsythe, ed., *The United Nations in the World Political Economy* (London: Macmillan, 1989), 36–53.

[42] Lawrence J. LeBlanc, *The Convention on the Rights of the Child: United Nations Lawmaking on Human Rights* (Lincoln: University of Nebraska Press, 1995).

[43] Thomas J. Biersteker and Cynthia Weber, eds., *State Sovereignty as Social Construct* (Cambridge: Cambridge University Press, 1996).

[44] Among many sources, see C. Wilfred Jenks, *The Common Law of Mankind* (London: Stevens, 1958).

that individual rights were a matter of national rather than international concern.[45] In war, or international armed conflict, from the 1860s belligerent states were obligated to allow neutral medical assistance to the sick and wounded under their control, and from the 1920s a humanitarian quarantine to prisoners of war. In peace, foreigners residing in a state, called legal aliens, were granted some minimum civil rights. Also in peace, from 1920, laborers might be legally protected under conventions developed and supervised by the International Labour Organization. Finally in what passed for peace in the European interwar years of 1919–1939, certain minorities in some of the defeated states were officially afforded certain international rights as supervised by the League of Nations. Furthermore, certain of the European Great Powers claimed a right to act in foreign states when events shocked public morality. As noted below, these claims to "humanitarian intervention" were never collectively approved, and most European interventions for supposedly humanitarian purposes were heavily affected by political calculations.[46] Otherwise, while European states and private actors might debate human rights, they remained a matter of national rather than international law and policy.[47]

The situation summarized above represents the basic legal view. Rules for organizing international relations and centering on the central notion of state sovereignty (with few restrictions) was always "organized hypocrisy," because states often violated in practice the rules that they endorsed in theory.[48] Nevertheless, international relations was indeed affected by the notion derived from state sovereignty, that states should not intervene in the domestic affairs of other states; and while this norm was violated, it also exerted considerable influence.[49]

International human rights trends since 1945, summarized in the first paragraph of this chapter, have, in tandem with certain other developments in international relations, caused some to see a radical reformulation of state sovereignty. Javier Perez de Cuellar, UN Secretary-General 1981–1991, saw "an irresistible shift in public attitudes toward the belief

---

[45] See in general David P. Forsythe, *Human Rights and World Politics*, 2nd rev. edn. (Lincoln: University of Nebraska Press, 1989).

[46] See especially Gary J. Bass, *Freedom's Battle: The Origins of Humanitarian Intervention* (New York: Vintage, 2008).

[47] Herman Burgers, "The Road to San Francisco: The Revival of the Human Rights Idea in the Twentieth Century," *Human Rights Quarterly*, 14, 4 (November 1992), 447–477.

[48] Stephen D. Krasner, *Sovereignty: Organized Hypocrisy* (Princeton: Princeton University Press, 1999).

[49] R. J. Vincent, *Human Rights and International Relations* (Cambridge: Cambridge University Press, 1986).

that the defense of the oppressed in the name of morality should prevail over frontiers and legal documents."[50] This statement was made during the high tide of multilateral optimism immediately after the end of the Cold War. His successor during 1992–1996, Boutros Boutros-Ghali, believed that, "The time of absolute and exclusive sovereignty . . . has passed."[51] Because of aggression against Kuwait and subsequently renewed abuse of Iraqi citizens, Iraq was placed in a kind of "receivership" by the international community and denied the normal perks of state sovereignty during 1991–2003. Baghdad was not allowed to develop weapons of mass destruction, to engage in full trade with others, or even to have full control of parts of its territory. Because of Milosevic's repression of the Albanian Kosovars in 1999, other western states overrode his claims to state sovereignty and tried to coerce him into a change of policy.

Outside Europe, one should not overstate, however, the importance of various "humanitarian interventions" in international relations after the Cold War.[52] As suggested above, international law had never codified a clear right of humanitarian intervention for the benefit of nationals oppressed by their own government. Particularly developing countries, fearful of the action of the most powerful states, and ever mindful of their colonial experience, remained opposed during the 1990s to any such effort at codification. Even developed countries such as the USA and UK resisted international review of national policy in the name of human rights when the issue was something like racial discrimination in the application of the death penalty or UN debate on Northern Ireland. In fact, these western states were not eager to have their national decisions reviewed by international bodies.

By 2005, however, as already briefly noted, states agreed on the abstract notion of an international responsibility to protect (R2P): that if a sovereign state failed to exercise its primary responsibility to prevent gross violations of human rights, being unable or unwilling to do so, outside states inherited a responsibility to act. But, as also already noted, norms do not implement themselves. Thus the question arose after 2005 of the political will to make the principle of R2P meaningful in the real world of failed, failing, and repressive states. In some cases, e.g., Sudan (Darfur) and Democratic Republic of Congo (Ituri province), political will to decisively end atrocities was lacking despite some international involvement. The endorsement of R2P at a UN meeting in New York

---

[50] Quoted in Thomas G. Weiss, ed., *Collective Security in a Changing World* (Boulder: Lynne Rienner, 1993), 14.

[51] "Agenda for Peace," A/47/277 and S/24111, June 17, 1992, para. 17.

[52] Kelly Kate Pease and David P. Forsythe, "Human Rights, Humanitarian Intervention, and World Politics," *Human Rights Quarterly*, 15, 2 (May 1993), 290–314.

was not the first time that progressive principles had been agreed to, only to find subsequently that state enthusiasm for the agreed norm waned in the face of complex situations and disagreeable estimates of the costs of implementation.[53] But in other cases, e.g., Kenya wracked by ethnic tensions in 2008, timely diplomacy and various actions by the International Criminal Court, *inter alia*, brought the country back from the brink of major instability-cum-human rights violations. The long-term effect of diplomatic agreement on R2P was not yet clear.

By comparison especially with the statement of Perez de Cuellar above, a more analytical view was that the nature of state sovereignty had indeed changed, but that the "reality of state power and authority cannot be ignored."[54] So the principle of R2P was almost always joined by outside states' calculations about expending blood or treasure to protect the rights of "others."

More generally, state consent was still a bedrock principle of international law. But increasingly states were using their sovereign consent to create international institutions that restricted the subsequent operation of state sovereignty. Almost all of the states of Eastern Europe emerged from the control of the Soviet empire only to stand in line to join the Council of Europe, the European Union, and NATO. Each of these international organizations would reduce the operational independence of the state. Even the USA, the one superpower on the planet, chose to use its sovereign authority to join international institutions like NAFTA and the World Trade Organization that restricted its subsequent freedom of choice. In general, virtually all states felt the necessity to choose to participate in international legal regimes that "enmeshed" the state in international governing arrangements.[55] International arrangements concerning human rights constituted an important part of this trend.

States came to share jurisdiction over human rights issues with various international organizations and even foreign governments. Routinized international diplomacy confirmed the legality and legitimacy of state

---

[53] For a discussion of R2P and the literature it has generated, see Jennifer Welsh, "Implementing the Responsibility to Protect: Where Expectations Meet Reality," *Ethics & International Affairs*, 24, 4 (Winter 2010). For a discussion of how Winston Churchill joined with FDR in issuing the Atlantic Charter in 1941 promising broad human rights guarantees, then later tried to preserve the British Empire by saying the promises of the Atlantic Charter did not pertain to India, Nigeria, etc., see Richard Toye, *Churchill's Empire: The World that Made Him and the World He Made* (New York: Henry Holt, 2010), 212–216.

[54] Oscar Schachter, "Sovereignty and Threats to Peace," in Weiss, ed., *Collective Security*, 20.

[55] Mark Zacher, "The Decaying Pillars of the Westphalian Temple: Implications for International Order and Governance," in Rosenau and Czempiel, eds., *Governance Without Government*, 58–101.

and IGO discussion of almost all human rights issues. This debate, and resulting forms of diplomatic pressure, constituted an international attempt at *indirect* protection of human rights. IGOs, and also NGOs, tried to get states to meet their responsibilities under international rights standards. Emerging practice suggested that if a state failed to meet its responsibility to protect internationally recognized human rights, then the UN Security Council or some other entity might override traditional notions of state sovereignty and try international *direct* protection of rights. Where political will was adequate, the UN Security Council might declare large-scale human rights violations to constitute a threat to, or breach of, international peace and security, permitting authoritative action under Chapter VII of the UN Charter. The Council, using Cold War precedents stemming from Rhodesia and South Africa, had done so after the Cold War in places like Iraq, Somalia, the former Yugoslavia, and Haiti. The result might be military coercion, economic coercion, or the creation of international courts entailing mandatory cooperation, etc.[56]

While some observers had been predicting the decline of the territorial state for a considerable time,[57] international relations on the eve of the twenty-first century remained a modified state system. The territorial state and its claim to sovereignty remained important features of this international political system. But increasingly the territorial state was obliged to share the international stage with other actors. On some issues the state might retain supreme or ultimate authority. But in Western Europe on migration issues the national executives became intermediate authorities, sandwiched between individual claims on the one hand and the rulings of courts about international law on the other.[58] On still other issues the state might be legally superseded by another organization such as the European Court of Human Rights, the European Court of Justice, the UN Security Council, a dispute resolution panel of the World Trade Organization, etc. It was states themselves that found it desirable to create these processes that some called supranational. Others referred to "pooled sovereignty." States themselves recognized that state independence might need to be restricted for the achievement of other public goods such as prosperity, security, or human rights. Once these international organs that transcended state sovereignty were created, they might

---

[56] See further Oliver Ramsbotham and Tom Woodhouse, *Humanitarian Intervention in Contemporary Conflict* (Cambridge: Polity Press, 1996), on the various forms of international involvement in conflict situations.

[57] John Herz, *The Nation-State and the Crises of World Politics* (New York: D. McKay, 1976).

[58] David Jacobson, *Rights Across Borders: Immigration and the Decline of Citizenship* (Baltimore: Johns Hopkins University Press, 1995).

in certain cases override the particular wishes of a particular state. This was the price paid for orderly and beneficial international relations, a situation long recognized in most national societies. As President Eisenhower remarked about binding international decisions, "It is better to lose a point now and then in an international tribunal and gain a world in which everyone lives at peace under the rule of law."[59] (Ike's view might be seen as heresy if not treason to later Republican presidents such as Ronald Reagan and George W. Bush.)

The changing nature of state sovereignty, and along with it the changing nature of international norms and organizations, was produced by many causes. Science and technology had produced both terribly destructive wars and globalized markets. Following in the wake of each was a process of social globalization, with human rights as the cutting edge. The Geneva Convention of 1864, mandating neutral medical assistance to the sick and wounded in war, came about in part because improved communications allowed news of the wounded to reach the home front more quickly. European governments realized they had to do more for the wounded, in an era in which armies had more veterinarians to care for horses than doctors to care for the wounded,[60] in order to preserve support for the war back home.[61] Especially by 1945 there was a widespread moral revulsion against large-scale industrialized warfare,[62] and the idea took hold that internationalizing the concept of human rights might help erect barriers against the destruction so evident in the two world wars.[63] By about 2000, globally integrated markets had also led to increased emphasis on the plight of workers worldwide, such as the estimated 250 million child laborers.

In sum, science and technology had produced changing material and psychological conditions so that state sovereignty was no longer what it once was. Reference to the idea of state sovereignty no longer provided an automatic and impenetrable shield against international action on issues once regarded as essentially domestic. But then, human rights was also not what it had been. Human rights was essentially a western concept, first put into widespread political and legal practice by western

---

[59] Quoted in David P. Forsythe, *The Politics of International Law: US Foreign Policy Reconsidered* (Boulder: Lynne Rienner, 1990), 55.

[60] François Bugnion, *Le Comité International de la Croix-Rouge et la Protection des Victimes de la Guerre* (Geneva: ICRC, 1994). An English edition was published subsequently.

[61] John Hutchinson, *Champions of Charity: War and the Rise of the Red Cross* (Boulder: Westview, 1996).

[62] John Mueller, *Retreat from Doomsday: The Obsolescence of Major War* (New York: Basic Books, 1989).

[63] Nolan, *Principled Diplomacy*.

states.[64] But over time and for various reasons human rights had become internationalized.[65] Modern war, modern markets, modern repression all presented similar threats to human dignity. Human rights was widely seen as a useful means to help achieve human dignity in contemporary international relations.

Conclusion

As we look at global, regional, national, and sub-national actors for international human rights, we will see time and time again that liberal norms have indeed been injected into international relations, and that:

(1) the notion of human rights is here to stay in international relations – certainly for the immediate future,
(2) human rights as soft law is important and pervasive – which is not to denigrate the role of hard law through court cases,
(3) private actors – not just public ones – play a very large role, and
(4) state sovereignty is not what it used to be.

Because of these changes, one can be guardedly optimistic about the future of human rights in international relations – of liberalism in a realist world.

Case study: from humanitarian intervention to the responsibility to protect

It is generally agreed that the territorial state system of international relations began to emerge from the middle of the seventeenth century with its central notions of state sovereignty and domestic jurisdiction. It is also generally agreed that after the great destruction from the "Great War" of 1914–1918 there was a concerted effort to restrict state use of force to self-defense and to outlaw the aggressive first use of force. This left open the question of the use of force for other purposes, such as to protect human rights within the domestic jurisdiction of another sovereign state.

Already in the nineteenth century, improvements in communications technology made possible the rather rapid knowledge of atrocities in foreign states. In Britain and France, two of the leading powers at this

---

[64] See especially Burns Weston, "Human Rights," in Richard P. Claude and Burns Weston, eds., *Human Rights in the World Community*, 2nd rev. edn. (Philadelphia: University of Pennsylvania Press, 1992), 14–30; and also Jack Donnelly, *Universal Human Rights in Theory and Practice* (Ithaca: Cornell University Press, 1989).

[65] David P. Forsythe, *The Internationalization of Human Rights* (Lexington: Lexington Books, 1991).

time, governments faced the question of whether to take action to stop atrocities in places such as Greece and Bulgaria, the western Balkans, and the eastern Mediterranean. The Ottoman Empire was in decline and a humane order was not guaranteed. In Britain and France foreign policy realists were mostly in key positions. They therefore tended to be reluctant to use military force for humanitarian reasons, preferring to concentrate on power struggles and other disputes among leading states. Yet these realist national officials faced such domestic and international pressures that they wound up authorizing military action to stop what today we would call gross violations of human rights.

These interventions were obviously carried out by the stronger against the weaker, with no centralized approval from any international organization (there not being any of a general political nature), and with many other atrocities being ignored (as in the case of, somewhat later, the fate of Christian Armenians under Ottoman control). And no state intervened to stop, for example, British atrocities in colonial India. Still, it was clear that, at least sometimes, leading states could be pressured to deal with mass killings in foreign lands. Liberal transnational activism was relatively effective, at least sometimes – as shown by the British and French interventions mentioned earlier.

Subsequent events for a time only accentuated the tension between, on one hand, state power and authority and, on the other, the fate of individuals inside states. The German Holocaust certainly gave sovereignty a bad name. German Jews and other German outcasts were not protected by the international law of that time and were, legally speaking, at the mercy of Nazi persecution and murder. Yet in 1945 the UN Charter codified traditional thinking, namely that the organization was prohibited from intervening in matters that were "essentially within the domestic jurisdiction" of member states (Article 2 [7]). While the UN Security Council was given the authority to take action, including forceful action, in order to guarantee international peace and security, it was not at all clear from 1945 that outside parties, whether states or the UN Security Council, could "intervene" (whatever that meant) regarding human rights violations *per se*, particularly those not seen as affecting *international* peace and security. The 1948 UN Convention against Genocide obligated ratifying states to take action to prevent and correct genocide, but without specifying any precise action. And what about human rights violations falling short of genocide?

It was NATO's intervention against Serbia over the issue of Kosovo in 1999 that brought some new normative developments concerning humanitarian intervention. European and North American governments had not been persistently decisive, to put it mildly, in their responses to mass starvation in Somalia in the early 1990s, to genocide in Rwanda in 1994, and to various atrocities in the first Balkan wars of 1991–1995 with the epicenter of distress being in Bosnia. But when Serbia escalated the persecution of ethnic Albanians in the Kosovo region, the United States led a delicately unified NATO into a bombing campaign with the ostensible purpose of compelling Belgrade and Slobodan Milosevic to stop the policy of ethnic cleansing or forced displacement. NATO did not claim self-defense nor did it have the advance approval of the UN Security Council, China and Russia possessing the veto and being opposed to NATO's role. NATO "won ugly" in the sense of compelling a shift in Serb policy, but only with much controversy, damage to civilians and civilian structures, and help from Russian quiet diplomacy. The status of, and conditions within, Kosovo at the time of writing cannot be treated here.

For present purposes the point to be emphasized is this: given a widespread view in the West that the NATO operation in Serbia/Kosovo was "technically" illegal but morally justified, some parties tried to clarify the status of the idea of humanitarian intervention. They sought to close the gap between legality and legitimacy. In particular, the Canadian government appointed a panel of private eminent persons to consider the issues. This process led to the influential report (2001) of the International Commission on Intervention and State Sovereignty (ICISS). This report gave a renewed push to the notion of the permissibility of outside involvement to deal with gross violations of human rights.

The ICISS report in turn led to new developments at the UN. "Norm entrepreneurs" such as Gareth Evans from Australia and Francis Deng from Sudan, among others, argued that what was really at issue was not outside punishment of recalcitrant states. Such a formulation tended to conjure up visions of powerful western states imposing their will in a neo-colonial process. Rather, so it was argued, what was involved was a broad and largely diplomatic process to guarantee responsible sovereignty. Hence, what was at issue was not an attack on sovereignty, but a broad, largely diplomatic process to redefine sovereignty to ensure it was compatible with human rights. It was this approach that led in 2005 to consensus endorsement at the UN of the idea of R2P, a responsibility to protect. Concerning genocide, crimes against humanity, war crimes, and ethnic cleansing, states had the primary responsibility to prevent such mass atrocities – as they did for other human rights. But if a state was unwilling or unable to handle this responsibility, the undefined "international community" had a responsibility to become involved concerning gross violations.

One could reasonably be cautious about the importance of this apparent agreement. The Outcome Document of the 2005 UN Summit consisted of 178 paragraphs. Two paragraphs, nos. 138 and 139, made up the principle of R2P. Other paragraphs reaffirmed virtually all ideas normally endorsed at the UN every year: peace, security, international law, human security, etc. This sort of ritual lip service often means very little.

It was evident this 2005 UN document did not lead to a radically transformed international relations and certainly not in the field of human rights. In fact, more or less as soon as the ink was dry on the summit outcome document, various delegations at the UN tried to undermine the apparent agreement. There was certainly only a little increased determination by outsiders to stop gross violations of human rights in Sudan (e.g., Darfur) or in Democratic Republic of Congo (e.g., Ituri province). These situations were terribly complex, the USA and much of the West were preoccupied with Islamist militants not to mention being overstretched in military commitments and having a weakened economic foundation, and those carrying out the atrocities were both brutal and persistent.

Still, once the language was in the UN summit outcome document, various state and non-state personnel made reference to it as they sought to improve the fate of individuals in places such as Burma (Myanmar), Kenya, Ivory Coast, and elsewhere. Those jousting for power in various national settings did not do so in a vacuum. They had to anticipate the possibility of various international involvements and pressures. One needs only to recall Libya in 2011 to realize the upper range of an international duty to protect that might come into play.

What are the lessons to be drawn from this case study? One conclusion is that decisive improvement for human rights in international relations is difficult, takes time, and is affected by the history of the subject. Another conclusion is that ideas matter, and once there is formal agreement on an idea, that new principle can be appealed to by a variety of actors interested in protecting human rights. Yet another conclusion runs in a somewhat different direction, namely that power matters. It is important to note whether powerful states are willing to take action for human rights abroad, whether one speaks of NATO and Serbia or Libya, or France and Ivory Coast, or South Africa regarding the Mugabe government in Zimbabwe, etc.

Discussion questions

- Is support for international human rights a form of western imperialism? Is Francis Fukuyama correct that history shows no better way to legitimize and limit government's power aside from human rights? Did the Arab Spring of 2011 confirm the accuracy of Fukuyama's views? Is it not true that those supporting "Asian values" are correct in pointing out excessive individualism and legalism and too much litigation in the West? How can human rights be a good thing when the western liberal democracies, based on human rights, show so many problems?

- Which is more important, hard law or soft law? How do we know when to pursue hard law options, viz., litigation, as opposed to soft law options, viz., extra-judicial policy? Is it sufficient for law to educate over time, as opposed to providing legal rules for litigation? Whatever our conclusions about sufficiency, is soft law a necessity much of the time in international relations?

- Are human rights statements by private advocacy groups more reliable than governmental statements? Does it depend on which group is under discussion? Are private human rights groups too rigid and one-dimensional in their focus? How do we separate out the influence of private groups compared to public authorities in the evolution of human rights?

- Is state sovereignty a good thing or a bad thing? Should the international community disregard claims to state sovereignty when gross violations of human rights are at issue? Is any subject essentially or totally within the sovereign domestic affairs of states? Is it not true that state power, state authority, and citizen loyalty to the nation-state are still very strong in modern international relations? Is it not true that the nation-state and state sovereignty will be with us for some time? But in what precise form?

SUGGESTIONS FOR FURTHER READING

Barber, Benjamin R., *Jihad v. McWorld* (New York: Ballantyne Publishing Group, 1995). Sees the world as a contest between universal secularism (human rights fits here) and romantic particularism such as renewed assertions of virulent nationalism as in the Balkans, Iran, and other places.

Bass, Gary J., *Freedom's Battle: The Origins of Humanitarian Intervention* (New York: Vintage, 2008). A highly readable account of how domestic public opinion, as led by liberal activists, compelled realists in high positions in Britain and France to take action to protect human rights in foreign countries during the nineteenth century.

Burgers, Jan Herman, "The Road to San Francisco: The Revival of the Human Rights Idea in the Twentieth Century," *Human Rights Quarterly*, 14, 4 (November 1992), 447–477. The best short treatment of the origins of human rights as practical politics and diplomacy in the twentieth century.

Carey, Sabine, Mark Gibney, and Steven Poe, *The Politics of Human Rights: The Quest for Dignity* (Cambridge and New York: Cambridge University Press,

2010). A clear introduction to the subject focusing on selected subject matter and based on much empirical information.

Claude, Richard P., and Burns Weston, eds., *Human Rights in the World Community*, 3rd rev. edn. (Philadelphia: University of Pennsylvania Press, 2006). A standard reader covering many important aspects.

Donnelly, Jack, *Universal Human Rights in Theory and Practice* (Ithaca: Cornell University Press, 1989). One of the best advanced treatments of human rights in international context. The second edition is now available.

International Human Rights, 2nd edn. (Boulder: Westview, 1997). A sound introduction by a leading social scientist on the subject. Strong on theory.

Doyle, Michael W., *Ways of War and Peace* (New York: Norton, 1997). A sophisticated discussion of liberalism, realism, and socialism in international context.

Evans, Gareth: *The Responsibility to Protect: Ending Mass Atrocity Crimes Once and for All* (Washington: Brookings Institution Press, 2008). An excellent discussion of the attempted move from the discourse on humanitarian intervention to that on the responsibility to protect. This involved an attempt to redefine state sovereignty as the primary responsibility of states to avoid gross violations of human rights, and the permissibility of outsiders to act when states were unwilling or unable to fulfill this responsibility.

Freeman, Michael, *Human Rights*, 2nd edn. (Cambridge: Polity, 2010). A very good introductory overview, strong on political theory.

Fukuyama, Francis, *The End of History and the Last Man* (New York: Free Press, 1992). A former US foreign service officer and leading conservative intellectual argues that the highest stage of history reflects recognition of human rights as the superior way to legitimize the exercise of power.

Goodhart, Michael, ed., *Human Rights: Politics and Practice* (New York: Oxford University Press, 2009). A good collection of essays by twenty authors covering leading issues about the development and application of human rights.

Hoffmann, Stanley, *Duties Beyond Borders: On the Limits and Possibilities of Ethical International Politics* (Syracuse: Syracuse University Press, 1981). A leading Harvard professor of United States foreign policy and international relations examines international ethics from a liberal perspective.

Ignatieff, Michael, *Human Rights as Politics and Idolatry* (Princeton: Princeton University Press, 2001). A short, provocative treatment, stressing the social construction of human rights and emphasizing the value of the individual.

Ishay, Micheline R., ed., *The Human Rights Reader: Major Political Essays, Speeches, and Documents from the Bible to the Present* (London: Routledge, 1997). A good selection of documents along the lines suggested by the sub-title.

The History of Human Rights: From Ancient Times to the Globalization Era (Berkeley: University of California Press, 2004). A thematic, conceptually interesting, and provocative history of human rights.

Krasner, Stephen D., *Sovereignty: Organized Hypocrisy* (Princeton: Princeton University Press, 1999). An analytical look at the theory and practice of this central concept. The author is a realist analyst who continues to emphasize the power of states and to suggest that all the ideas and diplomacy and laws about human rights, among other subjects, have not altered traditional understandings of world affairs very much.

Rosenau, James N., and Ernst-Otto Czempiel, eds., *Governance Without Government: Order and Change in World Politics* (Cambridge: Cambridge University Press, 1992). An excellent collection showing the extensive efforts to collectively manage problems in international relations, with a good chapter pertaining to human rights by Marc Zacher.

Singer, Max, and Aaron Wildavsky, *The Real World Order: Zones of Peace, Zones of Turmoil*, 2nd edn. (Chatham, NJ: Chatham House Publishers, 1996). Two conservatives indicate why they are optimistic about the future of international relations, believing that current authoritarian and failed states will learn the proper lessons about the benefits of democratic capitalism.

Vincent, R. J., *Human Rights and International Relations* (Cambridge: Cambridge University Press, 1986). A somewhat dated introduction, but still good on basic philosophical and legal points.

2   Establishing human rights standards

It is quite remarkable that the notion of human rights has played such a large role in western history, and now in international relations since 1945, and yet no one has been able to definitively settle questions about the origins and "true" nature of these rights. Despite continuing debate over such philosophical matters, the international community – mostly through the United Nations – has agreed on a modern version of human rights. States, the most important actors in that community, who supposedly follow "realist" principles of harsh self-interest, have used international law and organization to adopt "liberal" standards requiring attention to individual and collective human rights.[1] Internationally recognized human rights, as social construct, are a fact of international relations.

A philosophy of rights?

We do not lack for differing theories about human rights.[2] Even among western philosophers there is great variation. For Edmund Burke, the concept of human rights was a monstrous fiction.[3] For Jeremy Bentham, it was absurd to base human rights on natural rights, because *"Natural rights* is simple nonsense . . . nonsense upon stilts."[4] The contemporary

---

[1] David P. Forsythe, "Human Rights and US Foreign Policy: Two Levels, Two Worlds," in David Beetham, ed., *Politics and Human Rights* (Oxford: Blackwell, 1995), 111–130.

[2] In a voluminous literature see further David P. Forsythe, *Human Rights and World Politics*, 2nd rev. edn. (Lincoln: University of Nebraska Press, 1989), ch. 7; Morton E. Winston, ed., *The Philosophy of Human Rights* (Belmont: Wadsworth, 1989); part I of Tim Dunne and Nicholas J. Wheeler, eds., *Human Rights in Global Politics* (Cambridge: Cambridge University Press, 1999); James Nickel, *Making Sense of Human Rights*, rev. 2nd edn. (Malden, MA: Blackwell, 2007); and Charles R. Beitz, *The Idea of Human Rights* (New York and Oxford: Oxford University Press, 2009). For a concise overview, see Michael Freeman, "Philosophy," in David P. Forsythe, ed., *Encyclopedia of Human Rights* (New York: Oxford University Press, 2009), vol. IV, 228–238.

[3] Jeremy Waldron, ed., *Nonsense upon Stilts: Bentham, Burke and Marx on the Rights of Man* (London: Methuen, 1987).

[4] Quoted ibid., 53.

philosopher Alasdair MacIntyre tells us there are no such things as human rights; they are similar to witches and unicorns and other figments of the imagination.[5] Karl Marx, for that matter, was not born in Beijing. He too was western, both by birth and by principal area of concern. At the risk of oversimplifying his many and not always consistent writings, one can say that he regarded many civil rights as inherently good and tactically helpful in achieving socialism, while regarding property rights as contributing to the social ills of the modern world.[6]

John Locke has been subjected to many interpretations. In a dominant strain of western political philosophy, he seems to say natural law provides human rights as property rights – owned by each individual. Human rights are moral rights that no public authority can transgress. Individuals, in his liberal view, are equal and autonomous beings whose natural rights predate national and international laws. A primary purpose of public authority is to secure these rights in legal practice. Attracta Ingram tells us, on the other hand, that human rights are not property rights that derive from natural law.[7] They are constructed in a political process featuring self-government, not discovery of metaphysical principles. There are other constructivist or analytical theories of human rights.[8]

Ingram goes on to argue for the legitimacy of economic and social rights in addition to civil and political rights. She emphasizes the importance of the positive rights featuring entitlements to minimal standards of food, clothing, shelter, and health care. On the other hand, Maurice Cranston argues that human rights can only be civil-political, not economic-social.[9] He ends his list of fundamental personal rights with the so-called negative rights that block governmental interference into the private domain. Morris Abrams agrees,[10] but Donnelly disagrees – supporting Ingram on the validity of economic and social rights.[11] Henry Shue and John Vincent argue for the primacy of subsistence rights (mostly

---

[5] Alasdair MacIntyre, *After Virtue* (Notre Dame: University of Notre Dame Press, 1981), 61–69. See also Susan Mendus, "Human Rights in Political Theory," in Beetham, ed., *Politics and Human Rights*, 10–24.

[6] I am indebted to Professor Jack Donnelly for much of this formulation.

[7] Attracta Ingram, *A Political Theory of Rights* (New York: Oxford University Press, 1994).

[8] See especially Michael Ignatieff, *Human Rights as Politics and Idolatry* (Princeton: Princeton University Press, 2001).

[9] Maurice Cranston, "Human Rights, Real and Supposed," in D. D. Raphael, ed., *Political Theory and the Rights of Man* (Bloomington: Indiana University Press, 1967), 43–53; also Cranston, *What Are Human Rights?* (New York: Basic Books, 1964).

[10] Morris Abrams, "The United Nations, the United States, and International Human Rights," in Roger A. Coate, ed., *US Policy and the Future of the United Nations* (New York: Twentieth Century Fund Press, 1994), 113–138.

[11] Jack Donnelly, *Universal Human Rights in Theory and Practice* (Ithaca: Cornell University Press, 1989). See also Nobel laureate Amartya Sen, *Development as Freedom* (New York:

but not entirely socioeconomic) over procedural rights (which are civil and political).[12] Donnelly in turn says that human rights can only be individual, not collective. William Felice disagrees, arguing for the legitimacy of group rights.[13] Some go beyond the first generation of negative rights (said to be of the first generation because they were recognized first), and the second generation of positive rights, to a third generation of synthetic rights: the rights to peace, a healthy environment, development, and perhaps humanitarian assistance.[14]

One could continue with arguments and citations, but almost every notion put forward in regard to foundational arguments about human rights has become what political scientists like to call a "contested concept." Ingram notes that "propositions of rights are a pervasive and contested feature of our political practice."[15] Chris Brown writes that "Virtually everything encompassed by the notion of 'human rights' is the subject of controversy."[16] Belden Fields, in an excellent review of differing theoretical justifications for human rights, notes that none are perfect and that all have strong and weak points; he then puts forward his own grounding and justification, centering on development of the human personality.[17] Especially given the lack of intellectual agreement on the sources and nature of fundamental personal rights, and the fact that foundational theories continue to be published all the time, one might well agree with Vincent "that the list of objections to the idea of human rights seems formidable."[18]

In so far as the notion of human rights is associated with the West (and it is only western scholars that have been cited above), the unity and coherence of western civilization on the rights question have been greatly

---

Anchor Books, 1999), on the importance of socioeconomic rights in order to eliminate various "unfreedoms" that impede human development.

[12] Henry Shue, *Basic Rights: Subsistence, Affluence, and US Foreign Policy*, 2nd edn. (Princeton: Princeton University Press, 1997); John Vincent, *Human Rights and International Relations* (Cambridge: Cambridge University Press, 1986).

[13] William Felice, *Taking Suffering Seriously: The Importance of Collective Human Rights* (Albany: SUNY Press, 1996). See further A. Belden Fields, "Collective/Group Rights," in *Encyclopedia of Human Rights*, vol. I, 345–353; and also Gene M. Lyons and James Mayall, eds., *International Human Rights in the 21st Century: Protecting the Rights of Groups* (London: Rowman & Littlefield, 2003).

[14] See, e.g., William F. Felice, "Right to Development," in *Encyclopedia of Human Rights*, vol. II, 21–31.

[15] Ingram, *Political Theory of Rights*.

[16] Chris Brown, "Universal Human Rights: A Critique," in Dunne and Wheeler, eds., *Human Rights in Global Politics*, 103.

[17] A. Belden Fields, *Rethinking Human Rights for the New Millennium* (New York: Palgrave Macmillan, 2003). See also Michael Freeman, *Human Rights*, 2nd edn. (Cambridge: Polity, 2010), for a good introduction with much attention to political theory.

[18] Vincent, *Human Rights and International Relations*, 35.

overstated. It remains true, however, that the dominant western view of rights comprises some version of liberalism. Individuals, at least, are said to have rights that public authority must respect. They are to be written into law and defended via independent courts. Debate then ensues over which individuals should have recognized rights (women, racial minorities, gays, members of certain political groups?), who besides individuals have rights (animals, human groups, which groups?), whether rights should go beyond traditional civil and political rights (socioeconomic rights, cultural rights, solidarity rights to peace, or economic development, or a healthy environment?), where rights originate (god, natural law, human construction?), and what is the best way to implement them (courts, extra-judicial policy, private action, education?).[19]

Despite these disagreements, human rights as intellectual construct and as widespread political-legal practice was indeed first associated with the West. Other regions or cultures displayed moral principles and movements in favor of some version of human dignity, but they were not grounded in a rights discourse.[20] It was in the West that individuals were first said to be entitled to fundamental personal rights, giving rise to institutionalized claims that public authority had to respect them. Britain pioneered the development of constitutionalism, in this case monarchical government limited by the rights of other elites. France and the USA began to practice a type of democratic politics based on individual rights from the 1780s – at least for white males. In most non-western cultures individuals were still dependent on rulers to recognize abstract principles of good governance; individuals were not seen as having personal rights and the means (such as access to independent courts) to compel rulers to respect them.

Thus western states, some earlier and some later, became associated with a set of liberal principles: personal rights matter, the vulnerable and marginalized should be accorded special attention, public authority should respect personal autonomy and preferences, reason should prevail

---

[19] See further Rhoda E. Howard-Hassmann, *Compassionate Canadians: Civic Leaders Discuss Human Rights* (Toronto: University of Toronto Press, 2003). This work, based on interviews with civic leaders in Hamilton, Ontario, Canada, shows, among other things, that it is possible to have a conception of human rights and a sense of community at the same time.

[20] Jack Donnelly, "Human Rights and Human Dignity: An Analytic Critique of Non-Western Human Rights Conceptions," *American Political Science Review*, 76, 2 (June 1982), 433–449. For a different view, see Paul Gordon Lauren, *The Evolution of International Human Rights: Visions Seen* (Philadelphia: University of Pennsylvania Press, 1998); and Micheline Ishay, ed., *The Human Rights Reader: Major Political Essays, Speeches, and Documents from the Bible to the Present* (London: Routledge, 1997).

over emotionalism, violence should give way to negotiated arrangements, progress is possible.[21]

For present purposes, as stated in the previous chapter, and consistent with John Locke, I consider liberalism to connote above all attention to the essential moral and legal rights of the person. These fundamental rights, these human rights, are supposed to be trumps in that public policies must respect them.

Also for present purposes, I want to distinguish a modern version of classical political liberals from pragmatic liberals. The former emphasize peaceful and rational discussion to the point that sometimes they become judicial romantics and opposed to forceful action to stop human rights violations. They overemphasize the role of adjudication by courts, either national or international, and they overemphasize as well what diplomacy can achieve when divorced from considerations of coercion.

A pragmatic liberal, by comparison, while starting from the same assumption that human rights in general are a good thing, recognizes that there is morality or ethics beyond the human rights discourse. Thus a pragmatic liberal believes there are forms of justice apart from criminal justice, and is therefore sometimes prepared to suspend court action on behalf of personal rights for other values such as peace or reconciliation. A pragmatic liberal also believes that, while one of the important goals of international relations should remain peaceful and rational diplomacy, at times the only realistic way to end some calculated human rights violations by evil persons is through coercion.

The discourses on "human security" and/or "complex humanitarian emergency" can be noted here. They came into usage partly as diplomatic devices to try to do good for individuals in situations when reference to specific human rights and humanitarian law might in fact impede human dignity. If, for example, UN officials and state representatives referred to a situation as one of internal war and implied the possibility of war crimes, this would necessarily suggest that the government in question had lost much control of national territory and faced serious challenge. Many if not most governments are hesitant to admit this, or to invoke specific rules about what could and could not be done. But if one referred to a concern for "human security" and/or a "complex humanitarian emergency," it might be possible to obtain governmental cooperation for remedial action through international efforts. The same

---

[21] In addition to the fine synthesis of liberalism by Michael Doyle cited in Chapter 1, see further Andrew Moravcsik, "Taking Preferences Seriously: A Liberal Theory of International Politics," *International Organization*, 51, 4 (Winter 1997), 513–554.

logic might prevail where a weak, ineffective government confronted situations such as serious drought and/or plague. If a government resisted the notion of socioeconomic rights, it might be moved to progressive action by reference to the ideas of human security or humanitarian emergency. Bypassing individual responsibility and threat of legal action for war crimes or crimes against humanity might actually improve the lives of large numbers of persons in certain circumstances.

On the other hand, if the fuzzy, imprecise, a-legal language was used frequently, it might undercut the long struggle to develop clear human rights and humanitarian legal standards under which officials could be held responsible for doing – or allowing – evil. Like most policy options, reference to the language of human security, complex emergency, or even human rights held the potential for positive or negative effect. Recall the effort to label militia leader General Mohamed Farrah Aideed in Somalia a war criminal. This led to more violence, the withdrawal of various outside actors from that complicated situation, and then a reluctance by various outsiders to intervene decisively in the subsequent genocide in Rwanda. Policy decisions have to be evaluated in particular context, with "bounded rationality" or lack of certainty about what the future holds. Use of the discourse on human rights with attendant notions of violation of law and criminal responsibility may or may not be superior to other efforts to do good in particular circumstances.[22]

While there are many varieties of liberalism and liberals, the classical idea of liberalism remains centered on respect for personal moral rights, based above all on the equal worth of the individual, whose preferences should be followed in the public domain. Classical liberals emphasize above all legal rights derived from political morality, independent court judgments, and peaceful policy making.[23] Pragmatic liberals, depending on context, may emphasize the importance of other values *in addition*

---

[22] For a concise introduction, see Gerd Oberleitner, "Human Security," in *Encyclopedia of Human Rights*, vol. II, 486–493. For a discussion of the relationship between the notions of human security and human rights, see Rhoda E. Howard-Hassmann, "Working Paper: Human Security," *Human Rights and Human Welfare*, January 2011, on-line via hrhw@du.edu. See also Tom Farer, "Human Security: Defining the Elephant and Imagining Its Tasks," *Asian Journal of International Law*, 1, 1 (Fall 2010), 43–55, who confirms the imprecise notion of human security and discusses its links to human rights. See further Edward Newman and Oliver P. Richmond, eds., *The United Nations and Human Security* (New York: Palgrave, 2001). For a discussion of the idea of complex humanitarian emergency, see E. Wayne Nafziger, et al., eds., *War, Hunger, and Disease: The Origins of Complex Humanitarian Emergencies* (New York and Oxford: Oxford University Press, 2000).

[23] It is true that Locke argued for a right of rebellion as a last resort in the face of tyranny, but short of persistent and systematic gross violations of human rights, Locke emphasizes the role of independent courts to protect human rights.

to human rights, other modes of conduct *in addition to rational discourse*, and wind up recognizing the necessity of difficult choices in the context of how to better human dignity and social justice. In the face of human rights violations the classical liberal almost always looks to the rule of law and court decisions, whereas the pragmatic liberal may well favor diplomatic compromises and other extra-judicial action. For both the classical and the pragmatic liberal, the good or welfare of the person remains their touchstone for policy making.[24] Realists remain focused on the power of the state as their primary concern.

Bringing some closure to this brief synopsis about especially a liberal philosophy of rights, Susan Mendus correctly observes that the more philosophers find theories of rights to be wanting, the more public authorities proceed to codify human rights in public law.[25] There is a remarkable lack of connection between philosophical or theoretical debate on the one hand, and, on the other, considerable agreement on behalf of internationally recognized human rights – "one of the twentieth century's most powerful ideas."[26] According to Zbigniew Brzezinski, who was national security advisor to President Jimmy Carter, "Human rights is the single most magnetic political idea of the contemporary time."[27] Whether he has changed his view after the end of the Cold War saw the rise of Islamist terrorism and tough counterterrorism policies is an interesting question. However, broad-based opposition movements against longstanding autocrats in places such as Egypt and Tunisia in 2011 indicated that the idea of human rights still had broad appeal, even in areas long dominated by illiberal forces.

The American lawyer Cass R. Sunstein, when noting agreement on the 1948 Universal Declaration of Human Rights, quotes Jacques Maritain's explanation: "Yes, we agree about the rights but on condition that no one asks us why."[28] Sunstein then notes that "A nation's constitutional rights are often respected without anything like agreement about what best justifies them."[29] The Canadian Michael Ignatieff provides a good reason

---

[24] My concern is with liberalism as a political (and legal) philosophy. Liberalism applied to economics is mostly a separate subject, except that political liberalism suggests the right to personal property, which may have some role in also producing limited (constitutional) government. Liberalism and economics form an important subject, but it is not necessary for my primary purposes to go into it in great detail here.

[25] Mendus, "Human Rights in Political Theory."

[26] Tony Evans, *US Hegemony and the Project of Universal Human Rights* (New York: St. Martin's Press, 1996), 41.

[27] Zbigniew Brzezinski, *The Grand Failure: The Birth and Death of Communism in the Twentieth Century* (New York: Collier Books, 1990), 256.

[28] Cass R. Sunstein, *The Second Billl of Rights: FDR's Unfinished Revolution and Why We Need It More than Ever* (New York: Basic Books, 2004).

[29] Ibid., 177.

why: historical awareness. "Our grounds for believing that the spread of human rights represent moral progress . . . are pragmatic and historical. We know from historical experience that when human beings have defensible rights . . . they are less likely to be abused and oppressed."[30]

So we have in the notion of human rights perhaps a matter of secular religion, something which is metaphysical and cannot be proved but often taken on faith, or different versions of faith. But by reading history, we can see and study the results of that belief, that human beings are usually more secure, free, and prosperous when they exist in a society that takes human rights seriously.[31] After all, other ideas, like Locke's social contract, cannot be proven to exist independently of belief. But when believed, such ideas often have affected behavioral reality and have bettered lives. Still, context matters. Had all efforts to devise liberal laws and protect human rights ended up like Weimar Germany certainly in the 1930s, with great economic distress and political instability, we would not sing the praises of human rights quite so much. Or maybe we would, seeing the Nazi regime that followed Weimar.[32]

An international politics of rights

As discussed in Chapter 1, western power has been dominant in international relations for about two centuries, which means for present purposes that powerful western states have been in a central position to advance or retard ideas about the human being in world affairs.[33] From more or less the middle of the nineteenth century, western transnational moralism made itself felt in international public policy. Nineteenth- and early twentieth-century action occurred against slavery and the slave trade, on behalf of war wounded, for the protection of industrialized labor, and on behalf of legal aliens. Most of this western-based moralism was of a liberal nature, focusing on downtrodden individuals and seeking to legally require changes in public policy.

Even Marxism can be seen as part of this western-based international moralism.[34] Marx's concern for the industrialized laborer under crude capitalism occurred at more or less the same time as Henry Dunant's

[30] Ignatieff, *Human Rights as Politics and Idolatry*, 4.
[31] For an examination of the idea that practicing human rights contributes to secure societies and peaceful international relations, see David P. Forsythe, "Peace and Human Rights," in *Encyclopedia of Human Rights*, vol. IV, 187–196.
[32] See Deborah E. Kipstadt, "Holocaust," ibid., vol. II, 412–423.
[33] See further Eivind Hovden and Edward Keene, eds., *The Globalization of Liberalism* (New York: Palgrave, 2002).
[34] See especially John Hutchinson, "Rethinking the Origins of the Red Cross," *Bulletin of the History of Medicine*, 63 (1989), 557–578.

concern for victims of war and the start of the Red Cross, as well as widespread western concern about slavery and the African slave trade.

Within western states, it was accepted that the legitimate purposes of public authority extended beyond defense against external threat and maintenance of minimal public order. Such a libertarian or "night watch-man" view was superseded everywhere, to varying degrees, by the view that the state should advance the health and welfare, defined rather broadly, of its citizens. This same expansive view about public authority, which led to the welfare state everywhere in the West, but again to vary-ing degrees, has produced similar developments in international relations. For example, the magnitude of refugee and disaster problems outstripped private charitable efforts, leading to expanding public policies.[35] Other regions of the world also displayed moral principles and movements,[36] but they were not in a position to influence the western states that dom-inated world affairs.

Curiously enough, the discourse of human rights was largely absent from western-inspired transnational moral developments during roughly 1845–1945.[37] Private groups such as the Anti-Slavery Society in London or what became the International Committee of the Red Cross in Geneva pushed western states to adopt treaties obligating governments to cor-rect injustices (stop the slave trade from Africa, provide neutral medical assistance to the sick and wounded in war). The International Labour Organization was created. But for the most part personal human rights were bypassed. In the anti-slavery movement, some took the approach of Christian charity toward the less fortunate and not the approach of human rights based on equality of persons.[38] Human rights as such remained largely a national rather than international matter. The most notable exception pertained to the minority treaties and declarations in Central and Eastern Europe after World War I, in which individuals from minority groups were afforded certain rights of petition to international bodies in order to hopefully offset any prospect of discrimination by a tyranny of the national majority.[39] The League of Nations did guarantee,

---

[35] David P. Forsythe, "Humanitarian Assistance in US Foreign Policy, 1947–1987," in Bruce Nichols and Gil Loescher, eds., *The Moral Nation: Humanitarianism and US Foreign Policy Today* (Notre Dame: University of Notre Dame Press, 1989), 63–90.

[36] Donnelly, "Human Rights and Human Dignity."

[37] Jan Herman Burgers, "The Road to San Francisco: The Revival of the Human Rights Idea in the Twentieth Century," *Human Rights Quarterly*, 14, 4 (November 1992), 447–477.

[38] Adam Hochschild, *Bury the Chains: Prophets and Rebels in the Fight to Free an Empire's Slaves* (Boston and New York: Mariner Books for Houghton Mifflin, 2005, 2006).

[39] See especially Inis L. Claude, Jr., *National Minorities* (Cambridge, MA: Harvard Uni-versity Press, 1955).

with deployment of military force, a democratic election in the Saar in 1934, and did allow individual petitions to the Mandates Commission which "supervised" certain territories not deemed ready for legal independence or statehood.[40] Some efforts would have transformed moral concern for individuals into internationally recognized human rights. A few European non-governmental organizations were active in this regard, as were a few states, during the 1920s and 1930s. Poland and Haiti, for example, were advocates of universal human rights during the League era. Britain and the United States had tried to write the principle of individual religious freedom into the Versailles Peace Treaty and League of Nations Covenant, but withdrew the proposal in order to block Japan from advancing the principle of racial equality.[41] Thus the League was largely silent about human rights, although it later developed social agencies and programs dealing with refugees, slave-like practices, etc.

Key developments that were to lead to the international recognition of human rights occurred when Franklin D. Roosevelt and others drew the conclusion that human rights were connected to international peace and security. It cannot be stressed too strongly, because the point has not been sufficiently emphasized, that human rights as such became a formal part of international relations when important states believed that universal human rights affected their own self-interests. The human rights language that was written into the United Nations Charter had less to do with a western moral crusade to do good for others than with the expediential concerns of particularly the United States. It is not by accident that the UN Charter's Article 55 reads: "*With a view to the creation of conditions of stability and well-being which are necessary for peaceful and friendly relations among nations*, based on respect for the principle of equal rights and self-determination of peoples, the United Nations shall promote . . . universal respect for, and observance of, human rights and fundamental freedoms for all without distinction as to race, sex, language, or religion" (emphasis added).

President Roosevelt was familiar with the British intellectual H. G. Wells and his proposals for an international code of human rights.[42] In the summer of 1941 FDR and Winston Churchill issued the Atlantic Charter in order to contest fascism and militarism. This document stressed, among various topics, political freedom and national self-determination. Then in late 1941 FDR made his famous "four freedoms" speech in which he tried to give both an ideological framework for US

---

[40] See Neta Crawford, *Argument and Change in World Politics: Ethics, Decolonization, and Humanitarian Intervention* (Cambridge: Cambridge University Press, 2002).
[41] Burgers, "The Road to San Francisco," 449.   [42] Ibid., *passim*.

participation in World War II and a blueprint for the post-war peace. The four freedoms (freedom of speech, of religion, from want, and from fear) were to presage much of the International Bill of Rights. In the early 1940s US planning moved ahead with regard to a post-war international organization, with continuing attention to human rights. Roosevelt, along with Truman after him, was convinced that attention to a broad range of human rights in international relations was needed in order to forestall a repeat of the kind of aggression witnessed in the 1930s from Japan, Germany, and Italy. In this view the United Nations was needed not just to coordinate traditional interstate diplomacy, but to adopt social and economic programs in order to deal with the national conditions that led to dictators and military governments – and eventually to world wars. Roosevelt believed strongly that aggression grew out of deprivation and persecution.[43] International attention to universal human rights was in the security interests of the USA, western states, and everyone else. So much the better if self-interest dovetailed with political morality.

The US Executive, aware of racists and ultra-nationalists at home, a skeptical United Kingdom still interested in maintaining colonialism, and a brutally repressive Soviet Union, abandoned plans for writing into international law immediately binding human rights language of a specific nature. Human rights proposals were extremely modest at Dumbarton Oaks and other Allied conferences during the war. Eventually the USA led a coalition at the San Francisco conference, which created the United Nations, that was in favor of general human rights language in the Charter.[44] This general language was slightly expanded by several western NGOs and Latin American states, that were, nevertheless, unable to get the USA to agree to specific commitments to protect rights in the here and now.

Here we see a basic and still incompletely unresolved contradiction about international human rights. Violations of human rights domestically may lead to aggression abroad. But if you establish a global rule of

---

[43] In the context of American politics in the 1990s, and in particular in the context of attacks from the American right wing stating that the UN was somehow injurious to US security, two authors present FDR as a classic power politician who saw the UN as part of his realist plans to keep the peace after 1945. There are realist elements to FDR's thinking, but he and Truman saw the UN as also advancing peace by attacking human rights violations and poverty. See further Townsend Hoopes and Douglas Brinkley, *FDR and the Creation of the UN* (New Haven: Yale University Press, 1997). Compare Ruth B. Russell, *A History of the UN Charter: The Role of the US 1940–1945* (Washington: Brookings, 1958).

[44] Antonio Cassese, "The General Assembly: Historical Perspective 1945–1989," in Philip Alston, ed., *The United Nations and Human Rights: A Critical Appraisal* (New York: Oxford University Press, 1992), 25–54. See also Cathal Nolan, *Principled Diplomacy: Security and Rights in US Foreign Policy* (Westport: Greenwood Press, 1993), 181–206.

law to deal with the human rights violations of others, you will restrict your own freedom of maneuver and highlight your own defects. Roosevelt and Truman were convinced that the origins of World War II lay in Germany's internal policies of the 1930s. But if they created precise international law with strong enforcement mechanisms, these arrangements would reduce US freedom of choice in the making of public policy at home. A strong international legal regime for human rights costs something in national discretion. In fact, FDR had not been a vigorous advocate for civil rights at home primarily because he wanted the cooperation of Southern senators, in whose states persecution of African-Americans was still rampant, for his New Deal approach to economic recovery. And Harry Truman knew, in similar fashion, that robust language on human rights in the UN Charter would undermine its chances of obtaining Senate advice and consent, owing to the key position of those same Southern senators in the mid-1940s. Both presidents saw internationally recognized human rights as important, but both adjusted their policies to the realities of domestic politics.[45] The compromises were frustrating to many human rights advocates at the time but laid the foundations for important developments later.

Despite contradictions, the UN Charter came to be the first treaty in world history to recognize universal human rights. Yet no Great Power proposed a radical restructuring of international relations to benefit individuals after the two immensely destructive world wars of the twentieth century. Human rights were vaguely endorsed, but they were to be pursued by traditional state diplomacy. The theory of rights was revolutionary: all individuals manifested them, and even sovereign states had to respect them. But neither the United Nations nor any other international organization in 1945 was given clear supranational authority to ensure their respect. The UN Charter allowed the Security Council to take binding decisions on security questions, but not on social questions. The Charter also contained a prohibition on UN interference in national domestic affairs. The International Court of Justice, the so-called World Court that was technically part of the UN system, could address only those cases that states chose to submit to it. Much of world politics in subsequent years was to deal with this contradiction between the affirmation of universal human rights and the reaffirmation of state sovereignty over domestic social issues.

---

[45] David P. Forsythe, "Human Rights and Humanitarian Intervention," in David Coates, ed., *The Oxford Companion to American Politics* (New York: Oxford University Press, in press). See also Carol Anderson, "United States: Race Relations in the 1940s and 1950s and International Human Rights," in *Encyclopedia of Human Rights*, vol. V, 224–233.

At about the same time as the UN Charter was adopted, the victorious states in World War II organized the Nuremberg and Tokyo international criminal tribunals for the prosecution of some German and Japanese leaders. International prosecutions for war crimes and crimes against peace solidified the notion that individuals could be held legally responsible for violating the laws of war and for waging aggressive war. But the idea of a "crime against humanity," while somewhat new and thus raising questions about due process, implied that individual leaders could be held responsible for violating certain human rights of their own citizens.[46] Certain gross violations of human rights, such as murder, enslavement, deportation, and pseudo-medical experiments, when practiced on a mass scale, could lead to prosecution, conviction, and even the death penalty. These two international criminal proceedings were not free from well-founded charges of bias and "victor's justice," but they did further the idea that all individuals had fundamental rights in both peace and war.[47]

One dimension to the Nuremberg tale is important but not very well known. While the USA was an early champion of international criminal justice at the end of World War II, it eventually changed course. Many Germans saw those trials as more political than legal, particularly since the USA, UK, and USSR had also committed war crimes but did not have to answer to an international proceeding. Thus much West German opinion was not entirely supportive of German politicians associated with the USA. So in the context of the Cold War, to get the pro-western Konrad Adenauer elected as Chancellor of a West Germany firmly integrated into NATO, the USA led the way in abandoning the Nuremberg process and its results. Various convicted Germans were released and new rounds of trials were suspended. The United States engaged in "strategic legalism," pushing criminal justice when it seemed a good idea and abandoning it when it interfered with larger foreign policy goals. Abandoning Nuremberg was not simply to secure West Germany as a reliable NATO ally,

---

[46] The notion of a crime against humanity was articulated by the British after World War I with regard to the Ottoman Empire and its atrocities against the Armenian community of that empire. But since the defeated Ottomans, or Turks, still held some British prisoners of war, Britain dropped the subject of crimes against humanity by the Turks in order to secure the release of its POWs. During World War II, no treaty covered crimes against humanity, nor was this latter legal notion part of international customary law. Yet some German leaders were prosecuted for violating this "rule" nevertheless. See further Gary Jonathan Bass, *Stay the Hand of Vengeance: The Politics of War Crimes Tribunals* (Princeton: Princeton University Press, 2000), 114–146. See also Peter Balakian, "Armenians in the Ottoman Empire," in *Encyclopedia of Human Rights*, vol. I, 92–103.

[47] Christian Tomuschat, "International Criminal Prosecution: The Precedent of Nuremberg Confirmed," *Criminal Law Forum*, 5, 2–3 (1994), 237–248.

but also to lock in genuine democracy, thereby undercutting extremists.[48] Once again, context mattered in a calculation of complicated trade-offs. Norms mattered, as did the rule of law and independent courts, but when to push them, and how hard, was a complex policy decision.

An international bill of rights

Because the Charter made references to universal human rights but did not specify them, early UN diplomacy sought to fill that void. On December 10, 1948, the General Assembly adopted the Universal Declaration of Human Rights, which was, according to Eleanor Roosevelt, then chair of the UN Human Rights Commission, a statement of aspirations.[49] Its thirty principles covered the same range of rights long endorsed by many western leaders and private parties: rights of political participation and of civic freedom; rights to freedom from want in the form of entitlements to adequate food, clothing, shelter, and health care; and rights to freedom from fear in the form of a pursuit of an international order in which all other rights could be realized. Even this Declaration, which in international law was not immediately binding, proved too much for Saudi Arabia, South Africa, and the Soviet Union and five of its allies – all of which abstained. (All successor governments excepting Saudi Arabia publicly disavowed their abstentions later.)

For the remaining forty-six members of the UN in 1948, the Declaration could be negotiated rather rapidly by international standards, although there were many specific points of controversy.[50] Most of the General Assembly members represented governments that were comfortable with the notion of individual fundamental rights in the abstract and who did not object to their elaboration in this general way. During 1946–1948 there was relatively little acrimonious debate about universalism versus relativism, or about various generations of rights. Especially the West European democracies were comfortable with the values found in the Universal Declaration, as it closely paralleled the domestic policies they wanted to pursue. Moreover, it cannot be stressed too much that in the mid-1940s the US Executive was in favor of socioeconomic as well as civil-political rights. The Democratic Party, through its long control of the White House, had coped with economic depression after 1932

---

[48] Peter McGuire, *Law and War: An American Story*, rev. edn. (New York: Columbia University Press, 2010).

[49] Mary Ann Glendon, *A World Made New: Eleanor Roosevelt and the Universal Declaration of Human Rights* (New York: Random House, 2001).

[50] See further Johannes Morsink, *The Universal Declaration of Human Rights: Origins, Drafting, and Intent* (Philadelphia: University of Pennsylvania Press, 1998).

with broad governmental programming that responded to the failures of capitalist markets to provide for the people (and, it must be noted, with participation in World War II which finally conquered high unemployment). Roosevelt had proposed an economic bill of rights in 1944.[51] Truman strongly advocated a right to national health care, although he was never able to get his proposals approved by Congress. (Members of the Democratic Party from the states of the former Confederacy, however, were mostly opposed to internationally recognized human rights.)

Women's organizations were highly active in negotiating the Declaration and achieved a number of semantical changes to their liking.[52] The Indian representative in the Human Rights Commission, Hansa Mehta, was highly assertive on substantive matters, unlike Eleanor Roosevelt who made her contributions mainly through procedural diplomacy and liaison with officials in Washington. Feminist critiques of mainstream UN human rights developments were largely absent. With a female as chair of the Human Rights Commission, and with the creation of the UN Commission on the Status of Women, dominant opinion within the UN believed that sufficient attention was being paid to gender issues – especially since the UN Charter spoke of equality without regard to sex. The negotiating process entailed a broad range of views, not just western ones, although Africa and Asia were underrepresented.[53] Beyond Western Europe and North America, Latin American political elites were essentially western. Their governments reflected Iberian, and hence western, values in the abstract, rather than indigenous Indian values.[54] The Latin American social democrats, working with the Canadian social democrat John Humphrey, who was a UN international civil servant, were largely responsible for the wording on socioeconomic rights. This language was not the product of the communist states.[55] Lebanon was also strongly in favor of international human rights, being greatly affected by French influence. The same was true for the Philippines, being affected by American influence. The relatively easy adoption of the 1948 Universal Declaration, a "mere" General Assembly non-binding recommendation, was to prove a major step in the evolving attention to

[51] Bertram Gross, "The Human Rights Paradox," in Peter Juviler and Bertram Gross, et al., eds., *Human Rights for the 21st Century: Foundations for Responsible Hope* (Armonk: M. E. Sharpe, 1993), 128.
[52] Morsink, *Universal Declaration*, ch. 3 and *passim*.   [53] Ibid., *passim*.
[54] On the compatibility of abstract Latin American Iberian values with international human rights standards, the many violations of these rights notwithstanding, see David P. Forsythe, "Human Rights, the United States and the Organization of American States," *Human Rights Quarterly*, 13, 1 (February 1991), 66–98; and see below, Chapter 5.
[55] Morsink, *Universal Declaration*, chs. 5, 6, and *passim*.

internationally recognized human rights. According to one source, it is "the essential document, the touchstone, the creed of humanity that surely sums up all other creeds directing human behavior."[56] This most basic statement of international ethics is liberal in tone and content. In late 1948 the Cold War had not fully emerged, and so the Universal Declaration was approved. Had it been delayed for any reason beyond December 1948, it might never have passed the General Assembly. The Cold War soon deeply divided that body.

It proved much more time-consuming and controversial to translate the Universal Declaration into supposedly enforceable treaties. The Great Powers were preoccupied by the Cold War. It was to take from 1948 to 1966 to accomplish the task of producing the International Covenant on Civil and Political Rights, and also the International Covenant on Economic, Social, and Cultural Rights. These two treaties, discussed in Chapter 3, together with the Universal Declaration, against the background of the UN Charter, make up the International Bill of Rights. Despite the fact that substantive negotiations for the two treaties were completed by 1966, it took another decade for the required number of legal adherences to be obtained in order to bring the treaties into legal force for full parties. This indicated a certain caution by states in moving from general principles to specific treaty provisions that might prove to limit their freedom of choice in foreign and domestic policy – or what had been domestic policy prior to international legislation.[57]

The negotiations after 1948 were complicated by several factors.[58] The USA was in no hurry to move things forward, since the Executive Branch was under attack by certain powerful domestic groups fearful of international pressures to change the existing American way of life. The Executive was sometimes seen as in favor of a domineering federal government that would introduce foreign and excessively permissive principles and thus destroy the existing *status quo* as protected by the US Constitution and state/provincial governments. The Soviet bloc and the developing countries seized the opportunity to push for economic and social rights in ways, and to an extent, that troubled the western bloc. The western group finally accepted socioeconomic rights in treaty form only as realized gradually over time, and when two separate Covenants were

---

[56] Nadine Gordimer, "Reflections by Nobel Laureates," in Yeal Danieli, Elsa Stamatopoulou, and Clarence J. Dias, eds., *The Universal Declaration of Human Rights: Fifty Years and Beyond* (Amityville, NY: Baywood, 1998).

[57] See further Stephen James, *Universal Human Rights: Origins and Development* (El Paso: LFB Scholarly, 2007).

[58] See further Evans, *US Hegemony.*

drafted – with different supervisory mechanisms.[59] The developing countries, supported by the communist coalition, pressed hard for rewriting the principle of national self-determination as a collective human right. The western states finally accepted political reality and agreed to a common Article 1 in the two Covenants focusing on a highly ambiguous right to collective self-determination. It has never been clear in international law as to what exactly comprises a people entitled to self-determination, what form self-determination should take, or who can pronounce authoritatively on these controversies.[60] There was also controversy about whether ratification of the Covenants obligated a colonial state to apply human rights provisions in dependent territories. Thus many of the disputes between the East and West, between the North and South, played themselves out in UN debates about human rights.

It bears emphasizing that the General Assembly changed in composition, especially from the mid-1950s. Many non-western states were added to UN membership. This complicated negotiations concerning human rights compared with 1948. Most of these newer states were not only non-western, but also non-affluent and non-democratic. They were therefore not hesitant in expressing concern about an emphasis on democratic rights and a civic society replete with many civil rights, or in emphasizing economic rights to an extent that troubled particularly the USA.[61] These developments were welcomed by the Soviet Union and its allies. Moreover, as noted above, a number of states were hesitant to place themselves under specific international legal obligation in the field of human rights, even though they had voted for the Universal Declaration – and even though a UN human rights court had not been created. The Covenants always entailed weak supervisory or enforcement mechanisms, as we will see. Many states sought to preserve considerable

[59] It should be stressed that many western societies had long accepted socioeconomic rights in their domestic arrangements, although this was more controversial in the USA. See further Daniel J. Whelan and Jack Donnelly, "The West, Economic and Social Rights, and the Global Human Rights Regime: Setting the Record Straight," *Human Rights Quarterly*, 29, 4 (November 2007), 908–949. In that journal the reader can follow a subsequent debate over several issues about this article.

[60] From a vast literature, see especially Hurst Hannum, *Autonomy, Sovereignty, and Self-Determination: The Accommodation of Conflicting Rights* (Philadelphia: University of Pennsylvania Press, 1992); and Morton H. Halperin and David J. Scheffer, with Patricia L. Small, *Self-Determination in the New World Order* (Washington: Carnegie Endowment, 1992). The UN Charter endorses human rights in the name of promotion of international peace and security. But in writing the national self-determination of peoples into subsequent human rights legal instruments, the international community endorsed a principle of collective human rights that has caused much mischief and no little instability in both national and international politics.

[61] See further Upendra Baxi, "North–South Views on Human Rights," in *Encyclopedia of Human Rights*, vol. IV, 131–136.

independence in policy making, even as they found it prudent to be associated with the notion of human rights.

Be all that as it may, by 2010 many states had become parties to the International Covenants on Civil and Political Rights (166), and also to the International Covenant on Economic, Social, and Cultural Rights (160). With UN membership at 192 states in 2010, it is apparent that most states found it desirable to at least give formal endorsement to the liberal notion of universal human rights. There is something about the idea of human rights that has proved widely attractive, as Francis Fukuyama predicted, even as endorsement has not always been followed by compliance. As we will see, many states including liberal ones like the USA wish to have it both ways. They wish to identify with support for human rights, but they wish to maintain national independence in policy making both at home and abroad.

Legal regimes without hegemonic leadership

One of the central problems in the development of international human rights law at the United Nations was that the USA was compelled by domestic politics to abandon a position of clear leadership in the setting of international human rights standards.[62] FDR had led on human rights, up to a point. But Truman, Eisenhower, and other presidents were severely constrained by American domestic politics. The start of the Cold War between the USA and the USSR caused some members of Congress to view socioeconomic rights as a form of creeping socialism on the road to communism. The conservative and fanatical movement known as McCarthyism made rational congressional discourse about international rights difficult if not impossible; that movement only allowed in Washington's policy debates a mindless defense of a chauvinistic version of American moral superiority and security. Racists took courage from the overall situation and demanded an end to international developments in support of racial equality and freedom from racial discrimination. Nationalists championed the supremacy of the US Constitution compared with treaty law. The American Bar Association acted irresponsibly, manufacturing and exaggerating problems supposedly entailed in US adherence to the International Bill of Rights. When the Bricker movement in Congress sought to undermine the Executive's authority to negotiate and ratify self-implementing treaties (with the advice and consent of a supermajority in the Senate), the Eisenhower Administration agreed to back away from open support for human rights treaties. In this way the

[62] Evans, *US Hegemony*.

Executive preserved its overall position in tugs of war with Congress, but at the sacrifice of leadership on international human rights matters. UN human rights developments were left without the full support of the most powerful state in the world, despite the US penchant for seeing itself as a human rights model for others.[63]

In other parts or issue-areas of international relations, a hegemonic power had taken the lead in the construction of norms and organizations to manage important issues.[64] For example, the USA had taken the lead in both Western Europe and the Western Hemisphere to construct security arrangements for the defense of multilateral interests. NATO and the workings of the InterAmerican system reflected broad deference to, or cooperation with, US views on security. The USA did not have to coerce other states into compliance with its views (Cuba excepted after 1959) but rather exercised hegemonic leadership through a series of initiatives, burdens, payments, etc.

But with regard to global human rights, the USA was not able to play this role of hegemon, not so much because of clear Executive disagreement with the course of UN human rights developments. Rather, congressional and public views relegated the Executive Branch, under both Republicans and Democrats, to a background and low-profile role regarding international rights. From Dwight Eisenhower through Gerald Ford, the USA did not emphasize international human rights in its foreign policy, and this orientation certainly was evident in UN proceedings. It was only when Congress shifted position in the mid-1970s, and began to stress what it had rejected in the 1940s, namely an emphasis on human rights in foreign policy, that presidents like Jimmy Carter felt free to make human rights a more salient issue in world politics.[65] Even after 1976 and Carter's election, the USA did not ratify the International Covenant on Economic, Social, and Cultural Rights or the Convention on the Rights of the Child or the Convention on the Elimination of Discrimination against Women; it ratified other human rights treaties only with restrictive conditions; still manifested evident and widespread problems of racism; and utilized the death penalty for common, non-political

---

[63] In addition to Evans, *US Hegemony*, and Forsythe, "Human Rights and US Foreign Policy," see Natalie Hevener Kaufman, *Human Rights Treaties and the Senate: A History of Opposition* (Chapel Hill: University of North Carolina Press, 1990); and Lawrence J. LeBlanc, *The United States and the Genocide Convention* (Durham: Duke University Press, 1991).

[64] See especially Stephen D. Krasner, ed., *International Regimes* (Ithaca: Cornell University Press, 1983); Volker Rittberger and Peter Mayer, eds., *Regime Theory and International Relations* (New York: Oxford University Press, 1993).

[65] See further David P. Forsythe, *Human Rights and US Foreign Policy: Congress Reconsidered* (Gainesville: University Press of Florida, 1988).

crime far more than any other industrialized democracy. Thus the USA still found it difficult to play the role of hegemonic leader at the UN on human rights issues, although from 1977 it tried to a greater extent than during 1953–1976.

Beyond the International Bill of Rights

Despite the absence of hegemonic leadership from the USA, other states, international civil servants, and non-governmental organizations combined their efforts to provide at the UN a relatively large body of treaties and declarations about universal human rights. Through the UN General Assembly, in 1948 states adopted the Convention on the Prevention and Punishment of the Crime of Genocide, making individuals responsible for prosecution if they intend to destroy a national, ethnic, religious, or racial group, in whole or in part. Only four groups fall under this treaty, and the very notion of genocide is vaguely defined.[66] Nevertheless, the convention represents some progress in humane matters. The Assembly adopted a treaty regulating prostitution in 1949, and in 1951 it adopted the Convention Relating to the Status of Refugees, adding a protocol in 1967. The central rule in international refugee law obliges states to give temporary asylum to those who have fled their homeland because of a well-founded fear of persecution. In 1953 the Assembly amended the 1926 Slavery Convention. In the same year it adopted the Convention on the Political Rights of Women, and the following year the Convention Relating to the Status of Stateless Persons. In 1956 the Assembly approved the Convention on the Abolition of Slavery, the Slave Trade, and Institutions and Practices Similar to Slavery, thus supplementing earlier treaties and protocols on this subject. The treaty on the Reduction of Statelessness was adopted in 1961. Reflecting the impact of many new non-western member states, the General Assembly in 1965 adopted the Convention on Racial Discrimination. This was followed in 1973 by the Convention against Apartheid, referring to legal racial segregation primarily as then practiced by the Republic of South Africa. In 1979 the Assembly adopted the Convention on General Discrimination against Women and the UN Convention against Torture was approved in 1984. In a highly popular move, the Assembly in 1989 adopted the Convention on the Rights of the Child.

During this same era, the International Labour Organization, a carry-over from the League of Nations period but after 1945 technically part of

---

[66] See further William A. Schabas, "Genocide," in *Encyclopedia of Human Rights*, vol. II, 294–304.

the UN system, adopted a series of treaties dealing with such subjects as freedom of association (1948), the right of labor movements to engage in collective bargaining (1949), freedom from forced labor (1957), freedom from social discrimination (1958), and the protection of indigenous peoples (1989). The United Nations Educational, Scientific, and Cultural Organization adopted a convention in 1960 dealing with discrimination in education.

Outside the United Nations, but still concerning universal standards, states agreed to further develop international humanitarian law – sometimes also referred to as international law for human rights in armed conflict.[67] In 1949 they adopted the interlocking four Geneva Conventions of August 12 for Protection of Victims of War. In a subsequent diplomatic conference during 1974–1977, also called by the Swiss government, the depository state for humanitarian law since 1864, two protocols were added to the 1949 law. The first protocol increased humanitarian regulation of international armed conflict. The second provided a mini-convention, the first ever, on internal armed conflict, sometimes called civil war. In 1980 many states agreed to a framework convention on conventional weapons that might cause indiscriminate or unnecessary suffering. The sum total of this Geneva law or Red Cross law, so named because of the supporting role played by the Geneva-based International Committee of the Red Cross (ICRC), an independent component of the International Red Cross and Red Crescent Movement, focused on victims of war.

The thrust of international humanitarian law was nothing less than to humanize war, in the sense of trying to protect and assist those fighters held as prisoners or otherwise inactive through sickness or wounds; civilians; those in occupied territory; those separated from and without information about family members; those in a war zone and in need of food, clothing, shelter, and medical care; and those victimized by certain weaponry – among other subject matter.[68] A fundamental point is that

---

[67] See Hans-Peter Gasser, "Humanitarian Law," ibid., vol. II, 462–472.

[68] From a vast literature which frequently focuses on strictly legal aspects, see especially the following: Geoffrey Best, *War and Law Since 1945* (Oxford: Clarendon Press, 1994); Caroline Morehead, *Dunant's Dream: War, Switzerland, and the History of the Red Cross* (New York: St. Martin's Press, 1998); Francois Bugnion, *The International Committee of the Red Cross and the Protection of War Victims* (Geneva: ICRC, 2003); John Hutchinson, *Champions of Charity: War and the Rise of the Red Cross* (Boulder: Westview, 1996); Stephen C. Neff, *War and the Law of Nations: A General History* (Cambridge: Cambridge University Press, 2005); Gary D. Solis, *The Law of Armed Conflict: International Humanitarian Law in War* (Cambridge: Cambridge University Press, 2010); David P. Forsythe, *Humanitarian Politics: The International Committee of the Red Cross* (Baltimore: Johns Hopkins University Press, 1977); Forsythe, *The Internationalization of Human*

even in war, international or civil, fighting parties are not legally free to engage in wanton destruction, but rather must direct military action only to permissible targets in an effort to minimize human misery. This general principle is formally accepted by all professional military establishments, even as many civilians still wonder how there can be a humane law of war in the midst of intentional killing.

Much has been written about the relationship between the international law for human rights in peacetime, and international humanitarian law for situations of international and non-international armed conflict. The essential and non-legalistic point is that these two bodies of international law share the objective of creating minimal standards designed to protect human dignity in different situations.[69] Human rights law is general law, and the law of armed conflict is specialized law. However, some parts of human rights law apply in situations of armed conflict. For example, the prohibition on torture applies both in peace and war. The United Nations, which historically dealt with human rights in peace, has increasingly developed policies and programs for humanitarian action in war. The ICRC, the theoretical coordinator for the private Red Cross Movement in wartime, increasingly interacts with UN bodies (and other actors) about its humanitarian action. Legal distinctions should not be allowed to obscure common objectives and cooperation in programs.[70]

If one adds together the human rights and humanitarian treaties negotiated through the UN General Assembly, the ILO, UNESCO, and the diplomatic conferences called by Switzerland in consultation with the ICRC, it is clear we do not lack global or universal humane standards in both peace and war. One could add to the list certain declarations and other forms of soft law adopted by various international organizations on

---

Rights (Lexington: Lexington Books for D. C. Heath, 1991), ch. 6; and Forsythe, *The Humanitarians: The International Committee of the Red Cross* (Cambridge: Cambridge University Press, 2005).

[69] It has never been clear how international law can obligate non-state parties in a non-international armed conflict. International law is state centric. The rebel side in a civil war did not participate in the drafting of the laws of war, and cannot deposit a signature of adherence with the depository agent giving its consent to be bound. Nevertheless, a number of rebel movements have promised to abide by humanitarian law, whatever their subsequent behavior. It is not legal technicalities but political calculation that is important. If a rebel side seeks recognition as a responsible party, it frequently is an asset to have a reputation for humane conduct.

[70] See further David P. Forsythe, "The International Committee of the Red Cross and Humanitarian Assistance: A Policy Analysis," *International Review of the Red Cross*, 314 (September–October 1996), 512–531; Larry Minear and Thomas G. Weiss, *Mercy Under Fire: War and the Global Humanitarian Community* (Boulder: Westview, 1995); and Thomas G. Weiss, David P. Forsythe, and Roger Coate, *The United Nations and Changing World Politics*, 2nd edn. (Boulder: Westview, 1997), ch. 5.

these same subjects. States clearly wish to picture themselves as standing for something besides harsh realist principles of narrow self-interest. Many non-western and non-democratic states have become legal parties to human rights treaties. Actual behavior in concrete situations will be examined later. Enough was said at the start of Chapter 1 to suggest a yawning chasm between statements of noble principle and the reality of political action under the pressures of winning and losing power struggles – or perhaps under the weight of sheer indifference to human suffering. Still, human rights standards are indeed a liberal fact of international relations, and the possibility of their actually generating some beneficial influence on behalf of human dignity cannot be discounted out of hand. As has been said of the United Nations, so it can be said of international human rights standards: their purpose is not to get us to heaven, but to save us from hell.[71]

Continuing debates

It was clear at the 1993 UN Vienna Conference on Human Rights that a number of states harbored serious reservations about internationally recognized human rights as codified and interpreted up to that time. In the view of the USA, which took the lead in an effort to reaffirm universal human rights, a number of states tried to say at Vienna that international human rights were essentially western and therefore inappropriate to other societies. In this group of states at that time were China, Cuba, Syria, Iran, Vietnam, Pakistan, Malaysia, Singapore, Yemen, and Indonesia.[72] From Singapore's view,[73] it was legitimate to note that certain Asian countries were so crowded as to call into question the wisdom of pursuing a highly individualistic human rights orientation that might jeopardize the welfare of the community as a whole.[74] Moreover, Asian societies had long emphasized precisely that emphasis on collective welfare that seems notably lacking in the West. Some western observers found it hypocritical that the USA should push for universal human rights

---

[71] Weiss, et al., *The United Nations*, 282.   [72] *New York Times*, June 14, 1993, A3.

[73] For a concise overview, see Ian Neary, "East Asian Values," in *Encyclopedia of Human Rights*, vol. II, 73–77. See further Mark Hong, "Convergence and Divergence in Human Rights," in David P. Forsythe, ed., *The United States and Human Rights: Looking Inward and Outward* (Lincoln: University of Nebraska Press, 1999); Fareed Zakaria, "A Conversation with Lee Kuan Yew," *Foreign Affairs*, 73, 2 (March/April 1994), 109–127; Bilahari Kausikan, "Asia's Different Standard," *Foreign Policy*, 92 (Fall 1993), 24–41. In general see Joanne R. Bauer and Daniel A. Bell, eds., *The East Asian Challenge for Human Rights* (Cambridge: Cambridge University Press, 1999).

[74] See further Brian Orend, "Communitarianism and Community," in *Encyclopedia of Human Rights*, vol. I, 377–386.

in international relations while itself refusing to fully endorse socioeconomic rights as approved by the international community, continuing to
employ the death penalty for common crime despite considerable opposition from the rest of the democratic community, and violating refugee
rights when convenient – as in dealing with Haitians in the late 1980s
and early 1990s.[75] As noted above, the USA intentionally abused some
detainees in its "war on terrorism" after September 11, 2001.

As so often happens in international conferences, basic differences were
not fully resolved. The Vienna Final Declaration reaffirmed "universal
respect for, and observance of, human rights and fundamental freedoms
for all . . . The universal nature of these rights and freedoms is beyond
question." But the Declaration also stated, "While the significance of
national and regional particularities and various historical, cultural and
religious backgrounds must be borne in mind, it is the duty of states,
regardless of their political, economic and cultural systems, to promote
and protect all human rights and fundamental freedoms." This latter
language gave some "wiggle room" to the Singapores of the world who
claimed they were not in fact authoritarian but had devised a successful
and regionally particular Asian-style democracy.

It cannot be denied, however, that those in favor of universal human
rights, with only a weak form of particularism allowed, constituted a
majority at the end of the Vienna meeting, even if that position did not
fully convert those on the other side of the question.[76] The dominant
view was that universal human rights responded to universal problems
such as governmental repression and harsh capitalistic markets. This was
recognized by any number of non-western observers.[77] Persons need protection from these problems regardless of civilization, region, or nation.
States might well differ, for example, on whether presidential or parliamentary models best implemented the right to political participation in
policy making, but they were obligated to provide a genuine and not
bogus right to democratic governance. It was a historical fact that the
human rights discourse arose in the West, but so did the discourse about
state sovereignty. Just as the idea of state sovereignty had found broad
acceptance in the non-western world, it was argued, so should the notion
of human rights. Like state sovereignty, there was nothing in the history

[75] Beth Stephens, "Hypocrisy on Rights," *New York Times*, June 24, 1993, A13.
[76] On combining universal principles with weak cultural relativism, or some particular/local
variation in how the principles are implemented, see especially Jack Donnelly, *Universal
Human Rights in Theory and Practice* (Ithaca: Cornell University Press, 1989), part III.
[77] See the clear exposition by Onuma Yasuaki, *In Quest of Intercivilizational Human Rights:
"Universal" vs. "Relative" Human Rights Viewed from an Asian Perspective*, Occasional
Paper No. 2, Center for Asian Pacific Affairs, the Asia Foundation (March 1996), 15.

of human rights that made it *ipso facto* inappropriate to non-western societies. A simple analogy might not be out of place: whether the bicycle was invented in France ca. 1790 or Germany ca. 1815, that European origin did not mean the bicycle was inappropriate in other parts of the world.

There were other critiques of the International Bill of Rights toward the close of the twentieth century. In the final chapter I discuss a number of these further – especially feminist perspectives. For the moment it suffices to note that the most important critique of liberalism has come from the realists.

Contemporary realists like former National Security Advisor and Secretary of State Henry Kissinger regard international human rights as mostly an unfortunate and sentimental intrusion into the real stuff of international relations – interstate power calculations. Realists barely tolerate diplomacy for human rights because they know states like the USA or the Netherlands will insist sometimes on attention to democracy and hence civil and political rights, but they still think an emphasis on such things is unwise. Rational states in anarchic international relations concentrate on the power relations that can protect their existence and domestic values. Unique and sentimental states, above all the USA, unwisely try to project their domestic values and conditions into international relations, where the situation of anarchy and lack of moral and political consensus means a very different context.[78]

A widely cited version of this realist position regarded international action to stop gross violations of internationally recognized human rights as "social work" more properly in the domain of the late Mother Teresa, known for her charitable works with the poor in India.[79] In this view, United States' and others' actions to stop mass misery in Somalia or misrule in Haiti and Kosovo were not things that rational states did. Such action was supposedly best left to private social agencies, not rational great powers. States needed to keep their powder dry and their military forces prepared for traditional wars involving traditional vital national interests, and not dissipate their power in what the Pentagon called "operations other than war." If this realist approach meant ineffective policies to cope with human suffering abroad, this might be unfortunate. But the wise policy maker or diplomat was not moved by sentiment, only by hard-headed calculations of power and security. The touchstone for

[78] See especially Henry Kissinger, *Diplomacy* (New York: Simon & Schuster, 1994).

[79] Michael Mandelbaum, "Foreign Policy as Social Work," *Foreign Affairs*, 75, 1 (January/February 1996), 16–32. See the rejoinder by Stanley Hoffmann in the same journal, "In Defense of Mother Teresa," 75, 2 (March/April 1996), 172–176.

realist policy was narrow and expedient national interest, not personal
welfare and certainly not universal human rights. Condoleezza Rice,
National Security Advisor to President George W. Bush, reflected this
realist tradition when she wrote that the USA should focus on transcen-
dent national interests; by implication she was suggesting that the Clinton
Administration had wrongly used the US military for nation-building in
the Balkans and other diversions from true national interests.[80]

It does not go too far to say that a central problem of contemporary
international relations is how to reconcile the liberal framework of international human rights law with the widespread practice of realist foreign
policy based on the fact that in anarchic international relations each state
must provide for its own security and economic welfare. International
law and organization demand liberalism, but traditional international
relations has produced realism.

In the dialectical clash of liberalism and realism, questions of human
rights remain central. The liberal concept of human rights is a malleable
and evolving notion. Without doubt new human rights norms would be
adopted and new meanings read into existing documents, as new threats
to human dignity emerged. When science made the cloning of animals
possible, it gave rise to a new debate on the ethics of cloning, with laws
sure to follow. When science made possible the freezing of sperm and
delayed *in vitro* fertilization of the human egg, it produced both ethical
debate and new legislation. Threats to human dignity change with time
and place. International human rights standards, as means to ensure
minimal standards of human dignity, change as well. It is a normal, even
necessary, process to debate universal human rights in an effort to retain
what is still sound and valid, and to make changes as moral and political
judgment dictate. But how to protect human rights, however defined, in
international relations remains a perplexing question.

Case study: more on crimes against humanity

There is no treaty specifically focused on crimes against humanity as there
is, for example, on genocide or torture. Yet the crime exists in international law. Both international and national prosecutions have found
individuals guilty of a crime against humanity. The history of the subject
shows that international norms to protect against abuses of the individual
or of individuals can evolve in various ways over considerable time.

[80] Condoleezza Rice, "Promoting the National Interest," *Foreign Affairs*, 79, 1 (January/
February 2000), 45–62.

In the more distant history of international relations one finds semantics about crimes against humanity, violations of the laws of humanity, enemies of the human family, crime against the whole world, and similar phrases. By 1907 and the Hague Regulations on the laws and customs of war, one can find reference to customary international law and crimes against humanity. But the particular act or acts said to make up this crime were not specified. The "law of humanity" remained vague, as well as the customs that gave rise to it. Sporadically there was moral outrage at certain acts, but translating this moral intuition into clear law was not quick or easy.

After World War I, the victorious powers discussed proceedings against the defeated Ottoman leadership for crimes against humanity as represented by the deaths, deportations, and other atrocities inflicted on ethnic Armenians particularly during that war. But no institutionalized measures resulted as other concerns took priority – from the return of prisoners of war to coping with the massive dislocations and epidemics that followed the war.

After World War II again the victors took aim at the losers, and this time the Nuremberg and Tokyo criminal courts addressed German and Japanese crimes against humanity in more specific terms. In the wake of the German Holocaust and Japanese atrocities particularly against Chinese and Koreans, both panels dealt with acts such as murder, extermination, enslavement, pseudo-medical experiments, deportation, and more. At this time it was fairly clear that the victors had in mind acts just before or during the war that were directed against the civilian population, whether domestic or foreign. The notion of war crimes did not clearly cover all of this subject matter, and the concept of genocide had not yet been codified.

Whatever the merits and demerits of these two examples of international criminal courts, the new United Nations General Assembly endorsed the broad outlines of these developments. But the entire subject of international criminal justice, with crimes against humanity as a subset, went into the deep freeze because of the Cold War. A thaw first occurred in 1993 with the creation of the International Criminal Tribunal for the former Yugoslavia (ICTY), followed the next year by the International Criminal Tribunal for Rwanda (ICTR). Both courts were created by the UN Security Council and were mandated to deal with genocide, war crimes, and crimes against humanity. Thus the two international criminal courts from 1945, warts and all, led to proceedings that were more procedurally correct some fifty years later. The ICTY and the ICTR demonstrated less victor's justice and more careful attention to due process than previously was the case.

The rules, regulations, and case law of these and subsequent international proceedings changed somewhat the notion of crimes against humanity. Torture and rape were added to the list of acts that could, in some contexts, constitute such crimes. Other treaties also expanded the definition; for example, enforced disappearance was added to the list of proscribed actions. Civilians remained the main target of protection, but some experts held that military personnel could also be victims. It came to be accepted that the crime could be committed in peacetime as well as during war, in internal as well as international armed conflict. How systematic and pervasive the act or acts had to be remained a matter of some dispute. Reports from the Office of the UN Secretary-General and from private organizations might or might not clarify changes as compared to muddying the definitional waters.

During the 1980s and 1990s there were also national laws, proceedings, and convictions for crimes against humanity in states such as Canada and France. These national judgments added complexity to definitions, as the wordings chosen by a set of judges did not always prove consistent with international or other national documents. In some states such as the United States, there were no statutory or judicial developments pertaining to the concept of a crime against humanity. What Washington endorsed in international relations was not translated into US domestic law.

In 1998 states, pushed by various advocacy groups, met in Rome to negotiate a permanent or standing International Criminal Court (ICC). This was in large part to eliminate the "transition costs" involved in creating various *ad hoc* criminal courts, which entailed considerable time, money, and diplomatic or political "capital." The resulting ICC again was delegated by states the task of addressing genocide, war crimes, and crimes against humanity. (These legal concepts could overlap; depending on facts, a defendant might be found guilty of all three for the same or similar actions.) States retained the primary responsibility for action in this domain, but when they proved unable or unwilling to discharge their responsibility through proper investigation and, when warranted, prosecution, the ICC was to be brought off the shelf and into action.

The treaty called the Rome Statute that created the ICC contained a modern formulation for the core notion of crimes against humanity. According to the Rome Statute, crimes against humanity entailed "particularly odious offences in that they constitute a serious attack on human dignity or grave humiliation or a degradation of one or more human beings. They are not isolated or sporadic events, but are part either of a government policy (although the perpetrators need not identify themselves with this policy) or of a wide practice of atrocities tolerated or condoned by a government or a *de facto* authority. Murder; extermination; torture; rape; political, racial, or religious persecution; and other inhumane acts reach the threshold of crimes against humanity only if they are part of a widespread or systematic practice."

Some experts maintained that the idea of crimes against humanity as found in customary international law was broader than that found in the Rome Statute. Nevertheless, from 1907 if not before, one found an intermittent political and legal process that spasmodically advanced and refined the idea of crimes against humanity.

In the ICTY the Serbian leader Slobodan Milosevic faced charges not only of war crimes and genocide but also of crimes against humanity. (He died of natural causes in UN custody before the completion of his trial.) The ICC public prosecutor brought charges against the Sudanese leader Omar Hassan al-Bashir not only of war crimes and genocide but also of crimes against humanity. (The ultimate effect of this indictment and a subsequent arrest warrant was not clear at the end of 2010.) These and other developments in the early twenty-first century were very different from the vague reference to a law of humanity found in the 1907 Hague Convention. The concept of crimes against humanity had been greatly improved in specificity, even if not fully agreed upon, and both international and national courts sometimes carried out fair and independent proceedings to enforce this aspect of criminal justice. The core objective was to punish for, and hopefully deter against, certain gross violations of human rights.

Discussion questions

- Do human rights derive from basic humane principles that are found in various societies around the world, as Professor Lauren argues, or do human rights derive from western liberal principles as Professor Donnelly argues? Should we expect non-western societies, without a long history of exposure to liberalism, to accept and protect human rights on a par with industrialized western democracies? Is it philosophical tradition that matters for the protection of human rights, or economic development? Where does India fit in this debate? South Korea? Botswana?
- Given the lack of connection between philosophical argument on the one hand, and on the other the widespread acceptance of human rights treaties, is the philosophy of human rights irrelevant to the practice of human rights? Or do we have great problems in applying human rights standards because we do not sufficiently understand the difference

between liberalism and other "isms" like conservatism, communitarianism, and realism?

- What is the significance of widespread formal acceptance by states of the international law of human rights? When states consent to human rights treaties and diplomatic practice, is this realist hypocrisy? Is it sincere commitment to liberalism that they are sometimes unable to implement in specific situations? Why do states that practice liberalism and human rights at home sometimes find it difficult to advance human rights in international relations?
- Do international organizations (IOs) always reflect the policies of their most powerful members? Can international civil servants, less powerful states, and private organizations advance human rights through these IOs, even if the major states are not always in favor?
- Do we have human rights in the UN Charter because of a concern for the human dignity of persons, that is because of some sort of liberal crusade; or because of a concern for the security of states, that is because of realist concerns? Is it possible that human rights contribute to security? Is liberalism sometimes compatible with realism? And sometimes not?
- Do human rights properly encompass only civil and political rights, as Professor Cranston (and the USA) argues, or also economic and social rights as Professor Shue (and most of the rest of the world) argues? Should we recognize a third generation of solidarity rights including rights to development, peace, and a healthy or safe environment? Should we have a moratorium on further internationally recognized human rights until we can better implement the ones already recognized?

SUGGESTIONS FOR FURTHER READING

Best, Geoffrey, *War and Law Since 1945* (Oxford: Clarendon Press, 1994). A readable account of the modern development of international humanitarian law, its content, and efforts to apply it.

Brownlie, Ian, ed., *Basic Documents on Human Rights*, 3rd edn. (New York: Oxford University Press, 1992). An extensive and useful collection.

Claude, Inis L., Jr., *National Minorities* (Cambridge, MA: Harvard University Press, 1955). A classic study of the effort to use international law to protect minority rights in Europe in the interwar years, and of the causes of failure.

Cook, Rebecca J., *Human Rights of Women: National and International Perspectives* (Philadelphia: University of Pennsylvania Press, 1994). An excellent overview of a subject of growing importance.

Cranston, Maurice, "Human Rights, Real and Supposed," in D. D. Raphael, ed., *Political Theory and the Rights of Man* (Bloomington: Indiana University Press, 1967). A classic defense of civil and political rights, especially as utilitarian to state stability and security, and an attack on economic and social rights. Other chapters in this book are useful as well.

Crawford, Neta, *Argument and Change in World Politics: Ethics, Decolonization, and Humanitarian Intervention* (Cambridge: Cambridge University Press, 2002). A good study of the impact of ideas and arguments over time to delegitimize colonialism and other violations of human rights. In the last analysis, she is vague about the exact interaction of ideas, military power, and economic resources.

Donnelly, Jack, "Human Rights and Human Dignity: An Analytic Critique of Non-Western Human Rights Conceptions," *American Political Science Review*, 76, 2 (June 1982), 433–449. A seminal article noting the distinction between human rights and other means to advance human dignity. Argues that human rights in history was an essentially western construct.

Dunne, Tim, and Nicholas J. Wheeler, eds., *Human Rights in Global Politics* (Cambridge: Cambridge University Press, 1999). Advanced discussions of the conceptual bases of human rights and their relations to different cultures and societies. Addresses the question of whether human rights are violated because there is something fundamentally wrong with the concept of human rights in international relations.

Evans, Tony, *US Hegemony and the Project of Universal Human Rights* (New York: St. Martin's Press, 1996). A European academic takes a critical look at the US role in the evolution of international human rights standards, stressing the nefarious impact of American domestic politics on international developments.

ed., *Human Rights Fifty Years On: A Reappraisal* (Manchester: University of Manchester Press, 1998). A critical, even hypercritical, evaluation of international human rights fifty years after the adoption of the 1948 Universal Declaration of Human Rights.

Fields, A. Belden, *Rethinking Human Rights for the New Millennium* (New York: Palgrave Macmillan, 2003). A good introduction to the theory of human rights. A review of major thinkers is followed by Belden's own attempt at justification, centering on what is needed for proper development of the human personality.

Glendon, Mary Ann, *A World Made New: Eleanor Roosevelt and the Universal Declaration of Human Rights* (New York: Random House, 2001). A readable history showing how Roosevelt made her contributions through social diplomacy rather than engaging on the substantive wording of different articles in the Declaration.

Hannum, Hurst, *Autonomy, Sovereignty, and Self-Determination: The Accommodation of Conflicting Rights* (Philadelphia: University of Pennsylvania Press, 1992). A lawyer provides a sound review, with case studies, of how various claims to the collective human right of national self-determination have been handled in different parts of the world. A good blend of general legal principles with knowledge of specific problems.

Hunt, Paul, *Reclaiming Social Rights: International and Comparative Perspectives* (Aldershot: Dartmouth, 1996). One of the earlier books to give serious and in-depth treatment to economic and social rights, arguing that they are important, and some of them can be adjudicated.

Hutchinson, John F., *Champions of Charity: War and the Rise of the Red Cross* (Boulder: Westview, 1996). Takes a critical look at the International Red Cross and Red Crescent Movement from its origins in about 1859 to just after World War I. Stresses the strength of nationalism and militarism in the face of private efforts for victims of war.

Ignatieff, Michael, *Human Rights as Politics and Idolatry* (Princeton: Princeton University Press, 2001). Two short but provocative essays by a prolific Canadian thinker. He defends civil and political rights on the basis of historical pragmatism. He also sees human rights as individuals "worshipping" their own worth and agency.

Krasner, Stephen D., ed., *International Regimes* (Ithaca: Cornell University Press, 1983). Reprint of a special issue of the journal *International Organization* dealing with the concept of international regimes. Useful background for discussion of one or more international human rights regimes, a popular concept among social scientists.

Lauren, Paul Gordon, *The Evolution of International Human Rights: Visions Seen* (Philadelphia: University of Pennsylvania Press, 1998). Emphasizes the role of private organizations and individuals, including non-western ones, in advancing human rights over time in international relations. Argues that the human rights idea is not a strictly western one.

Maguire, Peter, *Law and War: An American Story*, rev. edn. (New York: Columbia University Press, 2010). An eye-opening account of the Nuremberg trials and their aftermath, showing that the USA was not fully committed to international criminal justice over time, making the complex judgment that there were other ways to advance pro-western democracy in West Germany.

Morsink, Johannes, *The Universal Declaration of Human Rights: Origins, Drafting, and Intent* (Philadelphia: University of Pennsylvania Press, 1998). The definitive treatment, fifteen years in the making, about this legislative process.

Sen, Amartya, *Development as Freedom* (New York: Anchor, 1999). A Nobel laureate in economics argues, like FDR, that persons in socioeconomic need are not free persons. Thus for him a certain socioeconomic development, especially in education and health care, is necessary for real freedom.

Shue, Henry, *Basic Rights: Subsistence, Affluence, and US Foreign Policy*, 2nd edn. (Princeton: Princeton University Press, 1997). An influential book arguing that the most important human rights cut across traditional categories, thus including some civil rights such as the right to life in the form of freedom from summary execution, and the right to life in the form of adequate food, clothing, and shelter. In his view, some economic and social rights are fundamental, being necessary for the enjoyment of certain other rights.

Sunstein, Cass R., *The Second Bill of Rights: FDR's Unfinished Revolution and Why We Need It More than Ever* (New York: Basic Books, 2004). An argument, grounded in American history, for socioeconomic rights, at least as "constitutive principles" if not as full-fledged constitutional or international law.

Winston, Morton, ed., *The Philosophy of Human Rights* (Belmont: Wadsworth, 1989). A sound overview.

Part II

Implementing human rights standards

3   Global application of human rights norms

In this chapter we examine more closely the evolving process for applying universal human rights standards on a global basis. We inquire whether there is now more commitment to liberalism, as shown through institutionalized procedures to protect human rights.

International law has traditionally been clearer about "What?" than "Who?"[1] The law has emphasized what legal rules apply in different situations. It has frequently not explicitly addressed who is authorized to make authoritative judgments about legal compliance. By default this means that states remain judge and jury in conflicts involving themselves – a principle accepted by no well-ordered society. Certainly the global law on human rights and humanitarian affairs has traditionally been characterized by decentralized decision making leading to much ambiguity about compliance. As this author concluded some time ago, "Most states, in negotiating human rights agreements, do not want authoritative international means of protection."[2] Many states have asserted an apparently liberal commitment to internationally recognized human rights. But states have often elevated national independence, particularly the supremacy of national policy making, over the realization of universal human rights. States have wanted to retain the authority to delay or opt out of human rights commitments, for whatever reason.

Is this conventional wisdom still valid? This chapter will show that, first, global enforcement of human rights, in the form of international court judgments and other forms of direct international responsibility for the application of human rights standards, is still a relatively rare event. Direct protection by international agencies exists, but not often. Neither the International Court of Justice, nor other international courts, nor the UN Security Council frequently assumes direct responsibility in seeing

---

[1] David P. Forsythe, "Who Guards the Guardians: Third Parties and the Law of Armed Conflict," *American Journal of International Law*, 70, 2 (January 1976), 41–61.

[2] David P. Forsythe, *Human Rights and World Politics*, 2nd rev. edn. (Lincoln: University of Nebraska Press, 1989), 46.

that universal human rights norms prevail over competing values. This is so especially outside Europe. There may be some change under way on this point in the early twenty-first century. But the generalization still holds. The global international community does not often frontally and flagrantly override state sovereignty in the name of human rights despite the 2005 norm of an international responsibility to protect (R2P).

At the same time, states generally find themselves enmeshed in global governance.[3] By their own consent, they find themselves part of international legal regimes that generate diplomatic pressure to conform to human rights standards. While direct international protection or enforcement of human rights is mostly absent, attempts at indirect international implementation of human rights are frequently present. There still is no world government to systematically override state sovereignty. But there are arrangements for global governance to restrict and redefine state sovereignty. The effectiveness of these many implementation efforts, which still fall short of direct enforcement, is a matter requiring careful analysis.[4] (The matter of human rights treaties leading to compliance with their norms because of domestic politics is addressed later in this chapter and in Chapter 6.)

State sovereignty is not likely to disappear from world affairs any time soon, but it is being restricted and revised in a continuing and complex process.[5] Human rights norms are at the core of this historical evolution. States may use their sovereignty to restrict their sovereignty in the name of human rights. In general, the importance of internationally recognized human rights is increasing, and the value placed on full national independence decreasing. This pattern is more evident, with some exceptions, in the global north than the global south. Again in general, but again with some exceptions, moral interdependence accompanies material interdependence – albeit with a time lag. As will become even clearer after Chapter 5 on regional developments, for some states, especially in Europe, achieving human rights through international action is more important than maintaining full freedom of strictly national policy making. Liberalism is relatively more important in international relations than

---

[3] Mark W. Zacher, "The Decaying Pillars of the Westphalian Temple: Implications for International Order and Governance," in James N. Rosenau and Ernst-Otto Czempiel, eds., *Governance Without Government: Order and Change in World Politics* (Cambridge: Cambridge University Press, 1992), 58–101.

[4] See further B. G. Ramcharan, *The Concept and Present Status of the International Protection of Human Rights* (Dordrecht: Martinus Nijhoff, 1989), 37 and *passim*.

[5] The realist Stephen Krasner, in *Sovereignty: Organized Hypocrisy* (Princeton: Princeton University Press, 1999), reminds us states have long endorsed state sovereignty and violated that norm when power allowed. See also his *Problematic Sovereignty* (New York: Columbia University Press, 2001).

it used to be. But realism, especially in times of insecurity, is still a potent force.

Principal UN organs

The Security Council

A fair reading of the UN Charter, as it was drawn up in 1945, indicates that the Security Council was given primary responsibility for the maintenance of international peace and security, which meant issues of peace and war. On security issues the Council could take legally binding decisions under Chapter VII of the Charter pertaining to enforcement action. In addition, there were economic, social, cultural, and humanitarian issues. On these issues the Council, like the General Assembly, could make recommendations under Chapter VI. Presumably human rights fell into one of the categories other than security – such as social or humanitarian. But the Council was authorized by the Charter to take action to remove threats to the peace. Logically, threats to the peace could arise from violations of human rights. In political fact, early in the life of the Security Council some states did attempt to bring human rights issues before it, precisely on grounds of a relationship to security. The early Council responded to these human rights issues in an inconsistent fashion,[6] being greatly affected by the Cold War. From about 1960 to the end of the Cold War, the Council began to deal more systematically with human rights issues as linked to four subjects: racism giving rise to violence – especially in southern Africa; human rights in armed conflict; armed intervention across international boundaries; and armed supervision of elections and plebiscites.[7] During this era the Council sometimes asserted a link between human rights issues and transnational violence.

After the Cold War the Security Council, building on some of these earlier decisions, especially those pertaining to Southern Rhodesia and the Republic of South Africa, expanded the notion of international peace and security.[8] The line dividing security issues from human rights issues

---

[6] Sydney D. Bailey, "The Security Council," in Philip Alston, ed., *The United Nations and Human Rights: A Critical Appraisal* (Oxford: Clarendon Press, 1995), 304–336. The second edition, with Frederic Megret as second editor, is forthcoming.

[7] Ibid.

[8] The Council invoked Chapter VII in the mid-1960s in dealing with the situation in Southern Rhodesia (now Zimbabwe) without making clear whether the central issue was illegal secession from the United Kingdom, racism, and other violations of human rights including denial of national self-determination and majority rule, or fighting between the Patriotic Front and the Ian Smith government. The Council invoked Chapter VII in the late 1970s in dealing with the situation in the Republic of South Africa without making

was often blurred. In these developments the Council was aware that, when dealing with especially internal conflicts, it was difficult to wind down the violence without addressing the human rights violations that drove much of the rebellion.[9] The Council thus expanded the range of Chapter VII enforcement action and stated, much more often compared with the past, that human rights violations were linked to international peace and security, thus permitting invocation of Chapter VII and even leading to an occasional enforcement action. In the process the Council shrank the scope of domestic jurisdiction protected by state sovereignty. In so doing, the Council implied more than once that security could refer to the security of persons within states, based on their human rights, and not just to traditional military violence across international frontiers. All these developments, mostly during the 1990s, held out the potential of increasing the UN Security Council's systematic action for human rights, based on pooled or collective sovereignty, relative to autonomous state sovereignty.

Five summary points deserve emphasis. First, there were numerous situations of violence in world affairs around the close of the Cold War; the UN Security Council did not address all of them. Vicious wars in places like Chechnya, Sri Lanka, and Algeria never drew systematic Council attention, much less bold assertions of international authority. Realist principles still mattered; if major states, especially the United States, did not see their narrow interests threatened, or believed a conflict resided in another's sphere of influence, the Council might not be activated.

Second, on occasion the Council has continued to say that human rights violations inside states can threaten international peace and security, at least implying the possibility of enforcement action under Chapter VII to correct the violations. In early 1992 a Council summit meeting of heads of state issued a very expansive statement indicating that threats to security could arise from economic, ecological, and social causes, not just traditional military ones.[10]

Third, the Council sometimes made bold pronouncements on behalf of Council authority, but then proceeded to seek extensive consent from the parties to a conflict. Sometimes, as in dealing with Iraq in the spring of 1991, there were enough votes in the Council to declare the consequences of repression a matter that threatened international peace and

---

clear whether the issue was denial of majority rule or political violence and instability. For political reasons, the Council sometimes acts in ways that make life difficult for professors of international law.

[9] Thomas G. Weiss, "United Nations Security Council," in David P. Forsythe, ed., *Encyclopedia of Human Rights* (New York: Oxford University Press, 2009), vol. V, 204–209.

[10] S/23500, January 31, 1992, "Note by the President of the Security Council."

security, but not enough votes to proceed to an explicit authorization to take collective military action. Sometimes, as in dealing with Somalia during 1992–1994, or Cambodia 1993–1996, or Bosnia in 1992–1995, the Council would adopt a bold stand in New York, asserting broad international authority, but in the field UN officials made every effort to obtain local consent for what the Council had mandated.[11]

Fourth, the Council has frequently deployed lightly armed forces in "peacekeeping operations" under Chapter VI, with the consent of the parties, to help ensure not just simple peace based on the constellation of military forces, but a more complex liberal democratic peace based on civil and political rights.[12]

Fifth, the Council has asserted the authority under Chapter VII to create *ad hoc* criminal courts, to prosecute and try those engaging in war crimes, crimes against humanity, and genocide. In this last regard the Council has asserted that all member states of the UN are legally obligated to cooperate with the *ad hoc* courts in order to pursue those who have committed certain gross violations of internationally recognized human rights. These courts are reviewed in Chapter 4. Other uses of Chapter VII are discussed below.

Other sources provide detailed information on the Security Council's invocation of Chapters VI and VII to deal with putative security issues since the end of the Cold War.[13] Aside from Iraq's invasion of Kuwait in 1990, and South Africa's involvement in Namibia, most of these situations drew international attention because of the death and debilitation of civilians inside states. The Security Council, no longer paralyzed by Cold War divisions, responded in various ways to: repression, oppression, and civil war in El Salvador from 1990; attacks by the Iraqi government

---

[11] On Somalia, see Mohamed Sahnoun, *Somalia: The Missed Opportunities* (Washington: US Institute for Peace Press, 1994). On Cambodia, see Steven J. Ratner, *The New UN Peacekeeping* (New York: St. Martin's Press, 1995).

[12] In addition to Ratner, *The New UN Peacekeeping*, see Ramesh Thakur and Carlyle A. Thayer, eds., *A Crisis of Expectations: UN Peacekeeping in the 1990s* (Boulder: Westview, 1995); Paul F. Diehl, *International Peacekeeping* (Baltimore: Johns Hopkins University Press, 1993); William J. Durch, *The Evolution of UN Peacekeeping: Case Studies and Comparative Analysis* (New York: St. Martin's Press, 1993).

[13] Lori Fisler Damrosch, ed., *Enforcing Restraint: Collective Intervention in Internal Conflicts* (New York: Council on Foreign Relations Press, 1993); James Mayall, ed., *The New Interventionism: United Nations Experience in Cambodia, Former Yugoslavia, and Somalia* (Cambridge: Cambridge University Press, 1996). See also Richard M. Price and Mark W. Zacher, eds., *The United Nations and Global Security* (New York: Palgrave, 2005); and Michael J. Matheson, *Council Unbound: The Growth of UN Decision Making on Conflict and Postconflict Issues After the Cold War* (Washington: US Institute of Peace, 2006). Finally, see Vaughan Lowe, et al., eds., *The United Nations Security Council and War: The Evolution of Thought and Practice Since 1945* (New York: Oxford University Press, 2008), for an encyclopedic overview.

on Iraqi Kurds and Shi'ites in the spring of 1991; systematic rape, ethnic cleansing, and other gross violations of human rights in the former Yugoslavia from 1992 to 1995; widespread malnutrition and starvation in Somalia during 1992–1994; the absence of liberal democracy and political stability in Cambodia during 1991–1997; the absence of liberal democracy and economic wellbeing in Haiti during 1993–1996; ethnic violence constituting genocide in Rwanda from 1994; and a longrunning low-intensity conflict in Guatemala from 1996. The Council also paid considerable attention to murderous wars in places like Angola and Mozambique during this same era.

At the time of writing the Council was still dealing both with the Democratic Republic of the Congo (DRC), where more persons had been killed in political conflict than any other place on the planet during a five-year period since 1945,[14] and Sudan, where millions were affected by displacement, rape, disease and malnutrition, and political killing. At one point the USA labeled the situation in the latter case as genocide.[15]

With due respect to the continuing importance of interstate conflict in places such as Afghanistan and Iraq when invaded by the USA, nevertheless the most striking feature about Security Council action in the past fifteen years was its willingness to deal with conflicts whose origins and most fundamental issues were essentially national rather than international. In El Salvador, Iraq, Somalia, Cambodia, Haiti, Rwanda, Guatemala, Liberia, Angola, Mozambique, the DRC, and Sudan, central issues of conflict revolved around "who governs" and "how humanely." This was precisely the issue in Ivory Coast in 2011, where a UN security field mission was caught up in disputes about free and fair elections and who should rule the country. The UN mission was trapped between demands that it leave from the politician trying to cling to power, and instructions from the Security Council that it stay in order to contribute to legitimate order and good governance. In fact, in Afghanistan and Iraq international armed conflict evolved into something close to internal armed conflict, or some mixture of the internal and international. In both states the violence eventually revolved around the stability of national governance.

In a few of these situations there were indeed international dimensions to the conflict that pushed the Council into action. Iraqi flight into Iran and Turkey, Haitian flight to the United States, Rwandan flight

---

[14] See further Emizet F. Kisangani, "Democratic Republic of the Congo," in *Encyclopedia of Human Rights*, vol. II, 12–20.

[15] See further Linda Bishai, "Darfur," in *Encyclopedia of Human Rights*, vol. I, 470–480.

into Tanzania and eastern Zaire, for example, did call for an international response. The protracted political instability of the DRC invited unauthorized military intervention by a handful of neighboring states, interested either in natural resources or eliminating sanctuaries for enemies. In places like El Salvador and Bosnia, among others, there was real concern that the violence might expand to engulf nearby states. Yet in places like Somalia, Cambodia, and Guatemala, the international dimensions were not so pressing. In Ivory Coast there was some movement of fighters across borders and some transnational flight of civilians. The really core issues, however, remained those pertaining to effective and democratic and humane governance – which inherently raised questions about human rights.

The bright aspect of this picture was the willingness of the Council to expand the notions of both security and Chapter VII to try to improve the personal security of citizens inside various states by improving attention to their human rights. "Human security" became a new buzzword at the United Nations.[16] The not-so-bright aspect of this picture was the gap between the blizzard of Council resolutions endorsing human rights and even making reference to Chapter VII enforcement actions, and the paucity of political will to take the costly steps necessary to make Council resolutions effective on the ground. In Somalia in the early 1990s, the Council declared that to interfere with the delivery of humanitarian assistance was a war crime. But when certain Somalis not only continued to interfere with relief, but killed eighteen US Rangers in one incident, the US removed most of its military personnel from the country. Extensive starvation was eventually checked in Somalia, but national reconciliation and humane governance were not quickly established. US casualties in Somalia caused Washington to block deployment of a significant UN force in Rwanda, despite clear and massive genocide.[17] It was one thing for diplomats in New York to say the right words. It was another thing for nations to accept costs when protecting the rights of "others" when not seen as involving their vital national interests.

In Cambodia the first national election was successfully organized by the UN, but the Khmer Rouge were not brought to heel at that time,

---

[16] Lloyd Axworthy, "Human Security: An Opening for UN Reform," in Richard M. Price and Mark W. Zacher, eds., *The United Nations and Global Security* (New York: Palgrave, 2004), 245–260. See also Edward Newman and Oliver P. Richmond, *The United Nations and Human Security* (New York: Palgrave, 2001). The discourse on human security might or might not be expressly linked to human rights as noted in Chapter 2.

[17] The ethics of non-intervention in Rwanda are well discussed in Michael A. Barnett, *Eyewitness to a Genocide: The United Nations and Rwanda* (Ithaca: Cornell University Press, 2002).

and the UN mission was terminated prematurely – setting the stage for a coup in 1997 and the return of controversial and contested rule by Hun Sen and his supporters. In former Yugoslavia 1992–1995, the Council focused in large part on human rights and humanitarian issues in order to avoid tough decisions about self-determination of peoples and later collective security for Bosnia. When the Council did authorize strong measures particularly against Bosnian Serbs and their supporters, and when the Serbs responded in tough ways, such as by taking UN personnel hostage, the Council generally backed down. The Council was willing to declare "safe areas" within Bosnia, but then it refused to provide the military forces necessary to effectively defend them, which again set the stage for massacres at Srebrenica and elsewhere.[18] The key states on the Council, meaning the USA, France, and Britain, had no stomach for decisive but costly action in places like Bosnia and Cambodia, Somalia and Rwanda.[19]

In the DRC, the UN Security Council only put a small contingent of blue helmets on the ground, policing just a small area of that very large state. A later expansion of this force was much less than what the Secretary-General recommended. In Sudan, to cope with massive misery in the area of western Darfur, the Council tried to mobilize troops through the African Union (formerly the Organization of African States). But the process proceeded slowly, with much foot dragging by the government in Khartoum and various other parties not tremendously concerned about death and destruction in the African part of that tormented country.

This trend of limited and indecisive action by the international community to guarantee human security made NATO's intervention in Kosovo in 1999 all the more remarkable. With the western states bypassing the Security Council because of Chinese and Russian opposition to what the West wanted to do, NATO and particularly the United States expended considerable treasure and prestige to try to stop and then reverse the repression, ethnic cleansing, and other violations of human rights being visited upon ethnic Albanians by the Serbian-dominated government of Yugoslavia.[20] In a portentous development, members of NATO declared that the absence of liberal democracy in Yugoslavia – especially in the internal province of Kosovo – constituted a vital interest, justifying the

---

[18] Srebrenica represented the worst massacre in Europe since World War II. See David Rohde, *End Game: The Betrayal and Fall of Srebrenica* (Boulder: Westview, 1997).

[19] Edward Luttwak, "Where Are the Great Powers?," *Foreign Affairs*, 73, 4 (July/August, 1994), 23–29.

[20] A good inside look at the details of the process can be found in Wesley Clark, *Waging Modern War* (New York: Perseus, 2002).

use of military force despite the absence of explicit Security Council authorization.

Yet the main problem for most situations of human insecurity remained lack of humanitarian intervention, not too much of it. NATO's intervention in Kosovo and Libya remained the exceptions that proved the general rule. The international community normally did not intervene decisively and quickly in response to gross violations of human rights. This was true in Burma/Myanmar, Sri Lanka, and other places. Transnational morality remained thin or weak. Often, third parties with the military muscle to make a difference perceived no self-interest at risk in the situation. Sometimes former colonial powers roused themselves to action, as did the British in Sierra Leone and the French in Ivory Coast. At other times the former colonial power was part of the problem, as were the French in Rwanda with their support for militant Hutus.

Despite the inconsistency of state policies, some improvements were achieved. El Salvador and Namibia were clearly more humane places after extensive UN involvement, especially when compared with the preceding decade. Mozambique and Guatemala eventually stumbled toward improved respect for many human rights. If the Council could help conflicting parties move toward accommodation and humane governance through Chapter VI peacekeeping, which did not entail large-scale combat or other costly enforcement measures, then its record was commendable in many respects. The UN spent more than $2 billion in trying to advance liberal democracy in Cambodia, and some improvements – however incomplete – were made. A study by the Rand Corporation showed that when the UN undertook moderately challenging field operations directed to establishing humane governance after violent conflict, the organization used its experience and soft power to manage matters reasonably well, although some problems were evident – such as delay in the arrival of resources and inconsistency in quality of personnel loaned by states.[21] This study concluded that the UN record in this regard was not inferior to that of the USA, although the latter took on tougher situations in places like Afghanistan and Iraq from about 2002–2003.

The overall record of the Council on human rights issues after the Cold War was complex, defying simple summation. Clearly the Council was more extensively involved in trying to help apply human rights standards than ever before. It had demonstrated on a number of occasions that human rights protections could be intertwined with considerations of peace and security. It had certainly blurred the outer boundaries of

[21] James Dobbins, et al., *The UN's Role in Nation-Building: From the Congo to Iraq* (Santa Monica, CA: Rand, 2005).

state sovereignty and its corollary, domestic jurisdiction. If it lacked the collective political will to make effective on the ground some of its bolder pronouncements from New York, it had nevertheless expanded second-generation peacekeeping to encompass more attention to a rather broad range of human rights.[22] The Council also increased its references not just to human rights but also to humanitarian affairs.[23]

A continuing problem was the inconsistent record of the Permanent Five (P-5) members of the Security Council when dealing with human rights and conflict. This was certainly true of the USA, which took much more interest in Kosovo than in almost all problems in Africa (even before it became preoccupied with Afghanistan and Iraq after September 11, 2001). Britain and France had not been on the front lines of those pressing for action in Rwanda and Sudan. Yet they did press for military action under a UN mandate in Libya in 2011. Russia and China were consistently hesitant about using the UNSC to endorse military action to protect human rights, yet they too were inconsistent – threatening to veto action to protect the Kosovars but abstaining on the resolution authorizing all necessary means to protect civilians in Libya. Clearly the Council was a political as well as legal institution.

Office of the Secretary-General

Although relatively little has been published about the Office of the UN Secretary-General and human rights, it appears that two factors explain a great deal about the evolution of events in this area. On the one hand, as human rights have become more institutionalized in UN affairs, Secretaries-General have spoken out more frequently and been generally more active in this domain.[24] There is almost a straight line progression on increasing action by Secretaries-General on human rights over time. Second, while all Secretaries-General have given priority to trying to resolve issues of international peace and security, increasingly they

[22] For an overview of UN second-generation peacekeeping and human rights, see David P. Forsythe, "Human Rights and International Security: United Nations Field Operations Redux," in Monique Castermans-Holleman, et al., eds., *The Role of the Nation-State in the 21st Century* (The Hague: Kluwer, 1998), 265–276.

[23] Weiss, "UN Security Council." See further George Nolte, "The Different Functions of the Security Council with Respect to Humanitarian Law," in Lowe, et al., eds., *UN Security Council and War*, 519–534.

[24] David P. Forsythe, "The UN Secretary-General and Human Rights: The Question of Leadership in a Changing Context," in Benjamin Rivlin and Leon Gordenker, eds., *The Challenging Role of the UN Secretary-General: Making "The Most Impossible Job in the World" Possible* (Westport: Praeger, 1993), 211–232. See also Kent J. Kille, ed., *The UN Secretary-General and Moral Authority: Ethics and Religion in International Leadership* (Washington: Georgetown University Press, 2007).

have found human rights intertwined with security. In so far as security issues can be separated from human rights, rights issues tended to be either downgraded or dealt with by quiet diplomacy – because UN officials, to be effective, have to avoid a rupture with major states.[25] If U Thant had been outspoken in condemning communist violations of human rights, it is doubtful he would have been acceptable to the Soviet Union for sensitive mediation in the 1962 Cuban missile crisis. In contemporary times, with human rights increasingly institutionalized within the UN and meshed with many security concerns, a Secretary-General like Kofi Annan appeared to be more willing to take firm stands for the protection of human rights. The fate of his nomination of Mary Robinson, former President of Ireland, to be the second High Commissioner for Human Rights, however, indicates that all executive authority in the UN, as an intergovernmental system, remains fragile – as explained below.

From the earliest days of the UN there were Secretariat officials active in the promotion of human rights through setting of standards, even if they were not able to achieve a great deal in specific protection efforts.[26] At the highest level, however, neither Trygve Lie nor Dag Hammarskjöld showed much direct and clear interest in internationally recognized human rights. Lie became ineffective and eventually resigned because of his clear opposition to the communist invasion of South Korea, and there is no reason to think the result would have been any different had he strongly opposed communist violations of human rights. During the Cold War, forthright and public stands on any major issue were likely to make any Secretary-General *persona non grata* to one coalition or the other. Hammarskjöld was, surprisingly enough given his Swedish nationality and overall dynamism and creativity, not to mention his religious mysticism, not much interested in human rights at the UN. While he was willing to take a strong stand on security issues in the Belgian Congo (now Zaire), even to the point of serious friction with both the Soviet Union and France, he never devoted much effort to more than a handful of rights issues via quiet diplomacy.

After U Thant, a transitional figure for present purposes, both Kurt Waldheim and Perez de Cuellar showed relatively more interest in the protection of human rights. Given the personal histories of the two men,

---

[25] In addition to Forsythe, "The UN Secretary-General and Human Rights," see Theo van Boven, "The Role of the United Nations Secretariat," in Alston, ed., *United Nations and Human Rights*, 549–579.

[26] John P. Humphrey, *Human Rights and the United Nations: A Great Adventure* (Dobbs Ferry: Transnational, 1984).

this trend is partly explained by the institutionalization factor. The Austrian Waldheim had been in the Nazi army and had consistently misrepresented that part of his past. De Cuellar had been a traditional Peruvian diplomat well versed in diplomacy based on state sovereignty, whose first major act as Secretary-General was to decide not to renew the contract of the then activist UN Director of Human Rights – the Dutchman Theo van Boven.[27] Van Boven had proved an irritant to both the military junta in Argentina and the Reagan Administration in Washington, then aligned with Buenos Aires. Yet both Waldheim and de Cuellar turned out to be more active in the protection of human rights than their predecessors, clearly so in de Cuellar's case.[28] Particularly in dealing with Central America, de Cuellar came to realize that peace and security in places like Nicaragua and El Salvador depended on progress in human rights. He therefore helped arrange deeply intrusive rights agreements, especially in El Salvador, and persistently acted to rein in death squads and other gross violators of human rights through his mediation and other diplomatic actions.[29] By the end of his second term, de Cuellar held quite different views on the importance of human rights, compared with when he entered office and got rid of van Boven.[30]

Boutros Boutros-Ghali was the most outspoken Secretary-General on human rights up to that time, making a strong case in particular for democracy. His *Agenda for Development* strongly advocated democratic development, based on civil and political rights, at a time when the General Assembly and the World Bank were, to put it kindly, less than clear in their support for civil and political rights.[31] He thus sought to correct what had been a major deficiency in human rights programming at the UN, the lack of integration between human rights and development

---

[27] See further Theo van Boven, *People Matter: Views on International Human Rights Policy* (Amsterdam: Beulenhoff Netherlands, 1982).

[28] De Cuellar listed human rights second in importance only to disarmament among pressing issues. See his "The Role of the UN Secretary-General," in Adam Roberts and Benedict Kingsbury, eds., *United Nations, Divided World: The UN's Roles in International Relations*, 2nd edn. (Oxford: Clarendon, 1993), 125 and *passim*. See also Barbara Ann J. Rieffer-Flanagan and David P. Forsythe, "Religion, Ethics, and Reality: A Study of Javier-Perez de Cuellar," in Kille, ed., *UN Secretary-General*, 229–264.

[29] See the details in David P. Forsythe, "The United Nations, Democracy, and the Americas," in Tom J. Farer, ed., *Beyond Sovereignty: Collectively Defending Democracy in the Americas* (Baltimore: Johns Hopkins University Press, 1996), 107–131.

[30] This argument, already expressed in print, I recently reconfirmed via interviews with some of those close to de Cuellar during his time in New York and with the former Secretary-General himself in interviews in Paris.

[31] A/48/935 (1994). See further David P. Forsythe, "The United Nations, Human Rights, and Development," *Human Rights Quarterly*, 19, 2 (May 1997), 334–349. See further Anthony F. Lang, Jr., "A Realist in the Utopian City: Boutros Boutros-Ghali's Ethical Framework and Its Impact," in Kille, ed., *UN Secretary-General*, 265–298.

activities.[32] A human rights dimension was present in a number of his decisions in places such as Somalia (seeing militia leader Aideed as a war criminal) and Rwanda (expressing regret that he did not persuade the USA to take more action), but this dimension was not so evident in certain other decisions.[33]

As for Kofi Annan, he may have displayed the strongest commitment to human dignity of any of the UN Secretaries-General, and he once suggested that action for human rights should generally override state sovereignty.[34] Yet like the other UN Secretaries-General, his options and policy positions were constrained by member states and their interests. And so Annan was necessarily implicated in the UN's lack of decisive action for human rights in places such as the Balkans and Rwanda, among other situations. As noted below, he responded to US pressures by getting rid of Mary Robinson when she was UN High Commissioner for Human Rights, similar to de Cuellar's sidelining of van Boven. Still, both because of his own personal values and because human rights were institutionalized in UN affairs by the time of his tenure, Annan is generally associated with as strong a support for human rights as his political context allowed. Certainly by comparison to the early days of his successor, Ban Ki-moon, Annan was widely seen as having compiled a reasonable record on human rights overall.

The Secretary-General appoints the UN High Commissioner for Human Rights, a post created by the UN General Assembly in 1993, subject to the (pro forma) approval of that body.[35] Boutros-Ghali appointed the Ecuadoran, José Ayala Lasso, as the first UN High Commissioner for Human Rights, probably hoping to assuage the fears of developing countries that the new post would be used only to hammer them on issues of civil and political rights. Thus the Secretary-General probably hoped to encourage acceptance by developing countries over time of this new and somewhat controversial post. The new High Commissioner had been a foreign minister in a previous military government in Quito.[36] Upon

---

[32] Theo van Boven, "Human Rights and Development: The UN Experience," in David P. Forsythe, ed., *Human Rights and Development: International Views* (London: Macmillan, 1989), 121–136. Compare James Gustave Speth, "Poverty: A Denial of Human Rights," *Journal of International Affairs*, 52, 1 (Fall 1998), 277–292.

[33] See Lang, "Realist in the Utopian City."

[34] Courtney B. Smith, "Politics and Values at the United Nations: Kofi Annan's Balancing Act," in Kille, ed., *UN Secretary-General*, 299–336.

[35] For a concise overview of this office, see Theo van Boven, "United Nations High Commissioner for Human Rights," in *Encyclopedia of Human Rights*, vol. V, 173–182.

[36] Ayala Lasso did originate the operation of UN field offices for human rights, generating grassroots activities for human rights within consenting countries. See further Alfred de Zayas, "Jose Ayala Lasso," in *Encyclopedia of Human Rights*, vol. I, 130–132.

Ayala Lasso's resignation to return to Ecuadoran politics, Secretary-General Annan turned to Mary Robinson, a lawyer with a record of dynamism especially on issues affecting women and the less fortunate in Ireland, which gave the promise of more dynamism on rights issues. The Cold War was over, human rights had been integrated with many UN security concerns, and much of the powerful West was demanding more vigorous UN diplomacy for human rights. The USA, the most important of the P-5, was very happy with the nomination of Robinson and her subsequent approval by the General Assembly.

One of the reasons for having a UN High Commissioner for Human Rights was to free the Secretary-General in public diplomacy to concentrate on security issues. A dynamic High Commissioner might play the role that van Boven tried to play as Director of the UN Human Rights Program. But since the Director was nominated by the Secretary-General, and without an independent power base, disaffected countries like Argentina under military rule could bring pressure on him through having a patron – in this case the Reagan Administration – lobby the Secretary-General to rein in or get rid of a human rights official causing a state embarrassment.[37]

In theory, an independent High Commissioner, once appointed in a higher-profile position created by the General Assembly, had slightly more protection from such pressures. But the fate of Robinson, the second High Commissioner for Human Rights, suggested that things had not progressed much beyond the era of de Cuellar and van Boven. Robinson was so outspoken about rights violations in places such as China, Israel, and Russia – and also by the USA regarding treatment of enemy prisoners after 9/11 – that she raised questions about whether her activism was matched by enough diplomatic acumen. Especially after a UN conference at Durban, South Africa on the subject of racism and xenophobia, in which the USA and Israel walked out after repeated speeches denouncing Israel, Washington became deeply dissatisfied with Robinson. The George W. Bush Administration leaned on the Secretary-General, Kofi Annan, not to renew her contract. He finally did as Washington desired, although Robinson wanted to continue.[38] The critique of Robinson for being too outspoken in defense of human rights was somewhat ironic, given that the first High Commissioner, Ayala Lasso of Ecuador, had been criticized by a number of human rights advocacy

---

[37] See further Iain Guest, *Behind the Disappearances: Argentina's Dirty War Against Human Rights and the United Nations* (Philadelphia: University of Pennsylvania Press, 1990).

[38] See David P. Forsythe, "Mary Robinson," in *Encyclopedia of Human Rights*, vol. IV, 347–349.

groups for being too diplomatic and not assertive enough. This indicates the crosspressures that UN officials have to manage.

After Robinson, the Secretary-General then nominated, and the General Assembly approved, Sergio de Mello of Brazil, who was an experienced diplomat with a career in the UN refugee office. But he was killed by an insurgent bombing in Iraq, and so Louise Arbour of Canada became the UN High Commissioner for Human Rights. She was a jurist, formerly the prosecutor for the UN *ad hoc* criminal court for Yugoslavia (covered in Chapter 4). She was widely respected and had more of a "judicial temperament" than Robinson. Seeing what had happened to Robinson, early on she relied more on quiet diplomacy than public criticism. Yet over time she, too, spoke out on a number of issues and also was criticized by, in particular, the George W. Bush Administration in the USA.[39] Arbour was followed by Navi Pillay, a jurist of Asian descent from South Africa.

In sum, the Office of the Secretary-General, including after 1993 the related office of the UN High Commissioner for Human Rights, represented the purposes of the organization as found in the Charter. Among these purposes was international cooperation on human rights. Yet most decisions taken in the name of the UN were taken by states, and the Secretary-General, while independent, was also given instructions by states acting collectively through UN organs. Moreover, he (or she in the future) could only be effective when he retained the confidence of the more important states. Thus there was room for action on human rights, which Secretaries-General had progressively exercised as human rights became more and more a regular part of international and UN affairs. The Secretary-General's protective action, beyond promotional activities, consisted mostly of reasoning in quiet diplomacy.

But there were also major constraints imposed by states – such as lack of real commitment to international human rights, lack of consensus on priorities, and lack of adequate funding. Even as states endorsed human rights norms, they still did not like being criticized in public on human rights issues, as especially Theo van Boven and Mary Robinson discovered when they were eased out of office. It was certainly ironic that the USA, which often presented itself to the world as a model on human rights, undercut both van Boven and Robinson when an ally – military government in Argentina or Israel as occupying power – was publicly criticized by the UN High Commissioner for Human Rights. Particularly the George W. Bush Administration, with its strong unilateralist tendencies at times, did not take kindly to public criticisms of its detention and

---

[39] See further William A. Schabas, "Louise Arbour," ibid., vol. II, 88–91.

interrogation policies at Guantanamo and other places by Robinson and Arbour.

Other main organs: the General Assembly, ECOSOC, and the ICJ

The GA The UN General Assembly has been instrumental in the promotion of human rights, approving some two dozen treaties and adopting a number of "motherhood" resolutions endorsing various human rights in general. The Assembly has played a much less important role in the protection of specific human rights in specific situations, although much ambiguity inheres in this subject. The Assembly has mandated a number of new UN offices to deal with human rights.

One can take a minimalist approach and note that the General Assembly did not try to reverse certain decisions taken in the Economic and Social Council (ECOSOC) and the UN Human Rights Commission that were directed to specific protection attempts (see below).[40] Furthermore, since many of the treaty monitoring mechanisms report to the Assembly, the same can be said for the Assembly's review of those bodies (see below). More optimistically, after the Cold War as before, the Assembly adopted a number of specific resolutions condemning human rights violations in various countries.[41] During the Cold War, it is likely that repeated Assembly condemnation of Israeli and South African policies had little immediate remedial effect on those two target states, as they viewed the Assembly as inherently biased against them. This was certainly the case when the Assembly declared Zionism to be a form of racism in 1975, a resolution eventually rescinded in 1991. (Some of the standard arguments about Zionism as racism, however, were renewed at the Durban I conference of 2001 mentioned above. They did not figure prominently at Durban II in 2009.)[42] It is possible that repeated Assembly attacks on apartheid policies in South Africa contributed to an international normative climate in which powerful states eventually brought

---

[40] John Quinn, "The General Assembly into the 1990s," in Alston, ed., *United Nations and Human Rights*, 55–106.

[41] Soo Yeon Kim and Bruce Russett, "The New Politics of Voting Alignments in the United Nations General Assembly," *International Organization*, 50, 4 (Autumn 1996), 629–652.

[42] On the politics of victimhood as it relates to struggles over legitimacy, see Pierre Hazan, *Judging War, Judging History: Behind Truth and Reconciliation* (Stanford: Stanford University Press, 2007). Israel has sought to bolster its legitimacy by reference to its hosting victims of the Holocaust, while some developing countries present themselves as the victims of imperialism and colonialism, picturing Israel as part of those processes. These views played out in various UN meetings.

pressure to bear on racist South Africa.[43] How ideas as expressed in Assembly resolutions affect states' definitions of their national interests remains a murky matter.[44] In any event the Assembly shrank the realm of state sovereignty by demonstrating clearly that diplomatic discussion of specific human rights situations in specific countries was indeed part of routinized international relations, even if the Assembly displayed a tendency to adopt paper solutions to complex and controversial subjects.[45] As one expert noted, the UN General Assembly did not invent the politicization of human rights, as political debates are inherent in construction and interpretation of the concept. So it should come as no surprise that the Assembly was the scene of different disputes as state members from a diverse world contested meanings, priorities, and targets of action.[46]

ECOSOC ECOSOC, officially one of the UN's principal organs, very rapidly became little more than a mailbox between the Assembly and various bodies subsidiary to ECOSOC, transmitting or reaffirming instructions from the Assembly to a proliferation of social and economic agencies. ECOSOC is not, and has never been, a major actor for human rights.[47] The states elected to ECOSOC have taken three decisions of importance since 1945 regarding human rights, one essentially negative and two positive. First, ECOSOC decided that the members of the UN Human Rights Commission should be state representatives and not independent experts. This decision put the foxes inside the hen house. Later ECOSOC adopted its resolution 1235, permitting the Commission to take up specific complaints about specific countries. Resolution 1503 was also eventually adopted, permitting the Commission to deal with private petitions indicating a systematic pattern of gross violations of internationally recognized human rights. While ECOSOC resolutions 1235 and 1503 affected considerable diplomacy, they did not lead to sure protection of human rights on the ground.

---

[43] See further Audie Klotz, "Norms Reconstituting Interests: Global Racial Equality and US Sanctions Against South Africa," *International Organization*, 49, 3 (Summer 1995), 451–478.

[44] See further Judith Goldstein and Robert O. Keohane, eds., *Ideas and Foreign Policy: Beliefs, Institutions and Political Change* (Ithaca: Cornell University Press, 1993); and Albert S. Yee, "The Causal Effects of Ideas on Politics," *International Organization*, 50, 1 (Winter 1996), 69–108.

[45] Antonio Cassese, "The General Assembly: Historical Perspective 1945–1989," in Alston, ed., *United Nations and Human Rights*, 25–54.

[46] M. J. Peterson, "United Nations General Assembly," in *Encyclopedia of Human Rights*, vol. V, 165–172.

[47] Declan O'Donovan, "The Economic and Social Council," in Alston, ed., *United Nations and Human Rights*, 107–125.

In addition, ECOSOC maintains a committee that decides which non-governmental organizations (NGOs) will be given which category of consultative status with the UN system. The highest status allows NGOs to attend UN meetings and submit documents. Both before and after the Cold War, this committee was the scene of various struggles over human rights NGOs. Certain states that were defensive about human rights matters tried, with periodic success, to deny full status, or sometimes any status, to legitimate human rights NGOs. These problems diminished by the end of the twentieth century. Still, in the late 1990s, a western-based NGO that had antagonized the Sudanese government and engaged in a controversial policy of buying back hostages taken in Sudan's longrunning civil war (such a policy provided money to the fighting parties and led to the retaking of sometimes the same hostages) was denied consultative status.

Finally, ECOSOC officially supervises a number of UN agencies such as the UN Development Program (UNDP). UNDP remains primarily a development agency but clearly it has increased its activities pertaining to human rights associated with democracy and the status of women. Its Human Development Reports are widely cited; they chart indicators of sustainable human development – a broad concept that overlaps with human rights. Most of these initiatives came from UNDP itself and not from ECOSOC.[48]

The ICJ The International Court of Justice (ICJ), technically a principal UN organ but highly independent once its judges are elected by the Security Council and General Assembly, has not made a major imprint on the protection of international human rights.[49] This is primarily because only states have standing before the Court in binding cases, and states have demonstrated for a long time a reluctance to either sue or be sued – especially on human rights matters – in international tribunals.[50] As long as individuals lack legal standing, the ICJ's case load on human rights is highly likely to remain light.

From time to time the Court is presented with the opportunity to rule on issues of international human rights and humanitarian law. In 1986 in

---

[48] See further Elizabeth A. Mandeville, "United Nations Development Programme," in *Encyclopedia of Human Rights*, vol. V, 50–157. Compare Carmen Huckel Schneider, "World Health Organization (WHO)," ibid., vol. V, 388–394.

[49] For a concise introduction with mention of several cases, see Ralph G. Steinhardt, "International Court of Justice," ibid., vol. III, 103–112.

[50] A. S. Muller, D. Raic, and J. M. Thuranszky, eds., *The International Court of Justice: Its Future Role After Fifty Years* (The Hague: Martinus Nijhoff, 1997), especially the chapter by Mark Janis.

Nicaragua v. the United States it reaffirmed some points about both human rights and international humanitarian law while dealing primarily with security issues such as what activity constitutes an armed attack giving rise to a right of self-defense.

In the Belgian arrest warrant judgment of 2002, the ICJ held that an individual state (in this case Belgium) could not on its own exercise the principle of universal jurisdiction and pursue legal charges for gross violations of human rights against a sitting state official (in this case the foreign minister of Democratic Congo). In the Court's view such sitting officials were protected by the principle of sovereign immunity, which should be respected in the interests of orderly international relations. On the other hand, one might conclude from other developments that, if a centralized body like the UN Security Council, and/or its derivative agencies, sought similar legal proceedings, they might continue. One could note that Slobodan Milosevic, when an official of Serbia, and Omar Hassan al-Bashir, when an official of Sudan, were both required to answer to legal proceedings about human rights violations (in the first instance via the International Criminal Tribunal for the former Yugoslavia, and in the second via the International Criminal Court).[51]

In 2004 in the Avena judgment, the ICJ handed down a ruling ostensibly about a treaty on consular relations but in substance about the death penalty in the USA. Under the 1963 Vienna Convention on Consular Relations, a state party is obligated, when detaining aliens, to notify defendants of a right to contact their consular officials in order to guarantee adequate defense counsel. This the state of Texas did not do with regard to several defendants from Mexico. Mexico sued the USA at the ICJ, particularly since the death penalty was facing a number of its nationals detained in the USA. By overwhelming majority the ICJ held the USA in violation of its treaty obligations. A central problem for the USA was its federalism and the fact that the Mexican prisoners had been processed in state, not federal, courts. A subsequent US Supreme Court decision, the Medellin judgment, held that US authorities in Washington had no

---

[51] Pieter H. H. Bekker, "World Court Orders Belgium to Cancel an Arrest Warrant Issued Against the Congolese Foreign Minister," *ASIL Insights* (February 2002), www.asil.org/insigh82.cfm. In the 1999 Pinochet case in the UK, not involving the ICJ but involving this same subject matter, the British court held that Pinochet, as a *former* head of state, could indeed be extradited to Spain to stand trial for allegations of past torture in Chile under Spain's exercise of universal jurisdiction. Britain eventually returned Pinochet to Chile on supposedly humanitarian grounds (ill health) but probably because he had been a staunch anti-communist ally of Britain during the Cold War. The legal principle about prosecution for torture remained, even if Pinochet died without having to stand trial for his actions.

authority under the US Constitution to instruct Texas courts as to proper procedure. José Medellin was eventually executed in Texas for murder, the USA remained in violation of its obligations under international law, and states such as California, but not Texas, changed their state law to provide the requirement of notification required via the Vienna Consular Convention.[52]

Also in 2004 the ICJ gave an advisory opinion on the legality of Israel's new security wall, part of which was built on territory beyond "the green line" or Israel's *de facto* borders in 1949. In this case the ICJ showed evident concern for the fate of Palestinians adversely affected by the wall, with the Court paying much attention to the Fourth Geneva Convention of 1949 dealing with occupied territory. (The ICJ is allowed to give advisory as well as binding judgments; such advisory rulings might become binding over time, dependent on whether they enter customary international law.)[53]

In 2007 the ICJ made a ruling on genocide in the Balkans that satisfied very few analysts. In responding to a petition from Bosnia against Serbia, the Court held on the one hand that it could not find evidence of genocide by Serbia. On the other hand it found that Serbia had failed in its legal obligations to prevent genocide in cases such as the Srebrenica massacre of 1995. This complex judgment, obviously a compromise, did little to improve the situation in the Balkans or to enhance the status of the Court.[54] In sum, the Bosnian Serb massacre at Srebrenica was held to be genocide, Serb authorities in Belgrade were held not to be responsible, but those same authorities were held liable for not preventing the genocidal massacre.

In general, while the ICJ's case load has increased on average from two or three cases per year to ten or eleven after the Cold War, it is still rare for the Court to make a major pronouncement on human rights. States still generally regard human rights as too important a subject to entrust to some fifteen independent judges of various nationalities who make their judgments with reference to rules of law rather than national interest or public opinion. Thus, for example, while the 1948 Genocide Convention contains an article providing for compulsory jurisdiction for the ICJ in

---

[52] William J. Aceves, "Consular Notification and the Death Penalty: The ICJ's Judgment in *Avena*," *ASIL Insights* (April 2004), www.asil.org/insigh130.cfm; *Medellin v. Texas*, 552 U.S. 491 (2008).

[53] For a variety of reactions to the ICJ advisory ruling on Israel's security wall, see *American Journal of International Law*, 99, 1 (January 2005), 1–141.

[54] For a short overview see Jason Morgan-Foster and Pierre-Olivier Savoie, "World Court Finds Serbia Responsible for Breaches of Genocide Convention, but Not Liable for Committing Genocide," *ASIL Insights* (April 2007), www.asil.org/insights070403.cfm.

resolving disputes under this treaty, states like the USA reserved against this article when ratifying the treaty.

Under the Court's statute, states can give a blanket jurisdiction to the ICJ to rule on all or some legal issues, but few states have done so in unambiguous fashion. In this respect the end of the Cold War has made no difference. State defense of sovereignty still trumps interest in orderly and humane international relations, at least in so far as the ICJ is concerned. The ICJ case load shows that realism is alive and well, as states protect their claims to sovereign decision making so as to pursue their national interests as they define them. In general, states, certainly most major military powers, are still reluctant to place the ICJ in a supranational position and do not often give it legal authority to have the final say on human rights issues.

Major subsidiary bodies

In addition to the principal UN organs, there are several subsidiary bodies that concern themselves with the application of human rights standards. The focus here is on the UN Human Rights Council (formerly the Human Rights Commission), the International Labour Organization, and the Office of the UN High Commissioner for Refugees. The Sub-Commission on Prevention of Discrimination and Protection of Minorities, first renamed the UN Sub-Commission on Human Rights, and since 2006 recast again as the Human Rights Advisory Committee, has been active but reports to the Council. Space constraints oblige its omission. The Commission on the Status of Women has been primarily engaged in promotional and assistance activities rather than protection efforts.[55] The two *ad hoc* criminal courts are addressed in Chapter 4. UNESCO can be mentioned in passing. Its activities too are primarily promotional rather than protective.[56]

The Human Rights Commission, now Council

It used to be said of the UN Human Rights Commission that it was the organization's premier body, or diplomatic hub, for human rights issues. After the Cold War this was no longer completely the case. If

---

[55] Stephanie Farrior, "United Nations Commission on the Status of Women," in *Encyclopedia of Human Rights*, vol. V, 142–149.

[56] Roger A. Coate, "United Nations Educational, Scientific, and Cultural Organization (UNESCO)," ibid., vol. V, 158–164; and David Weissbrodt and Rose Farley, "The UNESCO Human Rights Procedure: An Evaluation," *Human Rights Quarterly*, 16, 2 (May 1994), 391–414.

the Security Council establishes a connection between human rights and international peace and security, then the Council becomes the most important, certainly the most authoritative, UN forum for human rights – as discussed above. What can be said is that until 2005 the Commission remained the center for traditional or routine human rights diplomacy, in addition to the Secretary-General's office, and in loose tandem with the UN High Commissioner for Human Rights. The UN system has never been known for tight organization and streamlined, clear chains of command.

The Commission for Human Rights was anticipated from the very beginning of the UN and first served as a drafting body for the International Bill of Rights and many other international instruments on human rights.[57] As noted above, it was composed of representatives of states, elected by ECOSOC, itself composed of states. Because of its composition as well as its focus on drafting legal standards, for its first twenty years the Commission avoided specific inquiries about specific rights in specific countries. In one wonderful phrase, it demonstrated a "fierce commitment to inoffensiveness."[58] Contributing to this situation was the fact that both the East and West during the Cold War knew that if they raised specific human rights issues, such inquiries could be turned against them. The West controlled the Commission in its early days, but its own record on racism and discrimination suggested prudence in the face of any desire to hammer the communists on their evident violations of civil and political rights. In any event, Cold War debates about human rights violations occurred in the UN General Assembly, and, it might be noted, without any notable effects on improving the actual practice of human rights on either side of the Cold War divide.

Beginning in about 1967 the Commission began to stumble toward more protection activities rather than just promotional ones. This change was made possible primarily by the greater number of developing countries in the organization. They were determined to do something about racism in southern Africa and what they saw as neo-imperialism and racism via the Zionist movement in the Middle East. They did not apparently anticipate how a focus on specific rights in specific places could also be turned against them in the future. Some western governments, pushed by western-based non-governmental organizations, then struck a deal with the developing countries in the newly expanded ECOSOC and

[57] This and many other points about the Commission are drawn from Alston, ed., *United Nations and Human Rights*, 126–210.

[58] Tom J. Farer, "The UN and Human Rights: More than a Whimper, Less than a Roar," in Roberts and Kingsbury, eds., *United Nations, Divided World*, 23.

Commission, agreeing to debates about Israel and South Africa in return for similar attention to countries like Haiti and Greece, both then under authoritarian rule. The door was thus opened for attempts under the Charter to monitor and supervise all state behavior relative to international rights standards, using the Universal Declaration of Human Rights as the central guide.

ECOSOC's Resolutions 1235 and 1503, mentioned above, authorized specific review of state behavior on rights, and a Commission response to private petitions alleging a pattern of gross violations of rights, respectively. In theory, both procedures represented a constriction of absolute and expansive state sovereignty. In practice, neither procedure resulted in systematic, sure, and impressive protections of specific rights for specific persons in specific countries. Lawyers sometimes got excited about the new procedures, but victims of rights violations were much less impressed. Mostly because of the 1235 procedure allowing a debate and resolutions on particular states, the Commission sometimes used "Special Procedures" and appointed country investigators, by whatever name, to continue investigations and keep the diplomatic spotlight on certain states, thus continuing the politics of embarrassment. This step, too, while sometimes bringing some limited improvement to a rights situation, failed to provide systematic and sure protection. The 1503 procedure on private petitions, triggered by NGOs as well as by individuals, took too long to transpire and was mostly shielded from publicity by its confidential nature. Somewhat more effective was the Commission's use of *thematic* investigators or working groups, such as on forced disappearances. These developed the techniques of "urgent action" and "prompt intervention." The Commission also started the practice of holding emergency sessions to give prominence to a subject. Yet if at the end of emergency sessions, and reports by the country, thematic, or emergency investigators, member states were not prepared to take further action, Commission proceedings still failed to generate the necessary impact on violative states.

Summarizing the protective role of the Commission has never been easy.[59] If one looks at what transpires inside Commission meetings, there was clear progress after about 1967 in attempts by this UN agency to pressure states into complying with internationally recognized human rights. States mostly took Commission proceedings seriously. They did not like to have the Commission focus on their deficiencies. Many went

---

[59] See further Howard Tolley, Jr., *The UN Commission on Human Rights* (Boulder: Westview, 1987). See also the relevant essays in Gudmundur Alfredsson, et al., eds., *International Human Rights Monitoring Mechanisms* (The Hague: Martinus Nijhoff, 2001).

to great efforts to block, delay, or weaken criticism by the Commission and its agents. This was true, for example, of Argentina in the 1980s and China in the 1990s. Despite these obstructionist efforts, at first a fairly balanced list of states was publicly put in the diplomatic dock via the Commission. Careful scholarship established that the actual record of the Commission over time in attempted protection was not as poor as often suggested, with much appropriate diplomacy directed at precisely those states with poor human rights records.[60]

The Commission, however, suffered a decline in reputation. The main reason for this was state foreign policy, since the Commission was made up of states. In the geographical caucuses of the UN, where many real decisions about the UN are made, member states elevated certain concerns like equitable geographical representation over concern for serious and impartial protection of human rights. Thus the Latin American caucus elected Cuba to the UN Human Rights Commission, despite its poor record on civil and political rights. Thus the African and Arab caucuses combined to ensure the election of repressive Libya as President of the Commission at one point. Also debilitating in the Commission were persistent double standards in rights debates, especially by the major countries. The P-5 countries were always elected to the Commission by tradition (with the USA denied a seat only one time in a controversial vote in its caucuses group). China, for example, was certainly not committed to systematic protection of human rights, going to great lengths, including use of foreign assistance, to try to ensure that its rights record was not the target of a critical resolution. The USA, for example, spent much time in focusing on the rights record of adversaries like Cuba, while remaining silent on egregious human rights violations in allies like Saudi Arabia. African and other developing countries were reluctant to address the rights violations of their compatriots in places like Zimbabwe, preferring to focus on Israeli policies in the occupied territories. So, given the very messy political process of the body, the Commission lost legitimacy in the eyes of many.

If one looks at the Commission in broad context, it is clear that many states were prepared to continue with rights violations, even if this brought various forms of criticism and condemnation. In places like

---

[60] J. H. Lebovic and E. Voeten, "The Politics of Shame: The Condemnation of Country Human Rights Practices in the UNCHR," *International Studies Quarterly*, 50, 3 (2006), 861–888. Note that this study was not published until after the Commission gave way to the Council. See the follow-on study by David P. Forsythe with Baekkwan Park, "Turbulent Transition: From the UN Human Rights Commission to the Council," in Scott Kaufman and Alissa Warters, eds., *The United Nations: Past, Present and Future* (Haupagge, NY: Nova Science Publishers, 2009), 85–110.

the former Yugoslavia or the Great Lakes region of Africa, numerous parties were prepared to go on killing and maiming in the name of ethnic group or political power, regardless of words spoken or written in Geneva where the Commission was based. Russia was the only P-5 country to be the target of a resolution of criticism in the Commission, but this did not change to any appreciable extent its brutal policies in the secessionist region of Chechnya.[61] In the last analysis the Commission was divorced from control of military, economic, and the more important diplomatic sanctions. If the Commission's thematic measures (such as Special Rapporteurs and special Working Groups) on forced disappearances could provide some protection to 25 percent of its persons of concern, this was considered a very good relative figure of success. Diplomatic pressure conducted with weak resources stood little chance of cracking the hard nut of intentional and systematic, rather than accidental and episodic, violations of human rights.

Such was the dissatisfaction with the UN Human Rights Commission, whether carefully considered or not, that during 2005 Secretary-General Kofi Annan proposed the dissolution of the Commission and its replacement by a Human Rights Council as a major organ of the UN. This change in fact transpired, with the new Council reporting to the General Assembly.[62] But changes turned out to be more superficial than substantive.

From 2006 the new Human Rights Council looked more or less like, and acted more or less like, the old Commission. While the western-style democracies and the non-western developing countries might agree on dissolution of the old Commission, for different reasons as it turned out, they could not agree on new arrangements that would guarantee improved protection of human rights. The new Council was still dominated by the numerous African and Asian states. As lobbied especially by the Arab League and Conference of Islamic States, the Council continued to vote disproportionate criticism of Israel compared to similar or greater human rights violations in various developing countries. The USA changed from a policy of boycott (under the George W. Bush Administration) to one of engagement (under the Obama Administration). But this did not much change the double standards and other weaknesses of the Council. The Council remained a politicized talking shop of minor

---

[61] See further Catherine Osgood, "Chechnya," in *Encyclopedia of Human Rights*, vol. I, 290–299.
[62] In addition to Forsythe and Park, "Turbulent Transition," see Paul Gordon Lauren, "To Preserve and Build on Its Achievements and to Redress Its Shortcomings: The Journey from the Commission on Human Rights to the Human Rights Council," *Human Rights Quarterly*, 29, 2 (May 2007), 307–345.

importance relative to many other developments concerning internationally recognized human rights. On occasion, but not consistently, it took a principled decision, as when it suspended Kaddafi's Libya from membership in 2011.

The change from Commission to Council amounted to a repackaging of old wine in a new bottle, although some held out hope for progress over time. There was a new Universal Periodic Review in which all states had to defend their human rights records, but the input from the UN High Commissioner for Human Rights was meager. And the so-called Special Procedures continued (Rapporteurs and Working Groups) which allowed relatively independent and non-politicized diplomacy on behalf of certain human rights problems.[63] But often the Council paid scant attention to their reports. If the Council, like the Commission, was engaged in a long-term effort to educate or socialize about human rights, this process might eventually bear some fruit. But serious and evident protection of human rights through the Council in the short run remained elusive. The Security Council was much more important, if also inconsistent as noted earlier.

International Labour Organization

The ILO has long been concerned with labor rights, first as a parallel organization to the League of Nations, then as a specialized agency of the UN system. It has developed several complicated procedures for monitoring state behavior in the area of labor rights. In general, certain differences aside, its record on helping apply international labor rights is similar to that of the UN Human Rights Commission, now the Council, in two respects: it proceeds according to indirect implementation efforts falling short of direct enforcement; and its exact influence is difficult to specify.[64]

---

[63] Surya P. Subedi, "Protection of Human Rights Through the Mechanism of UN Special Rapporteurs," *Human Rights Quarterly*, 33, 1 (February 2011), 201–228.

[64] For a positive overview see Lee Swepston, "International Labor Organization," in *Encyclopedia of Human Rights*, vol. III, 144–150. Along similar lines, see Virginia A. Leary, "Lessons from the Experience of the International Labor Organization," in Alston, ed., *United Nations and Human Rights*, 580–619. Compare Hector G. Bartolomei de la Cruz, Geraldo von Potobsky, and Lee Swepston, *The International Labor Organization: The International Standards System and Basic Human Rights* (Boulder: Westview, 1996); and Nicolas Valticos, "The International Labor Organization," in Karel Vasak, ed., *The International Dimensions of Human Rights*, edited for the English edition by Philip Alston (Westport: Greenwood, for UNESCO, 1982). For a historical treatment and optimistic evaluation, see Gerry Rodgers, et al., *The ILO and the Quest for Social Justice, 1919–2009* (Ithaca: Cornell University Press, 2009).

Of the more than 170 treaties developed through and supervised by the ILO, a handful are considered oriented toward basic human rights such as the freedom to associate in trade unions, the freedom to bargain collectively, and the right to be free from forced labor. States consenting to these treaties are obligated to submit reports to the ILO, indicating steps they have taken to apply treaty provisions. These reports are reviewed first by a committee of experts, then by a larger and more political body. Specialized ILO secretariat personnel assist the review committees. At both stages, workers' organizations participate actively. Other participants come from owners' organizations, and states. This tripartite membership of the ILO at least reduces or delays some of the problems inherent in the UN Human Rights Commission, such as states' political obstruction that makes serious review difficult. Nevertheless, at the end of the day the ILO regular review process centers on polite if persistent diplomacy devoid of more stringent sanctions beyond public criticism. Some issues remain under review for years. States may not enjoy multilateral criticism, but they learn to live with it as the price of continued political power or economic transactions.

All member states of the ILO are subject to a special review procedure on the key subject of freedom of association, regardless of their consent to various ILO treaties. Despite procedural differences, the outcome of these special procedures is not very different from the regular review. Workers' organizations are more active than owner and state representatives, and public criticism of state malfeasance must be repeated because amelioration comes slowly. Indeed, a study of freedom of association and the ILO during the Cold War concluded that those states most violative of freedom of association were also most resistant to ILO pressures for change.[65] There are procedures for "urgent cases," but these sometimes take months to unfold. If a Chile under Pinochet or a Poland under Jaruzelski was determined to suppress independent labor movements, the ILO was unable to protect them – at least in the short term.

There are still further actions the ILO can take in defense of labor rights, such as sending special representatives of the Director-General for contact with offending governments. Moreover, the ILO is not the only UN agency concerned with labor rights. UNICEF, for example, is much concerned with child labor, arguing in early 1997 that some 250 million child laborers were being harshly exploited.[66]

---

[65] Ernst B. Haas, *Human Rights and International Action: The Case of Freedom of Association* (Stanford: Stanford University Press, 1970).
[66] UNICEF helped develop the Convention on the Rights of the Child, which contains provisions relevant to child labor. See Lawrence J. LeBlanc, *The Convention on the*

All the ILO diplomacy for labor rights no doubt has an educational effect over time and constitutes a certain nuisance factor for states interested in their reputations in international circles. It remains true, however, that some states regard cheap and disorganized labor as part of their "comparative advantage" in international markets, and therefore useful in pursuit of economic growth for the nation as a whole. Suppressed labor organizations may also prove convenient to ruling elites. While some see labor rights as an essential part of human rights, others see labor rights as disguised claims to privileges or special benefits.[67] There are those who see the western emphasis on labor rights as part of neo-imperialism, designed to hamstring developing countries' drive for economic growth by saddling them with labor standards that the more developed countries never met in their "takeoff" stage of "crude capitalism" in the earlier years of the industrial revolution. The contrary view was that international labor rights were necessary to protect labor even in the developing countries, by mandating equal competition and a level playing field in global economic matters.

Then there was the very real problem of black market labor associated with human trafficking, certainly recognized by the ILO. Organized crime, both large and small, moved illegal labor across state borders for coerced prostitution, for compelled servitude as domestic servants, for indebted workers for migrant agricultural labor, and more. Given that often significant money could be made by those who controlled the trafficking (illegal human trafficking across the Mexican–USA border was worth about $6 billion annually), this proved a growing problem that both the ILO and its member states found difficult to deal with. A modern form of slavery, human trafficking belied the legal prohibitions on slavery established in the nineteenth and twentieth centuries.[68]

At the start of the twenty-first century, with more global markets than ever before, labor issues remained one of the more controversial features

---

Rights of the Child: United Nations Lawmaking on Human Rights (Lincoln: University of Nebraska Press, 1995).

[67] See further Lance A. Compa and Stephen F. Diamond, *Human Rights, Labor Rights, and International Trade* (Philadelphia: University of Pennsylvania Press, 1996). Note that in the USA in the state of Wisconsin and other internal states in 2011, political conservatives thought labor unions for public workers had negotiated contracts for "elevated" benefits that were unsustainable in a time of economic difficulties.

[68] See the concise but analytical coverage by Howard B. Tolley, Jr., "Human Trafficking," in *Encyclopedia of Human Rights*, vol. II, 494–502; Joel Quirk, "Slavery and the Slave Trade," ibid., vol. IV, 462–471. See also Kevin Bales, ed., *Understanding Global Slavery: A Reader* (Berkeley: University of California Press, 2005). See further Jorge Heine and Ramesh Thakur, eds., *The Dark Side of Globalization* (Tokyo: United Nations University Press, 2011). The latter note that labor rights are relatively poorly regulated on a global basis, accurately contesting some of the optimistic evaluations of the ILO.

of global efforts to apply human rights standards. I return to this subject in Chapter 8, dealing with transnational corporations.

The High Commissioner for Refugees

After World War II, such was the naïvety of the international community that it was thought the problem of refugees was a small residue of that war and would be cleared up rather quickly.[69] Over half a century later, refugees as defined in international law numbered about 13–15 million each year, perhaps another 25 million persons found themselves in a refugee-like situation, and the UN Office of the High Commissioner for Refugees (UNHCR) had become a permanent organization with an annual budget of around $1 billion.[70] Some 2 million persons fled genocide in the Great Lakes region of Africa in 1994–1995. Some 800,000 ethnic Albanians were forced out of Yugoslavia's Kosovo area in 1999.

International law provided for legal refugees – those individuals crossing an international boundary on the basis of a well-founded fear of persecution (also called social, political, or convention refugees). Such persons had the legal right not to be returned to a threatening situation, and thus were to be granted at least temporary asylum in states of first sanctuary. But in addition, many persons fled disorder without being individually singled out for persecution, and others found themselves displaced but still within their country of habitual residence (and thus internally displaced persons, or IDPs). Others needed international protection after returning to their original state ("returnees"). After the Cold War virtually all of the traditional states of asylum, historically speaking, adopted more restrictive policies regarding refugees and asylum seekers. Being protective of traditional national values and numbers, these western states feared being overwhelmed with outsiders in an era of easier transportation, not to mention an era of international organized crime and human trafficking.

The UNHCR started out primarily as a protective agency that sought to represent legal refugees diplomatically and legally. States retained final authority as to who was recognized as a legal refugee and thus who was to be granted temporary or permanent entrance to the country. Hence the

---

[69] On this and subsequent points, see in particular Gil Loescher, *Beyond Charity: International Cooperation and the Global Refugee Crisis* (New York: Oxford University Press, 1993, for the Twentieth Century Fund). See also his excellent overview, *The UNHCR and World Politics: A Perilous Path* (Oxford: Oxford University Press, 2001).

[70] See Geoff Gilbert, "United Nations High Commissioner for Refugees," in *Encyclopedia of Human Rights*, vol. V, 183–190; Joel R. Charny, "Internally Displaced Persons," ibid., vol. III, 70–79.

early role of the UNHCR was primarily to contact states' legal authorities and/or foreign ministries on behalf of those exiles with a well-founded fear of persecution. Increasingly the UNHCR was drawn into the relief business, to the extent that some observers believed it was no longer able to adequately protect refugees because its time, personnel, and budgets were consumed by relief operations. In its relief, the UNHCR felt compelled by moral concerns to disregard most distinctions among legal refugees, war refugees, and internally displaced persons. They were all in humanitarian need. This approach was approved by the General Assembly. Given that repatriation rather than resettlement became increasingly the only hope for a durable solution to refugee problems, the UNHCR increasingly addressed itself to the human rights problems causing flight in the first place. Thus the UNHCR became less and less a strictly humanitarian actor, and more and more a human rights actor dealing with the root causes of refugee problems.[71] In 1999, for example, High Commissioner Sadako Ogata testified to the UN Security Council that the primary cause of flight from Kosovo was not NATO bombing but mass persecution and terror by the Serbian authorities in Yugoslavia.

The UNHCR faced numerous and complex issues while trying to provide protection and relief to those who had broken normal relations with their governments. In Bosnia in the early 1990s the UNHCR found itself contributing to ethnic cleansing by moving persons out of harm's way in accordance with the desires of certain fighting parties, but it was morally preferable to do so rather than see the persons killed. In effect in the Balkans in the early 1990s, important states "hid behind" the UNHCR, insisting it stay on the scene to give the impression that "the international community" was doing something. In reality, these states wanted to avoid decisive military involvement that might prove unpopular at home; for this cynical reason the UNHCR (and Red Cross agencies) proved politically useful. But their humanitarian missions became compromised. In the Great Lakes region of Africa, armed militia were mixed with civilian refugees. The UNHCR had no authority or power to police refugee areas, and thus faced the dilemma of whether to provide relief to all or to withdraw in protest against the presence of armed groups interested in continuing the violence. While some private relief agencies pulled out, the UNHCR stayed – and tried to arrange the proper policing of refugee camps by certain local states. State members of the UN Security Council

---

[71] See further Gil Loescher, "Refugees: A Global Human Rights and Security Crisis," in Tim Dunne and Nicholas J. Wheeler, eds., *Human Rights in Global Politics* (Cambridge: Cambridge University Press, 1999), 233–258. More generally see Emma Haddad, *The Refugee in International Society: Between Sovereigns* (Cambridge: Cambridge University Press, 2008).

were clearly briefed as to the situation but refused to take the necessary steps to clear the brutal militias out of the refugee camps.[72]

Despite some evidence of accounting and other mismanagement, and charges that its bureaucracy in Geneva was not as committed to the needs of refugees as it could be, the UNHCR was often seen as one of the more respected UN agencies. It became one of the more important UN relief agencies, it was trying to re-establish a sound record of protection, and its legal staff had been a pioneer in addressing the special problems of female refugees.[73]

Treaty-specific bodies

The United Nations is a decentralized and poorly coordinated system. Since states are unwilling thus far to create a human rights court to centralize the juridical protection of internationally recognized human rights, each human rights treaty may (or may not) provide its own monitoring mechanism. (The 1948 Genocide Convention, with 140 parties as of early 2011, refers unresolved disputes to the International Court of Justice.) Since obviously the UN Human Rights Council, the ILO, and the UNHCR have not resolved all or even most human rights problems, the tendency is to respond to pressing problems via a specialized treaty with an additional supervisory system. States keep adopting human rights standards, but avoiding the hard issue of effective enforcement. The result is a proliferation of weak implementation agencies and a further lack of coordination. The heads of the treaty monitoring mechanisms, however, have started meeting together to exchange views. Sometimes human rights independent experts also try concerted or pooled diplomacy, as when in 2004–2005 they compiled a joint report about, and asked to visit, the US detention center at Guantanamo Bay. The existence of the post of UN High Commissioner for Human Rights since 1993 may eventually improve coordination in relative terms. (There is also the embryonic international criminal court analyzed in Chapter 4.) Here we cover the two monitoring mechanisms under the two basic Covenants, then make quick reference to other treaty-based bodies.

---

[72] See Sadako Ogata, *The Turbulent Decade: Confronting the Refugee Crises of the 1990s* (New York: Norton, 2005).

[73] Unfortunately some of its local personnel in East Africa were implicated in the sexual harassment of women and girls, in that special attention was offered in return for sexual favors. The problem also sometimes occurred in UN peacekeeping operations. A principal problem especially in peacekeeping was that the UN Secretariat lacked the authority to properly train, and in some cases ensure the punishment of, personnel loaned by states.

The Human Rights Committee

The International Covenant on Civil and Political Rights, with 167 parties as of early 2011, provides for a Human Rights Committee with two basic protective functions. Composed of individual experts nominated and elected by states that are party to the Covenant, the Committee reviews and comments on obligatory state reports. The Committee also processes individual petitions alleging violations of rights under the Covenant, from those states consenting to an optional protocol. As of early 2011, 113 states had provided that specialized consent. There is also a procedure for state-to-state complaints, but it has never been activated.

A second protocol forbidding the death penalty has many fewer ratifications (just over seventy), and has had no clear influence yet on states such as the USA, Japan, China, and Iran, *inter alia*, that widely use the death penalty for common crime (as compared to political crime like treason). In the case of the USA, it defends its position on use of the death penalty by arguing in human rights forums that: (1) it is not forbidden by general international law; (2) it is established by democratic process reflecting majority opinion and independent court judgments; (3) it is not much used by federal courts, but under US federalism it is up to state (provincial) authorities over which federal authorities have no control. Nevertheless, the USA does have to take into account opposition to the death penalty particularly in extradition matters, where the USA often has to agree to forego capital charges in order to secure the return of a fugitive. There are scholars who believe the USA is on the way to eliminating the death penalty, in part because of international criticism.[74]

States report on measures they have taken to make national law and practice compatible with their obligations under the Covenant. The Committee, however, was divided during the Cold War on its proper role. A minimalist view, articulated mostly by individuals from the European socialist states, maintained that the Committee was only to facilitate dialogue among sovereign states. A maximalist view was that the Committee was to pronounce both on whether a state had reported correctly, and on whether that state was in compliance with its legal obligations. Since the end of the Cold War the Committee has been more free to adopt the maximalist view.[75] But once again we see that the Committee

---

[74] See further William Schabas, *The Abolition of the Death Penalty in International Law*, 3rd edn. (Cambridge: Cambridge University Press, 2002).

[75] An optimistic account is found in Ineke Boerfijn, "Towards a Strong System of Supervision," *Human Rights Quarterly*, 17, 4 (November 1995), 766–793.

could not proceed beyond some public criticism of the states that were found to be wanting in one respect or another via their reports. The volume of Committee proceedings and comments appeared to be in inverse proportion to the actual protection of civil and political rights in violative states.[76] Some states, mostly western democracies, did make changes in their national law and practice in the wake of Committee questions. The USA, however, proved more recalcitrant. During an earlier era the US Senate Foreign Relations Committee, ironically identifying with the old European communist position, challenged the right of the Committee to pass judgment on US reservations, understandings, and comments concerning the Covenant.[77]

Committee practice has evolved so that it makes summary comments about a state's compliance report, and general comments about the meaning of the Covenant. The former provides an authoritative agenda for any state seeking to improve its record on civil and political rights. The latter may affect the evolution of legal standards, as when the Committee's comments on how to interpret the prohibition on torture fed into the drafting of the 1984 UN Convention against Torture and Cruel, Inhuman, and Degrading Treatment.[78] As might be expected, states sometimes challenge the validity of both the summary comments and the general comments.

When individuals bring complaints under the Optional Protocol, having exhausted national remedies, the situation is not so very different. The Committee, when justified, will make public its views, frequently holding states to be in violation of their obligations. The range of countries found to be in violation is rather broad, ranging from one case of technical deficiencies (Canada) to numerous cases of gross violations (Uruguay). It remains uncertain in how many of these cases ameliorative steps were taken by offending governments, and whether such steps, if taken, were due strictly to the Committee. Uruguay eventually moved away from massive repression, because of which at one time it had more political prisoners per capita than any other country in the world. Whether progressive change was due to the Committee, to any great extent, is

---

[76] Dominic McGoldrick, *The Human Rights Committee* (Oxford: Clarendon, 1991); Manfred Nowak, *UN Covenant on Civil and Political Rights: CCPR Comments* (Arlington: Engel, 1993).

[77] William A. Schabas, "Spare the RUD or Spoil the Treaty: The United States Challenges the Human Rights Committee on the Subject of Reservations," in David P. Forsythe, ed., *The United States and Human Rights: Looking Inward and Outward* (Lincoln: University of Nebraska Press, 2000).

[78] David Weissbrodt, "International Covenant on Civil and Political Rights," in *Encyclopedia of Human Rights*, vol. I, 339–344. For more substance on the specific interpretations of this monitoring mechanism, consult the index to the *Encyclopedia*.

dubious. One expert believes that most states comply with Committee recommendations concerning private petitions,[79] which may be true of this non-public process since the more repressive and/or contentious states do not accept this optional protocol to begin with.

The Committee on Economic, Social, and Cultural Rights

The International Covenant on Economic, Social, and Cultural Rights, despite 160 adherences by early 2011, has always been the stepchild of the international human rights movement. Certain states, when speaking in the General Assembly or another political forum, may give it some prominence in order to deflect attention away from violations of civil and political rights. But few states have paid serious and sustained attention to this convention. The same is true for the question of its application.

After the E/S/C Covenant came into legal force in 1976, it took a full two years for any monitoring mechanism to be put in place. This first body, a working group of states derived from ECOSOC, compiled a truly miserable record of incompetence and was replaced in 1986 by an independent Committee of Experts. This Committee has shown considerable dynamism in confronting some daunting tasks: imprecision of the Covenant's terms; lack of jurisprudence to clarify obligations; lack of broad and sustained governmental interest in the subject matter; paucity of national and transnational private organizations interested in socio-economic and cultural rights as rights and not as aspects of development; and lack of, *inter alia*, relevant information for arriving at judgments.[80]

The Committee has struggled first with the problem of states failing to submit even an initial report on compliance, although legally required. This problem is widespread across the UN system of human rights reporting, but it is a pronounced problem under this Covenant. It has also faced the usual problem that many states' reports, even when submitted, are more designed to meet formal obligations than to give a full and frank picture of the true situation of E/S/C rights in the country. The Committee has persisted in trying to serve as an effective catalyst for serious national policy making in this domain, and has tried mostly to establish minimum base lines for national requirements – rather than universal rules – regarding economic, social, and cultural rights.[81]

---

[79] Weissbrodt, "International Covenant."

[80] Philip Alston, "The Committee on Economic, Social, and Cultural Rights," in Alston, ed., *United Nations and Human Rights*, 473–508.

[81] See further Robert E. Robertson, "Measuring State Compliance with the Obligation to Devote the 'Maximum Available Resources' to Realizing Economic, Social, and Cultural Rights," *Human Rights Quarterly*, 16, 4 (November 1994), 693–714.

Some argue that socioeconomic rights are receiving more attention now than in the past, and that a new monitoring mechanism is in order.[82]

In 2008 state members of the UN approved an optional protocol to the socioeconomic covenant allowing for private communications, similar to the civil-political covenant. By early 2011 only three states had ratified this instrument, and thirty-five had signed as a first step to possible full acceptance. Thus the Protocol was not yet in legal force anywhere. The Protocol did show a continuing effort to make socioeconomic rights more important, but clearly there were more noteworthy developments concerning civil-political rights, which had always been the case since the 1940s.[83]

On the one hand it could be shown that many if not most of the members of the influential coalition of western-style democracies had long accepted the notion of socioeconomic rights as a matter of public policy.[84] On the other hand these and other states showed some reluctance to have third parties require the enforcement of socioeconomic rights in the short term. For example, even in Europe where social democracy and large welfare states were the norm, regional arrangements for protecting human rights were weaker for socioeconomic rights than for civil-political rights. This is covered in Chapter 5 on regional developments. Nevertheless, in various states such as India and South Africa one could indeed find court cases on socioeconomic rights.

Other treaty-based mechanisms

As of 2011, compliance committees exist under these major conventions: the Rights of the Child (192 state parties), Racial Discrimination (174 parties), Torture (147 parties), Discrimination Against Women (186 parties), and Apartheid (107 parties). Similar committees exist or will exist regarding treaties on Migrant Workers, Persons with Disabilities, and Enforced Disappearances.

---

[82] Mario Gomez, "Social Economic Rights and Human Rights Commissions," *Human Rights Quarterly*, 17, 1 (February 1995), 155–169.

[83] See further Shareen Hertel and Lanse Minkler, eds., *Economic Rights: Conceptual, Measurement, and Policy Issues* (Cambridge: Cambridge University Press, 2007); and Rhoda E. Howard-Hassmann and Claude E. Welch, Jr., eds., *Economic Rights in Canada and the United States* (Philadelphia: University of Pennsylvania Press, 2006).

[84] Jack Donnelly, "The West and Economic Rights," in Hertel and Minkler, eds., *Economic Rights*, 37–55; Daniel J. Whelan and Jack Donnelly, "The West, Economic and Social Rights, and the Global Human Rights Regime: Setting the Record Straight," *Human Rights Quarterly*, 29, 4 (November 2007), 908–949. See the follow-on debate on this subject in that journal.

State endorsement of international human rights in these areas is generally not matched by timely and fulsome reporting by the state, nor by a willingness to respond affirmatively and quickly to critical comments by the control committees – which are composed of individual experts. As with other human rights treaties discussed above, UN Secretariat assistance is meager owing to budgetary problems. Some NGOs do give special attention to one or more of these treaties. For example, Amnesty International gives considerable support to the Committee Against Torture.[85] But the Committee Against Racial Discrimination has adopted restrictive decisions about the use of NGO information, as has the Committee on Discrimination Against Women.[86] This latter committee operates under a treaty that does not allow individual petitions, in part because the UN Commission on the Status of Women does.[87] The Committee dealing with apartheid has faced few private petitions, because most state parties from outside Europe have not given their consent for them to be lodged. Most of these treaties contain a provision on interstate complaints, but these provisions have remained dormant. States do not like to petition other states about human rights, because of the boomerang effect on themselves. The Committee Against Torture exercises a right of automatic investigation unless a state expressly reserves against that article; relatively few parties have. But as of 2011 UN prison inspections had yet to become systematic, because of the lack of large numbers of ratifications of this legal instrument. The Committee on the Rights of the Child has functioned for such a short time that its influence cannot be judged. There has been some effort to improve the coordination of all of these treaty-based monitoring mechanisms, but one cannot yet discern any greater influence in the short term generated by the sum of the parts, or the separate parts themselves.

From one view, the international regimes that center on these human rights treaties and their monitoring mechanisms constitute weak regimes that have not been able to make a significant dent thus far in violations of various human rights on a global scale.[88] The control committees do make their contribution to long-term promotion via socialization or

---

[85] See further Howard B. Tolley, Jr., "Torture: Convention Against Torture," in *Encyclopedia of Human Rights*, vol. V, 51–59; Nigel S. Rodley, "Torture: International Law," ibid., vol. V, 65–80.

[86] See Marsha A. Freeman, "Women: Convention on the Elimination of Discrimination Against Women," ibid., vol. V, 331–340.

[87] See further Stephanie Farrior, "United Nations Commission on the Status of Women," ibid., vol. V, 142–149.

[88] Jack Donnelly, *Universal Human Rights in Theory and Practice* (Ithaca: Cornell University Press, 1989), ch. 11.

informal and practical education for human rights.[89] States have to report and subject themselves to various forms of review. Their sovereignty is not absolute but restricted. At the end of the day, however, it is not these regimes, but the Security Council and the Secretary-General – and perhaps the High Commissioner for Human Rights – that are best positioned among UN actors to effectively press states to improve their human rights records in the short term.

From another view, one that focuses on related national developments, it is possible that some of these treaties may sometimes give rise to important changes despite the weak legal authority of international agencies.[90] Once ratified, a treaty may change the nature of national legislation and politics if influential persons and organizations pursue the norms found in the treaty. In these cases, it is not so much the official international review that generates impact for human rights, but rather those in national politics who appeal successfully to treaty standards. According to the leading scholar on this matter: "Human rights treaties matter most where they have domestic political and legal traction . . . [D]omestic mechanisms [may allow] a treaty to effect elite-initiated agendas, to support litigation, and to spark political mobilization."[91] In her view, human rights treaties usually have the greatest impact in unstable or transitional polities where views on human rights are not fully institutionalized. The foundational point is that no treaty implements itself. Some political actor with clout, or at least determined persistence, needs to "adopt" the treaty and "run with it." A transnational focus, with due attention to national politics, seems required for full understanding.[92] (See further the case study at the end of this chapter.)

The World Bank and International Monetary Fund The World Bank (International Bank for Reconstruction and Development, IBRD) and the International Monetary Fund (IMF) are the major agencies of the Bretton Woods institutions and are officially part of the UN system, but historically they have operated in a highly independent manner with their own governing boards and constituent legal instruments. Voting by

---

[89] David P. Forsythe, "The United Nations and Human Rights 1945–1985," *Political Science Quarterly*, 100 (Summer 1985), 249–269; and Forsythe, "The UN and Human Rights at Fifty: An Incremental but Incomplete Revolution," *Global Governance*, 1, 3 (September–December 1995), 297–318.

[90] See especially Beth A. Simmons, *Mobilizing for Human Rights: International Law in Domestic Politics* (Cambridge: Cambridge University Press, 2009).

[91] Ibid., *passim*.

[92] See further an earlier study by David P. Forsythe, *The Politics of International Law: US Foreign Policy Reconsidered* (Boulder: Lynne Rienner, 1990).

member states in each agency is greatly affected by financial contributions, which makes them different from other parts of the UN system. This arrangement obviously gives great weight to developed as compared to developing states. In recent years the Bank, but not so much the IMF, has become more closely linked to other UN agencies, such as via the Global Environment Facility in quest of better funded ecological programs. Likewise the Bank, but not so much the IMF, has made halting steps to pay more attention to human rights. The Bank, which makes loans for development, has declared that "creating the conditions for the attainment of human rights is a central and irreducible goal of development."[93]

As the Bank funded a number of large infrastructure projects such as dams to generate energy, local populations were adversely affected. In response the Bank created an Inspection Panel to which various stakeholders had access under certain rules. This was, therefore, an effort to increase participation in decision making by community-based organizations (CBOs) and the NGOs who often worked with them. Over time a number of local and international human rights groups played a larger role in Bank processes. Yet formal power and authority still resided with national governments on the Bank governing board, in interaction with Bank staff headed by a president (who is always an American, named by the US government).

Likewise controversial, again often pitting the quest for national economic development against the welfare of local populations, were Bank structural adjustment programs (SAPs). In return for Bank loans, governments often had to agree to specific conditions intended to restructure national economic programs. Typically the SAPs required reduced governmental spending on programs such as aid or subsidies to the poor, in quest of greater earnings through exports and other revenue-enhancing measures. The formula of the so-called Washington consensus was more economic liberalization or privatization or expanded "free markets" and less governmental spending. This formula normally disadvantaged, at least in the short term, the most needy in a country, and not surprisingly research showed that SAPs correlated negatively with protection or fulfillment of socioeconomic human rights.[94] That same research also concluded that SAPs negatively impacted civil and political rights in

---

[93] Quoted in Marc Darrow, "World Bank and International Monetary Fund," in *Encyclopedia of Human Rights*, vol. V, at 374. See further Joel E. Oestreich, *Power and Principle: Human Rights Programming in International Organizations* (Washington: Georgetown University Press, 2007), ch. 3.

[94] See, for example, M. Rodwan Abouharb and David Cingranelli, *Human Rights and Structural Adjustment* (Cambridge: Cambridge University Press, 2007).

many cases, since some repression was required to implement painful conditionality.

In 2006 the legal counsel of the Bank issued a report entitled "Legal Opinion on Human Rights and the Work of the World Bank." While asserting that under the Bank's Articles of Agreement the agency had the legal duty to take into account the human rights implications of its work, in subsequent years the specifics of this duty have not been completely clarified.

In certain situations the state members of the Bank have pushed the agency into an active and open human rights posture, as when the Bank was utilized to bring economic pressure on Serbia to cooperate with the International Criminal Tribunal for the former Yugoslavia, or to likewise hold up loans to Ivory Coast until the results of a free and fair election were honored. But this type of open support for criminal justice or democratic elections has not been pursued consistently. Thus the Bank has sometimes served as the means to implement the political objectives of the moment by the wealthy countries rather than manifesting a consistent and carefully considered human rights program by the Bank as an independent international organization.

The Bank evolved a concern with "good government" but this was generally intended to focus on transparency and proper accounting, and other matters related to sound economic decisions, rather than on fidelity to democratic and other human rights standards. Bank loans have certainly flowed at times to various authoritarian governments, even those committing or allowing atrocities. Pinochet in Chile was a case in point. To cite a more recent example, Bank loans have gone to authoritarian but pro-western Ethiopia.

In general the IMF (which has been always headed by a European) more than the Bank adhered to the position that it was a technical organization focused on currency and balance of payments problems within the domain of international monetary policy. Not being officially a development organization, the IMF mostly maintained the position that it was independent from human rights norms and obligations.[95]

International humanitarian law

If states have been generally slow to enforce global human rights norms in peace, or what passes for peace in modern international relations, it is not surprising to find that they have been even more reluctant to engage in

---

[95] See further Bahram Ghazi, *The IMF, the World Bank Group, and the Question of Human Rights* (Leiden: Brill, 2005).

broad and systematic enforcement of international humanitarian law.[96] In all states, including liberal democracies, it is politically difficult to put the national military in harm's way and then prosecute its members or their civilian superiors for violating parts of the laws of war pertaining to humane values. Even prosecuting the enemy for war crimes can also prove difficult. Often one has control of neither the guilty person nor the documentary evidence that would stand judicial scrutiny. Obtaining such persons or evidence may require more combat, with more death and destruction. This is a main reason the USA did not move on Baghdad in 1991 at the end of major combat to force the Iraqi army out of Kuwait. Trying to gain custody of Saddam Hussein and his supporting cast of commanders for war crimes trials was judged to be not politically sustainable at that time. Also, attempting to prosecute enemy personnel may give rise to further steps against one's own interests, especially if the other side has certain leverage points. One can recall that after World War I the British gave up on plans to prosecute Turkish/Ottoman officials for crimes against humanity related to their treatment of Armenians. The Turks held a number of British POWs and would not release them until the idea of prosecutions was dropped. Given difficulties of enforcement via judicial action, or various forms of collectively organized sanctions, once again interested parties must look primarily to diplomacy or other means of political application of humanitarian norms.

Under the Geneva Conventions of 1949 and Additional Protocol I of 1977 pertaining to international armed conflict, fighting states are supposed to appoint a neutral state as a Protecting Power to oversee application of appropriate international rules. Few Protecting Powers have been appointed since World War II. This situation leaves the International Committee of the Red Cross, a private Swiss agency, to do what it can to encourage states to see that captured, wounded, and sick military personnel benefit from international legal provisions as written, and that civilians in occupied territory and other war zones likewise benefit from protective norms.

There is also the matter of reciprocity among fighting parties, and such considerations played a role in World War II. Allied POWs in German hands and German POWs under Allied control were, in general and for the most part, treated according to the terms of the 1929 POW Convention. Such was definitely not the case for Soviet POWs in German hands and vice versa, where death rates were appalling, as neither was legally bound to the other under that same Geneva Convention. In this

---

[96] Among many sources see Hazel Fox and Michael A. Meyer, eds., *Effecting Compliance* (London: British Institute of International and Comparative Law, 1993).

regard it is difficult to say whether the driving force was legal factors backed by positive reciprocity, for good treatment, or racial views, for ill treatment. German and non-Soviet Allied prisoners were mostly of the same ethnic and racial stock, whereas particularly the "Aryan" Germans looked down upon the Soviets as inferior Slavs. Between Germans and Soviets there was negative reciprocity, as each side abused and killed many of the other's prisoners. The workings of positive reciprocity are particularly problematic in asymmetric warfare, since the weaker party fighting via guerrilla tactics and terrorism usually controls little fixed territory for safe detention and generally does not pay much attention to the laws of war.[97]

The overall record of applying humanitarian law is not an altogether happy one, especially in internal armed conflicts where the rules are more lenient and some of the fighting parties usually woefully uninformed about humanitarian standards.[98] Even in international armed conflict perhaps a minimalist approach is in order, as when one expert remarked that, if it were not legally wrong to bomb hospitals, they would be bombed all of the time instead of only some of the time. Occasionally, as in the Falklands/Malvinas war of 1982, states like Argentina and the United Kingdom engage in combat more or less according to humanitarian law. Even in places like the former Yugoslavia during 1992–1995, perhaps more civilians benefited from humanitarian protection and assistance than were intentionally shot, raped, tortured, maimed, or otherwise attacked and persecuted. It is a difficult comparison and judgment to make. Never before in world history have civilians constituted such a high percentage of the casualties in armed conflicts. But never have there been so many rules and actors trying to humanize war.[99] I will continue this subject in Chapter 4, when I address criminal prosecution in more detail.

Conclusion

If one compares the United Nations and the League of Nations with regard to setting human rights and humanitarian standards and trying to

---

[97] From a vast literature, see David P. Forsythe, *The Politics of Prisoner Abuse: US Policy Toward Enemy Prisoners After 9/11* (Cambridge: Cambridge University Press, 2011); and Mark Osiel, *The End of Reciprocity: Terror, Torture, and the Law of War* (Cambridge: Cambridge University Press, 2009).

[98] A useful overview is Larry Minear and Thomas G. Weiss, *Mercy Under Fire: War and the Global Humanitarian Community* (Boulder: Westview, 1995).

[99] David P. Forsythe, "The International Committee of the Red Cross and Humanitarian Assistance: A Policy Analysis," *International Review of the Red Cross*, 314 (September–October 1996), 512–531.

apply them, one can clearly see the increased commitment to liberal values centering on personal human rights in international relations, both in peace and war. But one can also see that much of this commitment is *pro forma*, which is to say, insincere. The members of the United Nations are states, and they still express considerable interest in their independence and freedom from authoritative international supervision on rights issues. Yet gradually, as subsequent chapters will also demonstrate, they are beginning to redefine their national interests to include more attention to human rights and humanitarian values, even if realist concerns with independent power and a tough pursuit of narrow national interests have not vanished.

Case study: human rights and humanitarian law at Guantanamo

After the Al Qaeda terrorist attacks on the US homeland on 9/11/2001, the George W. Bush Administration responded with military and CIA operations in Afghanistan and other places. The Al Qaeda core leadership was then in Afghanistan, in liaison with the Taliban government of Mullah Omar. As a result of military and paramilitary operations in conjunction with the local Northern Alliance militia, the US military began to detain a number of prisoners, especially in Afghanistan. Local detention arrangements were inadequate and sometimes insecure. Also, the highest levels of the Bush Administration decided that the terrorist threat was significant enough that it was unwise to observe the normal legal rules pertaining to the treatment of enemy or security prisoners. It therefore opened a military detention center on the island of Guantanamo, leased in perpetuity from Cuba. The facility was secure, and Bush officials hoped it would be a legal black hole, immune from US judicial oversight given their claim that it was foreign territory. The Administration claimed that detainees there were "unlawful enemy combatants" who had no rights under international humanitarian law.

Bush officials were concerned above all with two human rights or humanitarian treaties to which the US was a full party, having ratified them without crippling reservations: the 1984 UN Convention against Torture and Cruel, Inhuman, and Degrading Treatment; and the 1949 Geneva Conventions for situations of armed conflict, which prohibited torture, cruel treatment, and humiliation. The United States had also ratified the International Covenant on Civil and Political Rights, which also prohibited major abuse of prisoners. But at the time of ratification the United States had submitted reservations which prevented its use in courts in the USA. From the beginning the Administration was worried about domestic review of its planned abusive policies toward prisoners.

As 2002 progressed, the US Department of Defense Under Secretary Donald Rumsfeld moved in fits and starts toward abusive interrogation of probably about 15–20 percent of the detainees at Guantanamo (or GTMO, or Gitmo in military parlance). In the winter of 2002–2003, for example, a suspected potential hijacker by the name of Mohammed al-Qahtani was subjected to an interrogation process that a US official later characterized as torture.

The United States continued to submit periodic reports to the CAT, the Committee against Torture, which is the monitoring mechanism under the Torture Convention. The United States, because of convoluted events, also wound up with the International Committee of the Red Cross having a permanent presence at GTMO. The ICRC is mandated under the 1949 Geneva Conventions (referred to as "Geneva" in military parlance) to visit all detainees in international armed conflict, and is also often given permission to visit detainees in internal war and domestic troubles and tensions. From January 2002 the ICRC did its usual prison visits at GTMO and as usual submitted its confidential reports to the detaining authority. So two normal review processes were in place regarding the treatment of what can be factually called enemy prisoners, regardless of debate over legal categories or labels.

Domestically the US Congress, being under Republican Party control and sympathetic to the claims of a Republican Administration, did not at first much involve itself in matters pertaining to GTMO. Congress had passed an AUMF (authorization to use military force) under which the Bush Administration claimed it had the authority to set prisoner policy. Congress deferred to that Executive claim for a time. It was only in 2005 that Congress mustered the effort to deal with policy toward enemy prisoners, after the release of unauthorized photos from the Abu Ghraib prison in Iraq showing horrific US treatment of Iraqi and other prisoners there. From 2005 under the Detainee Treatment Act (DTA), the Congress required the US military to return to the treatment of detainees specified in the US Army Field Manual which was based on the 1949 Geneva Conventions, especially concerning the interrogation of prisoners under military control. Certain Republican senators with an interest in military honor and military law, and traditional American values, took the lead in this legislative effort, which gave political cover to Democratic members of Congress interested in curtailing abuse of prisoners. The DTA passed by such margins that a presidential veto was not in play, and so the Bush Administration formally accepted this congressional restriction on its prisoner policy.

In parallel fashion, the US Supreme Court wound up making a number of judgments that had been initiated by American human rights advocacy groups, working with detainees, based on international as well as US law. In particular the US Supreme Court in 2006 ruled in the Hamdan case that part of the 1949 Geneva Conventions (Common Article 3) applied to all detainees at GTMO. While the case dealt with the subject of military commissions for the trial of detainees, the judgment clearly implied that no torture or cruel treatment could legally obtain at GTMO.

Therefore from 2005–2006 both Congress and the courts pushed back against Bush policies of abusive treatment of certain detainees at GTMO in ways that cemented a change in Bush policies. The significant push back, as far as the present analysis is concerned, came from human rights and humanitarian treaties "gaining traction" in American legislative and judicial processes, not simply from international actors reviewing the US record in Geneva or New York or other centers of international diplomacy. The process was transnational, with international law merging with national law and politics.

One might observe that all of this took time, and without doubt from 2002 until 2005–2006 a number of GTMO prisoners were subjected to torture and/or cruel treatment while in US military custody. Nevertheless the abusive policies were eventually rolled back because of national decisions in the framework of international law. One can also observe that still other prisoner policies were debated in the context of international human rights and humanitarian law, such as what kind of due process in the military commissions satisfied the requirements of the 1949 Geneva Conventions and their Additional Protocol I which had been added in 1977. Finally, one should observe that Bush policies toward prisoners under CIA control comprise an additional and somewhat separate subject, too lengthy for coverage here.

Discussion questions

- Can a decentralized or Westphalian system of international law and diplomacy, in which equal sovereign states apply human rights norms, be fully effective? To what extent have contemporary states moved away from this Westphalian system for the purpose of using the United Nations to protect internationally recognized human rights?
- Can one always draw a clear distinction between security issues and human rights issues? Can a putative human rights issue also be a genuine security issue? Is it ever proper for the UN Security Council to invoke Charter Chapter VII, thus permitting legally binding enforcement decisions, when dealing with violations of human rights?

- Is it ever proper for a state, or a collection of states, to use coercion in another state to protect human rights, without the explicit and advance approval of the UN Security Council? What lessons should be drawn from NATO's action in Kosovo? Is this a form of humanitarian intervention that should be approved and repeated by the international community?
- What is the difference between international and internal (civil) armed conflicts, from the standpoint of law, and from the standpoint of practical action, when it comes to protecting human rights in such conflicts?
- Beyond the Security Council, which parts of the UN system, if any, have compiled a noteworthy record in applying human rights standards? Is this because of direct protection, indirect protection, or long-term education? Is it possible to generalize about the UN and protecting human rights under Charter Chapter VI and peaceful or quasi-peaceful diplomacy? What is the relationship between human rights and UN complex peacekeeping?
- What is the relationship between the international law of human rights and international humanitarian law concerning practical action to advance human dignity in "failed states" and "complex emergencies"?

SUGGESTIONS FOR FURTHER READING

Alston, Philip, ed., *The United Nations and Human Rights: A Critical Appraisal* (Oxford: Clarendon Press, 1995). A broad and excellent survey by experts on the subject; indispensable. A second edition with Frederic Megret as second editor is forthcoming.

Cohen, Roberta, and Francis M. Deng, eds., *The Forsaken People: Case Studies of the Internally Displaced* (Washington: Brookings, 1998). An authoritative look at a growing human rights problem, as displaced persons do not always benefit from the protection and assistance given to official refugees.

Dobbins, James, et al., *The UN's Role in Nation-Building: From the Congo to Iraq* (Santa Monica, CA: Rand, 2005). A good analytical overview, noting several positive contributions.

Forsythe, David, *The Politics of Prisoner Abuse: US Policy Toward Enemy Prisoners After 9/11* (Cambridge: Cambridge University Press, 2011). An overview of how the George W. Bush Administration sought to obtain information via abusive interrogation after 9/11/2001, despite the human rights and humanitarian treaties to which it was a party.

Guest, Iain, *Behind the Disappearances: Argentina's Dirty War Against Human Rights and the United Nations* (Philadelphia: University of Pennsylvania Press, 1990). A journalist uncovers Argentina's extensive efforts, supported by the Reagan Administration in Washington, to block UN investigation into its brutal policies during military rule in the 1980s.

Humphrey, John P., *Human Rights and the United Nations: A Great Adventure* (Dobbs Ferry: Transnational, 1984). The first Director of the Human Rights

Division in the UN Secretariat reflects on his experiences. Humphrey, a Canadian social democrat, was influential behind the scenes in the drafting of the Universal Declaration of Human Rights, although others like the Frenchman René Casin were often given more credit in public.

Kille, Kent, ed., *The UN Secretary-General and Moral Authority: Ethics and Religion in International Leadership* (Washington: Georgetown University Press, 2007). The best overview of the UN Secretaries-General with regard to personal values. Thus a study of the interplay of commitment to human rights, international law, and ethics, but in the context of state power and policy.

Lebovic, J. H., and E. Voeten, "The Politics of Shame: The Condemnation of Country Human Rights Practices in the UNCHR," *International Studies Quarterly*, 50, 3 (2006), 861–888. An important study showing that the UN Human Rights Commission was not as politicized as often pictured.

Loescher, Gil, *The UNHCR and World Politics: A Perilous Path* (New York and Oxford: Oxford University Press, 2001). The best comprehensive treatment of the UN Refugee Office (UNHCR). His proposals for change in the future are well considered but stand little chance of being adopted by states.

Matheson, Michael J., *Council Unbound: The Growth of UN Decision Making on Conflict and Postconflict Issues After the Cold War* (Washington: US Institute of Peace, 2006). A former State Department lawyer examines the UNSC's expanding role in conflicts, with some attention to human rights.

Mertus, Julie, *The United Nations and Human Rights* (New York: Routledge, 2005). A basic survey of the different agents in the UN system, intended for students.

Ogata, Sadako, *Turbulent Decade: Confronting the Refugee Crises of the 1990s* (New York: Norton, 2005). Account by the former head of the UNHCR about the problems she faced in places like Bosnia and the Great Lakes region of Africa.

Roberts, Adam, and Benedict Kingsbury, eds., *United Nations, Divided World: The UN's Roles in International Relations*, 2nd edn. (Oxford: Clarendon, 1993). A good collection of essays, mostly by legal experts, with considerable attention to human rights. The chapter centering on human rights by Tom Farer and Felice Gaer was one of the best short analyses that existed at that time.

Simmons, Beth, *Mobilizing for Human Rights: International Law in Domestic Politics* (Cambridge: Cambridge University Press, 2009). An outstanding analysis of why states ratify human rights treaties and why some of the treaty norms come to be taken seriously by states – mainly because of certain developments in the domestic politics of transitional states rather than the international monitoring process.

Tolley, Howard, Jr., *The UN Commission on Human Rights* (Boulder: Westview, 1987). While this book is now dated, it remains the definitive treatment for its time. No one has written a comparable sequel.

Tyagi, Yogesh, *The UN Human Rights Committee: Practice and Procedure* (Cambridge: Cambridge University Press, 2011). A comprehensive legal treatise.

Weiss, Thomas G., David P. Forsythe, and Roger A. Coate, *The United Nations and Changing World Politics*, 6th edn. (Boulder: Westview, for Perseus, 2010). A widely used text devotes Part II to human rights and humanitarian affairs.

4 Transitional justice: criminal courts and alternatives

After gross violations of human rights, what is one to do? This is the subject of transitional justice, a growth industry for intellectuals and policy makers after the Cold War. Should one prosecute individuals in international courts, or in hybrid or special courts, or in national courts? Should one avoid courts and rely on truth commissions, or bar violators from public office, or just move on to concentrate on building a rights-protective state in the future rather than looking back via criminal prosecution? There are many complexities facing those interested in international criminal justice – meaning those interested in whether to prosecute against the background of international human rights and humanitarian norms. Beyond punishment of evildoers, one needs to keep in mind other possible goals of transitional justice: deterring future atrocities, bringing psychological closure to victims and/or relatives, producing reconciliation among divided communities, building a rights-protective polity in the future, adjusting to the lingering power of elements of the old regime.

In the last decade of the twentieth century the United Nations created two international criminal courts, the first in almost fifty years. Moreover a new International Criminal Court (ICC) came into legal existence in July 2002. Furthermore, special courts were created in the aftermath of atrocities in Sierra Leone, East Timor, Kosovo, and Cambodia, while a new court was created by the interim government of Iraq after the US invasion and occupation of 2003 to try Saddam Hussein and his lieutenants. The United Kingdom agreed that the former dictator of Chile, Augusto Pinochet, could be extradited to Spain to stand trial there for torture.

In the abstract it is hard to disagree with the proposition that those who commit gross violations of internationally recognized standards pertaining to genocide, war crimes, and crimes against humanity should face criminal justice. The principle of R2P, already noted as adopted by the UN in 2005, adds ethnic cleansing to this list of major violations (but

117

without changing the subject matter jurisdiction of existing courts).[1] If we had reliable criminal justice on a global scale, we could punish individual criminals with more certainty, bring some catharsis to victims and/or their relatives, try to break the vicious circle of group violence, and hope to deter similar future acts.

In international relations as it continues to exist in the early twenty-first century, however, while there may be an embryonic trend toward "legalization" and more use of adjudication,[2] many policy makers are obviously reluctant to pursue criminal justice – especially through international tribunals. Sometimes this hesitancy is the product of realist attitudes and/or chauvinistic nationalism. But sometimes these policies of hesitation are characterized by careful reasoning and serious liberal argument.

Hesitancy about international criminal justice is thus not always a reaction by those who wish to elevate repressive privilege over protection of international human rights. Caution is also sometimes evidenced by persons of relatively liberal persuasion who by definition are motivated by considerable concern for human dignity. In general they are in favor of human rights, but on occasion they find it both politically prudent and morally defensible to bypass the enforcement of human rights through criminal justice. I term this position pragmatic liberalism. This view can be contrasted with judicial romanticism, which brushes aside such political and diplomatic concerns in the belief that criminal justice is a panacea for violations of human rights, and that "impunity" for those violations ought never be allowed. Judicial romantics overestimate what courts can achieve and underestimate the role of soft law and essentially political approaches to advancing human rights and humanitarian norms.

Like Martha Minow, this chapter suggests that in the wake of atrocities there is no single response that is always appropriate everywhere, but rather a menu of choice in which the proper selection depends upon context.[3] Like Richard J. Goldstone, the first ICTY prosecutor, this chapter argues that considerations of peace and justice have to be carefully

---

[1] See further Jennifer Jackson Preece, "Ethnic Cleansing," in David P. Forsythe, ed., *Encyclopedia of Human Rights* (New York: Oxford University Press, 2009), vol. II, 163–168.

[2] See the special issue of the journal *International Organization* on "Legalization and World Politics," March 2001. See also Mary L. Volcansek, *Law Above Nations: Supranational Courts and the Leaglization of Politics* (Gainesville: University Press of Florida, 1997).

[3] Martha Minow, in *Between Vengeance and Forgiveness: Facing History After Genocide and Mass Violence* (Boston: Beacon Press, 1998), argues that neither trials nor truth commissions are always the most appropriate option. Compare Andrew Rigby, *Justice and Reconciliation: After the Violence* (Boulder: Lynne Rienner, 2001), and Ruti G. Teitel, *Transitional Justice* (New York: Oxford University Press, 2002). Teitel provides a concise overview in "Transitional Justice," in *Encyclopedia of Human Rights*, vol. V, 81–86. See further the various articles in the journal *International Transitional Justice*.

calculated, and that pursuit of justice does not always require criminal justice as compared to social and political forms of justice.[4]

Historical background to 1991: few trials, small impact

The history of criminal prosecution – both international and national – related to international events is reasonably well known, at least to some scholars.[5] Since books have been written on the subject, here I seek merely to highlight several important points. Even a cursory retrospective shows that many policy makers have found ample reason to avoid international trials, with a few exceptions. As is usually the case, political calculation precedes reference to legal rules. As Werner Levi has written, "[P]olitics decides who the lawmaker and what the formulation of the law shall be; law formalizes these decisions and makes them binding. This distribution of functions makes law dependent upon politics."[6]

International trials

While there was some discussion of criminal prosecution of German (and Turkish) leaders after World War I, movement in that direction was aborted.[7] It was only after World War II that the first international criminal proceedings transpired, with well-known defects.[8] For a time Allied leaders leaned toward summary execution of high German policy makers, but eventually concluded a treaty creating the Nuremberg tribunal. The stated objectives were lofty enough, but the taint of victor's justice was pervasive. At Nuremberg (and Tokyo) only the losing leaders were tried, even though Allied leaders had engaged in such acts as attacking cities through conventional, incendiary, and atomic bombings, thus failing to distinguish between combatants and civilians – a cardinal principle of international humanitarian law (viz., that part of the law of war oriented

---

[4] "Bringing War Criminals to Justice During an Ongoing War," in Jonathan Moore, ed., *Hard Choices: Moral Dilemmas in Humanitarian Intervention* (Lanham: Rowman & Littlefield, 1998), 195–210.

[5] Steven R. Ratner and Jason S. Abrams, *Accountability for Human Rights Atrocities in International Law: Beyond the Nuremberg Legacy*, 3rd edn. (Oxford: Clarendon Press, 2009; 1st edn., 1997; 2nd edn., 2001). See further Ramesh Thakur and Peter Malcontent, eds., *From Sovereign Impunity to International Accountability: The Search for Justice in a World of States* (Tokyo: United Nations University Press, 2004).

[6] Werner Levi, *Law and Politics in the International Society* (Beverly Hills: Sage, 1976), 31.

[7] James F. Willis, *Prologue to Nuremberg: The Politics and Diplomacy of Punishing War Criminals of the First World War* (Westport: Greenwood, 1982).

[8] A vast bibliography is recorded in Telford Taylor, *The Anatomy of the Nuremberg Tribunal: A Personal Memoir* (New York: Knopf, 1992).

to the protection of victims of war, especially now the 1949 Geneva Conventions). Soviet military personnel committed perhaps 100,000 rapes in Berlin after the defeat of the Nazis. Rapes were systematic practice, yet no commanding officers, much less lower ranking soldiers, were ever held accountable. The Soviet Union then sat in judgment of Germans at Nuremberg.[9]

There was also some prosecution and conviction via *ex post facto* laws (laws created after the act in question). The concept of individual responsibility for war crimes was reasonably well established through national laws by 1939. But crimes against peace and crimes against humanity were concepts that had never been the subject of precise legislation or prosecution until 1946. Also, procedural guarantees of a fair trial could have been improved.[10]

Twenty-two German leaders were prosecuted at Nuremberg in the first round of trials, nineteen of whom were convicted, with twelve of these being executed. Other individual German cases occurred, in both international and national courts. Similar proceedings were held at Tokyo for Japanese leaders, through fiat of the US military command.[11] A pronounced defect of especially the Tokyo tribunal was the total ignoring of gender crimes, despite a broad policy of sexual slavery carried out by Japanese officials.[12]

The effect of these trials on subsequent thinking in Germany and Japan remains a matter of conjecture. Did the Nuremberg and Tokyo trials, through emphasis on individual criminal responsibility, force those nations to confront the past and face up to the individual moral choices that existed? There is widespread agreement that Germany more than Japan has tried to come to terms with the atrocities of the past – although Japan made increased gestures in that direction toward the end of the twentieth century. Yet both nations experienced similar international criminal tribunals. A researcher for the *Congressional Quarterly* wrote that "The tribunals were viewed as illegitimate by the

---

[9] Anonymous, *A Woman in Berlin* (Boston: Henry Holt, 2005).

[10] Michael P. Scharf, *Balkan Justice: The Story Behind the First International War Crimes Trial Since Nuremberg* (Durham: Carolina Academic Press, 1997).

[11] Arnold Brackman, *The Other Nuremberg: The Untold Story of the Tokyo War Crimes Trials* (New York: Morrow, 1987). Compare Richard Minear, *Victor's Justice: The Tokyo War Crimes Trial* (Princeton: Princeton University Press, 1971). For a further comparison of the Nuremberg and Tokyo trials see Gerry Simpson, "Nuremberg and Tokyo Trials," in *Encyclopedia of Human Rights*, vol. IV, 137–144.

[12] For a concise review see Kelly D. Askin, "A Decade of the Development of Gender Crimes in International Courts and Tribunals: 1993 to 2003," in *Human Rights Brief*, American University, Center for Human Rights and Humanitarian Law, 11, 3 (Spring 2004), 16–19.

defendants and by much, perhaps most, of the German and Japanese publics."[13]

Archival research shows that the Nuremberg process was deeply unpopular in Germany through the 1950s, and that the USA backed away from it in order to get Konrad Adenauer elected Chancellor in West Germany and also to get that new state integrated into NATO. As noted earlier, the USA thus engaged in "strategic legalism" concerning German war crimes trials, pushing them as long as they did not interfere with other foreign policy objectives but abandoning them when judged expedient.[14] It is possible but not certain that later, when the West Germans themselves pursued criminal prosecutions for Nazi crimes, in conjunction with transnational pressures to never forget the Holocaust, this combined process had some considerable impact on evolving German political culture – with developments in Japan being quite different.[15]

Since Nuremberg and Tokyo were not followed by other international tribunals for almost fifty years, it is clear that the international trials of the 1940s did little to deter other atrocities through credible threat of sure prosecution. The two tribunals certainly did clarify relevant facts, perhaps providing some catharsis and relief. Most clearly, the trials provided punishment for some national leaders. The trials also expressed the West's aspirations for a liberal world order based on rule of law and accountability for human rights violations.

Yet realist concerns were not absent. Particularly in Germany but also in Japan, the USA shielded certain officials, especially scientists, from criminal prosecution and brought them to the USA for work in weapons development – given the start of the Cold War with the Soviet Union.

---

[13] "War Crimes," *CQ Researcher*, 5, 25 (July 5, 1995), 589. See further Wilbourn E. Benton and Georg Grimm, eds., *Nuremberg: German Views of the War Trials* (Dallas: Southern Methodist University Press, 1955).

[14] Peter Maguire, *Law and War: An American Story* (New York: Columbia University Press, 2000).

[15] David P. Forsythe, "Human Rights and Mass Atrocities: Revisiting Transitional Justice," *International Studies Review*, 13, 1 (March 2011), 85–95. I think it likely that the Nuremberg tribunal, especially when followed up later by German courts, combined with other reminders of the German past such as a widespread and persistent socialization project about the Holocaust, has caused Germany to be highly sensitive to most human rights issues today. Similar western pressure on Japan has been less, providing one major reason why Japan has been more reluctant to come to terms with its past. The Tokyo trial was less well known in the West, Japanese atrocities such as the rape of Nanking were less well known, and there has been no western-based project like that of remembering the Holocaust which is comparable in the Japanese case. Nuremberg is part of a much broader campaign to remind Germans of their history during 1933–1945, making it difficult to factor out the singular impact of international criminal justice.

In Japan, the USA shielded the Emperor from prosecution, judging him useful in democratic state-building after the war.[16]

In numerous situations between the end of World War II and the end of the Cold War international criminal proceedings were not practical. As in the Korean War, most international armed conflicts ended inconclusively, and certainly without unconditional surrender, thus preventing the trial of those not in custody who were suspected of violations of international law. (And in the Korean War, US and South Korean forces had fired indiscriminately into civilians, fearing that enemy agents were hiding among those fleeing.[17] So raising the issue of war crimes by the enemy might point embarrassing fingers toward one's own side.)

Those wars like the 1991 Persian Gulf War that ended in decisive military defeat still did not result in unconditional surrender and the victors gaining control over the losers. The George H. W. Bush Administration made the judgment, among other considerations, that pursuit of prosecution for Iraqi war crimes was not worth the continued death, injury, and destruction that would have been involved in the attempted capture of the Iraqi leadership. This was a reasoned policy, not devoid of moral considerations. It was almost universally accepted at that time as the proper policy. Later the US House of Representatives voted overwhelmingly in favor of Iraqi trials for war crimes. But based on congressional reactions to American casualties in both Lebanon in the 1980s and Somalia in the 1990s, that body would have been among the first to heatedly criticize a costly ground war designed to apprehend the Iraqi leadership had such been launched by the senior Bush or his successor. By 2005, a majority of the American public gave the George W. Bush Administration very low marks for its 2003 invasion of Iraq. Even though that Administration could point to the capture and forthcoming trial of Saddam Hussein (and others), the public was primarily concerned with American casualties and lack of a clear exit strategy.

In other situations international tribunals could have been organized but for the strength of nationalism. Decisive outcomes produced by such as the Soviet intervention in Hungary or the US intervention in Grenada did not result in international trials since the victors did not want an international tribunal to closely examine embarrassing aspects of the use of force. Clearly the preferred value was not impartial application of

---

[16]   See further Dapo Akande, "International Law Immunities and the International Criminal Court," *American Journal of International Law*, 98, 3 (July 2004), 417; and Timothy Brook, "The Tokyo Judgment and the Rape of Nanking," *Journal of Asian Studies*, 60, 3 (August 2001), 673–700.

[17]   See, for example, Robert L. Bateman, III, *No Gun Ri: A Military History of the Korean War Incident* (Mechanicsburg: Stackpole Books, 2002).

human rights, humanitarian law, or criminal justice but rather protection of the national record and safeguarding unfettered decision making in the future.[18]

Some war crimes usually occur during any use of force. This was made clear, *inter alia*, by eventual disclosure that Israelis had massacred a number of Egyptian prisoners of war during the 1956 Middle East War.[19] Either by design, in the context of what is judged to be pressing military necessity, or by loss of control, even personnel of democracies commit war crimes. I have already noted US involvement in massacres in the Korean War.

National trials

As for crimes against humanity, before the 1990s only the French and Israelis held national trials involving this concept. Britain, France, the Soviet Union, and the United States were willing enough to apply this concept *ex post facto* to Nazi Germany and Imperial Japan, but of these only France developed the concept (slightly) in its own national law. French and Israeli cases were exceedingly few in number, and, with the exception of the Eichmann trial in Jerusalem, pursued with considerable domestic political difficulties. This was especially so in France, as charges against French citizens for aiding in the Holocaust through crimes against humanity resurrected a painful episode in French history. Officials of the Vichy government administered half of France during World War II. Some of its French officials displayed a vicious anti-Semitism.

As for genocide, until the mid-1990s and events in Bosnia and Rwanda, no procedurally correct national trials were held entailing this concept, only procedurally suspect trials in places like Equatorial Guinea. Germany, being the temporary home of a number of refugees from the fighting in the former Yugoslavia, found itself the site of at least one

---

[18] After the USA deposed the Panamanian strongman Manuel Noriega in 1989 through military invasion, he was tried and convicted in a US federal court for drug smuggling and racketeering, not for war crimes or human rights violations. His history of being on the CIA payroll did not save him from US regime change and prosecution. The USA then extradited him to France for further prosecution. All of this was dependent on political factors, namely his falling out of favor with western states. The same was true for Saddam Hussein, who had received US and other western support for his containment of revolutionary Iran, before he became the target of US regime change and US-supported Iraqi prosecution.

[19] Barton Gellman, "Confronting History," *Washington Post*, National Weekly Edition, August 28–September 3, 1995, 12; Serge Schmemann, "After a General Tells of Killing POWs in 1956, Israelis Argue Over Ethics of War," *New York Times*, August 21, 1995, A1.

national trial pertaining to both war crimes and genocide in the 1990s.[20] Rwandan national courts were to pursue this subject in numerous cases.

By far the most numerous national trials for gross violations of human rights connected to international events concern war crimes, although they are not always technically called that when prosecuted under national military law. For the most part these trials involve western liberal democracies applying the laws of war to their own military personnel. Very rarely, a country such as Denmark, Switzerland, or Germany will hold a war crimes trial concerning a foreigner, usually pertaining to events in the former Yugoslavia. National war crimes trials have not been without problems. As noted above, the military personnel even of democracies do commit war crimes, for those democracies that have used force abroad have not lacked for courts martial for violations of the laws of war. This, for example, the Americans discovered at My Lai and other places in Vietnam, the Israelis discovered in Arab territory occupied since 1967, and the Canadians and Italians discovered in Somalia during the 1990s.

Even when such national trials are held in liberal democracies, it has not always proved easy to apply the full force of national military law (which is derived from international law). No US senior officers were ever held responsible for the massacre at My Lai in Vietnam in the late 1960s. Moreover, President Richard Nixon felt compelled by public opinion to reduce the punishment for Lt. Calley who was held responsible for the deaths of between twenty and seventy "Oriental" civilians at My Lai. At the time of writing US officials have moved only against low-ranking soldiers for prisoner abuse connected to Washington's "war on terrorism." The Israeli authorities have been quite lenient in punishing their military personnel for violations of various human rights and humanitarian norms in disputed territory. The Canadians have found it difficult to come to full terms with the actions of some of their troops in Somalia. Only the Italians moved rapidly and vigorously against some of their soldiers who had abused Somalis. Rome concluded that the incidents in question were the result of a few "bad apples" and not part of a systematic or structural problem.

More than anything else this national record suggests the continuing power of nationalism, rather than any carefully reasoned and morally compelling argument about national criminal justice associated with war. That is to say that no compelling political or moral argument explains

[20] In re Jorgic (www.domovina.net/calenddar.html), regarding the Bosnian Serb convicted in Germany for atrocities committed in Bosnia during 1992–1993.

why the US military justice system mostly failed in its handling of the My Lai massacre.[21] (First, the military attempted to suppress the facts. Then the military establishment focused the spotlight of inquiry at platoon level, mostly ignoring the training and orders given to foot soldiers by superior commanders. There was never punishment that fitted the extent of the crime.) A defensive and emotional nationalism has frequently overwhelmed aspects of proper criminal justice. If this is true in national trials, it indicates much difficulty for the prospects of international criminal justice. If national governments have trouble prosecuting their own, particularly those who authorized or allowed the wrongdoing, how much more difficult it will be for them to turn over their own for trial by others. Serbia and the United States are not so different in this regard, except in the power of the USA to resist the kind of pressures that caused Serbia to grudgingly cooperate in matters of international criminal justice. When Ratko Mladic was finally arrested in 2011 for his role in the genocidal massacre at Srebrenica in 1995 and earlier attacks on Bosnian civilians in Sarajevo, thousands of Serbs demonstrated in his support, seeing him as a national war hero.

In sum, international criminal proceedings were very rare before the end of the Cold War, and thus we do not know very much about their effects. Rare also have been national proceedings for crimes against humanity and genocide. Only national trials for war crimes have occurred with any regularity, and these – mostly in democracies – have been frequently constricted by the continuing strength of nationalism.

International criminal justice since 1991

After the Cold War and the demise of European communism, international relations saw the creation of two UN *ad hoc* criminal courts, several special hybrid criminal courts, and for the first time in history a standing – which is to say permanent – International Criminal Court. There were also important national developments in criminal justice linked to international human rights and humanitarian law. Paradoxically, this movement toward increased international criminal justice only intensified the debate about other forms of transitional justice – and whether some forms of justice might be preferred that downplayed criminal justice in favor of social or political justice. Some spoke of the difference between retributive and restorative justice.

---

[21] Joseph Goldstein, Burke Marshall, and Jack Schwartz, eds., *The My Lai Massacre and Its Cover-Up: Beyond the Reach of Law?* (New York: Free Press, 1976).

The ICTY

At first glance, the creation of the International Criminal Tribunal for the former Yugoslavia (ICTY) in 1993 by the UN Security Council seemed to usher in a new age in international criminal justice.[22] The Security Council voted to create a balanced and mostly procedurally correct international tribunal while the fighting and atrocities still raged, and legally required all UN member states to cooperate with the tribunal by invoking Chapter VII of the Charter. Those who committed war crimes, crimes against humanity, and genocide in that particular situation were to be prosecuted. The emphasis was on commanders who authorized or allowed the crimes.

Several commentators tried to create the impression that pursuit of criminal justice in the former Yugoslavia was a clear and simple matter. David Scheffer, soon to become head of a new office in the State Department for war crimes, wrote of the creation of the ICTY: "The Council recognized the enforcement of international law as an immediate priority, subordinate to neither political nor military imperatives."[23] A United Nations lawyer, Payam Akhavan, wrote: "there was a political consensus on the complementary interrelationship between the establishment of the Tribunal and the restoration of peace and security in the former Yugoslavia."[24] To critics, these quotes might reflect a continuation of legalistic-moralistic reasoning that characterized exaggerated hopes for the arbitration treaties of the 1920s.[25] To critics, this was judicial romanticism *par excellence*. Public documents (and public posturing) notwithstanding, the tribunal was created in large part because of realist reasoning, not because of moral or legal commitment to human rights

---

[22] A useful compilation of documents about the creation of the ICTY can be found in Virginia Morris and Michael Scharf, *An Insider's Guide to the International Criminal Tribunal for the Former Yugoslavia* (Irvington-on-Hudson: Transnational Publishers, 1995).

[23] David Scheffer, "International Judicial Intervention," *Foreign Policy*, 102 (Spring 1996), 38.

[24] Payam Akhavan, "The Yugoslav Tribunal at a Crossroads: The Dayton Peace Agreement and Beyond," *Human Rights Quarterly*, 18, 2 (May 1996), 267. See also his views in "Justice in The Hague, Peace in the Former Yugoslavia?," *Human Rights Quarterly*, 20, 4 (November 1998), 737–816. In this latter article he refers to me as a "realist," and acknowledges "judicial romanticism" while saying the latter concept does not apply to him. I am not a realist of either the classical (Hans Morgenthau) or structural (Kenneth Walz) variety, but a pragmatic liberal. I am in favor of attention to human dignity, frequently via human rights, but recognize the pervasive power and interests of the territorial state. See further Forsythe, "International Criminal Courts: A Political View," *Netherlands Quarterly of Human Rights*, 15, 1 (March 1997), 5–19.

[25] See further George Kennan, *American Diplomacy 1900–1950* (Chicago: University of Chicago Press, 1951).

standards.[26] States like the USA were under pressure to act to stop the atrocities being reported by the communications media. The USA and some other Security Council members did not want to engage in a decisive intervention that could prove costly in terms of blood and treasure. They saw no self-interest in a complicated intervention. As James Baker, Secretary of State during the George H. W. Bush Administration, was reported to have said, "We have no dog in that fight." But they felt the need to do something. So the Clinton Administration helped create the tribunal in a short-term, public relations maneuver, leaving various contradictions to sort themselves out later.

From the creation of the tribunal in 1993 to the conclusion of the Dayton peace agreement in 1995, many policy makers and observers found fault with the very existence of the ICTY for possibly impeding diplomatic peacemaking.[27] The logic was clear enough. Would one prolong the fighting, with accompanying atrocities, by requiring that the principal fighting parties make a just peace – after which their responsible officials would be subjected to criminal justice? Would they not prefer to fight on, rather than cooperate in a peace agreement that would make their arrest and trial more likely?

This classic dilemma between peace and justice, between stability and punishment, became pronounced with the creation of the new court. Thus particularly the British during the John Major government played a hypocritical double game, voting for the tribunal but operating behind the scenes to hamper its work. London preferred the diplomatic to the juridical track, arguing in private that diplomacy was a better path to peace and human security. Public posturing aside, Major's approach was a pragmatic liberal strategy, hopeful of ending atrocities via diplomacy, but not one that gave more than cosmetic support to adjudication. Even Scheffer, before he entered the State Department, perhaps with El Salvador or South Africa in mind where criminal justice had been bypassed or minimized, wrote that "Despite the hard hits human rights standards take in these [unspecified] cases and the risk of never breaking the cycle of retribution and violence, the choice of 'peace over justice' is sometimes the most effective means of reconciliation."[28] It can be a serious matter

---

[26] I lay out the evidence in "Politics and the International Tribunal for the Former Yugoslavia," *Criminal Law Forum*, 5, 2–3 (Spring 1994), 401–422; also in Robert S. Clark and Madeleine Sann, eds., *The Prosecution of International Crimes* (New Brunswick: Transaction Publishers, 1996), 185–206.

[27] See further Anthony D'Amato, "Peace v. Accountability in Bosnia," *American Journal of International Law*, 88, 3 (July 1994), 500–506; and Anonymous, "Human Rights in Peace Negotiations," *Human Rights Quarterly*, 18, 2 (May 1996), 249–258.

[28] Scheffer, "International Judicial Intervention," 37.

to question the wisdom of international criminal justice in certain cases, and whether its pursuit in those situations reflects judicial romanticism.

Even Judge Goldstone, the first prosecutor for the ICTY, noted that truth commissions had certain advantages over criminal trials as far as establishing facts in a form broadly understandable and thus in providing education and catharsis. He advocated both trials and truth commissions.[29]

The Dayton agreement showed that at least superficially or on paper one could have both relative peace and some criminal justice – one could end most of the combat and reduce much of the multifaceted victimization of individuals while at least promising criminal justice for those who had engaged in war crimes, crimes against humanity, and genocide.[30] However, one could secure the cooperation of Slobodan Milosevic, and the Serb-dominated Yugoslavian army that he controlled, only by an evident deal at Dayton exempting him from prosecution – at least for a time. At that time there was no public indictment against Milosevic who, more than any other single individual, was responsible for the breakup of former Yugoslavia and no doubt the Serbian strategy of ethnic cleansing. As far as we know from the public record and the logic of the situation, in Milosevic's case one had to trade away in 1995 criminal justice for diplomatic peacemaking, although lawyers for the ICTY argued that they simply did not have a good legal case against him. It seemed to be a fact that western states did not make a serious effort to go after certain individuals who were guilty of atrocities such as Milosevic, Ratko Mladic, and Radovan Karadzic until later – when the Dayton agreement was more secure.

The same dilemma resurfaced regarding Kosovo. Milosevic was both the arsonist and the firefighter in that situation, as in Bosnia earlier. He undertook repressive policies and forced expulsions in Kosovo, a province in new Yugoslavia (now Serbia), that inflamed discontent among the

[29] "Ethnic Reconciliation Needs the Help of a Truth Commission," *International Herald Tribune*, October 24, 1998, 6. See also Goldstone, "Bringing War Criminals to Justice During an Ongoing War." Given the difficulty of educating the public via technical trials, Mark Osiel proposes liberal show trials in *Mass Atrocity, Collective Memory, and the Law* (New Brunswick: Transaction Publishers, 1997). But liberal show trials are inherently contradictory, as Samantha Power notes in *New Republic*, March 2, 1998, 32–38.

[30] See further Richard Holbrooke, *To End a War* (New York: Random House, 1998). Holbrooke was the key mediator at Dayton. He wrote that his mandate was to secure peace, not pursue criminal justice. This indirectly confirms that Milosevic did not face any threat of criminal justice from US diplomatic officials. No doubt Milosevic could at least infer a *de facto* trade-off: if he signed the Dayton accord US officials would not go after him for human rights violations. Whether there were secret and/or explicit assurances is not known.

ethnic Albanians who made up 90 percent of the local population. But the West had to deal with him, since he possessed the authority and power to restrain the Yugoslav forces (of Serbian ethnicity) who were engaged in hostilities in the province. How could one solicit his cooperation in reducing human rights and humanitarian violations if one threatened him with criminal justice? The US Congress, on record earlier as in favor of prosecuting Iraqi war criminals, voted to urge the Clinton Administration to offer Milosevic a deal – sanctuary in a friendly country in return for his abdication of power within new Yugoslavia. The prosecutor's office of the ICTY finally indicted Milosevic and several of his high-ranking colleagues in Belgrade for ordering criminal acts in Kosovo, but this was after hope was lost for a negotiated deal with Milosevic, à la Bosnia, to end the atrocities in Kosovo.

Immediately after Dayton, the fear of doing more harm than good via criminal justice resurfaced in still other forms. One fear was that pursuit of indicted suspects would cause the fragile commitment to the Dayton accord to collapse. In early 1996 certain Bosnian Serb military officers wandered into areas controlled by the Bosnian Muslims by error and were arrested on suspicion of war crimes. Bosnian Serb parties then refused to cooperate with talks on continued military disengagement called for under the peace agreements and supervised by IFOR (the NATO implementation force). A political crisis resulted, entailing high-level mediation by US diplomats. The Serbian officers were eventually returned to Serbia rather than transferred to The Hague for trial. It was a vivid if small demonstration of how pursuit of legal justice could endanger the broader political agreements that had ended both the combat and related human rights violations.

A similar fear was that pursuit of criminal justice in Bosnia would produce another Somalia. In that East African country in 1993, the attempt to arrest one of the warlords, General Aideed, leading as it did to the deaths of eighteen US soldiers and the wounding of many more, produced an early US withdrawal from that country and more generally a US reluctance to support other UN-approved deployments of force in places like Rwanda the following year. The goal of national reconciliation with liberal democracy was never achieved by the international community in Somalia, arguably at least in part because of the defection of the USA from the international effort in 1994. The companion fear in Bosnia was that similar US casualties would force a premature withdrawal of NATO forces (via IFOR and SFOR – the latter being the stabilization force) and a collapse of the effort to make the Dayton agreement work. European contributors to NATO deployments made it clear that if the USA pulled out, they would also.

After a passive policy of non-arrests by NATO forces during 1993–1995, some arrests were made after 1995. But for considerable time NATO did not seek to arrest the Serbian leaders who had devised and commanded the policies of ethnic cleansing of Muslims in Bosnia. They were well connected and well protected. In Washington especially, it was feared that a costly shoot-out would undermine the shaky congressional tolerance of American military personnel on the ground in the Balkans. It was only later, when the Dayton agreement seemed more secure, as enforced by a sizable contingent of first NATO and then EU troops on the ground, that a more vigorous pursuit of Milosevic, Mladic, and Karadzic took place. Eventually, particularly because of US financial pressure, a newly elected Serbian government detained Milosevic in spring of 2001 and transferred him to The Hague for trial in the ICTY. Thus in 1995 the USA negotiated with Milosevic at Dayton, but by 2001 the USA was demanding his arrest and trial. Either policy might prove justified, taking into account the broader political context of the Balkans. Later Radovan Karadzic, the Bosnian Serb inflammatory leader, was arrested and sent to The Hague. Still later Ratko Mladic, immediate author of the Serb massacre of Bosnian Muslim males at Srebrenica in 1995, was finally arrested by Serb authorities after more than fifteen years of evasion – sometimes with Belgrade's connivance. Under persistent pressure from the western network backing the ICTY, the highest Serb authorities knew that their chances of joining the European Union would be greatly affected by such arrests.

What we see with regard to the ICTY is an early tension between pragmatic liberalism and classical liberalism in the form of international criminal justice, a tension that was resolved only with the negotiated Dayton peace agreement for Bosnia, plus NATO intervention regarding Kosovo. It was only after these political events that there was serious pursuit of various Serbian leaders (and some Croat and Bosnian Muslim officials) in order to hold them personally accountable for certain crimes. What we also see in the example of the ICTY is the creation of the Court for essentially realist reasons, but then the transformation of the Court into a serious enterprise of criminal justice largely through the office of its prosecutor, supported by many non-governmental organizations and a few states.

The USA, which had led in the creation of the Court for cosmetic and self-serving reasons, then became the key backer of the Court. Having authored the Court, Washington felt it had to make it a success. Until 1999 and the NATO bombing of Serbia because of Kosovo, Washington could support the ICTY as criminal justice for others, the Court's jurisdiction being limited to behavior within the boundaries of the former Yugoslavia. But with the 1999 NATO bombing, NATO personnel became subject to the jurisdiction of the Court. (The jurisdiction of the Court pertained to allegations of certain crimes committed in the territory of the former Yugoslavia – or in the air space above it. So in carrying out bombing raids on Serb targets, NATO put itself under the Court's jurisdiction. NATO states did not contest this logic.) The ICTY prosecutor declined, on the basis of a staff investigation, to pursue charges of war crimes articulated against certain NATO personnel. Some observers thought this was a political decision, it being difficult for NATO to carry out military actions over several months without questionable decisions about, for example, bombing targets. (Serbia also pursued a legal complaint in the International Court of Justice against certain NATO states for violations of international law in the bombing campaign, but this legal action also came to naught. There was also a case filed with the European Court of Human Rights against certain European states that were members of NATO, but this litigation also failed.)

Out of these complicated origins, the ICTY compiled a complicated record. Without question the Court was able to punish a number of persons, including some high officials; it also helped develop international law in important ways.

As of 2008 the ICTY had convicted fifty-four persons (twenty via plea bargains and thirty-four via full trials). The average sentence handed down was incarceration for 15.6 years (median of 15 years). Those who pled guilty got about 2 years' less jail time than those convicted. By 2011 it was clear that the Security Council was pressing the Court to complete its agenda as quickly as compatible with due process. By that time the Court had dealt with 161 indictments; 126 persons had been convicted, cleared, or entered a plea bargain arrangement.

The Court in various cases held that: the 1995 massacre at Srebrenica constituted genocide, in that there was an intentional attempt to destroy a substantial part of the Bosnian Muslim people through the killing of over 7,000 men and boys; that individuals could be held responsible for crimes committed in internal war, not just international war; that a detention camp commander was responsible for crimes, including sex crimes, that occurred under his command, whether committed against men or women; that rape crimes could constitute war crimes or crimes against humanity, not just individual illegal acts; that someone who did not participate directly in rapes could be convicted of rape for allowing or encouraging it to happen, and that rape was also a form of torture and discrimination. It can be seen that the ICTY was especially attentive to various gender issues, certainly by comparison to the Nuremberg and Tokyo tribunals.

The most important case, that of Milosevic, ended prematurely with the death of the defendant from natural causes. The Serb leader had insisted on defending himself. This fact prolonged the trial, both because of health-related delays and time he devoted to histrionics. There were also disputes between the defendant and his court-appointed lawyers. It took some two years for the prosecution to present its case, with the defense phase projected to last longer. Much of the trial centered on proof of Milosevic's role in various war crimes, crimes against humanity, and genocide. The latter seemed the most difficult to prove, given that any commands reflecting an intent to destroy a national, ethnic, religious, or racial people were not likely to be found in written documents or clear and uncontested statements. This case was one of several in different courts that raised serious questions about the time and costs associated with international criminal justice, especially when defendants were given rather wide latitude to request repeated delays and make long speeches of dubious relevance.[31] It was not only Milosevic but other defendants in other courts that used their trial as a political platform. Karadzic played the game the same way, and Mladic was expected to do so.

It was difficult to say whether the Court achieved goals beyond punishment and legal development, which is not to denigrate gains in those categories, since it was hard to gauge its effect on regional reconciliation and stability, and on closure for affected individuals.[32] The Court early on did not have a good outreach program, explaining its actions to parties in the Balkans. Certainly in much of Serbia and the Serb part of Bosnia, the ICTY was widely seen as anti-Serb. This was partially because of the large number of Serbs indicted, arrested, and made defendants. Also, the third prosecutor, Carla del Ponte of Switzerland, often had pointed things to say about the lack of Serb and Bosnian Serb cooperation with the Court.[33] On the one hand some analysts thought Serb cooperation was secured only in direct response to outside pressures; when those pressures waned, so did Serb cooperation.[34] On the other hand a few

[31] See further William Schabas, "Balancing the Rights of the Accused with the Imperatives of Accountability," in Thakur and Malcontent, eds., *Sovereign Impunity*.

[32] David Tolbert, "The Criminal Tribunal for the Former Yugoslavia: Unforeseen Successes and Unforeseeable Shortcomings," *Fletcher Forum of World Affairs*, 26, 2 (Summer/Fall, 2002).

[33] Misha Glenny, "The Prosecutor Muddies Serbian Waters," *International Herald Tribune*, February 17, 2004, www.iht.com/cgi-bin/generic.cgi?template=articleprint.tmplh@ ArticleId=129800. See further Heikelina Verrijn Stuart, "Carla Del Ponte," in *Encyclopedia of Human Rights*, vol. I, 481–486.

[34] Patrice McMahon and David P. Forsythe, "The ICTY's Impact on Serbia: Judicial Romanticism Meets Network Politics," *Human Rights Quarterly*, 30, 2 (May 2008), 412–435. See also Jelena Subotic, *Hijacked Justice: Dealing with the Past in the Balkans*

analysts saw some genuine improvement in human rights matters in various Balkan states because of the ICTY.[35]

It was certainly difficult for the ICTY to promote reconciliation among Bosnian Muslims, Serbs of various sorts, and Croats, when the Dayton agreement itself had recognized largely autonomous Serb, Croat, and Muslim sectors within Bosnia.[36] As of 2011 there was clearly substantial antagonism remaining among the various communities in the Balkans, with a rather fragile peace being mainly the result of interposition and enforcement by NATO and EU states, under UN aegis, rather than because of genuine intercommunal reconciliation. Despite various Court judgments, Muslim refugees and displaced persons had trouble returning to their homes in Serb portions of Bosnia. Tensions also remained high in Kosovo between the Serbs and Albanians. Croats often did not fully cooperate with the ICTY, it usually being difficult for any nation to prosecute those claiming to defend the nation from insidious opponents.

The ICTY, costing around $275 million per year, had been asked to finish its trials (but not appeals) by 2008. This was later extended to 2011, with all appeals supposedly finished by 2014. The existence of the Court did contribute to the move to create a permanent international criminal court, as noted below. According to one summary evaluation that stressed once again not political but legal achievements: "The Tribunal's accomplishments are many. It established that an international tribunal could conduct trials according to law... It has also established a large number of important legal and institutional precedents, notably those clarifying the elements of international crimes, affirming the applicability of international humanitarian law to internal armed conflict [and covering] sexual violence in wartime... the ICTY made a unique and major contribution to the development of international criminal law and practice."[37]

The Rwandan court

The reasons for the creation of a second *ad hoc* UN criminal court were similar to the first. States on the Security Council, principally the United

(Ithaca: Cornell University Press, 2009); and Christopher K. Lamont, *International Criminal Justice and the Politics of Cooperation* (Farnham: Ashgate, 2010).

[35] See, e.g., Diane Orentlicher, *Shrinking the Space for Denial: The Impact of the ICTY in Serbia* (New York: Open Society Initiative, 2008).

[36] See further Patrice McMahon and Jon Western, "The Death of Dayton: How to Stop Bosnia from Falling Apart," *Foreign Affairs*, 88, 5 (September–October 2009), 69–83.

[37] Bartram S. Brown, "International Criminal Tribunal for the Former Yugoslavia (ICTY)," in *Encyclopedia of Human Rights*, vol. III, 137.

States, did not want to incur the costs of a decisive intervention in Rwanda in 1994 to stop the longstanding conflict between Hutu and Tutsi communities which resulted in a genocide with perhaps 500,000–800,000 deaths.[38] They saw no vital self-interests in such action. Somalia in 1993 had shown that international intervention in a situation where persons of ill will engaged in brutal and inhumane power struggles could be a dangerous venture. The USA and others were eventually willing to pay billions of dollars for the care of those fleeing genocide in Rwanda. But loss of western life, even in a professional and volunteer military establishment, was another matter. This was certainly true of Belgium, a former colonial power in Rwanda, which, when faced with ten deaths in its peacekeeping unit there, was in favor of the withdrawal, not the expansion, of those forces. Feeling nevertheless the impulse to do something, states on the Council created a second criminal court with similar jurisdiction and authority. Thus, as in former Yugoslavia, it was not consistent attention to moral norms and legal rules that drove the Security Council to action. Rather, it was a search for a tolerable expedient that resulted in attention to criminal justice. The best that can be said for the USA and the Security Council was that evident unease at the absence of moral and legal consistency across roughly similar cases produced at least some action on the question of prosecution for atrocities via ethnic/tribal slaughter in Rwanda.

As was true for the ICTY, so for the ICTR, it fell to the prosecutor's office, supporting NGOs, and a few concerned states to turn a venture based on guilt and public relations into something more substantive. The prosecutor's position proved problematic. The initial shared prosecutor showed more interest in former Yugoslavia than in Rwanda, and a later prosecutor, del Ponte, developed major frictions with the Rwanda government (Tutsi controlled) that had triumphed in the fighting of 1994. So eventually a separate prosecutor was established for the ICTR in 2003.

---

[38] The difference between Hutus and Tutsis had been codified by Belgium when a colonial power and was originally more a class than biological or blood distinction. By the time of Rwandan independence the distinction had been solidified, and it had great political significance – as those identifying as Hutu made up a large majority of the country, controlling the outcome of elections. By 1994 the Hutu community was divided between militants advocating Hutu power to the detriment of Tutsis, and moderates interested in power sharing. By contrast to the perhaps 800,000 killed in Rwanda in 1994, eighteen US soldiers were killed in one day in Mogadishu, among a total of some thirty-five US military deaths in Somalia in the early 1990s overall. This is a modest cost for a "great power" or superpower in relative terms. The USA suffered nine deaths in one military air crash off South Africa in September 1997, but the media did not emphasize it and commentators did not call for a change of policy there. See further Edward N. Luttwak, "Where Are the Great Powers?," *Foreign Affairs*, 73, 4 (July/August 1994), 23–29.

The Court early on was hamstrung by petty corruption, mismanagement, lack of adequate support, and not so veiled hostility on the part of more than one Rwandan.[39] Despite all this, by fall of 2004 the Court had rendered 17 final judgments involving 23 persons.[40] Several high officials had been convicted, including a prime minister and a mayor. The ICTR produced the first conviction for genocide ever recorded in a proper court of law. This was the Akayesu case, in which, in the view of the trial chamber, the mayor of the Taba Commune "had reason to know and in fact knew that sexual violence was taking place . . . and that women were being taken away . . . and sexually violated."[41] In this same judgment, rape of women was seen as part of genocide and crimes against humanity.

A summary evaluation seems accurate. "The ICTR punished only Hutu[s], as Rwanda effectively blocked the indictment of Tutsi[s] . . . officers who [President] Kagame feared would stage a coup rather than submit to prosecution . . . The ICTR did succeed in bringing to justice the major leaders of Rwanda's genocide and in creating an irrefutable historic record of their crimes . . . Over half of the extremist regime's cabinet ministers, a significant number of military commanders, business leaders, and local administrators were convicted in fair trials."[42]

Ironically, high Hutu officials convicted of genocide and/or crimes against humanity in the ICTR received only a maximum sentence of life imprisonment, whereas lower Hutu officials or citizens convicted in Rwanda national courts – mostly staffed by Tutsis – could receive the death penalty.

In Rwanda after 2002 one also found Gacaca or community courts designed in part to ease the intense overcrowding in Rwanda prisons and backlog of defendants. Controversial because of the lack of trained judges and full judicial process, the Gacaca courts nevertheless went forward with mixed results.[43] They were scheduled for termination at the time of writing.

---

[39] For a brief summary see Paul Lewis, "UN Report Comes Down Hard on Rwandan Genocide Tribunal," *New York Times*, February 13, 1997, A9.

[40] Even early on, those so inclined had made a positive assessment of the ICTR. See Payam Akhavan, "Justice and Reconciliation in the Great Lakes Region of Africa: The Contribution of the International Criminal Tribunal for Rwanda," *Duke Journal of Comparative and International Law*, 7 (1997), 325–348.

[41] Prosecutor v. Akayesu, Judgment, Case No. 96-4-T (September 2, 1998).

[42] Howard Tolley, "International Criminal Tribunal for Rwanda (ICTR)," in *Encyclopedia of Human Rights*, vol. III, 127–128.

[43] Erin Daly, "Between Punitive and Reconstructive Justice: The Gacaca Courts in Rwanda," *New York University Journal of International Law and Politics*, 34 (2002), 355–396; and Christopher J. Le Mon, "Rwanda's Troubled Gacaca Courts," *Human Rights Brief*, 14, 2 (Winter 2007), 16–20.

Beyond punishment of individuals and development of legal concepts, the ICTR merits further discussion. It was highly unlikely that an international tribunal prosecuting Hutus during a time of Tutsi control of Rwanda could interject a decisive break in the cycle of ethnic violence that had long characterized that country. True, militant Hutus had planned, organized, and executed the wave of killing in 1994. But consider the parallels with former Yugoslavia. By most accounts, Serbs had committed the greatest number of atrocities during 1992–1995, even though Croats and Bosnian Muslims did not have clean hands. And Serbs had certainly persecuted ethnic Albanians in Kosovo. But when the prosecutor brought indictments mostly against Serbs, many in this latter ethnic group claimed bias by the ICTY.[44] Thus the early pattern of indictments and convictions did little to break down group allegiance and group hostility. In similar fashion, it was unlikely that many Rwandan Hutus would be led to re-evaluate their prejudices by trials focusing only on Hutus, especially when some Tutsi violence had not been met with international prosecution.[45] So one might punish leading Hutu criminals, but using the tribunal to break the cycle of ethnic violence was a tougher nut to crack. It was fairly clear, unfortunately, that the ICTR had not contributed to regional stability.

During the life of the ICTR ethnic violence continued on a large scale in the Great Lakes region of Africa, with only relative decline compared with 1994. There was mounting evidence that Tutsis had massacred Hutus in eastern Zaire during the struggle for control of that country. That is precisely why the late President Kabila in the new Congo, who owed his position to Tutsi support, among other factors, consistently tried to block a United Nations investigation into the reported massacre. Tutsis and Hutus continued to fight in both the Democratic Republic of the Congo and Burundi, as well as in Rwanda. Murder and torture continued to be practiced by both sides. Could one realistically expect one international court, with a lack of full respect and support from either ethnic group, to make any great difference in the evolution of events – at least in the foreseeable future?

So for both the ICTY and the ICTR, punishment and legal development were one thing; personal closure and reconciliation were something else. By late 2004, the ICTR, operating on an annual budget of about $235 million, had been asked to close up shop by 2008, excepting

---

[44] For a critique of the pattern of indictments by the office of the independent prosecutor, see Cedric Thornberry, "Saving the War Crimes Tribunal," *Foreign Policy*, 104 (Fall 1996), 72–86.
[45] See further Leo J. DeSouza, "Assigning Blame in Rwanda," *Washington Monthly*, 29, 9 (September 1997), 40–43.

appeals. Similar to the ICTY, this deadline for the ICTR was later extended. But it was clear by 2011 that the UN Security Council was interested in ending these two *ad hoc* courts, especially after the permanent International Criminal Court had been created. Like the ICTY, the ICTR made some contribution to the new ICC.

The International Criminal Court

On July 17, 1998, a diplomatic conference meeting in Rome, relying heavily on the experience of the ICTY and ICTR, approved the statute of a permanent criminal court to be loosely associated with the United Nations. The statute consists of 128 articles and is longer than the UN Charter.[46] Subject matter jurisdiction covers genocide, crimes against humanity, war crimes, and aggression (crimes against peace) when international law presents a sufficiently precise definition, which was said not to be the case in July 1998. Judges are elected by the states that are parties to the statute; these judges sit in their individual capacity and not as state representatives. An independent prosecutor is attached to the Court. The final vote was 120 in favor, 7 opposed (the USA, Israel, China, Iraq, Sudan, Yemen, Libya), and the rest abstaining.

The Court operates, as of July 1, 2002, sixty ratifications being obtained, on the basis of complementarity. This means that the Court does not function unless a state in question is unable or unwilling to investigate and, if warranted, prosecute for one of the covered crimes. Thus, whereas the ICTY and ICTR had primary jurisdiction and could supersede state action, the ICC only has complementary jurisdiction. It is a backup system, designed to encourage states to exercise their primary jurisdiction and authority in responsible ways. The prosecutor can go forward with a case if the state where the crime has been committed is a party to the statute, or is the state of the defendant. But the prosecutor must obtain approval of a pre-trial chamber of the Court, whose decision to approve prosecution is subject to appeal to another chamber. This is designed to prevent political or other improper action by the prosecutor, who is also elected by state parties to the statute. The UN Security Council can also refer cases to the Court, or can delay proceedings for up to a year, renewable. This latter provision is to allow for diplomacy to trump prosecution – to allow pragmatic liberalism to trump classical liberalism in the form of criminal justice.

---

[46] See especially Benjamin Schiff, *Building the International Criminal Court* (Cambridge: Cambridge University Press, 2008). See further Robert C. Johansen, "International Criminal Court," in *Encyclopedia of Human Rights*, vol. III, 113–120.

In the final analysis the ICC was the product of a group of "like-minded" states, led periodically by Canada, and a swarm of NGOs. They, as in Ottawa a year earlier with regard to a treaty banning anti-personnel landmines,[47] decided to move ahead despite belated but clear opposition from the USA. Ironically, part of the momentum for a standing criminal court had come from the latter. But in Rome the USA made very clear that it did not intend to have its nationals appear before the tribunal. According to Scheffer, Ambassador at Large for War Crimes Issues:

> There is a reality, and the reality is that the United States is a global military power and presence. Other countries are not. We are. Our military forces are often called upon to engage overseas in conflict situations, for purposes of humanitarian intervention, to rescue hostages, to bring out American citizens from threatening environments, to deal with terrorists. We have to be extremely careful that this proposal [for a standing court] does not limit the capacity of our armed forces to legitimately operate internationally. We have to be careful that it does not open up opportunities for endless frivolous complaints to be lodged against the United States as a global military power.[48]

This was largely a smokescreen argument. The rule of complementarity meant that if US personnel should be charged with international crime, a proper investigation by the USA and, if warranted, prosecution would keep the new court from functioning. A prosecutor who wanted to bring charges against the USA would need to secure approval from the pre-trial chamber, whose approval could be appealed to a different chamber. By simple majority vote, the UN Security Council could delay proceedings, renewable, against the USA. Yet the Clinton Administration was unyielding in opposition. This was largely in deference to the Pentagon, and to the ultra-nationalists in the Congress. Senator Jesse Helms, the Chair of the Senate Foreign Relations Committee at that time, declared the treaty dead on arrival should it ever be submitted to the Senate.

For a country that saw itself as a leader for human rights, and that had led the effort to create two *ad hoc* criminal tribunals with jurisdiction over others, its posture at Rome was not a policy designed to appeal to many states. The double standards were too evident. (The French did successfully insist on a seven-year grace period for war crimes proceedings

---

[47] Among many sources see further Richard A. Mathew, Bryan McDonald, and Kenneth R. Rutherford, eds., *Landmines and Human Security: International Politics and War's Hidden Legacy* (Albany: State University of New York Press, 2004).
[48] *New York Times*, August 13, 1997, A8.

against adhering states, apparently to give it some wiggle room in the event of investigations into its African policies.)[49]

The George W. Bush Administration "unsigned" the Clinton signature on the Rome Statute, sought through bilateral diplomacy to persuade or pressure other states into exempting US personnel from the coverage of the ICC, delayed UN peacekeeping deployments until the Security Council exempted any participating US personnel from any review by the ICC, and in almost every way imaginable tried to undermine the ICC. In 2005, however, the USA abstained on a UN Security Council resolution that authorized the ICC prosecutor to open investigations about possibly indicting certain Sudanese leaders for atrocities in the Darfur region of that country. In effect, the Bush Administration prioritized action on Darfur over trying to kill the ICC.

The follow-on Administration of Barack Obama was more sympathetic to the Court in quiet ways, but without any movement toward seeking the Senate's advice and consent for ratification of the Rome Statute. Obtaining such consent was perceived as a bruising and uphill battle.

In the Libyan crisis of 2011, as NATO states tried to coax Muammar Kaddafi from power in the face of significant rebellion, a majority in the UN Security Council voted to refer the question of human rights violations to the prosecutor's office for further investigation. This move was debated. If one wanted to facilitate Kaddafi's departure after many years of dictatorial rule, as was true of Saddam Hussein in Iraq and Slobodan Milosevic in Serbia, promising prosecution after stepping down created a dubious incentive. On the other hand, would not impunity after gross violation of human rights encourage other national leaders to engage in brutal repression?

Despite some shift in US policies, the ICC was not free from controversy. As all of the early investigations and cases involved African defendants, many African states began to rethink their support for the Court. True, African states such as Democratic Congo, Central African Republic, and Uganda had all referred cases to the Court. In effect, these governments were asking the Court to help suppress various opposition figures. But when, in particular, the ICC prosecutor began to consider indictments against Kenyan and Sudanese political figures, African state opinion began to shift to a more critical stance. Moreover, in Uganda

---

[49] The British, in breaking with the USA over this issue, issued the following statement: "we and other major NATO allies are satisfied that the safeguards that are built in to the International Criminal Court will protect our servicemen against malicious or politically motivated prosecution" (British Information Services, Press Release 214/98, July 20, 1998).

the prosecutor became entangled in a dispute about the wisdom of criminal justice for Joseph Kony, leader of the so-called Lord's Resistance Army, as compared to seeking a diplomatic solution to the longrunning violent conflict there.[50] Also, it was alleged that human rights violations had been committed by the government side as well, thus raising issues about the scope of ICC investigations. In general, after about a decade of the Court's existence, there were many debates about the exercise of prosecutorial discretion, as well as the conduct of the few trials that actually got under way. A broad review of the ICC's record in DRC, Uganda, and Kenya in 2011 by the Open Society Foundations showed just how complicated matters could be.[51]

Hybrid courts

After atrocities in Kosovo, East Timor, Sierra Leone, and Cambodia, courts were created that might be called special, hybrid, or transnational.[52] In Kosovo in 1999, the UN field mission (UNMIK), operating under Security Council resolutions, created a hybrid court with local and international judges, applying a mixture of local and international law. The focus was mostly war crimes. Particularly the Serb population preferred this court to any court that would be dominated by the local majority of ethnic Albanians. The respect earned by this court was impressive in the context of continuing Serb–Albanian frictions. But the jurisprudence of this hybrid court did not mesh well with the ICTY, since the former did not use the cases of the latter as precedent.

In East Timor in 2000, the UN field mission there (UNTAET), again under UN Security Council mandate, created another hybrid court since the local legal infrastructure was non-existent. Panels of three judges contained two international and one local judge. The focus was on serious violations of international humanitarian law. A rather large number of indictments by the special prosecutor did not lead to rapid trials, as both neighboring Indonesia and the new authorities in East Timor showed considerable hesitance about cooperating on criminal justice matters.

---

[50] See further Susan Dicklitch, "Uganda," in *Encyclopedia of Human Rights*, vol. V, 109–114.

[51] Kelly Askin, for Open Society Foundations, "Putting Complementarity into Practice: Domestic Justice for International Crimes in DRC, Uganda, and Kenya," www.soros.org/initiatives/justice/focus/international_justice/articles_publications/ publications/complementarity-in-practice-20110119/putting-complementarity-into-practice-20110120.pdf.

[52] For further information, with the exception of Cambodia, see Laura A. Dickinson, "The Promise of Hybrid Courts," *American Journal of International Law*, 97, 2 (April 2003), 295–310.

Indonesian authorities had much to hide about their brutal attempt to hang on to East Timor, while the new authorities in the latter were wary of antagonizing their powerful neighbor. From the latter's view, criminal justice might interfere with building a stable, rights-protective state respected by Indonesia. When an Indonesian commander (General Wiranto) was indicted, East Timor said it would not cooperate in the case. Overall this hybrid court manifested ample weaknesses.[53]

In Sierra Leone in 2002, the government that emerged from a brutal internal armed conflict signed an agreement with the United Nations to create a special criminal court. Local authorities wanted some hand in trials, but not total responsibility. This court operates outside, and has legal primacy over, local courts. Again, there are two international judges and one local judge in each case, and they use a mixture of local and international law. Judgments have been handed down against pro-government individuals as well as against rebel commanders.

In a special chamber of this hybrid court, Charles Taylor, the former President of neighboring Liberia was indicted. Taylor, given temporary asylum and immunity in Nigeria, was eventually extradited to The Hague where he was put on trial. So, similar to Milosevic in Serbia, this national leader was first dealt with gingerly, then made subject to criminal justice in a different political context. Taylor's trial lasted three years, and was full of histrionics and controversies, with a verdict anticipated in 2011.

Among rulings of the broader Sierra Leone special court was a noteworthy judgment that the recruitment of child soldiers constituted a war crime. In Sierra Leone there was also a truth commission to establish past facts, completely apart from considerations of criminal justice.[54]

Finally in this brief review, long and tortuous negotiations finally in 2004 produced a special criminal court in Cambodia, long after the agrarian communists known as the Khmer Rouge had killed about two million persons during 1975–1979. The government of Hun Sen, who himself had been a low-level member of the Khmer Rouge, was ambivalent about criminal justice, but finally agreed to panels entailing two local and one international judge. This arrangement, against the background of a very weak local judicial system, prompted criticism by international human rights advocacy groups, as well as from the UN Secretary-General. But certain circles of opinion thought that imperfect

---

[53] See, for example, Suzanne Katzenstein, "Hybrid Tribunals: Searching for Justice in East Timor," *Harvard Journal of International Law*, 16 (Spring 2003), updated on the internet through 2008, www.law.harvard.edu/students/orgs/hrj/iss16/katzenstein.shtml.

[54] See further William A. Schabas, "The Relationship Between Truth Commissions and International Courts: The Case of Sierra Leone," *Human Rights Quarterly*, 25, 4 (November 2003), 1035–1066.

legal justice was better than no legal justice, particularly since the senior Khmer Rouge leadership was rapidly dying off. So legal proceedings finally got under way some thirty years after the horrific Khmer Rouge reign of terror.[55]

One reason for having the ICC is to reduce the "transaction costs" so evident in the creation of the two UN *ad hoc* courts and these hybrid courts. It takes much time to negotiate the composition, jurisdiction, authority, and rules of the court – and sometimes the details of the related prosecutor's office. Moreover, these hybrid courts do not produce a uniform jurisprudence, as their rules of procedure and substantive judgments do not always follow similar tracks.[56]

National courts

It should not be forgotten that most international law, to the extent that it is adjudicated at all, is treated in national courts. Moreover, under the principles that undergird the ICC and also the norm of R2P (the responsibility to protect), it is the territorial state that has the primary responsibility to protect internationally recognized human rights. That being so, it is impossible here to review over 190 national legal systems and their treatment of major violations of international human rights and humanitarian law. Two points began to deal with the tip of this large iceberg.

First, after atrocities, particularly during and after war, real or metaphorical, it is often difficult for national courts to provide independent and impartial due process, leading to substantive judgments widely regarded as legitimate forms of criminal justice. After the fall of communism in Poland, for example, the subsequent trial of General Jaruzelski turned into a comical show trial, with numerous irregularities.

---

[55] For an informative website that is periodically updated on recent developments see www. trial-ch.org/en/resources/tribunals/hybrid-tribunals/criminal-court-for-cambodia. html.

[56] A further international special court was created by the US Security Council after the assassination of a Lebanese prime minister in 2005. Evidence mounted of Hezbollah responsibility. Hezbollah, having a Lebanese parliamentary faction, withdrew its support from the governing coalition, thus creating a political crisis in that country. Once again international juridical proceedings failed to constitute an easy and effective response to events. It was not clear how concerned parties should respond to violent events affecting Lebanese democracy and stability, especially given the probable involvement of Iran and its non-state proxies such as Hezbollah. An analytical summary of developments at the time of writing can be found in International Crisis Group, "Trial by Fire: The Politics of the Special Tribunal for Lebanon," Middle East Report No. 100 (December 2, 2010), www.crisisgroup.org/en/regions/middle-east-north-africa/iraq-syria-lebanon/ lebanon/100-trial-by-fire-the-politics-of-the-special-tribunal-for-lebanon.aspx.

At one point in his trial the presiding official said that "The hearings will continue, and the accusations will be formulated later."[57] Victor's justice is often easy to identify.

Against this background, the new criminal court created by the Interim Government in Iraq after the fall of the Saddam Hussein regime raised questions about proper criminal justice. Given the political instability of that situation after the US-led invasion and occupation, juridical problems were evident: the newness and transitory nature of the ruling authorities, the weakness of the embryonic Iraqi judicial system – if there was a real system, the lack of due process already evident in the interrogation of defendants, and so on. Thus it was hardly surprising that the UN Secretary-General and many international human rights advocacy groups were critical of the process. The execution process was highly irregular. Yet the USA, quite influential in such matters, was so opposed to the ICC and many international forms of criminal justice that it and its Iraqi allies pushed ahead with national legal measures that were sure to remain controversial in historical perspective. In Iraq it might have been better to proceed with a hybrid court, with some international judges and international standards of due process, in order to enhance independence, impartiality, and ultimately legitimacy.

Moreover, often remnants of the previous regime remain powerful for a time, as in Chile or Argentina, blocking serious national criminal justice based on due process.

Second, the principle of universal jurisdiction has had something of a renaissance, stimulated by the Pinochet case. But states like Britain and Belgium found the subject perplexing.

The concept of universal jurisdiction attaches to certain crimes like torture, genocide, and crimes against humanity – and also to serious violations of the Geneva Conventions of August 12, 1949, pertaining

---

[57] Tina Rosenberg, *The Haunted Land: Facing Europe's Ghosts After Communism* (New York: Vintage Books, 1996), 254. She argues that criminal trials were inappropriate for the violations of human rights committed under European communism. In passing she suggests that trials were more appropriate in Latin America for human rights violations under military regimes. But it was precisely in some Latin American situations that the military remained strong, and a threat to democracy, after the end of formal military rule. See also David Pion-Berlin, "To Prosecute or Pardon: Human Rights Decisions in the Latin American Southern Cone," *Human Rights Quarterly*, 15, 1 (Winter 1993), 105–130, who tries to explain different policies in Argentina, Chile, and Uruguay regarding investigations and trials for human rights violations. See further the special issue "Accountability for International Crime and Serious Violations of Fundamental Human Rights," *Law and Contemporary Problems*, 59, 4 (Autumn 1996). Most of the authors are lawyers who predictably endorse legal proceedings and oppose impunity. But see the articles by Stephan Landsman, Naomi Roht-Arriaza, and Neil J. Kritz.

to victims of war.[58] Thus the principle of universal jurisdiction permits national authorities to pursue foreign as well as domestic suspects. Certain crimes are seen as so heinous that prosecution is allowed regardless of the place of the crime or the nationality of the defendant. In general, however, states remain reluctant to exercise extensive universal jurisdiction. They remain reluctant to open Pandora's box by establishing themselves as a global judge that would complicate relations with other states by legally judging their citizens.

In 1998, Spanish legal authorities presented British authorities with a request to extradite the visiting former Chilean dictator to Spain, to stand trial for genocide, terrorism, and torture.[59] Britain arrested Pinochet, and in complicated and confusing rulings finally decided that the former head of state was indeed extraditable, since Britain had ratified, and incorporated into British law, the UN Torture Convention. This treaty recognized that universal jurisdiction was appropriate in the case of charges of torture.

While the British ruling technically was a matter of interpreting British law, it held among other things that Pinochet's status as former head of state offered him no immunity from Spanish charges. Indeed, Slobodan Milosevic had been indicted by the prosecutor of the ICTY while he was a sitting high Serbian official. And Charles Taylor had been indicted by the special court in Sierra Leone despite his being a high former official of Liberia. Moreover, the British ruling made clear that it made no difference that the victims of Pinochet's alleged abuses were Spanish or otherwise. For heinous crimes like torture, the nationality of the victims or the defendant is not a relevant factor.

It is true that under intense pressure from former Prime Minister Margaret Thatcher and other British arch conservatives, who were admirers of the staunch anti-communist Pinochet, British Executive authorities released Pinochet to Chile on grounds of alleged poor health. Thus he was in fact not extradited to Spain to face charges. But the importance of the Pinochet ruling was that he legally could have been extradited to Spain, that as a legal matter claims to sovereign immunity did not trump valid attention to gross violations of human rights, and that other high

<hr />

[58] Darren Hawkins, "Universal Jurisdiction for Human Rights: From Legal Principle to Limited Reality," *Global Governance*, 9, 3 (July–Sept., 2003), 347–366; and Stephen Macedo, ed., *Universal Jurisdiction: National Courts and the Prosecution of Serious Crimes Under International Law* (Philadelphia: University of Pennsylvania Press, 2004). For a concise overview, see Gabor Rona, "Universal Jurisdiction," in *Encyclopedia of Human Rights*, vol. V, 253–260; and Beth Stephens, "National Courts," ibid., vol. IV, 41–49.

[59] See further Darren Hawkins, "Chile in the Pinochet Era," in *Encyclopedia of Human Rights*, vol. I, 309–320.

officials in other situations might indeed have to face accountability for deeds done in office. There were other ripple effects from the British ruling in Chile, Argentina, and other places.[60]

As for Belgium, in 1993 its parliament passed a broad law opening the door to many suits in Belgian courts based on universal jurisdiction.[61] While the legislative history of this Belgian statute showed an intent to allow cases in Belgium stemming originally from Rwanda, very quickly enterprising lawyers filed cases against a variety of public officials including Ariel Sharon of Israel, Yasir Arafat of the Palestinian Authority, George H. W. Bush of the USA, and so on. The Belgian Executive was certainly not happy about that country being involved in so many controversial matters, and so successfully worked for a much narrower statute requiring some Belgian connection to charges. The USA brought heavy pressure on Belgium, including discussing the relocation of NATO headquarters from Brussels, to alter the broad assertion of Belgian judicial authority.

In both the British and Belgian examples above, it is clear that many Executive Branch officials are highly reluctant to see criminal justice proceedings interfere with good relations with other states. And the activation of the principle of universal jurisdiction, by an investigative judge like Baltasar Garzon of Spain, can certainly generate frictions that many national authorities, especially in Foreign Offices, would prefer to avoid. Noting this situation is not an argument for amnesty, immunity, or tolerance for heinous crimes like torture, genocide, crimes against humanity, or major breaches of international humanitarian law. It is only to note that political difficulties often arise in exercising universal jurisdiction in contemporary international relations.

Other aspects of national proceedings in the wake of atrocities certainly exist, and the matter of US treatment of enemy prisoners taken in its "war on terrorism" is addressed in Chapter 6, on foreign policy.

Alternatives to criminal justice

A large number of human rights activists, like Aryeh Neier, argue for consistent implementation of criminal justice and decry any amnesty or

---

[60] Stacie Jonas, "The Ripple Effect of the Pinochet Case," in *Human Rights Brief*, 36–38. See also Richard Falk, "Assessing the Pinochet Litigation," in Macedo, ed., *Universal Jurisdiction*, 97–120.

[61] Richard Bernstein, "Belgium Rethinks Its Prosecutorial Zeal," *New York Times*, April 1, 2003, A8.

immunity offered to those who have committed atrocities.[62] But our discussion above of criminal justice in places like Bosnia, Somalia, Rwanda, Sierra Leone, Poland, Iraq, etc. has already suggested that criminal justice might interfere with, or fail to make a contribution to, other desirable goals such as peace, stability, reconciliation, consolidation of liberal democracy, or full closure for affected individuals.

Criminal justice is not the only way to advance human rights, and the human rights discourse is not the only way to advance human dignity in international relations. Well-considered diplomatic/political steps also have their role to play in advancing a liberal international order beneficial to individuals.[63]

No less than Nelson Mandela, supported by others with impeccable liberal and human rights credentials like Bishop Desmond Tutu, thought that in the Republic of South Africa after the apartheid era, the best way to build a multiracial rights-protective society there was to avoid criminal justice as much as possible. They opted for a truth and reconciliation commission with apologies and reparations as the preferred course of action. If those responsible for political violence, on both the government and rebel sides, would acknowledge what they had done and express remorse, trials would be avoided and reparations paid to victims or their families. After all, trials focus on the past and often stir up animosities. Complicated rules of evidence can sometimes make it difficult to get the truth out in a clear and simple way. Truth commissions may be better than courts at getting to the "macro-truth" – the big social and political picture of why atrocities took place.[64] Since criminal courts focus on individual responsibility for particular acts, the larger context with its group responsibility may escape examination in judicial proceedings and remain in place to impede "social repair."[65]

---

[62] Aryeh Neier, "The New Double Standard," *Foreign Policy*, 105 (Winter 1996–1997), 91–101. See further Aryeh Neier's book extolling the virtues of criminal justice: *War Crimes: Brutality, Genocide, Terror, and the Struggle for Justice* (New York: Times Books, 1998).

[63] See further Jeffrey E. Garten, "Comment: The Need for Pragmatism," *Foreign Policy*, 105 (Winter 1996–1997), 103–106. This is a rebuttal to the Neier argument for consistent implementation of criminal justice.

[64] See Audrey R. Chapman and Patrick Ball, "The Truth of Truth Commissions: Comparative Lessons from Haiti, South Africa, and Guatemala," *Human Rights Quarterly*, 23, 1 (February 2001), 1–43. See especially Audrey Chapman and Hugo van der Merwe, eds., *Truth and Reconciliation in South Africa: Did the TRC Deliver?* (Philadelphia: University of Pennsylvania Press, 2008).

[65] Laurel E. Fletcher and Harvey M. Weinstein, "Violence and Social Repair: Rethinking the Contribution of Justice to Reconciliation," *Human Rights Quarterly*, 24, 3 (August 2002), 573–639.

Certainly the relatives of some victims of white minority rule in South Africa are not happy that the perpetrators of foul deeds have gone unpunished. A full accounting of the pluses and minuses of the South African T&R Commission is still in progress. But the South African model for dealing with transitional justice, which downplays criminal justice, is an interesting one – especially since the new South Africa features all-race elections and the attempted protection of many human rights.[66]

In other places like El Salvador after protracted civil war, again trials were avoided. Leading suspects in criminal behavior were eased out of public office and sometimes eased out of the country altogether. Two commissions made their reports. In this case, as in some other cases like Chile and Argentina, the continuing power of the supporters of the old regime made full and fair criminal justice exceedingly difficult in the short run. El Salvador is another country that has made progress toward stable liberal democracy without a prominent role for criminal justice after atrocities.[67] Still other countries like Spain and Portugal moved from dictatorships to stable liberal democracy without either criminal trials for past political behavior or even truth commissions. But not all countries can be like Spain and Portugal and join regional organizations like the Council of Europe and the European Union that strongly insist on liberal democracy in member states.

What is now the Czech Republic implemented a policy of barring former high communist officials from public office after the fall of communism in that country. Yet controversy and hard feelings were still evident long after 1989. A former judge in the communist era, not a party member but one who had supported the old regime with repressive rulings, was elevated to the Constitutional Court, as confirmed by the democratic

---

[66] Priscilla B. Hayner, *Unspeakable Truths: Facing the Challenge of Truth Commissions*, 2nd edn. (New York: Routledge, 2010; 1st edn., 2002). She places the South African experience in the context of some twenty other truth commissions dealing with human rights, concluding that there is no one way to create a model truth commission. She also deals with the relationship between such commissions and criminal justice. See further the substantive book review of the Hayner volume by Juan E. Mendez and Javier Mariezcurrena in *Human Rights Quarterly*, 25, 1 (February 2003), 237–256.

[67] I note in passing that not all relatives of victims were satisfied with the absence of criminal justice related to the past civil war. Some Salvadorans have pursued legal action in US courts under provisions allowing civil suits for aliens claiming violation of international law. Under the US 1879 Alien Tort Statute, these Salvadorans sought monetary compensation from former Salvadoran security officials now residing in the USA. So while avoidance of public criminal justice was part of the political deal to end fighting and atrocities in El Salvador, some civil litigation went forward in US courts. For a journalistic summary, see David Gonzalez, "Victim Links Retired General to Torture in El Salvador War," *New York Times*, June 25, 2002.

Senate. This provoked outrage on the part of some, but not on the part of others who felt the democratic state needed experienced judges.[68]

Through an act of Congress, the USA apologized for, and paid reparations for, the internment of Japanese-Americans during World War II. Since that time there has been considerable debate in the USA over an apology and reparations to African-Americans for slavery and racial discrimination in that country.[69]

Democracy was at least encouraged in Haiti by offering the high officials of the Cedras autocratic regime a pleasant amnesty abroad, a diplomatic move by the USA and others that managed to restore an elected President Aristide there without major bloodshed. Likewise, George W. Bush offered Saddam Hussein safe passage out of Iraq in 2003. In this latter case, more than 4,000 American lives, and no doubt tens of thousands of Iraqi lives, along with much injury and destruction, would have been saved had Saddam accepted the offer of asylum. True, criminal trials would not have been held for him and his equally despicable colleagues. But what price to human life and dignity did those trials entail, and did such trials – particularly given their irregular aspects – really contribute to liberal democracy and intercommunal reconciliation in Iraq? Avoiding war is also a liberal value.

In Uganda, the government sought the aid of the International Criminal Court in order to prosecute leaders of the vicious rebel movement known as the Lord's Resistance Army. Yet a number of traditional Ugandans preferred traditional rituals emphasizing forgiveness, rather than criminal prosecution.[70]

Conclusion

Suffice it to say that transitional justice can take, and has taken, many forms. None are perfect. All are controversial in that they entail pluses and minuses.

Pursuit of an effective rule of law in international relations is a noble quest. International criminal justice has manifested a renaissance in international law.[71] In general and from a liberal perspective this is probably

[68] Matt Reynolds, "A Top Judicial Posting Stirs Anger in Prague," *International Herald Tribune*, August 22, 2005.

[69] See further Mark Gibney and Erik Roxstrom, "The Status of State Apologies," *Human Rights Quarterly*, 23, 4 (November 2001), 911–939; and Max du Plessis, "Historical Injustice and International Law: An Exploratory Discussion of Reparation for Slavery," *Human Rights Quarterly*, 25, 3 (August 2003), 624–659.

[70] Mark Lacey, "Victims of Uganda Atrocities Follow a Path of Forgiveness," *New York Times*, April 18, 2005, A1.

[71] M. Cherif Bassiouni, *International Criminal Law* (Leiden: Brill Publishers, 2008, 3 vols.).

a good thing. But criminal justice in relation to international events is no simple matter. A morally pure and consistent approach to the subject advocated by the distinguished human rights activist Aryeh Neier is inadequate for both policy making and general understanding. Judicial romanticism is not an adequate policy; it is a moral posture. As such, it is widely endorsed by many private lawyers and human rights activists, but evaluated more carefully by most diplomats.

There are ways of doing good for individuals, and maybe even advancing certain human rights over time, through delaying or bypassing criminal justice. As noted in Chapter 1, litigation is only one human rights strategy. The liberal West did not try to shun or isolate Stalin for his various crimes, but actively supported him during World War II in order to defeat fascism. The liberal West brought a great reduction in violence to the former Yugoslavia by giving a temporary *de facto* immunity from prosecution to Slobodan Milosevic.[72] The liberal West supported legal impunity in South Africa, El Salvador and the Czech Republic and many other places with adequate if not perfect results. One does not always advance human welfare and human rights by criminalizing behavior, as the attempted arrest of General Aideed in Somalia shows. There is much to be said for pragmatic liberalism at times as one approach to international human rights, however morally mixed the outcome.[73]

The process of making complicated contextual analyses leads to competing judgments because of the inability of the legal and policy sciences, or of policy makers, to accurately predict the future. Will provisions on criminal justice impede peacemaking? Can suspects be arrested without undermining the limited peace already achieved? Will court judgments against gross violators of human rights really have any major impact concerning ongoing patterns of violence or future atrocities? Would more good be achieved, with less bad, via truth commissions rather than criminal proceedings? These are important questions, to which no one's crystal ball has adequate answers thus far.

Social science research is examining the above questions with considerable energy and determination. Results at the time of writing are not fully consistent. Some authors find that criminal justice at both international and national levels contributes to democracy and improved human rights

---

[72] The question can fairly be raised, however, of whether NATO would have bombed Yugoslavia in 1999 over Kosovo had Milosevic been indicted and arrested for his role in Bosnia. Then again, would NATO have had to fight in Bosnia if Milosevic had not cooperated in producing the Dayton peace agreement?

[73] See further Mahmood Monshipouri and Claude E. Welch, "The Search for International Human Rights and Justice: Coming to Terms with the New Global Realities," *Human Rights Quarterly*, 23, 2 (May 2001), 370–401.

protection. Other authors find that liberal progress can be made when trials are combined with amnesties. Still other authors find that truth commissions alone correlate *negatively* with consolidation of democracy and human rights protections. So there is a vigorous search for macro-patterns, which may or may not shed light on particular situations. What is clear is that the issue of transitional justice – viz., what to do after gross violations of human rights – will be with us for some time. Given that states and their intergovernmental organizations will face this issue as a policy matter, they can be expected to ask researchers if there is an empirically grounded science of transitional justice. An epistemic community (group of experts) now exists for this subject matter; its findings in the future merit serious attention.[74] Included in this debate is whether sufficient attention in transitional justice has been given to women's concerns.[75]

Case study: the ICC and Uganda

In 1986 Yoweri Museveni seized power in Uganda, after a series of authoritarian governments, and remained in office at the time of writing. His rise to power, based on the support of various ethnic groups mostly in the southern parts of the country, was met with armed resistance by various factions, the most notorious of which was the Lord's Resistance Army (LRA), led by Joseph Kony. The LRA was based in the northern regions populated mostly by the Acholi people. To maintain its numbers and political prospects, the LRA engaged in intimidation including via murder, rape, and disfigurement. It relied heavily on the forced recruit-ment of children for use as fighters, sexual slaves, and other forced labor. The tactics of Kony's movement belied its claims to be a religious faction intending to create a benign theocracy in Uganda.

As instability and fighting continued, the government side was also accused of gross violations of human rights mainly through the actions of the army, the Ugandan Public Defense Force (UPDF) but also by a rapid reaction division of the central police. Numerous reports accused Museveni of being indifferent to various abuses against those Acholi who had fled to supposedly secure relocation camps, as well as allowing vari-ous abuses against others – including active campaigners for gay, lesbian, transgendered, and bisexual rights. In UPDF actions against the LRA,

---

[74] See the overview in David P. Forsythe, "Responding to Mass Atrocities: Revisiting Transitional Justice," *International Studies Review*, 13, 1 (March 2011), 85–95.

[75] See further for a critical view, Fionnuala Ni Aolain, "Women, Security, and the Patri-archy of Internationalized Transitional Justice," *Human Rights Quarterly*, 31, 4 (Novem-ber 2009), 1055–1085.

there were numerous reports of "collateral damage" among civilians. The situation was further complicated by international terrorist attacks, which – as is often the case – led to harsh responses by government forces.

In 2000 the Ugandan parliament passed an amnesty law promising impunity to those of the LRA who laid down their weapons and gave up the rebellion. In 2003, however, the Museveni government, having ratified the Rome Statute of the International Criminal Court, which began to function in 2002, asked the ICC prosecutor, Luis Moreno Ocampo, to open an investigation of the LRA leadership with a view to criminal prosecutions. In 2005 Moreno Ocampo unsealed indictments against Kony and his top assistants.

The indictments met with both praise and criticism. Those supporting the indictments talked of moving toward the rule of law, ending impunity for gross human rights violations, and increasing pressure on the LRA to reach a peaceful settlement perhaps in return for the suspension of criminal proceedings. Those criticizing the indictments talked about undermining the prospects for a negotiated end to violence and turning a blind eye to violations of human rights by the government side. It appears that a peace agreement was almost reached between the LRA and the government in 2008, but negotiations collapsed at the last moment.

It was reported that the LRA was receiving some support from the government of Omar al-Bashir in Sudan, in the context of allegations that the Museveni government was encouraging a rebellion in the south of Sudan by the South Sudanese Liberation Movement. It appears to be the case that, as international pressures increased against al-Bashir for his policies mainly in the Sudanese western region of Darfur, he both curtailed his support for the LRA and agreed to a referendum on the independence of the Sudanese south. Whatever the facts of various motivations and maneuvers, Kony and some of his colleagues, under relentless military pressure from the UPDF, with assistance from its allies, moved their base of operations to other countries such as the Central African Republic. Violence and atrocities were reduced over time, but without a definitive end to the conflict.

At the time of writing, the ICC indictments had not been effectuated, Kony remaining elusive and not under arrest by any government. The ICC prosecutor remained in the center of controversy particularly for not having brought any indictments against those in the Ugandan government or military. Moreno Ocampo continued to defend his focus on bringing to trial the leadership of the LRA rather than on a negotiated end to the violence, while arguing that his office lacked credible and admissible evidence of wrongdoing by Museveni authorities (the ICC lacks jurisdiction over certain gross violations of human rights transpiring before summer 2002). A 2011 report by Human Rights Watch, documenting governmental violations of human rights including torture and summary execution, tended to dilute a singular focus on the LRA.

Controversy was intensified when the ICC Assembly of States Parties agreed to meet in Kampala, Uganda, during 2010. There was first of all the continuing controversy over Moreno Ocampo's exercise of prosecutorial discretion and his pushing for LRA trials at the possible expense of renewed diplomatic efforts to bring the LRA leadership in from the cold. Second, there was the continued violation of various human rights by Museveni's longrunning regime. The ICC had jurisdiction only over matters of genocide, war crimes, and crimes against humanity, and then only when the government in question was unwilling or unable to proceed on its own. Allegations continued about war crimes by the UPDF. Clearly the ICC had no jurisdiction over, for example, the murder of gay rights activists in Uganda. Nevertheless, the ICC and its Office of the Prosecutor were sucked into disputes about whether the Court was being used by unsavory African governments to suppress opposition movements in ways that might actually undermine efforts to end violence – and the human rights violations that accompanied it. Promising prosecution for Kony and his top colleagues was not much of an inducement for him to change policies, any more than it had been for Kaddafi in Libya or Milosevic in Serbia.

Discussion questions

- Did the Nuremberg and Tokyo trials make a positive contribution to the evolution of human rights in international relations, despite their procedural and substantive errors, not to mention their use of the death penalty?
- Was the indictment and perhaps arrest of certain persons in the Balkans during 1992–1999 an impediment to peace, or compatible with peace? Would the indictment and perhaps arrest of Saddam Hussein in Iraq after his invasion of Kuwait have been an impediment to peace, or compatible with peace?
- What explains the US opposition to the 1998 statute of the International Criminal Court, when US democratic allies like Britain, Italy, Canada, France, etc. all voted to approve the statute?
- What impact, if any, has the International Criminal Tribunal for Rwanda made on the politics of the Great Lakes region of Africa?
- In South Africa after apartheid and El Salvador after civil war, among other places, there was considerable national reconciliation, and more

liberal democracy, at least relatively speaking, while avoiding criminal prosecution for most political acts of the past. Is this a useful model for the future?

- What are the purported advantages and disadvantages of truth commissions as compared with judicial proceedings, concerning past gross violations of human rights?
- Given that international and hybrid criminal courts all manifest a public prosecutor, how have these persons exercised their prosecutorial discretion in conducting investigations and bringing charges, and is that evaluation strictly legal or also political?

SUGGESTIONS FOR FURTHER READING

Bass, Gary Jonathan, *Stay The Hand of Vengeance: The Politics of War Crimes Tribunals* (Princeton: Princeton University Press, 2000). An excellent historical overview of the political decisions preceding the establishment of, or in some cases the failure to establish, international criminal courts.

Cobban, Helena, *Amnesty After Atrocity: Healing Nations After Genocide and War Crimes* (Boulder: Paradigm, 2007). A sympathetic look at the option of avoiding prosecutions, with an emphasis on reconciliation, and with several good case studies out of Africa.

Garten, Jeffrey, "Comment: The Need for Pragmatism," *Foreign Policy*, 105 (Winter 1996–1997), 103–106. Criticizes consistent emphasis on legal punishment in international relations; emphasizes other ways of doing good for persons and improving the environment for human rights besides judicial action.

Goldstein, Joseph, et al., eds., *The My Lai Massacre and Its Cover-Up: Beyond the Reach of Law?* (New York: The Free Press, 1976). Excellent collection about an American military unit that committed a massacre in Vietnam, but whose members never were subjected to appropriate punishment because of the Pentagon's maneuvering and nationalist American public opinion.

Holbrooke, Richard, *To End a War* (New York: Random House, 1998). By the principal mediator at Dayton on dealing with Milosevic to end the war in Bosnia. Holbrooke was also influential in the West's dealing with Kosovo four years later. Upon his nomination to be US ambassador at the United Nations, at his Senate confirmation hearings Holbrooke said his job in 1995 was to end the war, not pass judgment on various leaders.

Minow, Martha, *Between Vengeance and Forgiveness: Facing History After Genocide and Mass Violence* (Boston: Beacon Press, 1998). Careful reflection about whether there is any particular policy response that is always appropriate after atrocities, suggesting that debates over peace v. justice and reconciliation v. punishment have to be resolved case by case.

Neier, Aryeh, "The New Double Standard," *Foreign Policy*, 105 (Winter 1996–1997), 91–101. A short form of the following book.

War Crimes: Brutality, Genocide, Terror, and the Struggle for Justice (New York: Times Books, 1998). Passionate but one-sided advocacy for criminal justice in all situations.

Olsen, Tricia D., Leigh A. Payne, and Andrew G. Reiter, *Transitional Justice in Balance: Comparing Processes, Weighing Efficacy* (Washington: United States Institute of Peace Press, 2010). An empirical study arguing for a combination of trials and amnesties. Contradicts some other research findings that argue for trials alone. Indicative of many timely studies of an empirical nature focused on the scientific examination of the impact of transitional justice options.

Ratner, Steven R., and Jason S. Abrams, *Accountability for Human Rights Atrocities in International Law: Beyond the Nuremberg Legacy*, 3rd edn. (Oxford: Clarendon Press, 2009; 1st edn., 1997; 2nd edn., 2001). An overview of legal developments about international criminal justice in contemporary times.

Roht-Arriaza, Naomi, and Javier Mariezcurrena, eds., *Transitional Justice in the Twenty-First Century: Beyond Truth Versus Justice* (Cambridge: Cambridge University Press, 2006). A group of experts delves into particular situations and issues associated with transitional justice. Evaluations vary about measures adopted in Africa, Latin America, and elsewhere, which is characteristic of the field.

Rosenberg, Tina, *The Haunted Land: Facing Europe's Ghosts After Communism* (New York: Vintage Books, 1996). A journalist gives a fascinating account of her travels and interviews on the subject of how to respond to communist violations of human rights in Europe after 1991, but her conclusions based on quick comparisons with Latin America are not fully persuasive.

Scheffer, David, "International Judicial Intervention," *Foreign Policy*, 102 (Spring 1996). Later a State Department official, Scheffer argues for criminal justice, but suggests in passing that there are some situations in which national peace and reconciliation may hinge on bypassing it.

Thakur, Ramesh, and Peter Malcontent, eds., *From Sovereign Impunity to International Accountability: The Search for Justice in a World of States* (Tokyo: United Nations University Press, 2004). A group of experts present views on international criminal justice and other forms of international accountability for gross violations of human rights.

Visscher, Charles de, *Theory and Reality in Public International Law* (Princeton: Princeton University Press, 1957). Classic treatment of, among other subjects, peace v. justice in international relations.

5 Regional application of human rights norms

The world may be a smaller place in the light of communication and travel technology, but it is still a large planet when it comes to effective international governance. Given the approximately 6 billion persons and the 190 states or so that existed at the turn of the twenty-first century, and given the weakness of global organizations like the United Nations, it was both logical and sometimes politically feasible to look to regional organizations for the advancement of human rights. This chapter will show that regional developments for human rights have been truly remarkable in Europe, decidedly ambiguous in the Western Hemisphere, embryonic in Africa, and otherwise weak. The key to the effective regional protection of human rights is not legal drafting, but underlying political culture, political will, and political acumen. In Europe where there are considerable cases and other regional human rights decisions to analyze, I provide a summary analysis. In the Western Hemisphere with substantial case law and other important regional decisions only recently, I provide mostly political analysis of underlying conditions but some attention to legal factors. I treat Africa briefly because of lack of impact through regional arrangements.

Europe

After World War II, significant US foreign aid to Europe in the form of the Marshall Plan encouraged regional cooperation, especially of an economic nature. Most West European elites endorsed this approach at least to some degree, both in pursuit of economic recovery and to defend traditional western values in the face of Soviet-led communism. One result was the creation of the Council of Europe (CE) with its strong focus on human rights. Separately, owing to reluctance of the UK to integrate fully with the rest of Western Europe, one had the development of the European Communities, which more or less evolved into the European Union (EU). By the start of the twenty-first century it was evident that this bifurcation, while it had "worked" to a considerable degree, was

155

not a completely happy situation. As European international integration proceeded, the contradictions of bifurcation were salient as never before. In addition to the EU and the CE, there was also the Organization for Security and Co-operation in Europe (OSCE), not to mention the North Atlantic Treaty Organization (NATO).[1] While trans-Atlantic, they had substantial European membership.

Council of Europe

European Convention on Human Rights

From the very beginning of European regionalism in the 1940s, West European governments made it clear that promotion and protection of civil and political rights lay at the core of these regional developments.[2] They created the Council of Europe in the late 1940s to coordinate social policies (originally it was supposed to coordinate economic policies as well); the centerpiece of the CE's efforts was the European Convention on Human Rights and Fundamental Freedoms (hereafter the Convention).[3] This legal instrument was approved in 1950 and took legal effect in 1953. It covered only fundamental civil and political rights. (The Convention covers property rights and rights to education, both of which are sometimes viewed as civil rights.) Slightly later these same governments negotiated the European Social Charter to deal with social and economic rights. Attention to labor rights lay at the center of this development. The CE, whose governing organs are entirely separate from the EU's, eventually produced still other human rights documents including a 1986 convention for the prevention of torture, and a 1995 framework convention for the protection of national minorities. The 1950 Human Rights Convention remains the principal achievement of the CE. It does not go too far to say that it comprises a quasi-constitutional regional bill of rights for Europe which has led to a declaration of fundamental human rights by the European Union. The Convention is the foundation for the "most successful system of international law for the protection

---

[1] For the sake of completeness one can also mention other European regional organizations, such as the Western European Union (WEU, now defunct), a strictly European military arrangement, and the European Free Trade Agreement (EFTA). They had little impact on human rights.

[2] Mark Janis, Richard Kay, and Anthony Bradly, *European Human Rights Law* (New York: Oxford University Press, 1995), 3.

[3] Donald W. Jackson, "European Convention on Human Rights and Fundamental Freedoms," in David P. Forsythe, ed., *Encyclopedia of Human Rights* (New York: Oxford University Press, 2009), vol. II, 175.

of human rights."[4] The influence of the Convention in European public law is "immense."[5]

Given especially Europe's history of fascism, anti-Semitism, and the wars derived therefrom, one theory holds that European states wanted to lock in to strong regional human rights protections to prevent any backsliding into repressive policies – with consolidated democracies such as Britain facilitating the process.[6] If valid, this view still has to acknowledge that state sovereignty was not restricted easily or quickly but rather in fits and starts over time.

The Convention specifies a series of mostly negative or blocking rights familiar to western liberals. These rights are designed to block public interference with the citizen's private domain; to block the government from overstepping its rightful authority when the citizen encounters public authority through arrest, detention, and trial; and to guarantee citizen participation in public affairs. Of course governmental positive steps are required to make these negative rights effective. Public monies have to be spent to supervise and sometimes correct governmental policies; to run police departments, prisons, and courts; and to hold free and fair elections. The state may need to take positive action to ensure the dignity of children born outside marriage and to prevent discrimination against them. None of this is very new to liberalism, except that in Europe these norms are articulated on a regional basis in addition to national norms.

The really interesting aspect to the CE's work on human rights concerns methods to ensure compliance with the norms. In this regard under the Convention, the CE proceeded cautiously. Despite general agreement on the desirability of international norms on civil and political rights, the original ratifying states differed over how much state sovereignty should be restricted by regional international organizations. Under the Convention and additional protocols, therefore, early ratifying states had the option of accepting or not the jurisdiction and supranational authority of the European Court of Human Rights. States also had the option of allowing private petitions to the separate European Commission of Human Rights. This latter body was a screening commission of first recourse, as well as a fact-finding and conciliation commission. Thus complaints about violations could be brought by one ratifying state

---

[4] Janis, et al., *European Human Rights Law*, 3.

[5] R. Beddard, *Human Rights and Europe*, 3rd edn. (Cambridge: Grotius Publications, 1993), 6–7.

[6] Andrew Moravscik, "Explaining International Human Rights Regimes: Liberal Theory and Western Europe," *European Journal of International Relations*, 1, 2 (Summer 1995), 157–189.

against another, with the Commission taking its findings to the Committee of Ministers if a state involved had not yet accepted the jurisdiction of the Court. Pending the consent of ratifying states, complaints could also be brought by private parties whether individuals, non-governmental organizations, or associations of persons. Again the Commission had the option of taking its conclusions to the Committee of Ministers or to the Court (the state involved also could pursue several avenues). Originally private parties had no legal standing before the Court, being dependent on representation by the Commission. But under Protocol 9, additional to the Convention, if the Commission ruled in favor of a private petition, the private party then appeared before a special chamber of the larger Court for a further hearing. Thus private parties gained rights of action in an international court.

Lest one become lost in legal technicalities, it is important to stay focused on summary developments. First, over time the number of states adhering to the Convention increased. This was particularly evident after the Cold War, when Central and East European states, having recovered their operational sovereignty from Soviet control, sought membership in the CE and legal adherence to the Convention. Such adherence was a sign of being European, as well as a stepping stone to possible membership in the EU. CE membership reached forty-seven states by early 2011, with all of these (except Monaco) ratifying the Convention. Belarus remained outside the CE; it applied for membership but its poor human rights record, including lack of what the CE called pluralist democracy, blocked admission.

Second, over time all of these states accepted the right of private petition, as well as the jurisdiction in all complaints of the European Court of Human Rights. Thus particularly the former communist states of Eastern Europe recovered their sovereignty only to immediately trade aspects of it away for enhanced international protection of human rights. It was also noteworthy that highly nationalistic states like France, with a long history of national discourse about human rights, finally also accepted the need for private petitions and binding adjudication at the regional level. Equally noteworthy was the decision by Turkey to accept the right of private petitions and the presumed supranational role of the Court, despite evident human rights problems – historically associated with the Kurdish question in that state. Again, some state motivation can be attributed as much to the desire to be considered for membership in the EU, with its projected economic benefits, as to a simpler or purer commitment to civil and political rights *per se*. Politically speaking, the Council of Europe, with the Human Rights Convention required for membership, became an ante-chamber leading to the doorway of the EU.[7] By 1998 the CE had decided that private petitions and acceptance of the Court were no longer options, but had to be part of a state's adherence to the Convention. From a cautious beginning the CE had developed rigorous standards for human rights protection. The newly independent states of Eastern Europe were immediately held to standards that the West European states were allowed to accept over time. As we will see, judicial enforcement existed on a regular basis.

Third, the Convention system has always been cautious about accepting private complaints for further action. The Commission, before it was replaced by a revised procedure, usually threw out around 90 percent of the private petitions filed in support of an alleged violation of the Convention as being ill-founded. From 1955 to 1994, the Commission accepted only 8 percent of the petitions submitted. In 2010, the new procedures resulted in similar figures: only 6 percent of private petitions were advanced to the next stage of consideration (362 out of 5,954, with 5,592 rejected). For the period 1999–2010, of 61,300 private petitions submitted, only 8,400 were advanced, an acceptance rate of about 14 percent. Some of these were later declared inadmissible, thus reducing the final acceptance rate to usual levels. (It might be noted that the US Supreme Court is petitioned to take up cases about 10,000 times per year, out of which it usually accepts about 100 cases.)

Fourth, despite the rejection rate, the overall number of such private petitions has been growing consistently. In 1955, the Commission had received a total of 138 private petitions. In 1997, it received 4,750. From 1999 to 2010, complaints increased significantly; during this time, it should be observed, CE membership expanded considerably, given the demise of the Soviet empire in Eastern Europe. Or, in a different summary indicating the same trend, as of 1991 the Commission had dealt with 19,000 petitions, all but 8 of which (13 if you count the same case presented in different forms) were triggered by private petitions. Of the 19,000 petitions, 3,000 were discussed seriously further, and 1,000 pursued by either the Commission, the Court, and/or the Committee of Ministers.

This trend manifested itself despite the fact that ratifying states were all either liberal democracies or aspired to be. Clearly, before 1991, the evident fact was that consolidated pluralist democracy at the national

---

[7] Hugo Storey, "Human Rights and the New Europe: Experience and Experiment," in David Beetham, ed., *Politics and Human Rights* (Oxford: Blackwell, 1995), 131–151.

level did not guarantee that there would be no further violations of human rights. Indeed, the early history of the CE and Convention indicated just the opposite: that even with liberal democracy at the national level, there was still a need for regional monitoring of human rights – there being evident violations by national authorities.

It bears emphasizing that contributing to the great number of petitions more recently was the presence in the CE after the Cold War of highly problematic states such as Romania, the Russian Federation, Ukraine, and a few others. Their human rights records were inferior to those of many older CE members and generated numerous complaints. The human rights NGO Freedom House, based in New York, for example, downgraded the Russian Federation from "free" to "partially free," which indicated problems with free and fair elections, suppression of dissent, and other important human rights issues.

One sees the pattern when one looks at cases pending as of 2010 in the European Court of Human Rights regarding particular states: Russia, 28.4 percent of cases; Turkey, 10.7; Romania, 8.7; Ukraine, 7.5; Italy, 7.5; Poland, 4.8; Serbia, 2.8; Moldova, 2.7; Bulgaria, 2.4; Slovenia, 2.4. With the exception of Turkey and Italy, it was some former communist states that seemed to have trouble adjusting to European human rights standards.

At the same time we can note that some former communist states in Europe seemed flexible in adjusting to the regional human rights regime. If for the period 1999–2010 we look at states that, in the face of accepted private petitions, reached a friendly settlement or other national accommodation, and thus did not insist on Court adjudication, we find that Hungary settled almost 40 percent of the time, Croatia almost 75 percent of the time.

Fifth, public confidence in the system was high. Whether one looks at consolidated pluralist democracies that made up early CE membership or later members from the communist zone of Europe, the trend line for private petitions was upward. This was even true in states long known for commitment to human rights such as Denmark, the Netherlands, or Switzerland, to take just three examples. It was clear that many persons within the jurisdiction of the CE thought their international rights were being violated, that they increasingly looked to the regional "machinery" of the CE for relief, and that they were not deterred by the evident "conservatism" of the procedures which screened out the overwhelming number of petitions at the very first stage of review.

Sixth, one could not rely on state action to consistently protect human rights in another state. If one moves from private to interstate complaints, the numbers change dramatically. Without doubt, private petitions, and within these, individual complaints, drive the work of the Commission and Court. Even in Europe, states do not like to petition each other about human rights. Under the principle of reciprocity, my complaint about you today may lead you to complain about me tomorrow. States normally put a premium on good relations, especially among trading partners and security allies. There have been only nine state-to-state complaints up to the time of writing, not counting second and third phases of the same dispute. Several of these occurred in the context of already strained relations: Greece v. the UK over Cyprus (twice), Ireland v. the UK (twice), Cyprus v. Turkey (four times), Georgia v. Russia (twice). Military government in Greece in 1967–1974 produced two complaints by a group made up of Denmark, Norway, Sweden, and the Netherlands. The same group plus France brought a complaint against Turkey. Denmark alone also brought a case against Turkey.[8] But these are small numbers over the life of the Convention. Between 1959 and 1985 the Court handled 100 cases; 98 of these started with private petitions.[9] This pattern has profound relevance for other efforts to apply human rights standards relying on state complaints. The only recent interstate cases involved Georgia v. Russia in 2007 and 2008. The two states engaged in a brief armed conflict during late summer 2008.

Seventh, if one can get a private petition cleared for admissibility in the first stage of technical review, one stands a rather good chance of prevailing on substance. One of the reasons that private petitions continue to mount is that if one's petition is declared admissible, if a friendly settlement cannot be achieved between petitioner and state, and if the matter goes to the Court of Human Rights, the petitioner stands a very good chance of winning the case. For many states, the success rate of complaints against it is over 50 percent. As of 2004, the Court had found at least one violation in 11 of 15 cases against Belgium; for France, 59 out of 75; for Greece, 32 out of 40; for Italy, 36 out of 47; for the Netherlands, 6 out of 10; for the UK, 19 out of 23. The total was 589 violations (at a minimum) out of 719 admitted petitions. When one includes multiple

---

[8] Turkey might be considered a special case by European standards. The military was highly influential, taking over the government on several occasions and conducting, by almost all accounts, a brutal suppression of the Kurdish separatist movement. NGOs were reporting torture and other gross violations of human rights, especially in connection with the Kurdish question. But many in the Turkish elite believed that some Christian European political circles were using the human rights issue in an effort to block Muslim Turkey's entrance into the EU. It was said that these Christian circles feared the free movement of Muslim Turks as labor within the EU.

[9] Janis, et al., *European Human Rights Law*, 70.

violations, it appears that petitioners usually win about two-thirds of their claims.[10]

These are good odds for the petitioner across all types of European states, including some of those with the best general reputations for serious attention to civil and political rights. The judges of the European Court of Human Rights, sitting in their personal capacity through election by the CE's European Parliamentary Assembly, were not hesitant to find fault with governmental policy. They had once been cautious about ruling against states, in order to build state support for the CE system. It took the Court ten years to make its first ruling against a state.[11] But things have changed.

Eighth, the Court was overburdened with cases. It took thirty years to decide its first 200 cases; it only took three years to decide the next 200.[12] During its lifetime, the European Court of Human Rights has decided more than twenty times the cases handled by the World Court – the International Court of Justice at The Hague, to which only states have access for legally binding cases.[13] The case load for the Court, and delays in reaching it, had become of such concern that a protocol (number 11) to the Convention that would expedite proceedings went into legal force during the fall of 1998. All details of that change need not concern us here, but Protocol 11 eliminated the Commission, created a chamber of the Court made up of several judges to take over the screening functions, and utilized other chambers of several judges in order to process more cases at once. The full Court still sat to hear certain cases, including all state-to-state complaints. Thus, far from withering away because of national commitment to civil and political rights, the European Court of Human Rights was trying to figure out how to accommodate increased demand for its services. In 2010 the Court issued 1,499 judgments (some involving combined cases). In that same year there was a backlog of 139,650 cases pending.

Given this backlog, which had been building for several years, to further improve the efficiency of the Court, Protocol 14 to the Convention was put into effect as of June 2010. The Protocol, with complicated wording, seeks to provide the Court with the procedural flexibility and means to expeditiously process cases. Particularly when a state has failed to comply

---

[10] Council of Europe, Survey of Activities 2004, www.echr.coe.int/NR/rdonlyres/461D3893-D3B7-4ED9-AC59-8BD9CA328E14/0/SurveyofActivities 2004.pdf.

[11] Janis, et al., *European Human Rights Law*, 71.

[12] D. J. Harris, M. O'Boyle, and C. Warbrick, *The Law of the European Convention on Human Rights* (London: Butterworths, 1995), 35–36.

[13] Janis, et al., *European Human Rights Law*, 71.

with the decision of the Court, the Committee of Ministers will be able to bring the state more quickly to the Court for non-compliance.

One can note the number of "high importance" cases. These have no set subject matter but can include cases of non-compliance. In 1999 there were 105 high importance cases; in 2010 there were 1,012. Thus in 1999 high importance cases made up 60 percent of the Court work load, whereas the numbers had grown to 83 percent in 2010. The back-log presented something of a crisis for the system. At present rates of processing, it would take an expanded Court with more judges years and years to catch up to the number of validly filed complaints.

It should be noted that before 1991 most breaches of the Convention did not concern what are sometimes called gross and systematic viola-tions. (The question of torture is covered below.) Most CE states were genuinely sympathetic to civil and political rights. But where the CE faced a government that was non-cooperative and determined to engage in gross and systematic violations, the CE functioned in a way not dissim-ilar to the United Nations or the Organization of American States. This is shown by the Greek case of 1967–1974, and also by Turkish policy in Cyprus. The CE system for protecting civil and political rights did not prevent or easily correct violations in those situations, because the target government was basically non-cooperative. Liberal democracies might sometimes violate civil and political rights here and there, perhaps inad-vertently, or due to delay or personal malfeasance, and therefore be in need of regional monitoring. But the presence of genuine liberal democ-racy at the national level was a *sine qua non* for an effective regional protec-tive system.[14] The situation has changed somewhat with the admission to CE membership of states that Freedom House regards as only "partially free" rather than "free." According to some analysts, a number of experts who followed details closely always thought the Convention would not work well regarding Russia. Its human rights problems were seen as fun-damental and the attitude of the elites basically non-cooperative. In this view, major West European policy makers agreed to have Russia join the CE and be eligible to ratify the Human Rights Convention because it would be politically awkward to block Russian membership. But the legal experts were not surprised that Russian full compliance with Court judgments has been problematic.

As for Turkey, leading legal experts there such as Isil Karakas (a judge on the European Court of Human Rights) openly acknowledged that

---

[14] Menno T. Kamminga, "Is the European Convention on Human Rights Sufficiently Equipped to Cope with Gross and Systematic Violations?," *Netherlands Human Rights Quarterly*, 12, 2 (1994), 153–164.

Turkey's political culture was not as supportive of basic democratic values as was the case elsewhere in western Europe. Consequently, Turkey was still trying to improve its legal record on such fundamental rights as right to life, freedom from torture and inhuman treatment, and freedom of expression, *inter alia*.

As for the Court's important jurisprudence, it covered, among other subjects, treatment while detained, freedom of expression, respect for private and family life, the right to liberty and security of person, the right to fair and public hearing, and the effect of the Convention in national law.[15] According to one summary, the Court is one of the most important international organizations yet created, has made numerous rulings of major importance to even established democracies such as Britain and Sweden, and routinely secures at least partial compliance with its decisions.[16]

A special consideration was the "margin of appreciation" afforded to states in applying the Convention. For example, Article 15 allowed states to derogate from many provisions of the Convention in "public emergencies threatening the life of the nation." A democratic state did have the right to defend itself. (Whether or not this is an example of a collective human right is an interesting question.) On the other hand certain articles could never be legally abridged, such as those prohibiting torture. States had to formally declare such emergencies and subject them to authoritative review. In the matter of the seizure of the government by the Greek military in 1967, the Commission held that such action was not justified under Article 15. The Committee of Ministers, however, was not able to take corrective action. (The junta collapsed of its own ineffectiveness in 1974.) But in general, under Article 15 and others, the review organs tend to give some leeway to states – a margin of appreciation – in highly controversial interpretations of the Convention. The Court did so in upholding invocation of Article 15 by the UK regarding Northern Ireland. "Margin of appreciation," perhaps like "executive privilege" in US constitutional law, was a matter of great complexity and continuing case law.[17]

---

[15] Ibid. More traditional legal analysis covers the details of actual cases. That is not my intent here, and space does not allow it. For a short summary of some of the leading cases, see Jackson, "European Convention on Human Rights and Fundamental Freedoms."

[16] Darrin Hawkins and Wade Jacoby, "Agent Permeability, Principal Delegation, and the European Court of Human Rights," *Review of International Organization*, 3, 1 (2008), 1–28.

[17] Yutaka Arat, "The Margin of Appreciation Doctrine in the Jurisprudence of Article 8 of the European Convention on Human Rights," *Netherlands Human Rights Quarterly*, 16, 1 (1998), 41–56.

In general there are three measures open to the Court and Committee of Ministers: just satisfaction (e.g., payment of compensation), individual measures (e.g., revocation of a deportation order), or general measures (e.g., adopt new legislation). The Court can order the first and the Committee can utilize the other two. It is up to the Committee of Ministers to supervise the implementation of Court judgments. Early on, compliance was not a great problem, as most states complied with most judgments most of the time.

Before 1991, and thus before the expansion of state parties to the Court, Britain and Italy had been found in violation of the Convention more times than any other of the thirty-eight states then subject to its terms. In Britain it is said that this is because of its unwritten constitution and lack of judicial review.[18] But these factors, if true, do not explain Italy's record. The slowness of Italian judicial procedures seems to account for a considerable number of Italian violations of the Convention. Over time, states such as Britain and Italy did eventually comply with European Court judgments. By 2005, however, the bulk of the findings of violations were against Turkey, rising from 18 in 1999 to 154 in 2004.[19] This trend continued at the time of writing, with the Russian Federation in second place concerning Court judgments against particular states. Compliance has become slower and more complicated.

The matter of compliance merits further commentary. In the Russian case, for example, the government may agree to pay compensation to individuals whose rights have been violated as per Court interpretation, but it may fail to make legislative and other structural changes ensuring that such violations are not repeated. Thus there may be partial compliance by a state. The growing number of repeat cases on the same legal subject within a country is an indicator of the lack of fundamental, structural, or systematic change.

In general, given the changed CE membership after 1991, with states such as Russia and Romania in the mix, along with Turkey, the Court's record of securing compliance was not quite as stellar as in previous years. Ultimate responsibility then devolved to the Committee of Ministers in the tough cases. It was clear in the Russian situation, for example, that such major violations of human rights as fatal attacks on investigative journalists and arbitrary detention for those challenging the primacy of the existing elite were tough nuts to crack. It did not help

---

[18] Donald W. Jackson, *The United Kingdom Confronts the European Convention on Human Rights* (Gainesville: University Press of Florida, 1997).
[19] See further Arthur Bonner, "Turkey, the European Union and Paradigm Shifts," *Middle East Policy*, 7, 1 (2005), 44–71.

that some desires for progressive developments by President Dmitry Medvedev were undercut by the actions of Prime Minister Vladimir Putin.[20] Whether a new procedure that allows the Committee of Ministers to sue a recalcitrant state will better protect human rights remains to be seen.

In the past, the role of the Committee of Ministers has been generally underappreciated in human rights matters. When the Commission reached a decision on a petition, and could not advance the matter to the Court because of lack of state consent, its decision was only intermediate – with the final decision up to the Committee of Ministers. At least one observer holds that the Committee, made up of state representatives, was overly "statist" in its orientation by comparison with the Commission made up of independent experts.[21] All states have now accepted the Court's jurisdiction, and all new ratifiers of the Convention must do the same. Under Protocol 11, the Commission is eliminated, the Court will judge all well-founded petitions, and the role of the Committee will remain solely that of supervising the execution of Court judgments.

In all CE states the guarantees of the Convention can be invoked before the domestic courts, once the petitioner has exhausted local remedies (meaning, has tried national and sub-national norms and procedures first). There was a cottage industry for lawyers and law professors deciding on the exact legal effects of the Convention at the national level, either via direct effects or via domestic legislation. Yet almost fifty European states remain bound by the Convention and subject to the rulings by the Court, however the legal specifics might play out in national courts and other national public bodies.

Potentially troublesome was a 2004 judgment in the German Federal Constitutional Court (Gorgulu case) asserting a national right in some situations to challenge decisions by the European Court of Human Rights if the latter contradicted fundamental principles of German constitutional law. This German juridical assertion, if implemented by it and/or other national high courts in certain ways, could be seen – but does not have to be seen – as undermining the supranational authority of the European Court. As of 2011, this complicated case involving the subject of conflict of laws had not undermined the Convention system.[22] In

---

[20] See in general Amnesty International, "Human Rights Russian Federation," www.amnestyusa.org/all-countries/russian-federation/page.do?id=1011228.

[21] Adam Tomkins, "Civil Liberties in the Council of Europe: A Critical Survey," in C. Gearty, ed., *European Civil Liberties and the European Convention on Human Rights* (The Hague: Martinus Nijhoff, 1977), 1–52.

[22] See further www.humboldt-forum-recht.de/druckansicht/druckansicht.php?artikelid=135; and www.germanlawjournal.com/article.php?id=898.

the last analysis this controversy is about conflict of laws and the assumed supremacy of regional law in Europe.

Clearly, the European Convention had evolved in impressive ways, fueled by the underlying political agreement among national policy makers that protection of civil and political rights was central to their self-identification and self-image. This commitment was so strong that significant elements of state sovereignty were to be yielded in order to achieve it. Because of CE norms and judgments, the United Kingdom felt compelled to introduce a written bill of rights despite its long history of having an unwritten constitution. To be sure there was some grumbling in many states about the intrusiveness of regional norms and the assertiveness of the Court. Yet, overall, trends were clear. National decisions about human rights would be authoritatively reviewed by the European Court of Human Rights. One question for the future, in addition to how to maintain a good record of compliance with Court judgments, was how these decisions could be coordinated with other human rights judgments handed down by the EU's supranational court, the European Court of Justice. As of the time of writing, twenty-seven European states were subject to a potential double human rights review by supranational courts – once in the CE and once in the EU when human rights controversies fell within the purview of both organizations.

CE Social Charter

This 1961 legal instrument covers social and economic rights, originally workers' rights in and out of the work environment.[23] As of 1996 it had been comprehensively revised into a new document, and there was talk in the advisory European Assembly of converting some of its ideas into a new protocol that would be added to the European Convention on Human Rights, and thus made subject to the authoritative review of the European Court of Human Rights.[24] But this had not transpired at the time of writing. Thus there was increased attention to social (and economic) rights in Europe, and some effort was being made to deal with their secondary or inferior status. Still, it remained clear that even in Europe, with much social democracy and relatively large welfare states, socioeconomic rights received less attention, and less vigorous enforcement, than civil-political rights.

---

[23] See www.oneworld.org/oxfam/policy.html.
[24] This and other specific information about the status of the Charter is drawn from links to the home page of the Council of Europe: www.coe.fr.

By 2011 almost forty states had consented to be bound by various versions of the European Social Charter. (States that accepted an earlier version remained bound by it, if they did not accept the 1996 version.) There was no court dealing with economic and social rights, but a European Committee of Social Rights, composed of independent experts, made recommendations to superior intergovernmental bodies about application of the Charter. This Committee was advised by the International Labour Organization. It frequently found states to be in violation of their reporting obligations under the Charter, doing so, for example, in forty-seven cases in early 1999. It lacked the authority, however, to compel a change in policy by the states in violation. Its superior bodies also pursued the path of persuasion over time, rather than punitive enforcement.

A 1995 protocol adding a right of collective private petition, by trade unions and certain human rights groups, for alleged Charter violations had been accepted by fewer than half of the states that have accepted various versions of the Charter. Hence there was some effort to profit from the lessons drawn from the experience with civil and political rights. As noted above, private petitions drive the work of the European Court of Human Rights. As of 2006, thirty-one collective complaints lodged under this protocol have been declared admissible. Of these, twenty-nine have been heard on the merits and seventeen held to document violations of Charter rights by states. The Committee has found states in violation in a diversity of areas: child labor in Portugal, forced labor in Greece, right to organize in Sweden, discrimination on basis of disability in France, and protection of children against corporal punishment in Ireland and Belgium among others.

The revised Charter specified a number of new rights in addition to existing labor rights: the right to protection against poverty and social exclusion, to housing, to protection in case of termination of employment, to protection against sexual harassment and victimization, etc. Certain existing economic and social rights were revised: reinforcement of the principle of non-discrimination, increased equality between genders, better maternity protection and social protection for mothers, increased protection for children and disabled persons. Some rights were designated core or non-core rights (in non-legal terms), owing to the different levels of economic development in a CE of more than forty-five states. The non-core rights seem to be the ones considered more expensive to implement, such as fair remuneration. Unlike some other socioeconomic treaties, the rights codified are to be implemented immediately upon ratification and not over time depending on economic factors.

Still, even under the 1996 revisions of the Social Charter, the highest control mechanisms remained unchanged. That caused the Parliamentary Assembly of the CE in 1999 to call for a new protocol to the European Convention on Human Rights covering certain economic and social rights. Outside experts had agreed that some economic and social rights could be adjudicated, being not very different in some substantive respects from civil rights.[25] Should such a protocol to the European Convention be adopted, the question of subject matter jurisdiction between the European Court of Human Rights and the European Court of Justice (part of the EU system) would be brought into bold relief. Both would be dealing more with labor rights and economic matters. But a number of experts thought such a protocol was unlikely to be accepted by very many member states, and events thus far have borne out this skepticism.

As of 2011 one could not say what the effect of the revised Social Charter might be in the long run. In general it was still true to say that European states were not prepared to subject themselves to the same type of authoritative third-party review concerning economic and social rights as they had accepted for civil and political rights. On the other hand, they were experimenting with procedures of application that might direct more attention to labor rights, the right to housing, and various forms of social security. Unlike the USA, most European states, including those in Central and Eastern Europe, were social democracies that believed in extensive economic and social rights, as well as civil and political ones – even if European states were hesitant to encourage binding adjudication in this subject area. One expert believed that the Charter in its various versions had had "pervasive, though not spectacular impact," as many European states made small changes to their socioeconomic legislation to conform to its norms; the Charter seemed to have had some impact in the newly independent states of Eastern Europe after the demise of communism there.[26]

CE Prevention of Torture

All of the states that ratified the European Convention on Human Rights and Fundamental Freedoms also ratified the European Convention for the Prevention of Torture (CPT). Under this treaty a committee of uninstructed persons had the right to regularly visit ratifying states to inquire into measures and conditions pertaining to torture and inhuman or degrading treatment. The committee could also make *ad hoc* visits with minimal advance notification. The committee initially operated

---

[25] Paul Hunt, *Reclaiming Social Rights: International and Comparative Perspectives* (Aldershot: Dartmouth, 1996).
[26] Robin Churchill, "European Social Charter," in *Encyclopedia of Human Rights*, vol. II, 181–185.

on the basis of confidentiality. Similar to the detention visits of the International Committee of the Red Cross, if a state did not show adequate progress over time in meeting the norms of the Convention, the committee might publicize its conclusions. However, in practice most states ask the CPT to release its report after a visit. A few states, most prominently the Russian Federation, have declined to follow this practice, with the result that outsiders assume major problems exist. At times the CPT has itself taken the initiative to publish its findings in the context of clear non-cooperation by a state. This situation obtained in places such as Turkey (1992, 1996) and Russia/Chechnya (2001, 2003, 2007).[27] Over time the committee interpreted its mandate broadly, so that general prison conditions, and not just torture and cruel treatment, were reviewed. The committee also developed the tradition of making very specific recommendations to governments.

Some might assume that this treaty was made possible by the absence of torture in Europe. Such an assumption might be mistaken for several reasons, partially evident in the above paragraphs. First, older CE member states such as Britain, when dealing with perceived public emergencies such as Northern Ireland, had been known to engage in controversial interrogation techniques. Whether these techniques should be properly labeled torture, inhuman mistreatment, or something else was for review bodies to determine.[28] In the summer of 1999 France, having abused a suspected drug dealer while detained, was found guilty of torture by the European Court of Human Rights. Second, some of the newer members of the CE, especially the former communist states, displayed a history that was not free of a pattern of controversial interrogation techniques. Third, Turkey, and also Russia, which ratified the European Torture Convention, were regularly charged with using torture as public policy by various human rights groups, as well as the media. As noted above, the CPT also found some states to have engaged in torture or inhuman treatment of prisoners over time.

CE Protection of Minorities

The European Convention on Human Rights and Fundamental Freedoms deals explicitly only with individual civil and political rights.

---

[27] Malcolm D. Evans, "Torture: European Convention on Prevention of Torture," ibid., vol. V, 60–63.

[28] At one point the European Commission on Human Rights held that the UK had employed torture in dealing with Northern Ireland, whereas the European Court of Human Rights held only that the UK had engaged in mistreatment. In any event, because of domestic as well as international criticism, the British government presumably altered the interrogation techniques in question – at least officially in that particular controversy.

Likewise, the European Social Charter does not mention national minorities. Given the changing membership of the CE, and the historical importance to public order of national minorities not only in Central and Eastern Europe, but also in West European states such as Spain, the CE in 1995 concluded a Framework Convention for the Protection of National Minorities. The question of the protection of national minorities within nation-states has long bedeviled world affairs, starting with problems of definition, so it is no surprise that many problems are evident in European approaches to this subject. The UN Sub-Commission on Protection of Minorities, when it existed, also encountered many problems in its work for minority protection.

The CE Convention on Minorities entered into force in 1998 and had been ratified by forty-one states as of early 2011. It contains no special monitoring mechanisms aside from an unspecified role for the CE's Committee of Ministers. The Committee of Ministers has, however, created an Advisory Committee of eighteen independent experts to assist in the monitoring of state compliance. The Advisory Committee examines state reports and gives an Opinion on the measures taken by the reporting state. The Advisory Committee had also introduced country visits as part of its monitoring mandate. It is the Committee of Ministers, however, that adopts Conclusions and issues Recommendations to states. It has also started the practice of issuing commentaries on particular themes such as education or participation.

The treaty, rather than endorsing assimilation of all groups into one homogeneous society, endorses the preservation of national minorities. It urges governments to accommodate national minorities, although they are not defined in the treaty, through public policies on language, state services, etc. Parts of the treaty repeat non-discrimination norms found in other international human rights instruments. Other parts mandate states to enable individual members of national minorities to maintain their language, religion, and culture. These provisions give rise to questions such as whether the state, in public documents and processes, must accommodate minority languages.

France and Turkey are strongly opposed to the treaty in general, having neither signed nor ratified it. France thinks it unwise to focus on minorities at the expense of national unity; Turkey has long been concerned with its ethnic (national?) Kurdish minority in its southeastern region. The lack of definition has allowed individual states to pick and choose which groups are covered by the treaty. Estonia tends to see its Russian minority as a potential Trojan horse put at the service of the neighboring Russian Federation and thus labels that group as linguistic and not national. Germany has excluded Turkish residents from treaty coverage. A number of states watch Belgium with dismay, as elements in the north, Flemish speaking, talk of secession which is opposed by most French speakers in the south of that state. Are these linguistic groups to be properly viewed as national minorities? Despite the treaty, Roma are often discriminated against in both West and East European states.[29]

Despite these problems and more, some experts believe the treaty and its supervisory mechanism have political utility, even with their legal difficulties, in focusing on a troublesome subject and encouraging a dialogue designed to reduce frictions and misunderstandings.[30]

European Union

In the treaties during the 1950s that lay at the origin of the present EU, there was no mention of human rights. This anomaly was formally corrected in the 1992 Maastricht Treaty transforming the Communities into the EU, whereby it was stipulated (in Article F.2) that "the Union shall respect fundamental rights, as guaranteed by the European Convention for the Protection of Human Rights and Fundamental Freedoms . . . and as they result from the constitutional traditions common to the Member States, as general principles of Community law." This treaty provision codified important human rights developments that had already been occurring in the EU.

The European Court of Justice (ECJ), the supranational court of the EU, had been encouraging European integration by, among other things, declaring the supremacy of Community law compared with national law. German and Italian courts, against the background of their countries' experience with fascism, balked at supranational economic integration without explicit protections of human rights.[31] These and eventually other national bodies feared that national bills of rights and other national protections of human rights – primarily civil and political rights – would be washed away by Community law geared to purely economic considerations. The ECJ, therefore, began to address human rights issues as they related to economic decisions by Community institutions – the Commission (the collective executive), the Council of Ministers (officially a

---

[29] Geof Gilbert, "The Council of Europe and Minority Rights," *Human Rights Quarterly*, 18, 1 (Winter 1996), 160–189. See further Safia Swimelar, "Roma in Europe," in *Encyclopedia of Human Rights*, vol. IV, 350–360.

[30] Tove H. Malloy, "Minority Rights: European Framework Convention," in *Encyclopedia of Human Rights*, vol. IV, 1–5.

[31] See especially Nanette A. Neuwahl, "The Treaty on European Union: A Step Forward in the Protection of Human Rights?," in Neuwahl and Allan Rosas, eds., *The European Union and Human Rights* (The Hague: Martinus Nijhoff, 1995), 1–22.

meeting of cabinet ministers of the member states), and the Parliament (a mostly advisory body). Later the Council, a meeting of heads of state, came into being.

All of these other EU organs eventually took up human rights subjects. EU bodies addressed human rights issues from the late 1960s, and in 1977 the European Commission, Council, and Parliament issued a joint declaration saying what Article F.2 was to say in 1992 – namely that human rights were to be protected as found in the European Convention on Human Rights and in the constitutional traditions of member states. In 1989 the European Parliament proposed a European declaration of human rights. This was not immediately acted upon by the Commission and Council, but the proposal did contribute to later developments noted below.

Indeed, by 1992 the EU aspired not only to protecting human rights within its jurisdiction but also in a "common foreign and security policy" (Article J.1[2]).[32] The EU pledged to "develop and consolidate democracy and the rule of law, and respect for human rights and fundamental freedoms" in its dealings with other states. EU resources are devoted to this objective, as the EU is the largest donor of international development assistance and also a major donor of international humanitarian assistance in emergency situations. References to human rights and particularly democracy are included in treaties with other developing countries. Occasionally development assistance is suspended on human rights grounds as in Haiti, Myanmar, or Uzbekistan. The EU instituted an arms embargo after the Chinese massacre in Tiananmen Square in 1989. The EU has helped supervise elections in numerous countries. It was a major player in efforts to deal with human rights violations in the western Balkans throughout the 1990s. The EU Council sometimes tries to coordinate the foreign policies of its member states at the United Nations Human Rights Commission, now the Human Rights Council, and General Assembly, but without total success. For example, EU member states split badly on how to deal with China at the UN Commission in 1997.[33] EU unity is not always evident in the new UN Human Rights Council from 2006.

Clearly the EU emphasis on human rights affects aspiring members. Slovakia was delayed admission until certain human rights changes were effectuated. Turkey has yet to gain membership in part because of human

---

[32] Daniela Napoli, "The European Union's Foreign Policy and Human Rights," ibid., 297–312.

[33] See further Marine Fouwels, "The European Union's Common Foreign and Security Policy and Human Rights," *Netherlands Quarterly of Human Rights*, 15, 3 (September 1997), 291–324.

rights controversies. In the case of Turkey, observers debate whether that state's difficulty in entering the EU is genuinely because of human rights issues, or whether certain European states use the subject of human rights to block admission of a largely Islamic nation. Does France really want more Islamic workers to have open access to the French labor market?

It was the ECJ that had led the way in interjecting human rights into EU proceedings, and some observers – but certainly not all – thought the Court might rule on foreign policy decisions in the future. Some case law by the ECJ suggests that human rights values must be respected not only by EU organs but also by member states when taking decisions within the EU framework.[34]

In Europe at the beginning of the twenty-first century there were two supranational courts making judgments on regional human rights law – the EU's ECJ and the CE's Court of Human Rights. There was no explicit coordination between the two. The latter worked from an explicit human rights treaty containing specified human rights. The former did not, at least early on, but rather worked from "principles" vaguely derived from other sources, including the CE treaty. The potential for conflict and confusion was considerable between the CE's Strasburg court and the EU's Luxemburg court. The Strasburg court was staffed by human rights specialists. The Luxemburg court was staffed by judges primarily interested in economic law, but they had shown remarkable flexibility and creativity in adapting EU law to broad concerns – including human rights.[35]

For some time there has been discussion about whether the EC, as it then was, and which has some legal personality in international law, should try to formally adhere to the European Convention on Human Rights. The CE/EU Commission was in favor, but the ECJ held that under current law this was not possible, as the European Convention was open only to states and the CE did not have comparable legal personality. The state members of the CE/EU declined to change the appropriate law to make such an adherence possible, perhaps fearing the further loss of influence for national constitutions as the cost of Community law. The continued bifurcation in Europe between economic and social institutions no doubt would demand sorting out in the future, especially if there is ever to be a "United States of Europe."

[34] Neuwahl, "The Treaty on European Union," 9.
[35] G. Federico Manchini, "The Making of a Constitution for Europe," in Robert O. Keohane and Stanley Hoffmann, eds., *The New European Community: Decisionmaking and Institutional Change* (Boulder: Westview Press, 1991), 177–194.

By 2005 events had progressed to the point that an EU Charter of Fundamental Rights was negotiated by the leaders of the then-25 EU member nations as part of the projected EU Constitution. This Charter represented a further integration among the member states, as well as providing the most detailed legal obligations yet in the area of human rights. In effect, the Charter moved the members further toward what was in reality an EU bill of rights.[36] As it turned out, some of the nations of Europe were not completely sold on the constitutional project, and voters in both France and the Netherlands refused to accept the Charter in referenda. Since approval by all states was required, the movement for a more tightly unified Europe was thrown into turmoil. It was not clear what the outcome of the situation might portend over the long run.

As for the Charter of Fundamental Rights, it has already been separately accepted as a stand-alone document in 2000 and had been applied from time to time by the European Court of Justice as part of "the general principles of Community law." The Charter is one of the most extensive and innovative human rights documents anywhere, with most of its provisions pertaining to all individuals within the EU zone. Some political norms pertain only to nationals of EU member states. Increasingly the Charter, which is now legally binding within the EU, has affected juridical and legislative developments.[37] In the future the EU is likely to accede to the European Convention on Human Rights, in which case the Charter will be merged with, and supplement, that treaty.

After the no vote in France and the Netherlands, the *status quo ante* prevailed. This meant that the EU, while not fully integrating its member states, was still an actor for human rights both within its own jurisdiction and through its emerging but often disjointed foreign policy.[38] In general the EU joined the Council of Europe in being a major actor for human rights both in the region and in the larger world. But this certainly did not mean that all human rights issues had been resolved within the EU, whether pertaining to immigration, discrimination against minorities (e.g., the Roma), detention and interrogation of terrorism suspects, or other subject matter. The EU was still primarily an economic

---

[36] See further Victor Bojkov, "National Identity, Political Interest and Human Rights in Europe: The Charter of Fundamental Rights of the European Union," *Nationalities Papers* 32, no. 2 (2004), 323–353.

[37] See further Mielle Bulterman, "European Union Charter of Fundamental Rights," in *Encyclopedia of Human Rights*, vol. II, 195–199.

[38] See further Andrew Williams, *EU Human Rights Policies: A Study in Irony* (Oxford: Oxford University Press, 2004).

organization, but greater attention to human rights had changed its identity over time.[39]

Organization for Security and Co-operation in Europe

The diplomatic process known during the Cold War as the CSCE – the Conference on Security and Co-operation in Europe – became an organization, and hence OSCE, after the Cold War.[40] From 1973 to 1974, the communist East sought security and economic objectives *vis-à-vis* the democratic West. The West responded with an insistence that certain principles of human rights and humanitarian affairs be respected by all. The Helsinki Accord of 1975, plus various follow-up conferences, generated considerable pressure on European communist regimes to respect the principles they had formally endorsed. Individuals and private groups in the East, backed by western governments and private human rights groups, became more assertive in demanding respect for rights. The short-term response by communist party-state regimes was more repression, but the long-term outcome was to further undermine an increasingly discredited communist framework in Europe.

It is impossible to scientifically prove the exact role of the CSCE in the decline of European communism and the disintegration of the Soviet Union. As John J. Maresca, a high US diplomat, remarked, "It is a puzzle to analyze Helsinki's accomplishments, because it is impossible to establish what resulted from Helsinki and what was simply the result of history moving on."[41] Stefan Lehne, a high Austrian diplomat, argued that the primary factors leading to dramatic change in European communism were the internal contradictions of the system of political economy, combined with Mikhail Gorbachev's refusal to defend the *status quo* with force. But he goes on to argue that the CSCE process played a significant if secondary role.[42] This view was seconded by a number of other observers.[43]

---

[39] See Frederic Megret, "European Union," in *Encyclopedia of Human Rights* vol. II, 186–194.

[40] See Patrice C. McMahon, "Helsinki Accord and CSCE/OSCE," ibid., vol. II, 377–383.

[41] Quoted in David P. Forsythe, "Human Rights and Multilateral Institutions in the New Europe," in Forsythe, ed., *Human Rights in the New Europe: Problems and Progress* (Lincoln: University of Nebraska Press, 1994), 176.

[42] Stefan Lehne, *The Vienna Meetings of the Conference on Security and Cooperation in Europe, 1986–1989: A Turning Point in East–West Relations* (Boulder: Westview, 1991).

[43] See, e.g., William Korey, *The Promises We Keep: Human Rights, the Helsinki Process, and American Foreign Policy* (New York: St. Martin's Press, 1993). Korey gives pride of place to the US Congress and private interest groups, especially Jewish ones, in generating influence on European communists. See further Sandra L. Gubin, "Between Regimes and Realism – Transnational Agenda Setting: Soviet Compliance with CSCE Human

After the Cold War the new OSCE increased its membership from thirty-five to about fifty-five states, which broadened its jurisdiction but weakened its capability. A number of the new states emerging from the old Soviet Union lacked early and firm commitment to human rights as well as the real capability to resolve human rights problems. Some states such as the former Yugoslavia descended into murderous armed conflict, about which the OSCE could do little since it had no enforcement authority and no military power, aside from suspending Belgrade from the organization. The OSCE operated as a diplomatic framework to try to advance internationally recognized human rights, especially the civil and political rights associated with liberal democracy. To the extent that it manifested a strong point or area of expertise, it lay in the area of minority rights, about which the Council of Europe had been mostly silent.[44] The first OSCE High Commissioner for National Minorities, the Dutchman Max van der Stoel, was widely respected. He operated through quiet diplomacy to try to prevent and resolve conflicts over national minorities. It was difficult to document his success, in part because successful prevention of disputes left very little to document, and in part because not all minority problems could be resolved. He concentrated mostly on Central and Eastern European affairs, there being political opposition to his taking on minority problems in certain West European states.[45] His office became a focal point for diplomacy on minority issues in Europe, effectively if informally coordinating other IGO and NGO efforts so as to try to make a concentrated impact regarding minority rights.[46]

NATO

While historically NATO had been a traditional military alliance, and not a "regional organization" as per the terms of the UN Charter, increasingly after the Cold War it took on human rights duties – such as trying to lay the groundwork for liberal democracy in the former Yugoslavia,

---

Rights Norms," *Human Rights Quarterly*, 17, 2 (May 1995), 278–302, who argues it was a combination of international and domestic politics in the West that brought effective pressure on the USSR with regard to Jewish emigration.

[44] Jane Wright, "The OSCE and the Protection of Minority Rights," *Human Rights Quarterly*, 18, 1 (Winter 1996), 190–205. See above for coverage of the European Framework Convention on Minority Rights which was developed in weak legal form after the fall of European communism.

[45] Rob Zagman and Joanne Thorburn, *The Role of the High Commission on National Minorities in OSCE Conflict Prevention* (The Hague: Foundation for Inter-Ethnic Relations, 1997). See further Nigel Rodley, "Conception Problems in the Protection of Minorities: International Legal Developments," *Human Rights Quarterly*, 17, 1 (February 1995), 48–71.

[46] See further McMahon, "Helsinki Accord and CSCE/OSCE."

including the roles of arresting indicted war crimes suspects and ensuring the safe return of refugees and the internally displaced. Indeed, one of the reasons advanced for the 1998 expansion of NATO to include the Czech Republic, Hungary, and Poland was to provide an additional, military framework for reinforcing liberal democracy in those three formerly communist states. As already noted, in 1999 NATO undertook military force "out of area" in order to try to coerce the Milosevic government in modern Yugoslavia to stop its persecution and expulsion of ethnic Albanians in Kosovo. In fact, regardless of legal argument, NATO became an agent of humanitarian intervention and enforcer of liberal democracy in Europe. This trend was confirmed and expanded when NATO took military action in Libya in 2011, officially designed to stop the Kaddafi government from committing atrocities against its civilians.

A number of realists objected to this orientation, arguing that situations like Bosnia and Kosovo in the 1990s, and then Libya, did not engage the vital interests of the West and should not lead to tying down NATO through air campaigns and sometimes a presence on the ground. They argued that NATO military action should remain focused on traditional state security issues involving Russia, China, state-supported terrorism, and oil in the Middle East. They objected to military commitment to "minor" problems linked to self-determination and humanitarian assistance, as pushed by the communications media and private human rights groups.[47] For realists, priorities remained centered on individual and collective national interests traditionally defined in geo-political terms, not on alleviating human misery and distress in non-member states.

The different versions of realism have never been very precise about how states define their vital interests. Realist authors basically *assume* that states define their interests in terms of independent power, and then move on to emphasize competition that supposedly affects the "balance of power." In the third volume of his memoirs, Henry Kissinger refers repeatedly to the US "national interest."[48] He argues that his congressional critics (precisely because they were sentimental McGovernites) were not always interested in US national interests, rather than acknowledging that they had a *different* conception of the national interest. For Kissinger national interest centered on a geo-political power struggle with the old Soviet Union. But it is not self-evident that the USA should have expended blood and treasure in a place like Angola or the Horn of Africa during the Cold War, or that the Congress was in error in trying to block

---

[47] See, for example, the special section on NATO at fifty, in *Foreign Affairs*, 78, 3 (May/June 1999), 163–210, especially the articles by Robert E. Hunter and Michael E. Brown.
[48] Henry Kissinger, *Years of Renewal* (New York: Simon & Schuster, 1999).

national involvement in such places. After all, if the Soviets wanted to collect a handful of "basket cases" as allies, it is not self-evident that such expansion threatened US security. Thus there is room for reasonable persons to differ over what constitutes national interest, and within that, vital interests. Most realists like Kissinger do not acknowledge the subjective construction of national interests.

In Kosovo in 1999, NATO member states defined their vital interests to include a liberal democratic "neighborhood" in Europe. Just as European states had considered human rights important enough to merit two supranational regional courts that restricted state sovereignty in the name of human rights, so they, plus Canada and the USA, considered repression of ethnic Albanians in Kosovo important enough to merit military intervention – having come to feel highly uncomfortable with *not* undertaking military intervention in Bosnia during 1992–1994. Even Kissinger should have understood this, since he tried to justify his continued support of South Vietnam in 1975 and thereafter in terms of American honor – the moral obligation to help those who had relied on the United States – and not in terms of militarily affecting the balance of power or US security.[49]

Realists warned that western military power was stretched dangerously thin at the end of the twentieth century, with ground commitments in Bosnia and Kosovo, ongoing deployments of sizable numbers of troops on the ground in Afghanistan and Iraq, and longstanding military commitments particularly in East Asia. Should China flex its military muscles about Taiwan, or Russia revert to a more truculent foreign policy, for example, most realists argued that NATO would have to reduce its involvement in places like the Balkans – because traditional vital interests were not involved. It is for this reason that NATO yielded command of pacifying forces in Bosnia and Kosovo to the EU.

Regarding Libya in 2011, many of these same arguments resurfaced. Did the USA and NATO have an interest in intervening to preempt a possible slaughter of rebelling citizens, as Kaddafi seemed to promise? What would happen to NATO soft power in the event of non-intervention and atrocities? But should NATO have intervened in Libya and not in neighboring rebellions in Syria, Bahrain, Yemen, and other places? Would standing aside in Libya encourage repression by other autocrats? Was such a posture in the long-term interests of western states? Was it in the long-term interest of NATO states to be on the side of democratic change in the Arab world, and not just a matter of western "values"?

[49] Ibid.

After the Cold War, a relaxation of tensions among the great powers had allowed more liberalism in the form of human rights to be interjected into foreign policy through such instruments as NATO.[50] Realist thinking was not *passé*, but it did share the agenda more with a liberal conception of the national interest. The Al Qaeda attacks on the USA in 2001 supposedly brought a tough realism back to the fore, with a diminished interest in human rights. But NATO increasingly played a larger role in efforts to "secure" or "pacify" Afghanistan with an emphasis on democracy and broader human rights. So even in "an age of terrorism" or "an age of insecurity," the subject of human rights displayed considerable staying power. In post-combat situations, NATO was often expected to contribute to democratic nation-building and protection of human rights.

It bears emphasizing that developments pertaining to Libya in 2011 indicated that many basic questions had yet to be fully resolved within NATO. Among the supporters of NATO's intervention were both left-center humanitarian hawks wanting to prevent atrocities, and right-center nationalistic crusaders who wanted to go further and have Kaddafi removed. Among the critics were left-center policy circles concerned about a militaristic and expensive foreign policy, and right-center thinkers opposed to costly military steps not required by vital national interests centered on immediate self-defense. The USA handed off to NATO's leadership the military operations against Kaddafi, but at the time of writing many questions remained about that operation and its human rights dimensions, including not least the matter of core objectives over time and how best to achieve them.

The Western Hemisphere

By comparison with Europe, a major paradox exists with regard to regional organization and human rights in the Western Hemisphere. There we find, similar to Europe, an international organization, the Organization of American States (OAS), with human rights programs, a regional convention for the protection of human rights, and a commission and court to move beyond passive standards to active implementation. Yet we also find in that Hemisphere during much of the past fifty years an abundance of gross and systematic violations of human rights by OAS member states. How can it be that the states which are members of the Organization of American States engaged both in the repeated endorsement of well-known human rights standards, and at the same time, for

[50] Ryan Hendrickson, "North Atlantic Treaty Organization," in *Encyclopedia of Human Rights*, vol. IV, 119–123.

much of the time during the Cold War, in their repeated violation? The answer is to be found most fundamentally in a regional conflicted political culture.[51]

Supportive factors

Three hemispheric political values largely account for the creation and continued functioning of this regional regime for the promotion and protection of human rights. The first of these is widespread but abstract agreement that the legitimate state is the liberal democratic state. This is not a newly articulated value; most hemispheric states professed political liberalism from the time of their independence. More recent developments since 1945 mostly reaffirmed what had been preached if not practiced consistently since the early nineteenth century – namely that hemispheric republics aspired to be liberal democracies along the lines of the models in Europe and North America. The American Declaration on the Rights and Duties of Man, from 1948, and the InterAmerican Convention on Human Rights, from 1969, were but modern manifestations of this longstanding tradition of lip service to political liberalism. (One can note in passing that, whereas Europe developed its main human rights treaty in 1950, in legal force from 1953, the OAS took until 1969.)

A second widespread political value that undergirds regional developments in favor of human rights has been moral leadership for rights by OAS agencies and a shifting coalition of hemispheric states. A key player in this regard since the mid-1950s has been the InterAmerican Commission on Human Rights, now a principal organ of the OAS, and a persistent leader for human rights. This uninstructed body, charged with an active program of reporting, investigating, and diplomacy for human rights, also has duties under the InterAmerican Convention. The dynamism of this body has been supported by a variety of states with active and progressive human rights policies – although the composition of this group of states changes according to the government in power. Costa Rica and other states have been part of this pro-human rights coalition from time to time.

A third supporting factor has been erratic influence for human rights by the United States. Very little happens in the OAS that is strongly opposed by the USA. More positively, the USA on occasion has used the OAS to push for such things as the American Declaration, diplomatic pressure

---

[51] This section is drawn from a revision of David P. Forsythe, "Human Rights, the United States, and the Organization of American States," *Human Rights Quarterly*, 13, 2 (Spring 1991), 66–98.

against particular rights-violating governments at particular times, and OAS supervision of elections in places like Central America. US support for regional human rights standards and action has been highly selective, which is to say inconsistent, as I will note below. Nevertheless, periodic support by the USA for certain human rights developments via the OAS has been important – whether one speaks of efforts to rid Nicaragua of the Somoza dynasty, or efforts on behalf of a diplomacy generally supportive of liberal democracy in the 1990s.

Blocking factors

On the other side of the fence, however, three factors have historically constrained regional human rights developments in the Western Hemisphere. The first of these has been the historical trend on the part of Latin and Caribbean states to emphasize the principle of state sovereignty in the wake of repeated US interventions into their domestic affairs. This widespread endorsement of broad and traditional notions of state sovereignty was articulated to block OAS authority as well as US power, since the former (viz., OAS authority) was seen by many in the region to reflect the latter (viz., US power). By the turn of the twenty-first century there had been some movement away from historical patterns in this regard.

In 1991 the OAS declared unanimously, apart from Cuba, through its Santiago Declaration, that the question of democratic government within any state was an international and not strictly a domestic matter. But at approximately the same time the OAS continued to resist authorizing the use of force to create, recreate, or protect democratic government, as in Haiti, since such an authorization meant authorizing predominantly US use of force. In the latter situation, the USA had to turn to the United Nations Security Council for authorization of deployment of force to restore the elected government of Father Aristide in Haiti in the face of military usurpation. Thus the OAS remained unreliable for the direct protection of human rights in the Hemisphere, due to lingering widespread fears about US power.

This tension resurfaced over Venezuela in 2005, when the OAS refused to lend its name to a US plan to monitor democracy in the Hemisphere. Important OAS member states feared the plan was nothing more than a scheme to undermine the government of Hugo Chavez, whose left of center elected government in Caracas had incurred considerable criticism from Washington.[52]

---

[52] Joel Brinkley, "Latin Nations Resist Plan for Monitor of Democracy," *New York Times*, June 6, 2005, A9.

A second limiting factor on regional action for human rights in the Western Hemisphere stems from the fact that many national elites, while identifying with political liberalism in the abstract, have not really been able to bring themselves to practice liberal democracy when it meant recognizing human rights for indigenous peoples, the lower classes (the two are not mutually exclusive), those on the political left (the three are not mutually exclusive), etc. Military and other governments in the hemisphere have often found it "desirable" to emphasize a "national security state" and other departures from liberal democracy in order to save the nation from itself – viz., to save the state from control by some element deemed undesirable by the traditional elites made up of the military, the aristocracy, and conservative elements in the Catholic Church. Thus the abstract endorsement of liberal democracy has been frequently joined by the practice of authoritarian government, and even authoritarian government with a very brutal face, as a "necessary and exceptional" measure when the traditional elites have feared "subversive" movements. This was particularly the case in the Southern Cone of South America during the Cold War years of the 1970s and 1980s.[53]

Given the difficulties of securing agreement on equitable development in the Hemisphere, which has led both to polarized societies and radical movements, a backlash emerged against the "Washington consensus" and the pursuit of economic growth by relatively unregulated global capitalism from about 1980. The development course laid out by the Reagan Administration, the World Bank, and the IMF seemed to perpetually exclude from prosperity many on the lower rungs of society, particularly the indigenous Indian groups. Therefore in the early twenty-first century a leftist populism emerged (or in some cases re-emerged) in places such as Venezuela, Bolivia, Ecuador, and Nicaragua. This Latin American populism manifested at times certain authoritarian tendencies, as had been true, for example, in the populism of Huey Long in Louisiana in the USA.[54]

(There was also the problem of murderous narco-trafficking in states such as Colombia and Mexico, states where elected governments did not have full control over national territory and where the pursuit of the lucrative illegal drug trade entailed many human rights violations and even atrocities.)

---

[53] See further Jack Donnelly, *International Human Rights*, 2nd edn. (Boulder: Westview, 1998), ch. 3; and Rebecca Evans, "South American Southern Cone: National Security State, 1970s–1980s," in *Encyclopedia of Human Rights*, vol. IV, 492–504.

[54] Francisco Lopez-Bermudez, "Latin American Populism," in *Encyclopedia of Human Rights*, vol. III, 400–411.

A third and last limiting factor on human rights norms and practice was the preoccupation of the USA with containing if not rolling back Soviet-led communism during the Cold War. This orientation, a modern version of the Monroe Doctrine designed to keep the Hemisphere free from the influence of any external power, caused the USA to repeatedly emphasize national and regional freedom from communism as compared with individual freedom from non-communist repression. Until the Carter Administration of 1977–1981, the USA repeatedly aligned with repressive but non-communist governments in the Hemisphere. The goal may have been to protect human rights in the USA (along with the power of the USA in international relations), but the means entailed opposition to human rights developments in places like Guatemala in 1954 where the USA organized the overthrow of the genuinely elected and basically progressive Arbenz government. The murderous military governments that followed were propped up by Washington. After the Cold War this type of situation has obviously changed, and the USA has become less opposed to OAS actions for human rights in the Hemisphere. Cuba aside, there are no fully authoritarian governments and none consistently aligned with an external hostile power. (True, Chavez in Venezuela occasionally flirted with making a diplomatic alliance with the Iranian clerics but this was not seen by any government in Washington as posing a major security threat.)

Synthesis

The interplay of these three supporting factors (general commitment to liberal democracy, moral leadership for human rights by various actors, inconsistent leadership for human rights by the USA) and three limiting factors (fondness for traditional notions of state sovereignty, widespread if periodic practice of authoritarianism particularly of a brutal sort, US security concerns during the Cold War) meant that until about the end of the Cold War one found an ambitious regional human rights program that was mostly ineffective in the actual protection of human rights in most places most of the time. Human rights activities constituted the bright spot of the OAS, compared with security, economic, and environmental matters. At the same time regional action for human rights did not prevent or correct gross violations of human rights in many places between the 1940s and the 1990s. After the Cold War matters have been moving in a relatively progressive direction, but without radical change since the USA and Canada (and a few other states) remain outside the jurisdiction of the regional human rights court, neither having accepted the InterAmerican Convention on Human Rights.

Details

The American Declaration was voted into being (even before the UN Universal Declaration of Human Rights, and before the European regional instruments), and the InterAmerican Convention was eventually adhered to by twenty-four of the OAS thirty-five member states (Cuba being the thirty-sixth but suspended between 1962 and 2009). Twenty-four of these accepted the supranational jurisdiction of the InterAmerican Court.

The InterAmerican Commission basically tried to "referee the game of politics" in the Hemisphere by "blowing the whistle" on violations of human rights. But, to continue the analogy, the game continued in brutal fashion in many places as if that referee did not exist. To change the analogy, the InterAmerican Commission generated modest influence as a liberal ombudsman in the region.[55] Until the end of the Cold War, however, only sixteen of thirty-five states consented to supranational adjudication by the InterAmerican Court of Human Rights, which had come into being in 1979. Its case load remains less than those of the two European courts, as by 2004 the Court had handed down only forty-five binding and seventeen advisory opinions. Part of the reason for this low case load for the Court is the fact that only the InterAmerican Commission and states can present cases to the InterAmerican Court. In a sense, therefore, the Commission operates almost as a court of first instance handling over 12,500 cases since its creation.[56] No state so far has lodged a case at the Court. The USA continued to object to the Court's authority and jurisdiction, and to argue that the American Declaration had not passed into international customary law in whole or in part. In Europe, by contrast, all major states were supportive of most CE and EU human rights developments.

It is a measure of the positive evolution of the InterAmerican system, however, that in 1998 regionally important states like Brazil and Mexico accepted the Court's jurisdiction. Moreover, the countries that have accepted the jurisdiction of the InterAmerican Court have demonstrated a surprising willingness to comply with its decisions, when in the past they have often ignored the decisions of the Commission. However, while states have been more prepared to pay monetary damages to plaintiffs, they have been less willing to make further investigations and punish

---

[55] See, for example, Cecilia Medina, "The Role of Country Reports in the Inter-American System of Human Rights," *Netherlands Quarterly of Human Rights*, 15, 4 (December 1997), 457–473.

[56] Christina M. Cerna, "The Inter-American System for the Protection of Human Rights," *Florida Journal of International Law*, 16, 195 (2004), 195–212.

perpetrators.[57] About a decade after the Cold War it could be said that OAS developments pertaining to human rights were somewhat improved, with some of the Court's jurisprudence beginning to have broad effect particularly in Latin America.[58]

About a decade into the twenty-first century, the Commission reported that states had complied fully with its recommendations 12.5 percent of the time, partially 69.5 percent, and not at all in 18 percent. The Commission was overstretched, trying to process many complaints but with insufficient staff and budgets.[59] As for the Court, as of 2009 – with jurisdiction over twenty-five states – it had ruled on 211 cases and was still monitoring compliance in 114 of these. Overall, states had agreed, as ordered by the Court, to: pay reparations to victims 55 percent of the time; issue apologies or make other symbolic gestures 58 percent of the time; adopt new legislation and take other structural measures to ensure non-repetition of violations 23 percent of the time; etc. Commission and Court conclusions often became enmeshed in domestic politics, with the Executive often trying to signal to the Legislature and domestic groups its commitment to human rights.[60]

Resistance to the Court still remains, as attested by the withdrawal of Trinidad and Tobago from the InterAmerican Convention in 1999 to shield its death penalty regime from the Court's scrutiny – and Peru's short-lived intended withdrawal in the same year. Further, it is correct to generalize that while Latin American states have accepted the authority of the Court and the Commission (with the exception of Cuba), the English-speaking states of the hemisphere have only partially embraced the system.[61]

Overall, one found in the Western Hemisphere a regional system for the promotion and protection of human rights that resembled the European system on paper, but did not resemble it very much in reality.[62] For example, in both systems one found a right of private petition about

---

[57] Ibid., 203.
[58] Jo M. Pasqualucci and Christina M. Cerna, "Organization of American States," in *Encyclopedia of Human Rights*, vol. IV, 145–153.
[59] Robert K. Goldman, "History and Action: The Inter-American Human Rights System and the Role of the Inter-American Commission of Human Rights," *Human Rights Quarterly*, 31, 4 (November 2009), 856–887.
[60] See further Courtney Hillebrecht, "The Domestic Mechanisms of Compliance with International Law: Case Studies from the Inter-American Human Rights System," paper presented at the International Studies Association annual meeting, Montreal, 2011.
[61] Cerna, "The Inter-American System for the Protection of Human Rights," 203.
[62] See further Tom J. Farer, "The Rise of the Inter-American Human Rights Regime: No Longer a Unicorn, Not Yet an Ox," *Human Rights Quarterly*, 19, 3 (August 1997), 510–546.

human rights violations. But the results of such petitions in Europe provided consistent and real restraints on state policy through binding court judgments, whereas the results in the Americas had not through about 1991. One could hope that with the end of the Cold War both US policy and other factors would change toward more support for regional human rights values and processes. But some two decades after the end of the Cold War, the regional system for protecting human rights associated with the OAS remained much weaker than its European counterpart. The United States and Canada remained as strongly opposed to OAS review of their human rights record as during earlier times, although the Commission and Court were having broader impact in Latin American states.

Africa

African states, seared by the experience of colonialism and plagued by numerous problems of political instability, used the Organization of African Unity (OAU) early on, created in 1963, primarily to reinforce traditional notions of state sovereignty and domestic jurisdiction. The OAU Charter mentioned human rights. But for the OAU, concern with human rights was restricted to questions of racial discrimination by Whites against Blacks as in Rhodesia, South Africa, and the then remaining Portuguese colonies of Angola, Guinea-Bissau, and Mozambique. Even the most egregious violations of human rights in Idi Amin's Uganda or "Emperor" Jean-Bedel Bokassa's Central African "Empire" were met with a deafening silence from the OAU.

This embarrassing double standard contributed eventually to adoption of the African Charter on Human and Peoples' Rights – the so-called Banjul Charter – in 1981.[63] It received a sufficient number of ratifications to enter into legal force in 1986, at which time perhaps three states in Africa might be considered something relatively close to a liberal democracy and thus showing national commitment to civil and political rights. In brief summary, the Banjul Charter encompassed: an absolute endorsement of certain civil and political rights familiar to the liberal West; a conditional endorsement of other civil and political rights that were limited by "claw back" clauses permitting deviation from international standards on the basis of national laws; mention of fundamental economic and social rights requiring considerable material resources for their application; a list of individual duties; and a list of "people's"

---

[63] U. Oji Umozurike, *The African Charter on Human and Peoples' Rights* (The Hague: Martinus Nijhoff, 1997).

rights such as to existence, self-determination, and disposal of natural resources.[64] These regional developments mirrored an emphasis by developing states at the United Nations on, among other principles, the collective right to development and the collective right to freely dispose of national resources.

It was said by some that especially individual duties and people's rights reflected uniquely African approaches to internationally recognized human rights.[65] It was also said that since the Banjul Charter eschewed an African human rights court and established only an advisory African Human Rights Commission to oversee application of the Charter, this approach reflected African preferences for discussion and conciliation rather than adversarial adjudication. The fact remains that during the early stages of post-colonial Africa, political liberalism was in short supply on that continent. It would have been inconceivable for the OAU in the 1980s to adopt a human rights convention that was normatively strong and clear on behalf of individual rights, and subject to enforcement by a supranational regional court. Whether this was because of "African culture" or the political self-interests of those who ruled African states I leave to the historians and anthropologists.

What is undeniable, and entirely predictable, was that the Banjul Charter had only slight impact on anyone's behavior in the fifty-three states making up the OAU during the first ten years after 1986. As was true in general in other regions, African states did not avail themselves of the opportunity to petition other states about human rights violations. The only state petition lodged during this time was a bogus one: Libya petitioned against the United States. Since the latter was not a member of the OAU, the petition was properly dismissed. Moreover, African states were tardy at best, and frequently negligent, in submitting reports to the Commission about how they were applying the Charter. The Commission had neither the authority nor the power to correct the situation. When the Commission raised questions about the reports that were submitted, states tended toward silence. Likewise, when private communications were submitted to the Commission claiming a violation of the Charter, as best we can tell during the early days (the Commission at

---

[64] See further Rachel Murray, "African Union: Banjul Charter," in *Encyclopedia of Human Rights*, vol. I, 12–18.

[65] In addition to Umozurike, *The African Charter on Human and Peoples' Rights*, ch. 8, see Rhoda Howard, *Human Rights in Commonwealth Africa* (Totowa, NJ: Rowman & Littlefield, 1986), ch. 2; Timothy Fernyhough, "Human Rights and Precolonial Africa," in Ronald Cohen, Goran Hyden, and Winston P. Nagan, eds., *Human Rights and Governance in Africa* (Gainesville: University Press of Florida, 1993), ch. 2; and Abdullah Ahmed An-Na'im and Francis M. Deng, eds., *Human Rights in Africa: Cross-Cultural Perspectives* (Washington: Brookings, 1990).

that time interpreted its mandate as requiring full confidentiality), states tended to disregard the entire process of inquiry and friendly settlement that the Commission was trying to conduct.[66] It was well known that after 1986, as before, there were many gross and systematic violations of internationally recognized human rights throughout Africa, not to mention more mundane or quotidian violations, and that both types went uncorrected by regional (and other) arrangements.

Early on the Commission was poorly funded, its support staff or secretariat was weak, human rights non-governmental organizations in Africa were neither numerous nor well prepared for interaction with the Commission, and the imposition of confidentiality made the Commission's promotion and protection work exceedingly difficult.[67] Yet by the late 1990s the Commission, with the help of a number of European public and private parties, had managed to escape from some of the confidentiality restrictions, had improved both its staff and the quality of its decisions, had carried out several in-country investigations with the consent of the appropriate state, had taken some initiatives without waiting for petitions, and was in relative terms drawing slightly more support and praise.[68] Over time the Commission clearly became more active and assertive. The result was a determined socialization process by the agency, as it pronounced on various private petitions (there was only one state to state complaint) and in various ways tried to advance attention to human rights in Africa.[69]

In June 1998 the OAU adopted a protocol to the Banjul Charter approving the creation of an African human rights court.[70] The Protocol creating the court entered into force in 2004, but the court was not yet functional as of early 2011. It was true that Africa, like other regions, had been part of a "third wave" of democratization after the Cold War, and that in relative terms political liberalism had made some advances in Africa by the late 1990s. Large and important countries like South Africa

---

[66] Evelyn A. Ankumah, *The African Commission on Human and Peoples' Rights: Practice and Procedures* (The Hague: Martinus Nijhoff, 1996).

[67] Claude E. Welch, "The African Commission on Human and Peoples' Rights: A Five-Year Report and Assessment," *Human Rights Quarterly*, 14, 1 (February 1992), 43–61.

[68] Chidi Anselm Odinkalu and Camilla Christensen, "The African Commission on Human and Peoples' Rights: The Development of its Non-State Communication Procedures," *Human Rights Quarterly*, 20, 2 (May 1998), 235–280. See also Claude E. Welch, *Protecting Human Rights in Africa* (Philadelphia: University of Pennsylvania Press, 1995), especially ch. 5, on the interaction between the International Commission of Jurists, the NGO based in Geneva, and the African Commission.

[69] Rachel Murray, "African Union: Commission and Court on Human Rights," in *Encyclopedia of Human Rights*, vol. I, 19–25.

[70] Makau Mutua, "The African Human Rights Court: A Two-Legged Stool?," *Human Rights Quarterly*, 21, 2 (May 1999), 342–363.

and Nigeria were not the only ones in Africa to move from repression toward more liberal democracy.

In 2001 the African Union (AU) succeeded the old OAU. Its Constitutive Act gave a central place to human rights, including a right of humanitarian intervention in cases of genocide, war crimes, and crimes against humanity.[71] Yet authoritarianism, persistent political instability, violation of many basic civil rights, and even various atrocities remained a feature of much of Africa, especially in the Great Lakes region, parts of West Africa (Liberia, Sierra Leone), plus Somalia, Sudan, Central African Republic, Zimbabwe, etc. In this context, not to mention ongoing underdevelopment of the most dire economic sort, it would take a great deal of optimism to believe that a regional human rights court could make a major difference. It is still too early to judge whether the political initiative, the African Peer Review Mechanism, established as part of the African Union's development program, the New Partnership for Africa's Development (NEPAD), will improve or add confusion to Africa's nascent judicial institutions.[72] As of 2011 some twenty-six AU state members had submitted to this review process, which some saw as a search for certified good governance that might lead to increased foreign investment and/or foreign assistance.

The AU did participate with the UN in a security operation in the Darfur region of Sudan, in an effort to improve the human rights situation there. But the lightly armed military forces were too few in number and too poorly equipped to completely control the situation. In West Africa it was not the AU that either intervened or threatened to do so to stop atrocities in places such as Liberia, Sierra Leone, and Ivory Coast, but rather ECOWAS (Economic Community of West African States) under the leadership of Nigeria. (It was British military intervention, however, that finally stopped atrocities in Sierra Leone, and French military action that stabilized Ivory Coast.)[73]

Regarding both Europe and the Western Hemisphere, I have already noted in this chapter that, when regional human rights arrangements confront governments unsympathetic to human rights, the regional machinery is not very effective in its protection efforts. One cannot have robust regional protection of human rights without the necessary building

---

[71] Article 4 (h) and (j), Constitutive Act of the African Union.

[72] Christof Heyns, "The African Regional Human Rights System: The African Charter," *Penn State Law Review*, 108 (2004), 679–702.

[73] In places such as Ivory Coast and Democratic Republic of Congo, it was not the AU but the UN which put military forces on the ground in part to deal with gross violations of human rights. Sometimes the field missions had an enforcement mandate under UN Charter Chapter VII, and not just a more limited peacekeeping mandate.

blocks, which means a supportive national political culture and leadership genuinely committed to protecting the rights of nationals. Regarding international criminal courts, I have already noted the phenomenon of "judicial romanticism." If the International Criminal Tribunal for Rwanda has not made much of an impact on the Great Lakes region of Africa, and if the International Criminal Court has not quickly and easily made its mark in places such as Uganda, Sudan, Kenya, and elsewhere, as we saw in Chapter 4, surely there is not much reason to believe the impact of an African human rights court would be different – unless there were profoundly progressive changes in its context. By 2011 there were indeed some encouraging developments for human rights on the continent, even if many quite serious problems remained.

Conclusions

The Arab League's Human Rights Commission has mostly contented itself with one-sided attention to Israel's policies in territories controlled since 1967, while ignoring gross and systematic violations in many Arab countries. Only in 2011 did the Arab League's political organs confront authoritarianism and atrocity in Kaddafi's Libya, calling for outside intervention against his policies, and some observers thought this was because Kaddafi had uniquely managed to antagonize even the rest of the Arab League membership. The organization remained largely ineffectual regarding denial of many human rights in many other Arab states. The impact of the League and its human rights agency having been mostly negligible over the years, despite a few human rights developments, it does not merit analysis here.[74] It is possible, however, that if the Arab Spring of 2011, featuring street protests in several Middle Eastern nations for genuine democracy and good governance, were to produce different Arab governments, the human rights work of the Arab League might be transformed.

Asia, being large and extremely diverse, not to mention being the locus of much criticism of western models of political liberalism, manifests no intergovernmental organizations for human rights. However, ASEAN (Association of Southeast Asian Nations) did inch toward some human rights activity, but not very much.[75]

---

[74] See further details in David P. Forsythe, "The Arab League," in *Encyclopedia of Human Rights*, vol. III, 312–316.

[75] See further Kenneth Christie, "Association of Southeast Asian Nations (ASEAN)," ibid., vol. I, 119–125. Some Asian (and African) states were members of the Commonwealth of Nations, formerly the British Commonwealth. This transnational organization, while not a regional one, was not a global one either. The point here is that

Regional developments especially in Europe, the Western Hemisphere, and Africa make clear the paradox that in the absence of national commitment to political liberalism including human rights, it is impossible to build a regional system for protecting human rights that is genuinely effective. Where you have illiberal governments of various types, you lack the building blocks for effective regional intergovernmental action for rights. Conversely, however, the experience of Europe shows that just because you have liberal democracy at the national level, that does not mean that you do not need regional systems for review of state policies. Liberal democracy at the national level, meaning above all a commitment to civil and political rights, is a necessary but not entirely sufficient condition for achieving a truly rights-protective society. One needs regional review – and perhaps global action as well.

Case study: the OAS, democracy, and Honduras

Honduras is a small country of some eight million persons situated in Central America, bordered by Nicaragua on the south and by Guatemala and El Salvador on the north and northwest. An independent republic since the 1840s, it has experienced much multiparty democracy despite its persistent poverty. But it has also known periods of autocratic rule and is associated in some circles with the origin of the phrase "banana republic." From the 1980s pluralist democracy seemed increasingly stable under two dominant parties, human rights violations by the military were reduced, and the democratic constitution of 1987 seemed more durable than many others in the country's turbulent political history. The dominant political culture of this time seemed basically conservative, being pro-business and friendly to transnational corporations, with some analysts seeing the two dominant political parties as historically center-right.

Honduras was a founding member of the Organization of American States. That organization has long endorsed a regional version of human rights that was generally compatible with UN norms. OAS activities for human rights were more notable than in the domains of economics, security, and environment. In 2001 the OAS adopted the InterAmerican Democratic Charter, followed in 2003 by a resolution that became

the Commonwealth, under British influence, did have a human rights program and thus did involve its member states, as former British colonies, in various human rights questions, such as the suspension of the Robert Mugabe government in Zimbabwe for serious violations of rights. See Timothy Shaw, "Commonwealth of Nations," ibid., vol. I, 372–376. For a similar organization under French influence, also with a human rights program, see Emmanuel Decaux, "La Francophonie," ibid., vol. II, 261–265.

known as the Santiago Declaration. These steps made clear that all OAS members had to maintain genuine, liberal, pluralist, or constitutional democracy. These democratic norms were similar to other standards in the Council of Europe, European Union, Commonwealth of Nations, and about a dozen other intergovernmental organizations. Thus organizational "democracy clauses" were a prevalent feature of international relations.

In June 2009 the elected Honduran President, Manuel Zelaya of the Liberal Party, in office since 2006, was deposed by military coup. He had offended important sectors of the conservative elites of the country by several maneuvers including failure to enforce certain Supreme Court judgments and planning a referendum for a new constitutional convention that some thought might pave the way to his extended rule. As Honduran politics polarized, many conservatives feared that Zelaya was "moving left" and was positioning himself to become another Hugo Chavez in Venezuela – a relatively more authoritarian populist of the left, appealing to the poor while cracking down on dissent and opposition.

From the summer of 2009 Honduras was governed by a *de facto* administration of Roberto Micheletti of the National Party who had been speaker of the House in the Congress. His administration was endorsed by both the Honduran Congress and Supreme Court. In November of that year national elections saw the transfer of power from Micheletti to Porfirio Lobo, also of the National Party. A number of analysts noted that access to the media was restricted for those supporting Zelaya, and independent criticism of the Micheletti faction had become dangerous.

The international response to the events of June 2009 was at first remarkably uniform, vigorous, and opposed to the interruption of the 1987 Honduran Constitution. This was, after all, the first military coup in the region in several decades. The OAS suspended Honduras from membership by unanimous vote (the vote suspending Cuba had been split), and the OAS Secretary-General tried to persuade the Micheletti faction to change course. The InterAmerican Commission on Human Rights, having conducted an in-country investigation, condemned what it called a coup, then detailed a sizable list of human rights violations. The European Union imposed economic sanctions. The UN General Assembly also condemned the unconstitutional transfer of power, and various units of the UN system ceased dealing with Honduras. Most states withdrew their ambassadors from Tegucigalpa. The USA opposed the coup and imposed some sanctions, although it did not withdraw its ambassador and slightly later it tried to mediate a compromise solution to the crisis.

However, despite the inconvenience of economic and diplomatic sanctions, those opposed to Zelaya had a strategy of holding a firm course until the November 2010 elections. This was a broad coalition including elements of the Liberal Party, some state officials under Zelaya, most of the military, most of the Supreme Court, and much of the Congress. Their calculations proved to be a winning strategy, not only because economic sanctions take time to have full effect, but also and more importantly because the international coalition opposed to the extra-constitutional transfer of power fractured. With the election of Lobo, the USA, Colombia, Costa Rica, Guatemala, Panama, and Peru all recognized him as the legitimate head of state. Other OAS members continued their opposition, treating the Lobo Administration as a pariah government. Honduran membership in the OAS had not been restored at the time of writing but was foreseen, with Zelaya being allowed to return under a governmental promise of no prosecution.

It was not as if the removal of Zelaya had led to military government as in Chile in 1973 or in Argentina in 1976. Rather, by November 2010 one found in Honduras that one elected president had been replaced by another elected president, after about six months of interim civilian rule. This sequence made it difficult to hold the international line against interruption of the 1987 constitution, especially since a number of actors feared that Zelaya himself would not prove faithful to that constitution. In the view of some, however, in Honduras under the Lobo presidency one found illiberal democracy: elections had resulted in rule supported by the majority voting, but with many human rights violations directed at dissidents, independent journalists, etc. In this view Lobo was similar to Milosevic in Serbia: locally popular but using the state to stifle opposition and criticism, thus falling far short of genuine democracy.

In the USA several conservative Republican senators had taken an interest in the situation, had visited Honduras against the wishes of the Obama Administration, had supported the coup in the name of economic freedom and fear of another Chavez, and held up several Obama appointments to foreign policy positions dealing with the Hemisphere. These developments made it doubly difficult for the USA either to achieve some negotiated solution (since the Micheletti faction was encouraged to hold firm because of its support in US right wing circles), or to help hold together the international efforts to support the principle of constitutional democracy without military interference. Critics charged that the Obama Administration did a deal with conservative senators in order to get its nominees secured in office, at the expense of a robust defense of constitutional democracy in Latin America.

One sees in this case first of all the workings of transnational politics, or the blending of domestic politics with foreign policy and international relations. One also sees the continuing importance of the USA in hemispheric affairs; absent Republican senatorial pressures, it is likely that Obama policy would have remained more closely aligned with OAS positions. Finally, the outcome raised questions about the effect of OAS norms in favor of constitutional democracy. If the OAS could not reverse the coup in Honduras, a small and weak country, what precedent would this set for the future? On the other hand, a regional military coup strongly opposed by the USA might evolve according to different dynamics.

Discussion questions

- What explains the quality of regional protection of human rights in Europe, compared with the Western Hemisphere and Africa? Is it likely that the latter two regions will evolve so as to duplicate the European record?
- Is any one of these three regions seriously interested in the protection of economic and social rights? Can economic and social rights be adjudicated? Is there always a clear distinction between civil rights and economic or social rights?
- With regard to human rights, what is the relationship between the Council of Europe and the European Union? Have the OSCE and NATO carved out a special role for themselves regarding the protection of human rights in Europe?
- Does the United States have a reasonable and coherent policy toward the regional mechanisms for the protection of human rights in the Western Hemisphere? Is the Hemisphere evolving the political context in which the OAS can improve the regional protection of human rights?
- Is it likely that the projected African Court of Human Rights could function so as to make a major difference in the regional protection of human rights on that continent?

SUGGESTIONS FOR FURTHER READING

Ankumah, Evelyn A., *The African Commission on Human and Peoples' Rights: Practice and Procedures* (The Hague: Martinus Nijhoff, 1996). A generally sympathetic overview of historical developments, but with appropriate criticism. Some sections are mainly of use to practicing lawyers who want to use OAU regional procedures.

An-Na'im, Ahmed, and Francis M. Deng, eds., *Human Rights in Africa: Cross-Cultural Perspectives* (Washington: Brookings, 1990). A stimulating collection about universalism and cultural relativism with regard to Africa. Deals broadly and intelligently with the cultural context within which the OAU human rights initiatives occur.

Aziz, Miriam, *The Impact of European Rights on National Legal Cultures* (Oxford: Hart Publishing Ltd., 2004). A study of the interplay of regional and national standards on human rights in Europe.

Bartels, Lorand, *Human Rights Conditionality and EU External Relations* (Oxford: Oxford University Press, 2005). A timely update on a subject of growing importance.

Beddard, R., *Human Rights and Europe*, 3rd edn. (Cambridge: Grotius Publications, 1993). A good overview, widely used in specialized classes.

Cardenas, Sonia, *Human Rights in Latin America: The Politics of Terror and Hope* (Philadelphia: University of Pennsylvania Press, 2009). A very good and up to date survey of regional developments.

Davidson, Scott, *The Inter-American Human Rights System* (Aldershot: Dartmouth, 1997). A traditional legal overview.

Farer, Tom, "The Rise of the Inter-American Human Rights Regime: No Longer a Unicorn, Not Yet an Ox," *Human Rights Quarterly*, 19, 3 (August 1997), 510–546. One of the best short historical overviews.

Jackson, Donald W., *The United Kingdom Confronts the European Convention on Human Rights* (Gainesville: University Press of Florida, 1997). A thorough look at why Britain has encountered so much difficulty after becoming a party to the European Convention on Civil and Political Rights. A good reminder that even those Anglo-Saxon states with a long commitment to liberal democracy still violate international human rights and are in need of international (in this case, regional) review.

Janis, Mark, Richard Kay, and Anthony Bradly, *European Human Rights Law* (New York: Oxford University Press, 2008). A broad and analytical overview.

Kissinger, Henry, *Years of Renewal* (New York: Simon & Schuster, 1999). The former National Security Advisor and Secretary of State warmly endorses human rights in the CSCE process (for which he was not responsible) since it helped to generate problems for the Soviet empire, but generally, and explicitly in his African and Latin American diplomacy, he regarded human rights as frequently an unwelcome addition to his realist orientation. What caused him to work actively for majority rule in southern Africa was the appearance of Soviet and Cuban military personnel in Angola.

Korey, William, *The Promises We Keep: Human Rights, the Helsinki Process, and American Foreign Policy* (New York: St. Martin's Press, 1993). A favorable overview of the CSCE process that helped to de-legitimize European communism. Emphasizes the roles of the US Congress and private human rights groups, especially Jewish ones.

Neuwahl, Nanette A., and Allan Rosas, eds., *The European Union and Human Rights* (The Hague: Martinus Nijhoff, 1995). A solid reminder that the EU has a human rights dimension in addition to its economic activities.

Umozurike, U. Oji, *The African Charter on Human and Peoples' Rights* (The Hague: Martinus Nijhoff, 1997). A direct and to-the-point overview, with sensible interpretations.

Williams, Andrew, *EU Human Rights Policies: A Study in Irony* (Oxford: Oxford University Press, 2004). A study of the discrepancy between internal and external EU standards on human rights.

6   Human rights and foreign policy in comparative perspective

While intergovernmental agencies and private transnational groups dealing with human rights proliferate, one key to progressive developments remains states and their foreign policies.[1] As we have already seen, IGOs, from the UN through the OAS to the Organization for Security and Co-operation in Europe, have extensive human rights programs. Independent international officials for these organizations generate some influence. But it is usually state members of these IGOs that take the most important decisions, and it is primarily states that are the targets of reform efforts. Likewise, as we will see in Chapter 7, NGOs such as Amnesty International, Human Rights Watch, and Physicians for Human Rights, among others, are highly active in human rights matters and generate some influence. But, still, it is states that approve treaties and their monitoring mechanisms, states that sometimes manipulate foreign assistance in relation to rights, states that (may or may not) arrest war criminals – either singly or via international organizations such as NATO. NGOs mainly pressure *states* to do the right thing.

This chapter looks at human rights and state foreign policy in comparative perspective. It begins with a short discussion of three prominent mechanisms states can and do – at least sometimes – employ to influence another government's human rights policies: diplomatic, economic, and

The views in this chapter are my own, but I gratefully acknowledge the contributions of others who worked on a research project on this subject funded by the United Nations University: Peter Baehr (Netherlands), Sally Morphet (United Kingdom), Chiyuki Aoi and Yozo Yokota (Japan), Gabor Kardos (Central Europe), Sergei Chugrov (Russia), Sanjoy Banerjee (India), Cristina Eguizabal (Latin America), Tiyanjana Maluwa (South Africa), and Zachary Karabell (Iran). Jack Donnelly also participated in this project and wrote the final chapter in D. Forsythe, ed., *Human Rights and Comparative Foreign Policy* (Tokyo: United Nations University Press, 2000). An earlier version of this chapter was published in the *International Journal* (Canada), 53, 1 (Winter 1997–1998), 113–132. I am grateful to the editors for their helpful suggestions.

[1] An introduction can be found in Peter R. Baehr, "Foreign Policy," in David P. Forsythe, ed., *Encyclopedia of Human Rights* (New York: Oxford University Press, 2009), vol. II, 237–247.

military means. Different approaches may be taken in different situations, as states usually calculate the instruments available, the expected effect of the action taken, and anticipated reactions.[2] This is followed by a focus on the United States, the most important actor in international relations at the birth of the twenty-first century. I show that the USA has a particular slant to its foreign policy on rights, and that Washington is often more prone to preach to others than to take international rights standards very seriously in its own policies. The chapter then provides a comparative analysis of human rights in the foreign policies of some other states that either are liberal democracies or aspire to be so. I show that most differ from the US approach in one way or another, due to a varying combination of history and political culture, geo-political position, and perceived national interests. This is followed by a brief commentary on the human rights policies of some illiberal states such as Iran.

Finally, the chapter offers some concluding thoughts about human rights and foreign policy.[3] The accent is on the positive, despite ample reason for reserve about the immediate future. Despite the rise of Al Qaeda and other manifestations of radical Islamist groups prone to total war, with their attacks on civilians and abuse of prisoners, and despite a US tendency to respond in kind, at least during the George W. Bush Administration, with especially abuse of detainees, the historical trend remains in favor of a broad range of human rights. Arab popular movements in 2011 demanding human rights and democracy reinforce this interpretation.

Policy instruments

In the past, states have often proven reluctant to speak out on human rights violations by others, fearing interruption of "business as usual"– not only on business but also on other important matters like security cooperation. As indicated in Chapter 4, it is very clear that states do not like to sue each other about human rights in the International Court of Justice, the number of cases on human rights being very small. As shown in Chapter 5, even within the Council of Europe, neighboring states with numerous common concerns do not often sue each other in the European

---

[2] Peter R. Baehr and Monique Castermans-Holleman, *The Role of Human Rights in Foreign Policy*, 3rd edn. (New York: Palgrave Macmillan, 2004), 69.

[3] Compare Jan Egeland, "Focus on Human Rights: Ineffective Big States, Potent Small States," *Journal of Peace Research*, 21, 3 (1984), and his *Impotent Superpower – Potent Small State: Potentialities and Limitations of Human Rights Objectives in the Foreign Policies of the United States and Norway* (Oslo: Norwegian University Press, 1988).

Court of Human Rights, the overwhelming number of cases being triggered by private rather than state complaint. The same pattern is evident with regard to the InterAmerican Court of Human Rights. Nevertheless, many states do address human rights issues in other states short of judicial proceedings. Sometimes this public diplomacy on human rights is primarily to embarrass enemies, as was true of East–West debates in the UN General Assembly during the Cold War. And sometimes taking a public position on human rights abroad is designed for domestic consumption, as was true of Henry Kissinger's public comments about the importance of human rights in South America – even as he was committing the USA to quiet support for repressive regimes. But sometimes states are genuinely interested in advancing rights abroad; and then they seriously think about ends and means.

Diplomatic means

There are a number of ways a state may utilize diplomacy to try to influence the policies of states violating human rights. The traditional, classical method has been that of "quiet" diplomacy, that is, to hold a confidential discussion behind closed doors and away from public view. Emissaries may meet with foreign officials to discuss a particular human rights situation or to request a halt to certain actions. This is sometimes a useful way to bring objections and matters of concern to the offending party without risk of widespread controversy or public outcry. Sometimes a target government will prove flexible if it can avoid the public appearance of caving in to foreign pressure. Quiet diplomacy is of course hard to track and evaluate, precisely because it may be some years before outsiders know what has transpired.

From time to time private diplomacy for human rights is then followed by public statements, as when President George W. Bush met with Russian president Vladimir Putin in early 2005. President Bush, having devoted his second inaugural address to the theme of freedom, could hardly not raise the subject of Russian policies at home and abroad that touched on human rights. And by all accounts there was some private attention to human rights in places like Chechnya and the Ukraine during this presidential summit.

But when the dialogue moves to the public arena, states undertaking a human rights discourse frequently meet "blowback" or negative reactions. State leaders who are subjected to public criticism often become defensive and inflexible in the name of national pride, state sovereignty, or because they have domestic elements who are "hard liners" about resisting foreign pressure. When in the 1970s the US Congress passed the

Jackson–Vanik Amendment publicly requiring greater emigration (freedom of movement) from Romania, the Soviet Union, and other European communist countries, the numbers of those allowed out actually dropped in the short term, as the target governments did not want to be seen caving in to US public pressure.

On the other hand, sometimes some public pressure can be productive, and the human rights NGOs that engage in the "naming and shaming" game can cite a number of situations in which public pressure brought some progressive gains over time. European state pressure on Turkey to improve its human rights record, in the context of the debate over Turkey's admission to the European Union, clearly had some beneficial effect.

Other essentially diplomatic steps can be undertaken, such as cancellation or postponement of ministerial visits or recall of ambassadors. This is likely to draw attention to the issue at hand, particularly when done by prominent states. In early February 2005, in the wake of the assassination of a former Lebanese prime minister, the United States recalled its ambassador to Syria, believing that state bore at least some measure of responsibility. The USA used the opportunity to criticize Syria for its lax border-control policies, its anti-democratic domestic practices, and what it felt was an unnecessary Syrian military presence in Lebanon. While Syria condemned the assassination and denied involvement, greater international attention was being paid to its policies, including human rights policies.[4]

The large number of intergovernmental agencies dealing with human rights means that member states are confronted almost daily about taking a diplomatic position on some human rights question. This is certainly true in the sprawling UN system, but also true in more limited IGOs like the OSCE, Council of Europe, and OAS. Even in the Commonwealth of Nations, formerly the British Commonwealth, there are occasions for voting on human rights issues pertaining, for example, to governmental violation of rights in Zimbabwe.[5] Former British colonies in Asia, a region with no human rights intergovernmental organization, are compelled to address human rights issues through the Commonwealth.

---

[4] See Steve R. Weissman, "Bush Considers Syria 'Out of Step' with Democracy," *International Herald Tribune*, February 19, 2005, www.iht.com/articles/2005/02/18/news/syria.html.

[5] See further Rhoda Howard-Hassmann, "Zimbabwe," in *Encyclopedia of Human Rights*, vol. V, 399–406; and see her longer analysis in "Mugabe's Zimbabwe, 2000–2009: Massive Human Rights Violations and the Failure to Protect," *Human Rights Quarterly*, 32, 4 (November 2010), 898–920.

Often less influential, though undeniably symbolic, are various cultural or sports-related embargoes enacted by states. For example, many states refused to participate in sporting events with South Africa under white minority rule to protest the country's policy of apartheid. These actions were generally supported by apartheid's victims and often found favor with public opinion in criticizing states – in part because one could take a stand for human rights without paying much price in national blood or treasure. While these sports and cultural boycotts did not by themselves lead to the end of apartheid, such policies made their contribution to the broader effort to delegitimize repressive minority rule. Given white South Africa's love of sports such as rugby and soccer (often called football outside the USA, of course), etc., some effective pressure from sports diplomacy could not be discounted even if it could not be scientifically documented. (How is one to measure the impact of John McEnroe refusing to play tennis in South Africa during apartheid?)

The diplomatic methods discussed above are used to protest or draw attention to particular human rights violations. It can be noted, too, that not all diplomatic techniques are negative in nature. States may offer ministerial visits or invite foreign diplomats or heads of state to visit in an effort to support a country's human rights policies. Governments may be invited to participate in international conferences or to join international organizations, such as the Council of Europe or the European Union, in order to influence human rights policy. Organizations like the EU do note the domestic human rights policies of member states. One of the reasons for expanding NATO membership was to integrate militarily certain former authoritarian states into an alliance for constitutional democracies.

While diplomatic means may or may not be effective by themselves, they can be linked to other steps.

Economic means

Governments are often reluctant to undertake economic sanctions against another state – whether for human rights or other reasons – as they may hurt themselves. One of the reasons Switzerland did not join the United Nations until 2004 was that the economic sanctions it had imposed on Mussolini's Italy as voted by the League of Nations damaged the Swiss economy as well as proving highly unpopular in Italian-speaking Switzerland. One of the reasons that the USA violated mandatory trade sanctions on the breakaway white minority government of Ian Smith in Rhodesia, now Zimbabwe, was the damage otherwise done to American businesses, particularly Union Carbide. Economic sanctions mostly cut both ways.

States, however, do sometimes suspend full trade, and also development aid or other types of foreign assistance. This may be done for lack of other appealing options – e.g., diplomacy alone has proven ineffective but military action is not desired. But this type of sanctioning can have unintended or unwanted effects.[6] Former UN Secretary-General Boutros Boutros-Ghali expressed this concern succinctly: "[Economic sanctions] raise the ethical question of whether suffering inflicted on vulnerable groups in the target country is a legitimate means of exerting pressure on political leaders whose behavior is unlikely to be affected by the plight of their subjects."[7] Indeed, virulent debate ensued during the 1990s regarding sanctions imposed on the people of Iraq, as authorized by the UN Security Council. Supporters of the sanctions pointed to their efficacy in making life difficult for Saddam Hussein's abusive regime, while critics stressed their destructive effects on the people of Iraq, notably children.[8] Eventually the UNSC voted to allow Iraq to sell some oil, using the proceeds supposedly to purchase goods necessary for the civilian population. But the Council failed to supervise the program effectively. Money was siphoned off to the Hussein regime, and other problems manifested themselves.[9] The sanctions were generally ineffective in compelling more moderate policies from Saddam's brutal regime. We now know, however, that Saddam altered his policies on weapons of mass destruction. It is not clear whether this change stemmed from the UN mandated weapons inspections system, as compared to economic and military pressures, or some combination of the three.[10]

Most general economic sanctions undoubtedly do not decisively affect the elite in the short term, because the rulers and associated social circles are well positioned to avoid inconvenience. Such sanctions have never brought down a repressive regime, and the overall success rate of general economic sanctions, according to various measures, has been estimated

---

[6] Boutros Boutros-Ghali, quoted in Baehr and Castermans-Holleman, *The Role of Human Rights*, 74.

[7] Ibid.

[8] David P. Forsythe, *The Humanitarians: The International Committee of the Red Cross* (Cambridge: Cambridge University Press, 2005). The private ICRC was the first to raise the alarm, followed by UN agencies such as UNICEF and WHO.

[9] While much commentary focused on "UN" failures and corruption, the main difficulty was that western states turned a blind eye to such things as black market trade and profiteering, since western allies Jordan and Turkey were the main beneficiaries.

[10] Jean Krasno and James S. Sutterlin, *The United Nations and Iraq: Defanging the Viper* (New York: Praeger, 2003).

at about 33 percent or lower.[11] On the other hand, "smart sanctions" have been tried on occasion in an effort to affect target governments while avoiding harm to civilian populations. In Haiti, for example, after general sanctions had been tried with predictable results, smart sanctions were applied to the military elite associated with Lt.-General Raoul Cedras, that group then blocking the return of the elected president, Father Aristide. These smart sanctions, closing off elite bank accounts and freedom to travel, contributed to the departure of Cedras and his entourage – along with promises of safe passage and comfortable life in exile. Smart sanctions have been either debated or adopted regarding other situations, for example with regard to the Sudanese government because of its policies pertaining to the Darfur region in 2005. They were applied to leaders of the Kaddafi regime in Libya during 2011 – and then relaxed for some of those who defected.

One overview of economic sanctions and human rights concludes that: (1) multilateral rather than unilateral sanctions are to be preferred; (2) negative punishment should be combined with positive inducements; (3) even smart sanctions usually fail to produce complete compliance with demands; (4) economic sanctions that last more than two years are rarely effective; (5) economic measures should probably be combined with military threats; and (6) both ends and means should be clear.[12]

As with diplomatic means, economic steps do not have to be negative in nature. States may often provide loans or credits to governments who are willing to adopt measures conducive to human rights protection. Most liberal democracies, as well as the IGOs that they influence, manifest democracy promotion programs in order to provide economic and technical assistance to certain transitional states. The funding is used to sponsor and supervise free and fair elections, state-building (for example, the construction of vigorous parliaments and independent courts), and nation-building (for example, encouraging an active and rights-supportive civil society). At the time of writing western states were undertaking unilateral and multilateral democracy promotion and other rights-protective policies costing hundreds of millions of dollars in foreign assistance.

Military means

Finally, there is a range of military steps available at least to those states with effective military establishments. The most dramatic measure is

---

[11] George Lopez, "Economic Sanctions," in *Encyclopedia of Human Rights*, vol. II, 82–87.
[12] Ibid.

that of coercive military action. When undertaken without UN Security Council approval, such action is highly controversial, as seen by NATO's bombing of Serbia in 1999 to try to stop violent persecution and forced displacement of the ethnic Albanians constituting a majority of the Kosovars.

There is certainly the longstanding problem that states may claim to be engaged in "humanitarian intervention" whereas in reality they have other primary motives. The US-initiated war in Iraq from 2003, though it may have produced some positive long-term consequences for human rights there, along with many human rights problems, should not be defined as a humanitarian intervention. True, by 2005 the George W. Bush Administration's main justification for the war was advancing democracy. But the foundations for the war were steeped in the rhetoric of national security. At the time of the US invasion Washington argued that Iraq had ties to terrorist groups such as Al Qaeda, that it possessed illegal weapons of mass destruction, and that the Hussein regime needed to be removed because of future security problems. As Peter Baehr and Monique Castermans-Holleman note, however, "This regime had for a number of years been guilty of human rights violations, but to put an end to these violations was not [initially] mentioned as a main objective of military action."[13]

There have been numerous cases of "mixed motives" regarding the use of force in other states without UN approval. In 1971 India used force to stop Pakistan's Punjabi-dominated elites from slaughtering Bengalis, and in the process took the opportunity to weaken rival Pakistan by creating Bangladesh. In 1979 Tanzania used force to drive out the murderous Idi Amin from Uganda, after he had made a military incursion into Tanzania, which resulted in rule by the equally dictatorial but relatively more moderate Milton Obote. Also in 1979 Vietnam used force to topple the genocidal regime of the Khmer Rouge in Cambodia, then installed the pro-Vietnamese and anti-Chinese Hun Sen as leader. It is not just various western interventions over the years (by the Americans, British, and French, for example) that have made claims to humanitarian intervention so controversial.

There have not been many clear-cut cases of "humanitarian war." Most states have been reluctant to spill national blood for the protection of the rights of "others," and it is especially hard to justify such uses of force at home when loss of life by the intervening state(s) is not linked to traditional notions of security. Moreover, humanitarian intervention almost always makes the situation worse in terms of human costs in the short

[13] Baehr and Castermans-Holleman, *The Role of Human Rights*, 80.

run. NATO's bombing of Serbia in 1999 was initially met with Belgrade's expanded persecution and displacement of Albanian Kosovars.

Less controversial, at least initially, than unauthorized state military action in the name of human rights protection is state military support for a UN Security Council resolution designed to alleviate human rights problems. As discussed in earlier chapters, this may take the form of an enforcement or peacekeeping field operation. As already noted in Chapter 3, after the Cold War these multilateral security missions almost always entailed a human rights dimension. Whether these field operations were designed to be coercive, evolved into coercion, or remained mostly a matter of armed diplomacy, states were at the center of action. It was states in the UN Security Council that authorized the deployment, states that contributed the troops, and often states that pressed for termination of mission when difficulties occurred. In 2011 member states of the UN Security Council passed Resolution 1973 authorizing states to take "all necessary measures" to protect civilians in Libya: it was then states which chose the strategy and tactics of military action that implemented this vague resolution, which as usual contained no measure of follow-on supervision by any UN body. "The UN" had acted, but it was states that controlled developments. Furthermore, it was states that were responsible to see that military personnel were trained in international humanitarian law, and states that (perhaps) prosecuted military personnel who engaged in sex trafficking or other crimes.

As with diplomatic and economic means, there was a positive side to military options. I have already mentioned one reason for expansion of NATO membership, namely to shore up transitional democracies by linking them to more established democracies. Bilaterally, states may choose to expand military assistance to reward another state for democratic and rights reform. In 2005 the USA expanded military assistance to Guatemala, partly in response to some rights-protective reforms in that state. (At the same time the USA reduced military assistance to some states supportive of the ICC, thus using military assistance to try to undercut certain judicial developments.)

US foreign policy and human rights

To a great extent a state's foreign policy on human rights is bound up with its version of nationalism, which is to say with a nation's collective self-image, which is to say with its informal ideology. Since many nations in the past have thought well of themselves, many states' policies on human rights reflect the conviction that the state has some virtuous point to teach others. As Britain, France, Russia, and others extended their power in the nineteenth century, through formal colonialism or otherwise, they saw themselves as doing God's work in bringing a superior civilization to the inferior (and non-white) peoples of the world. As a matter of fact, this spreading of a "superior" civilization supposedly featuring freedom and the rule of law was accompanied by various atrocities.[14] When local attitudes were not very appreciative of the "benefits" of outside rule, the western response was not exactly charitable, but periodically vindictive toward the "unruly natives." In this sense we can understand why it has been written that American exceptionalism is not so exceptional: others, too, have seen themselves as exceptionally good and hence superior to others.

American exceptionalism

In the case of the United States, to understand the place of human rights in foreign policy it is initially important to understand that many in the elite and mass public view the USA as a beacon of freedom to the world. The notion of American exceptionalism is well known, but its precise application in public policy is open to various constructions.[15] Human rights in foreign policy is often a matter of Washington pressing others to improve personal and political freedom.[16]

Particularly for American ultra-nationalists, a powerful force in modern American politics since about 1980, human rights was equated with personal freedom as found in the US Bill of Rights appended to its constitution, and not with the broader and more complex conception found in the International Bill of Rights (as indicated, this means the UN Charter, the Universal Declaration, and the 1966 International Covenants on Civil-Political and Socio-Economic-Cultural Rights). Particularly the Ronald Reagan and George W. Bush Administrations – whether one calls them romantic nationalists, chauvinist nationalists, providential nationalists, Jacksonian nationalists, militant American exceptionalists, crusading neo-conservatives, nativists, or some other label – certainly did not try

---

[14] See, e.g., Peter Hopkirk, *The Great Game: The Struggle for Empire in Central Asia* (New York: Kodansha International, 1990, 1992). See also Juan Cole, *Napoleon's Egypt: Invading the Middle East* (Basingstroke: Palgrave Macmillan, 2007). See further Casper W. Erichsen, "Namibia: Germany's Colonial Wars Against the Herero and Nama," in *Encyclopedia of Human Rights*, vol. IV, 17–27.

[15] From a substantial literature, see especially Michael Ignatieff, ed., *American Exceptionalism and Human Rights* (Princeton: Princeton University Press, 2005). See also Tony Smith, *America's Mission: The Worldwide Struggle for Democracy in the Twentieth Century* (Princeton: Princeton University Press, 1995).

[16] See further David P. Forsythe, "Human Rights and US Foreign Policy: Situating Obama," *Human Rights Quarterly* 33, 3 (August 2011), 767–789.

to use internationally recognized human rights to improve US policies. Being disdainful of international law, they often preferred a strictly American conception of human rights in order to bypass many international rights standards and implementing agencies.[17]

More generally, from the early settlers in New England to the powerful Goldwater–Reagan–George W. Bush wing of the Republican Party in contemporary times, important political circles have seen the USA not as an ordinary nation but as a great experiment in personal liberty that has implications for the planet.[18] Well-known defects in American society such as a history of slavery, segregation, racist immigration laws, anti-Semitism, religious and other bigotry, gender discrimination, and grinding poverty have failed to alter this dominant self-image. American exceptionalism, the belief in the exceptional freedom and goodness of the American people, is the core of the dominant American political culture.[19]

The continuing strength of American exceptionalism should not necessarily be equated with an automatic crusade for human rights in US foreign policy. The belief in American greatness, as linked to personal freedom, can lead to involvement or isolationism. Two underlying schools of thought have long competed for control of US foreign policy. The first, associated with Washington, Jefferson, and Patrick Buchanan, would perfect American society at home and thus provide international leadership mainly by indirect example. This school was clearly dominant in the Congress in the 1930s. The second, associated with Hamilton and most presidents since Woodrow Wilson, would have the USA actively involved in world affairs – on the assumption that US impact would be for the better.[20] All modern presidents have manifested an activist foreign policy, including on human rights (to varying degrees). This activist stance leaves open the question of the general nature of decisions: realist, liberal, or "neo-con."

American exceptionalism does not so much guarantee specific foreign policy initiatives as it predisposes Washington to talk about freedom and democracy and to assume it can make a difference for the better when and if it gets involved. The American public and Congress were

---

[17] See further David P. Forsythe, *The Politics of Prisoner Abuse: The US and Enemy Prisoners After 9/11* (Cambridge: Cambridge University Press, 2011), ch. 2.

[18] T. Davis and S. Lynn-Jones, "City upon a Hill," *Foreign Policy*, 66 (1987), 20–38.

[19] See further David P. Forsythe, *American Exceptionalism and Global Human Rights* (Lincoln: University of Nebraska Distinguished Lecture Series, 1999); and Forsythe, "Human Rights and US Foreign Policy: Two Levels, Two Worlds," in David Beetham, ed., *Politics and Human Rights* (Oxford: Blackwell, 1995), 111–130.

[20] See Michael H. Hunt, *Ideology and US Foreign Policy* (New Haven: Yale University Press, 1987).

deferential if not supportive in 1992 when President Bush deployed military force to guarantee the secure delivery of humanitarian assistance in Somalia. But after difficulties there, especially in 1993, the American public and Congress were content not only to withdraw from Somalia but also to avoid military intervention in Rwanda during 1994. The Vietnam syndrome, now supplemented by Somalia, occasionally or inconsistently puts a brake on direct US military intervention by reminding of the complexity of deep involvement abroad. The prolonged and bloody engagement in Iraq from 2003 to 2009 reinforced those earlier experiences. Military operations for advancement of human rights in places such as Haiti, Bosnia, and Kosovo could only be sustained because combat casualties were avoided. But the more fundamental faith in American greatness as a symbol of freedom is alive and reasonably well, as shown by President Barack Obama's rhetoric (covered below).

Events in Serbian Kosovo can be understood against this background. The United States felt the moral obligation to oppose the 1999 repression and expulsion of ethnic Albanians, a Serbian policy that also contested NATO's hegemony and somewhat destabilized other European states, but fear of casualties caused the Clinton Administration and NATO to adopt the military strategy of high-altitude air strikes without ground troops. This approach failed to protect the Albanian Kosovars in the short term, contributed to continuing destabilizing pressures on neighboring states, and solidified Serb opinion behind the Milosevic government. But, in the long term, as noted in Chapter 5, the United States and NATO weakened Milosevic's ability to persecute the Albanian Kosovars, and weakened his power in Belgrade. In a quite remarkable if controversial military operation, Washington led NATO in using military force to protect human rights but without suffering more casualties (and civilian damage abroad) than domestic opinion would tolerate. (In fact, no NATO pilots were killed or captured during eleven weeks of bombings.) It was a delicate balancing act: to act militarily primarily for human rights abroad but maintain domestic support for an operation not linked to traditional security concerns. (Congress never voted yea or nay on the military venture.)[21]

US foreign policy toward Libya in 2011 fits well with themes discussed here. President Obama appealed to American exceptionalism in his televised national address on March 28, saying that, while other nations might be able to stand aside if Kaddafi threatened atrocities, the USA could not.[22] Bill Clinton's failure to stop the Rwandan genocide in 1994

---

[21] Ryan C. Hendrickson, *The Clinton Wars: The Constitution, Congress, and War Powers* (Nashville: Vanderbilt University Press, 2002).
[22] See www.whitehouse.gov/photos-and.../president-obama-s-speech-libya.

was a dark cloud in Obama's White House. But Obama then noted that military action, presumably to protect Libyan civilians, was occurring under UN mandate. American exceptionalism was thus combined with multilateral approval, hence presumably doubly legitimate. Actual military operations, whether led by the USA or NATO, were conducted with considerable prudence, both to avoid casualties and to avoid public responsibility for "regime change" and hence a possible long and costly involvement. The situation continued at the time of writing, with layers of policy. The "real" policy was indeed regime change, with western states trying to induce defections from the Kaddafi inner circle and hence the collapse of the regime. But the only way to get a UN mandate for military intervention (even with China, Russia, Germany, India, and Brazil abstaining in the Security Council vote) was to argue that the military operation was only to protect civilians. Of course some civilians were, in reality, fighters for the rebellion, so outside involvement to protect civilians inherently worked to enhance armed opposition to the government.

In sum to this point, one finds in US foreign policy on human rights much rhetoric about American exceptionalism – about a special US role to be active on human rights and democracy. But this periodic rhetoric does not always guarantee action (recall Rwanda) nor does it mean that the attentive public and elites in Washington are prepared to easily incur costs to protect the rights of others.[23] (The pattern of liberal rhetoric but realist hesitations is prevalent among liberal democracies. When Belgium suffered a few casualties in the early days of the 1994 Rwandan tragedy [about the same number as the USA suffered in Somalia in 1993], that state withdrew its remaining personnel and did not directly contest the genocide. When the Netherlands suffered one military fatality prior to the massacre at Srebrenica, Bosnia, in 1995, it withdrew its remaining personnel from a UN field operation and did not directly contest the ensuing genocide.)

More on bold rhetoric but limited measures

Even before the Libyan intervention, current public opinion on rights in US foreign policy indicated a blend of liberalism and realism – of universal concern for others and narrow self-interest. Polls showed that the general public as well as opinion leaders did indeed list "promoting and

---

[23] See further Julie A. Mertus, *Bait and Switch: Human Rights and US Foreign Policy* (New York and London: Routledge, 2004). See also Eric A. Heinze, "The Rhetoric of Genocide and US Foreign Policy: Rwanda and Darfur Compared," *Political Science Quarterly* 122, 3 (2007), 359–383. The George W. Bush Administration, having come to the conclusion of genocide in Darfur, still found reasons to avoid direct and major action in response.

defending human rights in other countries," as well as "helping to bring a democratic form of government to other nations" as "very important" goals of US foreign policy. But in 1995 these goals were in thirteenth and fourteenth place, respectively, with only 34 percent and 25 percent of the general public listing them as very important. Eighty percent or more of the general public listed "stopping the flow of illegal drugs into the USA," "protecting the jobs of American workers," and "preventing the spread of nuclear weapons" as much more important. Analysts concluded that there was considerable American popular support for pragmatic internationalism, but not a great deal of support for moral internationalism.[24] If human rights could be linked to self-interest, or if human rights do not interfere with self-interest, one could build a political coalition for action. But if one made only moral and altruistic arguments, it was difficult to sustain a principled foreign policy centering on rights. With regard to Kosovo, American public opinion was permissive as long as significant numbers of American casualties were avoided. But in the spring of 1999 polls showed that almost two-thirds of the public were in favor of early negotiations to end the NATO air strikes.

Public opinion polls in 2005 showed that in general or in the abstract, American public support for military means to advance democracy abroad was relatively low. It seemed very clear that had the George W. Bush Administration gone to the public and Congress in 2003 and asked for a mandate to use force to advance democracy in Iraq, that would have been a hard sell for the president. The actual rationale for that war was national security – links to terrorism, weapons of mass destruction, and general security fears for the future. It was only after clarification of facts – no substantive Hussein links to Al Qaeda, no weapons of mass destruction, and hence no clear and present security danger – that the Bush Administration stressed the role of advancing democracy in Iraq. Movement toward democracy in Iraq and Saddam Hussein being on trial and executed did not save George W. Bush from very low public approval at home regarding his Iraq policy during the last few years of his presidency.

Because of American exceptionalism, as well as a legal culture, Washington is full of private groups that lobby for some version of human rights abroad.[25] This subject is treated in detail in Chapter 7. The national

---

[24] Ole Holsti, "Public Opinion on Human Rights in American Foreign Policy," in David P. Forsythe, ed., *The United States and Human Rights: Looking Inward and Outward* (Lincoln: University of Nebraska Press, 2000).

[25] The USA manifests no national institute of human rights, as do several European states, to serve as a transmission belt between international norms and national policies on human rights. It has a Civil Rights Commission, but that body rarely takes an

communications media also report on international human rights issues with some regularity. But many of the human rights NGOs regularly bemoaned their inability to stimulate more action, and more consistent action, for rights in US foreign policy.[26] The polls cited above indicate why. There is no grassroots movement supportive of a costly crusade for human rights abroad. While "the CNN factor" was given some credit for pushing the USA into action in both northern Iraq (the flight of Kurds) and Somalia (domestic starvation and disorder), both Rwanda in 1994 and what was then Zaire (now Democratic Congo) in 1997, showed that Washington was not always moved to action by media coverage of human rights violations and humanitarian hardship. With regard to Kosovo, media pictures of trainloads of ethnic Albanians being forced from their homes, and other reports of refugee hardships, probably had something to do with western support for air strikes on Serbia despite mistakes and collateral damage. But those pictures did not cause a public demand for ground troops and costly humanitarian intervention in terms of soldiers' lives.

Similar commentary could be made about "the Arab Spring" or the "Arab awakening" in early 2011. Street protests in the name of human rights and democracy (and better economic opportunity) resulted in much media coverage, with Arab (and Iranian) repressive elites trying to shut off television and social media coverage. The Obama foreign policy team selectively and inconsistently aligned the USA with democratic change in places such as Tunisia and Egypt and belatedly Yemen (but not so clearly in Bahrain or Syria). In Libya, as noted, western military opposition to Kaddafi's policies was careful in trying not to entail western casualties and prolonged responsibilities. Obama faced fractured domestic opinion: some supported limited involvement, some wanted more open pursuit of regime change, some were critical of further military operations in the wake of fighting in Afghanistan and Iraq (and huge budget deficits at home). As per Rwanda, American media reported on atrocities in Syria, but the domestic pressure to intervene there was slight, partially because of military involvements elsewhere.

---

international approach to its limited subject. See further Julie Mertus, *Human Rights Matters: Local Politics and National Human Rights Institutions* (Stanford: Stanford University Press, 2009). See also Thomas Pegrane, "Diffusion Across Political Systems: The Global Spread of National Human Rights Institutions," *Human Rights Quarterly*, 32, 3 (August 2010), 471–501.

[26] Aryeh Neier, "The New Double Standard," *Foreign Policy*, 105 (1996–1997), 91–102; and Ellen Dorsey, "US Foreign Policy and the Human Rights Movement," in Forsythe, ed., *The United States and Human Rights*.

Samantha Power, who reportedly had some influence on Obama's decision to intervene in Libya, has shown that throughout its modern history, when the USA has faced situations of genocide or near-genocide abroad, there has never been a powerful domestic push from public opinion or Congress forcing the president into a decisive involvement. Presidents have felt free to pursue mostly realist policies of narrow self-interest, rather than liberal policies of protecting the rights of others.[27] When involvements have occurred more recently largely for human rights reasons in places such as Somalia (1992), Kosovo (1999), and Libya (2011), care has been taken to try to limit US casualties and other costs, as noted. As Obama mentioned in his television address on Libya, US involvement in Iraq from 2003 had cost at least one trillion dollars and many American and Iraqi lives. Hence Obama's intervention in Libya was no crusade to be pursued regardless of cost. Moreover, the Obama team, like the British government, tried to cast the Libyan intervention sometimes in self-interested terms – that it was in the national interest to be on the side of democratic change in the Arab world.

To take one further concrete example, the matter of religious persecution abroad is instructive regarding US foreign policy and human rights – and the blending of ethical consideration with self-interest. The subject of religious freedom has a nice ring to it in American society, founded partly as it was to secure freedom from religious bigotry in Europe. In the 1990s, especially social conservatives pushed hard to elevate the subject of religious freedom in US foreign policy. But a number of pragmatic conservatives, as well as some international liberals, objected to the bills introduced in Congress. These bills called for automatic sanctions against countries engaging in, or tolerating, religious persecution. As such, these bills would have created sanctions on such US allies as Saudi Arabia, Israel, Greece, Pakistan, etc. Only when the bills were weakened so as to give the president considerable discretion in dealing with religious persecution abroad did a law finally pass. So there was more attention to religious freedom in US foreign policy, and a new office for such was created in the State Department. But there was also concern not to interfere very much with traditional US economic and strategic interests.[28] Some religious conservatives had teamed with some secular liberals to produce more attention to religious freedom and religious persecution, but traditional self-interest in economic and security matters was hardly absent.[29]

---

[27] Samantha Power, *"A Problem From Hell": America and the Age of Genocide* (New York: Basic Books, 2002).

[28] See further Eric Schmitt, "Bill to Punish Nations Limiting Religious Beliefs Passes Senate," *New York Times*, October 10, 1998, A3.

[29] See further Allen D. Hertzke, *Freeing God's Children: The Unlikely Alliance for Global Human Rights* (New York: Rowman & Littlefield, 2004); and Felice Gaer, "Religious

Recent administrations

There is much more to say about modern diplomatic history pertaining to the USA and human rights. Space limitations impose considerable brevity. First of all, presidents do not have a free hand on this issue; Congress asserts itself periodically. It was Congress during the early Eisenhower Administration that forced the USA to abandon a high-profile posture on internationally recognized human rights, a conservative Congress being caught up in the hysteria of McCarthyism and seeing universal human rights as a subversive foreign influence. It was then Congress toward the end of the Nixon Administration that reintroduced human rights into the US foreign policy agenda, a Democratic Congress wanting to characterize the Nixon–Kissinger period as lacking in ethical values.[30] It was Congress, not Jimmy Carter, that first insisted on more attention to human rights abroad in the 1970s, and it was Congress, not Carter, that created a new human rights bureau in the State Department.

Second, particularly since the mid-1970s all presidents have had to fashion some sort of policy on human rights in world affairs, that subject being institutionalized at the UN and other international organizations, and Congress often being inclined to track developments.[31] Jimmy Carter (President 1977–1981), building on congressional developments, promised to make human rights the cornerstone of his foreign policy, a promise he largely abandoned after the Soviet invasion of Afghanistan in 1979. For his part Ronald Reagan (1981–1989) first attempted to collapse his human rights policy into his anti-communist orientation, but wound up reaching compromise with the Democrats on a bipartisan approach to democracy promotion, and on backing away from full support of anti-communist dictators such as Marcos in the Philippines and Pinochet in Chile.[32]

Giving somewhat more detailed treatment to later developments, we find that President Clinton's rhetoric on foreign policy, although spasmodically delivered, was squarely within the activist tradition of American exceptionalism. Enlarging the global democratic community was

---

Freedom," in *Encyclopedia of Human Rights*, vol. IV, 323–329, where one also finds brief discussion of US foreign policy on this issue.

[30] See further David P. Forsythe, *Human Rights and US Foreign Policy: Congress Reconsidered* (Gainesville: University Press of Florida, 1988).

[31] Once the USA became a party to treaties on human rights and humanitarian affairs, the domestic political process was altered to some extent, with various domestic groups making appeal to the treaties' provisions both in Congress and in the courts. See further Beth A. Simmons, *Mobilizing for Human Rights: International Law in Domestic Politics* (Cambridge: Cambridge University Press, 2009).

[32] A short summary can be found in Forsythe, "Human Rights and US Foreign Policy: Two Levels, Two Worlds."

supposedly one of the basic pillars of his foreign policy. The semantic emphasis was on personal freedom and democracy. He justified US
troops in Bosnia by saying Washington must lead, must hold the feet of
the European allies to the fire, must make a difference for a liberal democratic peace with human rights in the Balkans. The 1995 Dayton agreement was not just about peace, but about liberal democracy and human
rights. There was strong Clinton talk in support of human rights: for universal rights at the UN Vienna Conference on Human Rights in 1993,
which created the post of UN High Commissioner for Human Rights;
for criminal prosecutions at The Hague in the International Criminal
Tribunal for the former Yugoslavia; for containment of repressive states
such as Sudan, Iraq, and Iran; for sanctions on Burma/Myanmar. As
long as one did not have to pay a high national price, in blood or treasure, to advance human rights, the Clinton Administration was certainly
for them – at least for the civil and political rights congruent with the
American self-image. These were the rights stressed in Clinton's 1998
visit to China.

Self-interested economic and strategic concerns, however, were hardly
absent from US foreign policy during the Clinton era. His first Assistant
Secretary of State for human rights, John Shattuck, contemplated resign-
ing several times in frustration over the lack of systematic commitment
to human rights.[33] Not only did the Clinton Administration not intervene to stop genocide in Rwanda in 1994, after strong domestic criticism
concerning loss of American life in Somalia, but also that administration delinked trading privileges from basic civil and political rights in
China. Clinton's argument on that issue, not without reason, was that a
strong defensive nationalism prevailed in China, and thus the only route
to progress on human rights lay in economic growth and a larger middle
class over time. Presumably, when that middle class had met its basic
needs, it would then demand more personal and political freedoms.

President George W. Bush's foreign policy also stressed American
exceptionalism as its guiding principle, but in a way very different from
the Clinton era. Rhetoric promoting American ideals – namely freedom
and liberty – was omnipresent in his speeches, especially his second inaugural address.[34] Despite the originally declared justifications for invading
Iraq in 2003, which had little to do with human rights and much to do
with claims to national security, the president's post-war language was

---

[33] John Shattuck, *Freedom on Fire: Human Rights Wars and America's Response* (Cambridge,
MA: Harvard University Press, 2003).
[34] See georgewbush-whitehouse.archives.gov/news/releases/2005/01/images/20050120-1_
p44289.

replete with references to democracy and personal freedom. Whereas during his first term George W. Bush paid hardly any discernible attention to the decline of democracy in Russia, during the second term Bush himself laid great public and private stress on precisely that topic. Increasingly George W. Bush went beyond Clinton's rhetorical but sporadic forays into the human rights domain. Increasingly the Republican Bush took on the political coloring of a Jimmy Carter or a Woodrow Wilson to stress the advancement of democracy, and its civil and political rights, as a central pillar of his foreign policy.

A year after the September 11 terrorist attacks, the Bush Administration had presented its National Security Strategy statement, outlining a foreign policy with much semantic attention to personal rights. "Human rights" was not a privileged phrase, but freedom and democracy were. While the first major section of the outline declared an intention to "Champion Aspirations for Human Dignity," it was also the strategy's shortest portion, other than its initial outline.[35] References to "human rights" can be found sparsely strung about the document, but even more apparent were references to "human dignity." Throughout the document, "human rights" was offered as a vague matter to be dealt with by other states, while "human dignity" was outlined in substantial detail: "the rule of law; limits on the absolute power of the state; free speech; freedom of worship; equal justice; respect for women; religious and ethnic tolerance; and respect for private property."[36] Norms such as free speech, freedom of worship, and respect for private property are all values firmly embedded in American political discourse. "Human rights" abroad inevitably gets one into the domain of international law and organization, and in general this is not what the Bush Administration wanted to emphasize. The Bush team, much more so than the Clinton team, was in favor of unilateral assertions of hard power, as many commentators recognized.

Like all administrations, Bush foreign policy gave rhetorical emphasis to a freedom agenda and democracy promotion. And there was some substance behind the words. But also like other administrations, the Bush team continued close relations with a number of autocrats, notably the long-time dictator, Hosni Mubarak, in Egypt. Thus on the one hand Bush foreign policy claimed to be using the invasion of Iraq to start falling dominoes in favor of democracy in the Middle East. On the other hand the Bush team did not pressure Mubarak and other authoritarian

---

[35] See "The National Security Strategy of the United States of America," www.whitehouse.gov/nsc/nss.html.
[36] See further Mertus, *Bait and Switch*, 59.

allies to liberalize their political systems, much less to move toward genuine democracy. That would only come from the Arab street in 2011, an indigenous and largely secular regional movement that almost never mentioned developments in Iraq.

As for the Obama Administration at the time of writing, there was both continuity and change on human rights compared to the Bush II years. In the electoral campaign of 2008, human rights in foreign policy was not a leading issue, the country prioritizing concerns about economic recession. Candidate Obama did criticize the Republican Administration for sacrificing American values on the altar of national security.

As for change, President Obama undertook a high-profile stance to disassociate the USA from torture and cruel treatment of security prisoners. The Bush team, led by Vice President Richard Cheney, had gone to the "dark side" after 9/11 on grounds of national security, engaging in policies in CIA secret prisons that the International Committee of the Red Cross termed torture and inhuman treatment. At the Guantanamo prison facility on the island of Cuba, under military jurisdiction, and at other military prisons, there had also been torture and inhuman treatment, so characterized by some US military and legal officials.[37] On other issues one could also see some change, as in the Obama decision to rejoin (stand for election to) the UN Human Rights Council, boycotted by the previous Administration for its lack of evenhanded policies (mainly concerning Israel). The matter of new US policies concerning the Arab Spring of 2011 has already been noted, as Obama did slowly align the USA with democratic change in certain countries but not in others.

But there was much continuity as well. Some continuity was compelled by Congress despite Obama's wishes, such as in the continued operation of the Guantanamo prison for security prisoners, and the use of military commissions and administrative detention there as well. Some continuity came from the Obama team itself, as in efforts to keep courts from reviewing various prisoner claims of mistreatment. Initially the Obama Administration downplayed human rights issues in China, until NGO criticism and media coverage required increasing attention to rights there. Also regarding Russia, the Obama emphasis was on securing Moscow's cooperation on a variety of issues such as Iranian nuclear weapons, not on its backsliding on human rights in Russian domestic and foreign policy.

The fact was that across various administrations, with all being activist in foreign policy, and regardless of aspirations to being realist or liberal

---

[37] For overviews, see James P. Pfiffner, *Torture as Public Policy: Restoring US Credibility on the World Stage* (Boulder: Paradigm, 2010); and Forsythe, *Politics of Prisoner Abuse.*

or some version of ultra-nationalist, the balance sheet regarding human rights was normally very mixed with much inconsistency and muddling through. This was inherent in the subject, with many internationally recognized human rights, many countries and organizations on the US foreign policy agenda, many different conceptions of US interests, and much shifting domestic concern and pressure. Nixon and Bush I were not consistently realist, Clinton and Obama were not consistently liberal, and Reagan and Bush II were not consistently neo-conservative.[38] Some distinctions held up over time. For example, liberals gave greater weight to international law and organization, compared to realists and neo-cons.

Further observations

Further analysis reveals a major soft spot in the contemporary US approach to human rights, regardless of changing administrations. The USA, unlike all other developed democracies, refuses to accept cultural, economic, and social rights as real human rights. When the USA talks about its support for the Universal Declaration of Human Rights, it simply omits reference to those articles endorsing fundamental rights to adequate standards of food, clothing, shelter, health care, and social security. It has never ratified the International Covenant on Economic, Social, and Cultural Rights. Federal laws, and most internal state laws, do not provide for socioeconomic fundamental entitlements, as compared with optional benefits. There is no recognized right to health care, much less a recognized right to adequate food, clothing, and shelter. The USA is one of the few states not to adhere to the UN Convention on the Rights of the Child. The Convention appears to make encroachments on family privacy, arguably protected by the US Constitution. The Clinton Administration did rhetorically accept the right to development at the 1998 UN Vienna Conference on Human Rights, but this posture has been of no practical consequence.

The USA continues to exclusively emphasize civil and political rights, including the civil right to private property. But even on this subject the US support for international standards is highly qualified. The Senate has added many reservations, declarations, and understandings to its 1992 consent to the International Covenant on Civil and Political Rights (as well as failing to accept the Optional Protocol that would allow individual complaints about violations). It is clear the USA continues to emphasize

---

[38] See further Forsythe, "Situating Obama." On inconsistent US policies in Latin America, see Kathryn Sikkink, *Mixed Signals: US Human Rights Policy and Latin America* (Ithaca: Cornell University Press, for the Century Foundation, 2004).

a narrower national law rather than a broader international law of human rights. Even some of its international partners, like the Netherlands, have criticized this US orientation. It is well known that a number of Canadians view the US version of market democracy as unnecessarily harsh, overly individualized, and lacking in a sense of community.[39] Nevertheless, a powerful segment of the American political class remains strongly opposed to the "European nanny state." The phrase "social democracy" is a pejorative term in those circles of opinion. In the Republican Party in particular, the rhetorical emphasis continued to be on personal liberty and shrinking government, even if in reality both Reagan and Bush II expanded federal programs and federal deficit spending – while the latter Administration favored government bailouts to big investment banks in the major recession of 2008.

There are three strong points to recent US foreign policy on rights abroad. First, as noted in Chapter 3, all US administrations after the Cold War have led – albeit inconsistently – in expanding the scope of Chapter VII of the UN Charter, involving matters on which the Council can take a binding decision. As a result of US policy in the UN Security Council when dealing with northern Iraq, Somalia, Bosnia, Haiti, Rwanda, Angola, and Libya in 2011, the Council has effectively decided that the security of persons inside states can constitute a threat to international peace and security, leading to authoritative protection attempts by the international community. Deployments of military force, limited combat, economic sanctions, and deeply intrusive diplomacy have all occurred in recent years in relation to human rights issues under Chapter VII. International law still provides no doctrine of humanitarian intervention, although from 2005 one has the vague endorsement of R2P, as already noted, but the concept of international peace and security has been expanded to substitute for this lack. The USA has led in shrinking the domain of exclusive domestic jurisdiction, and in expanding the realm of authoritative decisions by the Council. This is a promising trend, at least in theory, for the international protection of human rights. In terms of sequence, UNSC decisions as they evolved after the Cold War in the 1990s laid the foundation for the adoption of R2P in 2005 – the responsibility to protect by outsiders, if a state proved unwilling or unable to protect the rights of its citizens. This was the diplomatic (and legal) background for events during 2011 in places like Libya and Ivory Coast where outside parties did indeed take forceful action to advance human rights concerns under UN mandate.

[39] Rhoda E. Howard, *Human Rights and the Search for Community* (Boulder: Westview, 1995).

Second, also noted in Chapter 3, the USA has also led in expanding the notion of peacekeeping so as to provide complex or second-generation peacekeeping with human rights dimensions. In places like Namibia, El Salvador, Cambodia, Guatemala, and Bosnia, and Sudan, *inter alia*, the USA has encouraged UN and other field missions under Chapter VI of the Charter not simply to oversee a cease-fire or other military agreement, but more broadly to try to establish and consolidate a liberal democratic peace. As might be expected, the actual record of results is mixed. There has been more success in Namibia and El Salvador than in Cambodia and Bosnia. Nevertheless, Washington has been a leader in these developments particularly where the local protagonists show signs of good faith efforts to reach and implement international agreements.[40] The trend continued in 2005, with the US encouraging a UN security operation in Sudan, long wracked by violence and instability and atrocities in the Darfur region, once it became clear that the African Union would not be able to decisively improve the situation. There was also a small UN security operation in the Democratic Republic of the Congo.

Third, as noted in Chapter 4, the USA led in the resurrection of the idea of international criminal courts, dormant since the 1940s at Nuremberg and Tokyo. True, as we saw in an earlier chapter, when the US-led Security Council created the 1993 *ad hoc* court for former Yugoslavia and the 1995 *ad hoc* court for Rwanda, it was searching for action that would not entail costly military intervention. The two courts were as much the product of escape from responsibility as of commitment to legal justice for gross violations of human rights such as grave breaches of the laws of war, crimes against humanity, and genocide. Be that as it may, the USA has contributed more money and personnel to particularly the Yugoslav court than any other state.

US support for an independent and authoritative standing UN criminal court, however, is an entirely different matter. Whereas President Clinton had signed the Rome Statute to keep the USA engaged in various negotiations about the ICC, President George W. Bush's opposition to the new court was so strong that he took the unprecedented step of "unsigning" that legal document. The Bush II Administration, like the Reagan Administration before it, was very clear in its hostility to many international agreements, including human rights agreements. For the

---

[40] See further David P. Forsythe, "Human Rights and International Security: United Nations Field Operations Redux," in M. Castermans, et al., eds., *The Role of the Nation State in the 21st Century* (Dordrecht: Kluwer, 1998), 265–276.

most part it was highly skeptical of supranational authority and international adjudication. Only on trade matters, centered on the WTO, did US governments allow an international organization to authoritatively review US policies. In 2005, however, the US did allow the UN Security Council to pass a resolution allowing the ICC prosecutor to conduct investigations of individual criminal responsibility by Sudanese leaders for atrocities in the Darfur region. Rather then vetoing that resolution the USA abstained. This action suggested that Washington might tolerate the ICC as long as US nationals were exempted from its jurisdiction. The Obama Administration followed up this shift in Bush II policies by continuing quiet cooperation with the ICC as long as there was no likelihood of Americans being defendants in that court. These and other developments caused the USA to back away from using the pressure of military assistance agreements to undermine the ICC.

Overall, and consistent with the analysis above, US foreign policy on human rights after the Cold War reflects a number of contradictions. The USA rhetorically supports universal human rights with great enthusiasm, but reserves to itself the practice of national particularism (elevation of national over international law, no socioeconomic rights, rejection of the treaty on rights of the child which is virtually unanimously endorsed, relative lack of legal protections for minors and the developmentally challenged in the criminal justice system, harsh prison conditions for common criminals, much injustice for security prisoners after 9/11, etc.).[41] Washington endorses development according to liberal democracy, but has extensive economic relations with numerous authoritarian states, from China to Kuwait, from Saudi Arabia to Ethiopia. The USA led in creating new *ad hoc* international criminal tribunals to respond to gross violations of human rights in certain states, but opposes the ICC having jurisdiction over Americans. Washington led in expanding the notions of enforcement action under Chapter VII of the Charter and of complex peacekeeping under Chapter VI, but blocked any significant UN deployments of force to protect persons in Rwanda. It then engaged in prolonged humanitarian intervention in Yugoslavia on behalf of Kosovar Albanians and in Libya in 2011. US leaders spoke out against torture, even while engaging in abuse of prisoners that on occasion was tantamount to torture, and even while turning prisoners over to countries that had a long history of

---

[41] See further Amnesty International, *United States of America: Rights for All* (London: Amnesty International Publications, 1998); and David P. Forsythe, "Human Rights Policy: Change and Continuity," in Randall B. Ripley and James M. Lindsay, eds., *US Foreign Policy After the Cold War* (Pittsburgh: University of Pittsburgh Press, 1997), 257–282.

torture. Whether other states have compiled a better or more consistent record in their foreign policy on rights abroad is an interesting question.

Other liberal democracies

Virtually all other liberal democracies and polities that strive to be liberal democracies display increasingly active policies on international human rights.[42] Like the USA, they take various initiatives on human rights abroad. Like the USA, they give a particular national slant to their policies. Like the USA, their general orientation to international human rights reflects their national political culture. Like the USA, most ascribe virtue to themselves in their orientation to internationally recognized human rights. Some, like Britain, are very similar to the USA in their rights policies abroad. Some, like Japan, are quite different. At the risk of superficiality, one can provide a brief summary of more thorough inquiries.

The Netherlands, for example, likes to picture itself as highly international and cosmopolitan.[43] It was the home of Grotius, the father of international law; it was a great trading nation; it was and is a country interested in world peace, for normal trade requires peace; and now it prides itself as a country highly active on human rights. This last orientation is affected both by its Protestant missionary tradition, and in some circles by a certain guilt about its colonial record and especially its handling of claims to independence by Indonesia in the 1940s. Both historical elements push the Dutch into activism on human rights. Thus Dutch governments engage in a friendly competition with like-minded states, perhaps especially Denmark and Norway, about who is the most progressive in foreign policy. The Dutch political classes see themselves as making a special contribution through their development assistance policies, perhaps because they know that the USA has one of the lowest ratios between gross domestic product and official development assistance of any western democracy (less than one-quarter of one percent). During the Cold War, if the USA had to sacrifice some attention to

---

[42] See further Alison Brysk, *Global Good Samaritans: Human Rights as Foreign Policy* (Oxford and New York: Oxford University Press, 2009).

[43] See further David Gillies, *Between Principle and Practice: Human Rights in North–South Relations* (Montreal: McGill-Queen's University Press, 1996); Peter R. Baehr, "The Netherlands and the United Nations: The Future Lies in the Past," in Chadwick F. Alger, Gene M. Lyons and John E. Trent, eds., *The United Nations System: The Policies of Member States* (Tokyo: United Nations University Press, 1995), 271–328; and Baehr, "Problems of Aid Conditionality: The Netherlands and Indonesia," *Third World Quarterly*, 18, 2 (June 1997), 363–376.

human rights in order to lead on security issues, some in The Hague wanted to fill that gap.

Because of the Dutch self-image and considerable Dutch activism at the United Nations on both human rights and peacekeeping issues, the Dutch role in the Srebrenica massacre in the former Yugoslavia in July 1995 proved to be a national trauma – perhaps roughly similar to Canadian reactions to charges of human rights violations against some of their military forces in Somalia. A lightly armed Dutch contingent in UNPROFOR, supposedly guaranteeing Srebrenica as a "safe area," was withdrawn – after which a massacre by Serbian partisans of thousands of remaining Muslim males occurred.

Also problematic, but not so traumatic, was the Dutch effort to combine development assistance with protection of human rights – especially civil and political ones. The Netherlands was inclined to assist poorer countries, and regularly was among the leading countries in amount of the gross domestic product contributed to official development assistance as a percentage of national economic productivity. But aid was not offered to some countries because of human rights problems. To other countries aid was offered but suspended for a time, for the same reason. Indonesia has posed a special case for Dutch governments, given the history involved and Jakarta's poor human rights record during times of authoritarian government. Certain Dutch statements led Indonesia in 1992 to indicate it would no longer receive foreign assistance from the Netherlands. So the aid relationship was terminated, leaving The Hague with no leverage on human rights developments in East Timor and other places controlled by Indonesia. Similar difficulties arose in relations with Suriname after a coup in that South American former colony, with the Dutch finally deciding to suspend assistance. Thus the Dutch, like the USA, have found it difficult to establish a consistent and principled policy on rights abroad, not only because of being entangled with other states via international organizations, but also because of wanting to pursue conflicting "public goods" – e.g., economic growth in poorer countries but with respect for civil and political rights.

British history, too, affects London's modern orientation to international human rights.[44] Political classes there strongly identify with civil and political rights and are proud of such early documents as the Magna Carta, the English Bill of Rights of 1689, laws on freedom of the press

---

[44] See further *Human Rights in Foreign Policy*, Foreign Policy Document No. 268 (London: Foreign and Commonwealth Office, July 1996); *Foreign Policy and Human Rights, Vol. 1*, House of Commons Sessions 1998–9, Foreign Affairs Committee (London: The Stationery Office, December 1998).

from 1695, etc. British leaders tend to see themselves as having generated great influence on subsequent developments for human rights in places like France and the USA, not to mention later developments in places like India and Zimbabwe. Like the USA, the UK prides itself on a strong legal culture emphasizing constitutionalism or limited government. Britain, like other colonial powers, tended to see its rule over foreign lands as benign and enlightening, rather than repressive and oppressive. Once it ended its colonial period, it became even more supportive of international human rights instruments – not having to be defensive about claims to national self-determination as a collective human right, or about the issue of individual petitions claiming rights violations in overseas territories.

Various British governments, unlike the USA, have not only accepted the full International Bill of Rights, along with European legal instruments, but also have undertaken concrete policies for specific situations – engaging in quiet diplomacy for the release of some Indonesian detainees, suspending foreign assistance to states like Chile and Uganda for human rights violations, supporting arms embargoes against South Africa and Chile, and so forth. It fought the Falklands/Malvinas war with Argentina with considerable attention to international humanitarian law. Like the USA, however, London has muted its criticism of some important states, such as Saudi Arabia which provides the British with important arms sales. On the other hand, Britain did join the USA in trying to have the UN Human Rights Commission adopt a resolution critical of China in 1997.

Some observers believe British governments are not as influenced by domestic human rights groups and media coverage as US policy, given the British tradition of parliamentary sovereignty but not necessarily popular sovereignty and radical interpretations of individual rights. Britain still does not have a written constitution or practice judicial review of parliamentary acts. On the other hand it has found its rights policies at home and abroad increasingly affected by its membership of the Council of Europe and the European Union. Britain has been far more affected by regional rights standards than the USA. These domestic and foreign factors interact to produce a foreign policy on rights somewhat similar to those of other European states – increasingly active and complicated, but inconsistent due to its variety of interests in international relations. In striking contrast to the USA, British governments support the ICC, even though Britain has sent its troops abroad in places like Iraq and Sierra Leone.

Britain, along with France, pushed hard for the use of force in Libya in 2011 to head off attacks on civilians by the Kaddafi regime. As usual European states found it impossible to present to the world a unified foreign and security policy, with Germany in particular unable to support the UN Security Council resolution providing a legal basis for attacks on Kaddafi's assets. Nevertheless the David Cameron coalition government in London framed the issue as a matter not just of humanitarianism but also of national interests – to be on the right side of history with new Arab governments and to deter further repression by other Arab trading partners, arguments which seemed to have had some effect on the Obama Administration.

Japan, by contrast, readily admits that the concept of human rights was not indigenous but was introduced from the West in the nineteenth century.[45] Obviously in a country with a history of imperial and military government, and with an era of atrocities during World War II, the notion of human rights did not take firm hold until the modern constitution was imposed during a time of military defeat and foreign occupation. Even so, and despite the existence of some indigenous "liberal" groups, Japan has still struggled at home with issues of equality or fairness for women, other races, and various ethnic and national groups. Given this history, it is not so surprising that Japan during the Cold War was a liberal democracy aligned with the other western liberal democracies, but was more passive than active on international human rights issues. In 1992, long after the US Congress put human rights back on the foreign policy agenda in Washington in the mid-1970s, Japan issued a white paper saying that human rights and democracy could be factors that affected foreign assistance and investment. But in general, and certainly in dealings with Peru which had a president of Japanese descent, human rights considerations did not appear to be a major factor in Japanese foreign policy.

As Japan has sought to show the world that it deserves a permanent seat in the UN Security Council, that it is more than an appendage of the USA, and that it has put its darker past behind it, Tokyo has become more active on rights issues abroad. Japan played a leading role, a far larger role than Washington, in trying to produce a liberal democratic peace with human rights in Cambodia. But it remains much less active in general on rights abroad than most other western-style liberal democracies. Tokyo has not pressed the human rights issue in its economic relations with other Asian states in particular, although it did suspend economic

---

[45] See further John Peek, "Japan, the United Nations, and Human Rights," *Asian Survey*, 32, 3 (March 1992); Seiichiro Takagi, "Japan's Policy Towards China After Tianan-men," in James T. H. Tang, ed., *Human Rights and International Relations in the Asia Pacific* (London: Pinter, 1995); and Yasuhiro Ueki, "Japan's New Diplomacy: Sources of Passivism and Activism," in Gerard Curtis, ed., *Japan's Foreign Policy After the Cold War: Coping with Change* (New York: M. E. Sharpe, 1997).

dealings for a time with China after the Tiananmen Square massacre of 1989. Tokyo has been more reluctant than Washington to press the rights issues in Burma. Given the history of Japanese relations with the Asian mainland during the 1930s and 1940s, it would be quite difficult for Japan to play a leading role on rights matters. This history reinforces those public officials who would like to concentrate primarily on Japanese economic interests. Likewise, Japan has not been one of the members of the World Bank that seeks to link loans with human rights performance, including democratic governance. Japan has, however, mostly voted with the western group at the UN on various rights matters in such bodies as the General Assembly and the Human Rights Commission and Council.

With regards to Japan's official development assistance (ODA) program, recent years have seen telling trends in Japanese policy making. While human rights have not been inextricably linked to foreign assistance, they are far from absent. In 2003, Japan reformed its ODA charter, citing domestic and international debate over its development policies and practices. The reformed document declares that its bedrock objective is "to contribute to the peace and development of the international community, and thereby to help ensure Japan's own security and prosperity." It even goes so far as to list paying "adequate attention to . . . the situation regarding the protection of basic human rights and freedoms" as one of four ODA principles of implementation, albeit behind such principles as environmental conservation and attention to military expenditures and WMD.[46] Later, in March 2005, Japan announced its Initiative on Gender Development, a new push to integrate gender concerns with other ODA considerations.[47]

Japan pressed North Korea on nuclear proliferation, but also on its human rights record, particularly with regard to its involvement in the abduction of up to fifteen Japanese nationals during the 1970s and 1980s. Japan threatened to withdraw food aid, and even considered sanctions against Kim Jong Il's regime.[48] It brought the issue to the United Nations Commission on Human Rights, helping to draft a resolution that dealt with North Korea's abduction of foreign nationals, among other human rights concerns.[49] But even as Japan sought to induce change in one of the

---

[46] See "Overview: Circumstances Surrounding Japan's Official Development Assistance (ODA) and Revision of the ODA Charter," www.mofa.go.jp/policy/other/bluebook/ 2004/chap3-d.pdf.

[47] See www.mofa.go.jp/policy/oda/category/wid/gad.html.

[48] See David Pilling and Jung a Song, "Tokyo Seeks Facts about Abducted Japanese," *Financial Times* (London), November 9, 2004, Asia edn.: Asia-Pacific, 2.

[49] See documents-dds-ny.un.org/doc/UNDOC/GEN/G05/101/97/pdf/G0510197.pdf and www.mofa.go.jp/policy/other/bluebook/2004/chap3-c.pdf.

world's most brutal regimes, it was forced to face its own tarnished past. While Tokyo was pressing Pyongyang to come clean on abductions, South Korea was demanding Japan follow Germany's example and apologize more completely for its wartime atrocities.[50]

Former European communist states like Hungary and Russia, to choose two almost at random, are now also active on international human rights issues.[51] Hungary strives to be like any other European state on these issues, although its relationship to ethnic Hungarians abroad generates clear differences. The Russian Federation is much more ambivalent about the place of human rights in foreign policy, although it too is propelled to considerable extent by concern for the protection of compatriots abroad. Both of these states stress minority rights in foreign policy much more than Washington.

Hungary presents an interesting situation in terms of foreign policy and human rights. Its history is mostly one of authoritarian rule, whether through empire or Soviet-imposed communism. Yet certain liberal tendencies were present, such as considerable respect for private property and a certain affinity for legal rules. Many politically active Hungarians considered themselves to be liberal and a part of the West. Considerable resistance to Leninist or Stalinist repression was much in evidence in the 1956 uprising, as was also the case at different times in what was then the German Democratic Republic, Poland, and what is now the Czech Republic. Many in these areas would have chosen western-style liberalism, had free choice been allowed. It was thus not very surprising that when the Soviet Union allowed Eastern Europe to go its own way in the late 1980s, Hungary embraced international human rights. This orientation came about not only because of a need to prove that it belonged in the Council of Europe, and perhaps the European Union and NATO, but also because of genuine domestic preferences.

Hungary has given special attention to minority rights in its foreign policy after the Cold War, given the number of ethnic Hungarians who reside in Romania, Slovakia, and Ukraine. Even while still officially communist, Hungary criticized its fellow communist neighbor, Romania, for

---

[50] Richard Lloyd Parry, "Seoul Searching for Japanese War Apology," *The Australian*, March 3, 2005, All-Around Country edn.: World 8.
[51] See further Bruce D. Porter and Carol R. Saivets, "The Once and Future Empire: Russia and the 'Near Abroad,'" *Washington Quarterly*, 17, 3 (1994), 75–76; Alexei Arbatov, "Russian Foreign Policy Thinking in Transition," in Vladimir Baranovsky, ed., *Russia and Europe: The Emerging Security Agenda* (Oxford: Oxford University Press, 1997); and Istvan Pogany, ed., *Human Rights in Eastern Europe* (Aldershot: Edward Elgar, 1995).

its treatment of the Hungarian minority. Hungary thus broke the unwritten rule that European communist regimes did not criticize each other on human rights issues. Since adopting liberal democracy, Budapest has continued to make the relationship with ethnic Hungarians abroad the centerpiece of its foreign policy. This has led to periodic friction with especially Romania, which fears too much local autonomy, if not separatism, for that sizable minority. Budapest has found more satisfactory relations on this issue with Ukraine and Slovakia. On other human rights issues Hungary has generally behaved as any other European state, voting with the western group at the UN and accepting regional human rights obligations through the Council of Europe.

Russia presents a fascinating study of human rights and foreign policy. Whether as Russia or the Soviet Union, this area has long manifested a conflicted political culture. The dominant aspect was and is authoritarian, illiberal, Slavic, and suspicious of the West. The tradition of legal rights, especially individual rights, is very weak – especially in the *mir* as a rural, organic community in which law and individualism were insignificant. But at least from the time of Peter the Great there was a weaker, more liberal aspect to Russian culture. These liberal tendencies have been encouraged since the Gorbachev and Yeltsin eras, yet one does not change the dominant culture by simply issuing legal documents and making proclamations. Russian policies, for example, directed toward suppression of a separatist movement in Chechnya were clearly brutal.

There is a part of the Russian political class that longs for the Stalinist days of order and superpower status, and believes that human rights equates with pornography, criminality, and foreign religious sects. There is another part of the political class that is more sympathetic to human rights,[52] but believes the West has not treated the new Russia with proper sensitivity and respect. In the view of this circle, Russia struggles to determine whether it should follow the US lead on certain human rights issues, align with a different European position, or strike out on its own. Like Hungary, Russia has given special attention to minority rights in foreign policy. Given the large number of ethnic Russians and Russian speakers in its "near abroad," and given its own problems with separatist movements, Russian foreign policy has been highly active on ethno-territorial-linguistic disputes in many former areas of Soviet control. Its still uncertain nationalism, reflecting a conflicted political culture, interacts with

---

[52] See further Anatoly L. Adamishin and Richard Schifter, *Human Rights, Perestroika, and the End of the Cold War* (Washington: United States Institute of Peace, 2009). This book is the joint effort of two diplomats, the first in Moscow and the second in Washington, who negotiated human rights issues toward the end of the USSR.

other factors such as an unsteady relationship with the powerful West to provide a most uncertain policy on rights abroad.

On human rights issues pertaining to the former Yugoslavia, Moscow tends to reflect the Slavic tendency of identifying as protector of the Serbs, but fears a further rejection by the West if it fully follows that course. It voted for the creation of the Yugoslav Criminal Court in the UN Security Council, but believes the prosecutor's office has been biased against the Serbs. At the Rome diplomatic conference in the summer of 1998, it aligned with the USA (and China, among a few others) in opposing a strong and independent standing criminal court. Likewise, it sought a relaxation of international pressure on dictatorial Iraq, believing that Baghdad had been punished enough (and wanting payment on existing commercial contracts), but again feared antagonizing the West, especially the USA, with that clear course of action. It wound up mediating the Kosovo crisis between NATO states and modern Yugoslavia. Russia was also not enthusiastic about UN sanctions on the government of Sudan for its policies in the Darfur regions, in part because it had a number of arms sales agreements with Khartoum.

Minority rights is not a moral sideshow for Moscow, any more than it is for Budapest. Minority rights in foreign policy is part of Russia's central effort to exercise influence in adjacent areas on the basis of nationalism. It does not necessarily want to encourage separatism, given its own problems in Chechnya and elsewhere (although it seems to have made an exception concerning Abkhazia and the various regions of Ossetia, which Moscow seems to want to pry away from Georgia). It may or may not want to encourage union – as in Belarus but without necessarily inheriting the problems involved. But it feels it cannot abandon Russians abroad. At the same time, it seems aware of how events are read in the West, lest foreign assistance and investment capital are restricted because of fears of Russian imperialism or illegal interference in another state's domestic affairs. So in Latvia Moscow thinks of sanctions to protect the interests of Russians there, but is cautioned by the western states about overreaction. Russian foreign policy on rights is not well grounded domestically, and is quite uncertain in its applications abroad.

Russian president Vladimir Putin, a staunch ally in the US "war" on terrorism, was particularly vocal over the controversial results of the Ukrainian presidential election in 2004. The number of ethnic Russians living in Ukraine at the time was around 17 percent,[53] the largest minority population in the country. The two candidates championed different

---

[53] Figure from the CIA World Factbook, www.cia.gov/cia/publications/factbook/geos/up.html.

visions of Ukrainian alignment. Viktor Yushchenko, former prime minister and more pro-West than his opponent, espoused stronger ties with the European Union (and survived an attempt on his life by way of deadly poison), while his opponent, then-Prime Minister Viktor Yanukovich, stressed a more prominent relationship with Russia. Putin was heavily involved in the political conflict to preserve Russian soft power in former Soviet spheres of influence, but also to ensure Russia retains a hand in protecting Russian minorities abroad. In so doing, Putin aligned Russia with a Ukrainian political faction known for corruption and authoritarianism. This orientation brought criticism from Washington and others, even as Putin played fast and loose with human rights at home by reducing press freedoms, the independence and authority of parliament, and the power of other competing power centers. According to the NGO Freedom House, by 2005 Russia was only a partly free country.

In the brief armed conflict in 2008 between Russia and neighboring Georgia, there was evidence of Russian disregard for some of international humanitarian law, with the media presenting evidence of military attacks on civilian structures. In general the Russian Caucasus area seemed at times beyond the reach of Moscow's legal arm.

At the time of writing, in Russia there were arbitrary arrests and politicized trials, not to mention impunity for the killings of some investigative journalists. One reading of events was that President Medvedev wanted to improve the Russian record on domestic human rights issues but that Prime Minister Putin was not so inclined. I have already noted in Chapter 5 the large number of cases involving Russia in the European Court of Human Rights. While Russia did not block UN authorization of use of force in Libya, but rather abstained, immediately thereafter it criticized the western states that were managing military operations.

One could look at any number of other liberal democracies – or would-be liberal democracies – and their foreign policies on human rights, from India to South Africa, from Canada to Costa Rica. Most such inquiries prove intriguing. France, origin of the 1789 Declaration on the Rights of Man and the state most like the USA in seeing itself as a universal model for human rights, presents a long history of support for corrupt and authoritarian rulers in Africa, not to mention a policy of torture and summary execution during the Algerian war of 1954–1962. Costa Rica, with some similarity to the USA, sees itself made up of an exceptionally good and peaceful people who therefore have a special and progressive role to play particularly in hemispheric affairs. However, the moralizing of Oscar Arias, like that of Jimmy Carter, was not always well received by other Latin American heads of state.

India, the most populous democracy, has become much more defensive and low key about international human rights matters.[54] This is so despite the fact that India was one of the first states to challenge apartheid in South Africa, India having many nationals there. In part Indian skepticism about international action stems from an awareness of certain domestic problems – including brutal treatment of terror suspects involved in the disputed region of Kashmir. Also, the collapse of the Soviet Union, its major strategic partner, reduced its standing in international relations. Its foray into Sri Lankan ethnic struggles under Rajiv Gandhi, by way of an Indian "peacekeeping" force which itself engaged in atrocities, proved disastrous, both personally and politically speaking, contributing to the current Indian low profile. In general, India now tends to favor the principle of state sovereignty when in conflict with international action for human rights, believing that the US-led Security Council has intervened too much in the affairs of the governments of the global south. The election of a clearly nationalistic government in 1998 intensified these trends. In 2011 it was still the case that India, given its colonial experience, was very sensitive about the USA or any other state engaging in public criticism of its human rights record. Some analysts were not at all surprised that India abstained on the UN Security Council vote regarding use of force in Libya in 2011.

Governments in South Africa emerging from all-race elections have identified strongly with international human rights, and – along with El Salvador – have pioneered official "truth commissions" to reveal the facts of past repression but without criminal prosecution for political crime. The Mandela government, however, was heavily involved in fairly disastrous gun-running in the Great Lakes region of Africa, and also defied UN sanctions on dictatorial Libya in order to repay Libyan support for the anti-apartheid movement. The Thabo Mbeki government that followed Mandela was certainly not at the forefront of the struggle against HIV/AIDS, even though that affliction was debilitating many African nations. The Mbeki team also was reluctant to press hard for decisive change in neighboring Zimbabwe where an aging Robert Mugabe was running the country into the ground with major human rights abuses over considerable time. It seems South African policy was based on fear of increased refugee flows into the country if Mugabe fell. Then the Jacob Zuma government seemed wildly inconsistent in its international human rights policies.

---

[54] See further R. Suresh, *Foreign Policy and Human Rights: An Indian Perspective* (Guragon: Madhav Books, 2009).

Canadian foreign policy has been generally progressive on rights abroad.[55] It is well known that Ottawa has long prided itself on its record especially in UN peacekeeping – including second-generation or complex peacekeeping that includes human rights dimensions. Canada, for example, joined the USA in practical efforts to bring liberal democracy to Haiti, no easy task given the history and impoverishment of that country. Canada has also been a leader in regard to a ban on anti-personnel landmines, and the creation of a UN criminal court. Limitations of space, however, compel us to move on.

Illiberal states

With due regard for gray areas and borderline cases, it can be said that liberal democracies are characterized by free and fair national elections based on broad suffrage, combined with protection of a wide variety of civil rights through independent courts and other mechanisms to provide fairness and tolerance. Limited government, or constitutionalism, is a key feature of liberal politics.[56] Whether or not a liberal democracy is also a social democracy depends on its commitment to socioeconomic rights. Illiberal democracies may have reasonably free and fair national elections based on broad suffrage, but they do not counteract the tyranny of the majority with effective protections for ethnic and religious minorities or various types of dissenters. States like Croatia under Tudjman and Iran under the rule of the clerics exemplify illiberal democracies, in which the rights of political participation are exercised to deny certain civil rights protecting minorities and dissenters. Authoritarian states do not reach the threshold of free and fair national elections in which the winners actually govern.

Iran presents an interesting case study of human rights and foreign policy in an illiberal state.[57] The comparison with the USA, with its long tradition of formal separation of church and state, could not be more striking. Yet there are similarities. Each sees itself as a leader for a certain way of life or culture.

---

[55] The standard work in this area is Robert O. Mathews and R. C. Pratt, eds., *Human Rights and Canadian Foreign Policy* (Montreal: McGill-Queen's Press, 1988).

[56] Fareed Zakaria, "The Rise of Illiberal Democracy," *Foreign Affairs*, 76, 6 (November–December, 1997), 22–43.

[57] See further Ali Mazrui, "Islamic and Western Values," *Foreign Affairs*, 76, 5 (Fall 1997), 118–132; Reza Afshari, "An Essay on Scholarship, Human Rights, and State Legitimacy: The Case of the Islamic Republic of Iran," *Human Rights Quarterly*, 18, 3 (Summer 1990), 544–593; and Anoushiravan Ehteshami, *After Khomeini: The Iranian Second Republic* (London: Routledge, 1995).

From the 1979 revolution, Iran instituted an Islamist theocracy which rejected the basic notion of secular and universal human rights as found in public international law. The clerics who wield ultimate authority in modern Iran believe that the Sharia, or fundamental Islamic law, has universal application for all Muslims. They do not accept the superiority of international human rights instruments. They just do not bother with the formalities of withdrawing Iran's adherence to international instruments on rights formally accepted by the previous government (and mostly ignored by the Shah in practice). Under the Sharia, as interpreted by contemporary Iranian leaders, the primary emphasis is on duties owed to the religious state, not individual rights that restrict the state. Individuals do not have human rights by virtue of being persons; they have those rights that Allah through the proper state provides them.

To a considerable extent, current Iranian rulers regard the international law of human rights, and related diplomacy in international organizations, as a product of the hated United States. That Iranian clerics might overstate the influence of the USA on international human rights developments does not mean that their critical beliefs are not firmly held. The Iranian leadership tends to dismiss foreign criticism on human rights issues, whether by the USA or other actors, including western-based NGOs, as being part of American neo-imperialism of a particularly evil nature. The fact that the USA employs double standards in its approach to human rights abroad, criticizing every defect in Iran vociferously, at least until a slight thaw in relations began in 1998, but remaining silent about major violations in Saudi Arabia and other allies, contributes to Iranian views.

Because Iran practices a type of cultural relativism with regard to human rights, its foreign policy on this subject is almost entirely defensive. It tries to reject foreign criticism, whether multilateral or bilateral, whether public or private, either by disputing facts or by claiming that a certain behavior is permitted under Islamic law. Iran tries to justify its discrimination against women on these latter grounds. Sometimes this defensive stance is difficult to make persuasive, for some Iranian policies fall short of Islamic as well as international law. This is apparently so, for example, concerning Teheran's vigorous persecution of the Iranian Ba'hai. The Sharia commands tolerance for minority religions as long as they are religions of the book – viz., Islam, Judaism, and Christianity. Only if one regards the Ba'hai as heretics from Islam, and not a branch of Islam, can one justify their severe persecution under Islamic law.

In 2011 there were blatant Iranian double standards regarding human rights. At home the Shi'ite clerics periodically suppressed, sometimes with loss of life, dissidents and protestors demanding more human rights and multiparty democracy. At the same time, the clerics criticized Sunni Saudi Arabia for helping quash demands for democratic change in Bahrain – where the rulers were Sunni and the street demonstrators, said to represent the majority population, were largely Shi'ite.

From 1997 the new Iranian President, Mohammed Khatami, had addressed some of these domestic shortcomings dealing with persecution, censorship, and other violations of internationally recognized human rights. He had even supported political pluralism. But he did so in the context of discussions on Islamic law. It is certainly possible that new interpretations of religious law might be forthcoming that would be more compatible with the international law of human rights. Other Muslim societies come up with different interpretations of the Sharia. At the end of 1997 an Egyptian court ruled against female genital mutilation. A continuing conflict between moderate and more fundamentalist interpretations of Islamic law was clearly in evidence in Iran during 1997 and 1998. All revolutions lose their radical zeal over time. This is beginning to happen in Iran. These domestic developments are intertwined with international ones – such as the desire of more moderate Iranian officials to reduce the country's status as international pariah, and in particular to take some steps toward repairing relations with the powerful USA. It is not inconceivable that Iranian policy on human rights might slowly evolve toward a less defensive posture, not exactly along the lines of the Turkish or Indonesian or Jordanian model but in that general direction.

On the other hand, by 2011 it was reasonably clear that the moderates, centered in and around former President Khatami, had lost ground to the clerics who were determined to continue the values associated with Khomeini. US pressure on the question of nuclear weapons encouraged the clerics, who stood for national defiance against the "great Satan" and weakened the hand of those favoring some rapprochement with the West. Should the USA, or even Israel, use the notion of preventive war to strike Iranian suspected nuclear weapons facilities, the cause of internationally recognized human rights, which were often associated with western democracies, would certainly suffer in the short run. There is the view that western pressure on Iran, because of issues such as terrorism and weapons proliferation, causes retrenchment and further repression by the regime of the clerics, and only in the context of relaxed international relations is it likely that Iran will become more progressive on human rights.[58]

---

[58] See Stephen Kinzer, *All The Shah's Men: An American Coup and the Roots of Middle East Terror* (Hoboken: Wiley, 2003, 2008), preface to the 2008 edn.

Conclusions

During the era of the League of Nations, this chapter could not have been written. The League Covenant did not mention universal human rights, and states did not address human rights in their foreign policies. There was some international humanitarian law for armed conflicts, and states did sometimes display humanitarian policies dealing with refugees, the nature of rule in colonies (via the League Mandates Commission), and other social subjects. But as late as 1944 human rights remained essentially a national rather than international matter (with the exception of the minority treaties for some Central European states in the interwar years, and international law governing aliens).

Increasingly all states, whatever their political character, have to deal with internationally recognized human rights. International relations or world politics is not what it once was. Much of international law codifies liberal principles of human rights. But in addressing human rights, states bring with them their national history, character, self-image, and nationalism. These national traits cause states to be more or less active on human rights issues, more or less confident and assertive, more or less defensive. This history, plus their contemporary situation and how they define their interests, causes states to take different slants or emphases on rights in foreign policy. When addressing human rights, the USA, for example, consistent with its national tradition, does not focus on socio-economic rights but rather on personal freedom. The Netherlands tries especially hard to link development assistance with rights behavior, and has a special focus on Indonesia. The Hungarians and Russians tend to emphasize minority rights for their ethnic and/or linguistic compatriots abroad. And so on.

It is significant that even states without a strong rights tradition or legal culture have been propelled to direct more attention to rights in foreign policy. This is true, for example, for both Japan and Russia. Even Iran, if it wishes to be accepted as a full or normal member of the international community, has found that it needs to respond to international criticism by addressing defects in Iranian society, even if it does so under the cover of a discussion of religious law rather than the secular law of international human rights.

Without downplaying the importance of international organizations, private non-profit groups, and even multinational corporations, it is still state foreign policy that plays a very large role in the promotion and protection of international human rights. So with regard to universal human rights and state foreign policy, it is both true and false to say: *la plus ça change, la plus c'est la même chose* (the more things change, the more they remain the same). True, because despite the fact that we have change in favor of human rights norms in international relations, we still have to deal with nationalism and national interests. False, because we do have real changes in foreign policy concerning human rights; there is much more attention to international human rights in 2005 compared with the foreign policies of 1925 or 1905.

Case study: French foreign policy, Ivory Coast, and human rights

Ivory Coast is a West African state of about 22 million persons that is rich in natural resources such as cocoa, coffee, and palm oil. It was a French colony from the 1890s until independence in 1960. For the first thirty years of independence the country was ruled by the strongman Felix Houphouet-Boigny, in close cooperation with France. The latter maintained a military base in the country, the nation being the hub of economic and political activity for French-speaking West Africa. Some analysts thought independence in 1960 brought little change in substance, such was the continuing influence of France.

The retirement and then death in 1993 of Houphouet-Boigny was followed by movement toward multiparty democracy, interspersed by coups and autocratic rule. As in other places, in Ivory Coast political parties and political leaders were frequently associated with particular ethnic and sectarian groups. By the late 1990s, as political leaders developed identity politics in order to mobilize voters and attract donor support, the country could be superficially seen as politically split between the largely Islamic north (perhaps 35–40 percent of the population) and the largely Christian south (of approximately the same percentage of the population), with other local beliefs covering the rest of the people. There were perhaps sixty ethnic groups in the country. Some analysts believe that sectarian divisions do not run deep and that a strong element of economic pragmatism and political opportunism are strong factors in public life.

In the widespread political violence that erupted in 2002 in the wake of disputed elections and various politico-legal maneuvers, France beefed up its military forces in the country in order to act as a stabilizing force. These French forces acted in tandem with first the troops, largely Nigerian, from ECOWAS (Economic Community of West African States), and then later from the United Nations. As of 2004 the UN field operation was given a Chapter VII mandate under the UN Charter, meaning that it was not just a peacekeeping force engaging in armed diplomacy, but rather was authorized to take enforcement action pursuant to a variety of goals pertaining to human rights as well as security. French troops acted as a rapid reaction force, taking on the more difficult military missions that the UN forces had difficulty handling alone.

A period of uneasy but relative calm from about 2003 was undermined by a disputed election in late 2010. The then President, Laurent Gbagbo, whose political base was largely in the south, refused to leave office after international election monitors agreed that his opponent, Alassane Ouattara, a Muslim from the north, had won the 2010 election. With remarkable international consensus running against Gbagbo, various public and private intermediaries tried to resolve the dispute. They appealed to the principle of R2P, the responsibility to protect, arguing that, if a national government was unable or unwilling to protect the human rights of the nation, outside parties had a duty to become involved.

Despite all the international activity, during early 2011 Ivory Coast was once again caught up in widespread violence. Both the forces loyal to Gbagbo and those supporting Ouattara were reported to have committed atrocities. There were many more political deaths in 2011 than had been the case in 2002.

In this violent context French military forces teamed with the UN forces to bring intense military pressure on Gbagbo, hunkered down in the presidential residence in Abidjan. The French government of Nicolas Sarkozy (teaming with Nigeria) had successfully pushed the UN Security Council to adopt a mandate (SC Resolution 1975) authorizing states and UN units to utilize "all necessary measures" to protect civilians in Ivory Coast. This was similar to French policy in Liberia at approximately the same time, in which French (and British) leadership resulted in Security Council approval for a limited if unclear military action in Libya. In both Libya and Ivory Coast, a UN enforcement mandate was worded in humanitarian terms but was applied for political purposes – namely to affect the central government. In both cases Russia and some other states protested how France and others interpreted UNSC resolutions. In the case of Ivory Coast, the combined effect of actions by UN and French troops, and militias loyal to Ouattara, led to the capture of Gbagbo and the tenuous control of the state apparatus by the Ouattara movement.

This case demonstrates above all the difficulty of establishing firm generalizations and expectations about western democratic foreign policy and democracy abroad. France's important role in supporting the duly elected Ouattara was at variance with its past support for many autocratic factions in Africa including the genocidal militant Hutus in Rwanda. The Sarkozy team continued to defer to autocrats in half a dozen African states even after its forceful role in Ivory Coast. But this inconsistency was not significantly different from the United Kingdom or the United States, *inter alia*, who continued close relations with (and arms sales to) Saudi Arabia and other autocratic regimes, even as they supported democratic change in Egypt and Tunisia. Local pressures for democratic change varied, as did media coverage of those pressures, as did state conception of its national interests. Consequently these factors, plus others such as historical relations, caused all states' foreign policy to be inconsistent but often important regarding democracy promotion.

Discussion questions

- Is there a theoretical or otherwise systematic reason why different states come up with different emphases and interpretations of international human rights standards? Even among liberal democratic states of the OECD, such as the United States, Britain, the Netherlands, and Japan, there are major differences in their approaches to international human rights: why is this?
- In general, are states paying more or less attention to human rights through foreign policy? Why?
- Why is it that democracies like India and the United Kingdom take very different approaches to questions of international human rights?
- Why is it that countries like France and the United States, which have a long national history of attention to human rights, repeatedly find it so difficult to apply international standards to themselves – even though the West has had great influence on the evolution of international human rights, both regional and global?
- What is the probability that traditionally illiberal states in places such as the Middle East (e.g., Iran) and Asia (e.g., China) will adapt their foreign policies to international standards of human rights?
- Is human rights in foreign policy primarily a matter of the executive branch, or do legislatures (and public opinion, with interest groups) play an important role?

SUGGESTIONS FOR FURTHER READING

Baehr, Peter, and Monique Castermans-Holleman, *The Role of Human Rights in Foreign Policy* (New York: Palgrave Macmillan, 2004). Thorough text examining the various aspects of the role human rights plays in state foreign policy, with particular attention to US and Dutch foreign policy.

Blau, Judith, David L. Brunsma, Alberto Moncada, and Catherine Zimmer, eds., *The Leading Rogue State: The US and Human Rights* (Boulder: Paradigm Publishers, 2009). A hypercritical treatment of the USA by a group of sociologists.

Brysk, Alison, *Global Good Samaritans: Human Rights as Foreign Policy* (Oxford and New York: Oxford University Press, 2009). A very good study of the foreign policies of Sweden, Canada, Costa Rica, the Netherlands, Japan, and South Africa on the subject of human rights.

Carothers, Thomas, *Assessing Democracy: The Case of Romania* (Washington: Carnegie Endowment, 1996). Shows how difficult it is to evaluate US foreign policy and democracy assistance, even in one country.

Curtis, Gerard, ed., *Japan's Foreign Policy After the Cold War: Coping with Change* (New York: M. E. Sharpe, 1997). Shows the changing nature of Japanese foreign policy, with some attention to human rights.

Egeland, Jan, *Impotent Large State – Potent Small State: Potentialities and Limitations of Human Rights Objectives in the Foreign Policies of the United States* (Oslo: Norwegian University Press, 1988). Argues that during the Cold War Norway had more room to maneuver for human rights in foreign policy than the United States, mainly because of US security obligations.

Forsythe, David, *The Politics of Prisoner Abuse: The US and Enemy Prisoners After 9/11* (Cambridge: Cambridge University Press, 2011). An overview of the policy by the George W. Bush Administration to gain intelligence by abuse of prisoners, and how the policy spun out of control because of poor design and weak oversight. Also covers the similarities and differences by the Obama Administration on this subject.

Forsythe, David, et al., eds., *American Foreign Policy in a Globalized World* (New York: Routledge, 2006). Contains chapters on US democracy promotion in places like Afghanistan, Iraq, and the Middle East in general, as well as a chapter on US policy toward "enemy detainees."

Gillies, David, *Between Principle and Practice: Human Rights in North–South Relations* (Montreal: McGill-Queen's University Press, 1996). A good comparative study of the role of human rights in foreign policy among several developed countries, when dealing with certain less developed countries. Shows how difficult it is to construct a principled foreign policy when trying to blend human rights and support for development.

Hunt, Michael H., *Ideology and US Foreign Policy* (New Haven: Yale University Press, 1987). Argues that while the United States see itself as an exceptionally good nation, it has done a great deal of harm in the world through its racism and commitment to the *status quo*. Argues for a reduced US role in the world, even at the cost of less attention to liberal causes like international human rights.

Ignatieff, Michael, ed., *American Exceptionalism and Human Rights* (Princeton and Oxford: Princeton University Press, 2005). Leading scholars from law and the social sciences examine the different meanings of American exceptionalism. They vary regarding the usefulness of the concept for understanding US foreign policy and human rights.

Kissinger, Henry, *Diplomacy* (New York: Simon & Schuster, 1994). As in his other modern works, Kissinger is critical of liberal views of foreign policy and international relations, which he calls Wilsonianism, and argues that the United States must beware of liberal crusades that go beyond American power and wisdom. He is suspicious of the validity of universal standards pertaining to democracy and human rights, believing them to have evolved in special western circumstances. But he says pure realism is not sustainable in American foreign policy.

Mathews, Robert O., and R. C. Pratt, eds., *Human Rights and Canadian Foreign Policy* (Montreal: McGill-Queen's Press, 1988). The definitive work for its time.

McGovern, Mike, *Making War in Cote d'Ivoire* (London: Hurst Publishing, 2010). An extremely well researched study by a former member of the International Crisis Group dealing with Ivory Coast.

Mertus, Julie, *Bait and Switch: Human Rights and US Foreign Policy* (New York: Routledge, 2004). Based on interviews with numerous current and former US officials, the author finds that international human rights norms predispose Washington to talk about human rights, while human rights considerations remain frequently absent from US foreign policy.

Power, Samantha, *"A Problem From Hell": America and the Age of Genocide* (New York: Basic Books, 2002). Examines the United States' response to genocide throughout the twentieth century, concluding that America's record has been consistently poor.

Sikkink, Kathryn, *Mixed Signals: U.S. Human Rights Policy and Latin America* (New York: Century Foundation, 2004). A scholarly overview of US human rights policy in most of the Western Hemisphere, stressing the mixed record emanating from Washington. Much rights talk is not always followed by consistent influence on behalf of that rhetoric.

Vogelgesang, Sandy, *American Dream, Global Nightmare: The Dilemma of US Human Rights Policy* (New York: Norton, 1980). One of the first studies of human rights and US foreign policy suggests the difficulty of establishing a foreign policy that is both principled and consistent.

Zakaria, Fareed, "The Rise of Illiberal Democracy," *Foreign Affairs*, 76, 6 (November–December 1997), 22–43. An important article noting the difference between liberal and illiberal democracy. Whereas the United States has in the past supported some illiberal elected governments, as in El Salvador, presumably the West now intends to enlarge the *liberal* democratic community.

7 Non-governmental organizations and human rights

By now it should be clear that states, acting frequently through international organizations and/or diplomatic conferences, produce the international law of human rights by concluding treaties and developing customary law. The resulting law obligates states, primarily. In Chapter 6 we examined state foreign policy against the background of the international law of human rights. But private actors can be important at both ends of this process, affecting legislation and implementation.[1]

This chapter starts with an analysis of non-governmental organizations and their advocacy of human rights ideas, which is directed both to the creation and application of human rights norms. Probably the best known of these groups is Amnesty International. This analysis is eventually set within the confines of social movements. Such actors push for more liberalism in the form of human rights protection in international relations. The chapter then turns to those private groups that are mostly called relief or development agencies, or sometimes PVOs (private voluntary agencies) or VOLAGs (voluntary agencies). A classic example is Oxfam. These private actors are crucial especially for grassroots action that directly or indirectly attends to social and economic rights. Most can be said to be liberal or pragmatic liberal actors, in that they emphasize policies for the betterment of individuals under legal norms, rather than emphasizing the collective national interests of states as pursued through the application of power. Chapter 8 addresses private for-profit actors, commonly called multinational or transnational corporations when they act across national borders.

---

[1] For an introductory overview, see Ann Marie Clark, "Nongovernmental Organizations: Overview," in David P. Forsythe, ed., *Encyclopedia of Human Rights* (New York: Oxford University Press, 2009), vol. IV, 87–96. See also William Korey, *NGOs and the Universal Declaration of Human Rights: "A Curious Grapevine"* (New York: St. Martin's Press, 1998). See further Claude E. Welch, Jr., *NGOs and Human Rights: Promise and Performance* (Philadelphia: University of Pennsylvania Press, 2001).

Private advocacy for human rights

There are perhaps 250 private organizations consistently active across borders that take as their reason for being (*raison d'être*) the advocacy of some part of the international law of human rights and/or humanitarian affairs on a global basis.[2] From this group a handful have the requisite budget, contacts, expertise, and reputation to get the global media and major governments to pay them at least periodic attention across a range of issues and situations: Amnesty International (AI), Human Rights Watch (HRW), the International Commission of Jurists, the International Federation for Human Rights, the International Committee of the Red Cross, Human Rights First, Lawyers Without Borders, Doctors Without Borders, Physicians for Human Rights, Anti-Slavery International, PEN (Poets, Essayists, Novelists), Article 19 (devoted to freedom of expression), etc. When there is an international meeting touching on human rights, private groups that identify themselves as working primarily for international law, peace, world order, and women's issues, etc. may swell the numbers of active advocacy groups to several hundred – 200 to 800 might be an expected range. The core advocacy groups are usually called NGOs or INGOS – non-governmental organizations or international non-governmental organizations. A related phenomenon is a governmentally created, quasi-private human rights organization, or GONGO. Some GONGOs have been surprisingly active and independent, as in Indonesia and Mexico.

The oldest and best-funded human rights NGOs are based in the West and concern themselves primarily with civil and political rights in peace-time and international humanitarian law in war or similar situations. Western societies have manifested the civil rights, private wealth, leisure time and value structures that allow for the successful operation of major human rights NGOs. To advocate human rights via a truly independent and dynamic NGO, there must be respect for civil rights and a civic society to start with. With the spread of liberal democracy and more open societies after the Cold War, the number of NGOs at least spasmodically active on some human rights issues has greatly increased. But the percentage of human rights groups, relative to the total number of NGOs active in international relations, has remained rather stable.[3]

---

[2] Jackie Smith and Ron Pagnucco with George A. Lopez, "Globalizing Human Rights: The Work of Transnational Human Rights NGOs in the 1990s," *Human Rights Quarterly*, 20, 2 (May 1998), 379–412.

[3] Margaret E. Keck and Kathryn Sikkink, *Activists Beyond Borders: Advocacy Networks in International Politics* (Ithaca: Cornell University Press, 1998), 11.

Many NGOs based in the global south manifest a different agenda from those based in the north or northwest. The former tend to emphasize the right to development and many socioeconomic rights, without neglecting entirely civil and political rights. Some of the better known NGOs based in the richer countries, like AI and HRW, have adopted mission statements that now pay some attention to socioeconomic rights, on the argument that they do indeed impinge on civil and political rights. But for these latter, their emphasis remains on civil-political rights and humanitarian affairs (including humanitarian relief).[4]

Complicating the picture is the fact that other private groups that exist for secular or religious purposes may become international human rights actors at particular times and for particular causes. The Catholic Church in its various manifestations and the World Council of Churches, *inter alia*, are examples of religious groups that fit this mold.[5] Some faith-based groups, for example, teamed with some secular human rights groups to help achieve greater attention to the right to religious freedom and the right to be free from religious discrimination in the recent past, at least in US foreign policy.[6] Labor unions that normally focus on domestic "bread and butter" issues, like the AFL-CIO in the United States, may – and increasingly do – have a private foreign policy on rights questions. Labor unions, in order to try to protect labor wages and benefits in their home country, may find it necessary to address labor rights in foreign countries. "Ethnic lobbies" such as "the Greek lobby" or "the China lobby" may and occasionally do take up human rights issues of concern. There are numerous national civil rights groups, such as the American Civil Liberties Union or the Center for Constitutional Rights in the United States, that occasionally turn to international rights issues under the 1949 Geneva Conventions or the 1984 Convention against Torture. Given the existence of transnational issues, or the penetration of international

---

[4] For a discussion of the lack of effective lobbying by NGOs such as HRW regarding socioeconomic rights, see David P. Forsythe and Eric Heinze, "On the Margins of the Human Rights Discourse: International Welfare Rights and Foreign Policy," in Rhoda Howard-Hassmann and Claude E. Welch, Jr., eds., *Economic Rights in Canada and the United States: Sleeping Under Bridges* (Philadelphia: University of Pennsylvania Press, 2006). Aryeh Neier, long-time Executive Director of Human Rights Watch, was strongly opposed to broadening the focus of HRW so as to include socioeconomic rights. See Aryeh Neier, *Taking Liberties: Four Decades in the Struggle for Rights* (New York: Public Affairs, 2003), introduction, xxx. For a discussion about NGOs and socioeconomic rights, see *Human Rights Quarterly*, 26, 4 (November, 2004), 866–881.

[5] See further Claude E. Welch, Jr., "Mobilizing Morality: The World Council of Churches and Its Program to Combat Racism, 1969–1994," *Human Rights Quarterly*, 23, 4 (November 2001), 863–910.

[6] Allen D. Hertzke, *Freeing God's Children: The Unlikely Alliance for Global Human Rights* (London and New York: Rowman & Littlefield, 2004).

relations into domestic affairs, it is increasingly difficult to separate national from international human rights groups. A good example was the ACLU interest in US policy toward "enemy detainees" during the George W. Bush Administrations, leading to a focus on international humanitarian law among other concerns.

Increasingly this amalgam of private actors is referred to as civic action groups, or as making up civil society. In global civil society, there was a great variety of private, non-profit groups, some of them clearly opposed to internationally recognized human rights.[7] Some of these groups seemed to generate so much influence on certain issues that some observers saw a "power shift" in international relations, with governments becoming less important and private groups decidedly more important.[8] On various issues the human rights NGOs could sometimes be influential, without doubt. Under CEDAW (Convention on the Elimination of Discrimination against Women), when governments submitted the required report about national implementation, the International Women's Rights Action Watch submitted a "shadow report" usually providing a more honest evaluation of the situation. This shadow report was then used in subsequent deliberations in the review process.

Along with the growing numbers, salience, and maybe even influence of civil society organizations came growing criticism. If one wanted to contest the activism of Human Rights Watch, one might say that it was elitist, non-democratic, non-transparent, and unaccountable. It was true that aside from AI, most human rights NGOs were not mass-membership organizations and held no elections for their leaders. They were indeed self-appointed.

On the other hand, there was the view that arguments about democracy and accountability for governments were inappropriate for human rights NGOs.[9] Human rights NGOs might be perceived as legitimate, or playing a correct role, if they impartially and neutrally worked in a non-partisan way to advance norms that had been approved by states. And they might be considered accountable if they were transparent about the sources and uses of their funds, and how they reached their advocacy positions. It was illogical to argue that NGOs were illegitimate when they

---

[7] See especially A. Florini, *The Third Force: The Rise of Transnational Civil Society* (Washington: Carnegie Endowment, 2000); and Michael Edwards, *Civil Society* (Cambridge: Polity, 2004). In general, see the *Global Civil Society Yearbook*, published by the London School of Economics and Political Science.

[8] Jessica Tuchman Mathews, "Power Shift," *Foreign Affairs*, 76, 1 (Jan.–Feb. 1997), 50–66.

[9] For background, see M. Edwards, *NGO Rights and Responsibilities: A New Deal for Global Governance* (London: Foreign Policy Center, 2000).

were approved to attend UN and other IGO meetings. The International Committee of the Red Cross, technically a private Swiss civic association, was even recognized – and given rights and duties – in the international humanitarian law approved by states.

Because traditional international human rights groups may indeed join with a variety of other actors to deal with particular human rights situations or issues, some prefer to speak of movements, coalitions, or networks rather than separate organizations.[10] Thus it was said that there was a movement to ban landmines, or a movement in support of an international criminal court. According to Keck and Sikkink, such movements may include NGOs, local social movements, foundations, the media, churches, trade unions, consumer organizations, intellectuals, parts of intergovernmental organizations, and parts of national or sub-national governments.[11] Hence it was said sometimes that the movement in support of a UN criminal court was made up of "like-minded states" plus over 200 human rights NGOs plus elements of the communications media, along with individuals. The foreign minister of Canada, in his efforts to achieve a strong international criminal court, wrote in 1998: "With lessons learned from the successful campaign for a treaty banning land mines, we are engaging not only political leaders but also nongovernmental organizations, media and citizens around the world."[12] Such movements or coalitions were indeed made up of diverse partners.[13]

Increasingly individuals or organizations that operate websites on the internet may be part of a coalition active on one or more human rights issues. The collection and spreading of information about human rights on the internet was a relatively new development in the 1990s that had the potential for considerable impact. For example, the International Monitor Institute started documenting human rights violations in the Balkans, moved to providing information on war crimes trials from the former

---

[10] See, for example, Jackie Smith, Charles Chatfield, and Ron Pagnucco, eds., *Transnational Social Movements and Global Politics: Solidarity Beyond the State* (Syracuse: Syracuse University Press, 1997); and Keck and Sikkink, *Activists Beyond Borders*.

[11] On the important but little studied matter of funding of NGOs by charitable foundations, see Jay Ovsiovitch, "Feeding the Watchdogs: Philanthropic Support for Human Rights NGOs," *Buffalo Human Rights Law Review*, 4 (1998), 341–364.

[12] Lloyd Axworthy, "Without Justice, No Security for Ordinary People," *International Herald Tribune*, June 16, 1998, 6. See further Benjamin N. Schiff, *Building the International Criminal Court* (Cambridge: Cambridge University Press, 2008), for a good analysis of the interaction of states and NGOs.

[13] See further Henry J. Steiner, *Diverse Partners: Non Governmental Organizations and the Human Rights Movement* (Cambridge, MA: Harvard Law College, 1991, for the Harvard Law School Human Rights Program and the Human Rights Internet). See also Laurie Wiseberg, "Human Rights Non-Governmental Organizations," in *The Role of Non Governmental Organizations in the Promotion and Protection of Human Rights* (Leiden: Stichting NJCM-Boekerig, n.d. [1989?]); and Keck and Sikkink, *Activists Beyond Borders*.

Yugoslavia, and then created the Rwanda Archive.[14] This and other relevant electronic activity fed into the Rome diplomatic conference of July 1998 that approved a statute for an international criminal court.

In the so-called Arab Spring of 2011, in which grassroots demonstrations broke out across the Arab world and Iran demanding more democracy and human rights, social networking and social media utilizing instruments such as Facebook and Twitter were central. A number of local and international NGOs were active, and the response of governments was crucial. But much networked activism arose through previously unknown informal groups. An individual in Tunisia set himself ablaze in frustrated reaction to economic distress in the context of repressive governmental policies. This incident was transmitted widely among individuals not only in Tunisia but then in Egypt. Demonstrations in Egypt then affected other protests in Bahrain, Libya, Syria, Jordan, Yemen, Morocco, and elsewhere. As far away as China, the nervous government cracked down on dissidents, human rights activists, journalists, and others, fearing that knowledge of street protests in the Middle East would generate similar demands for liberalization in China. The so-called mainstream media also transmitted images and played a role in helping to set the policy agenda of various governments. But in Egypt, for example, some of the early protests were led and organized by secular liberals utilizing the internet and cell phones, who then had to face competition from certain highly organized private groups such as the Muslim Brotherhood for control and direction of the movement. A key organizer of the early demonstrations was an employee of Google "on leave" from his job. The Arab street, loosely linked by social media, forced governmental change in Tunisia and Egypt, destabilized Yemen, Syria, and Bahrain, threatened the *status quo* in Jordan and Morocco, and led to civil war in Libya with major outside intervention by NATO and various states.[15]

The process

If we focus on the advocacy of traditional human rights organizations, either as separate entities or part of a network or movement, it is reasonably clear what these groups do.[16] First, the bedrock of all their activity is

[14] See www.imisite.org.

[15] See PBS Newshour, "Social Media's Role in Egyptian, Arab World Protests," February 15, 2011, www.pbs.org/newshour/extra/video/blog/2011/02/social_medias_role_in_egyptian.html. For background, see Sydney G. Tarrow, *Power in Movement: Social Movements and Contentious Politics*, 3rd edn. (Cambridge: Cambridge University Press, 2011). For further background see John Lannon, Steven F. Hick, and Edward F. Halpin, "Internet," in *Encyclopedia of Human Rights*, vol. III, 182–194.

[16] For a different approach, see Howard J. Tolley, Jr., *The International Commission of Jurists: Global Advocates for Human Rights* (Philadelphia: University of Pennsylvania Press, 1994).

the collection of accurate information and its timely dissemination. For a group to generate influence on governments and other public authorities like the UN Human Rights Council, it must manifest a reputation for accurate reporting and dissemination of information. States do not exist primarily to report the truth. They exist primarily to exercise power on behalf of national interests as they see them. Relevant is the old maxim about the role of ambassadors: they are sent abroad to lie for their country. Private human rights groups, on the other hand, do not fare very well if they do not develop a reputation for accurate reporting of human rights information.

Amnesty International has developed a general reputation since its founding in 1961 for accurate reporting primarily about prisoners of conscience – those imprisoned for their political and social views expressed mostly non-violently – and about torture and the death penalty, *inter alia*.[17] It has a research staff in London of about 320 persons (plus about 100 volunteers) that is much larger than the staff of the UN Human Rights Centre in Geneva.[18] AI's record is not perfect regarding accuracy, and in several instances it has had to retract public statements and reports, as when it got caught up in Kuwaiti propaganda in 1990 and erroneously repeated the story that invading Iraqi forces had torn incubators from premature Kuwaiti babies. But in general, AI is known for reliable reporting. One study found that AI's reporting was affected not just by the severity of human rights violations in a nation, but also by such factors as: the nation's links to US military assistance and prominence in the global media; and AI's opportunities to maximize advocacy, chance to shape norms, desire to raise its own profile, and other factors.[19]

The International Committee of the Red Cross (ICRC) has built up a reputation since 1863 for meticulously careful statements about prisoners of war and other victims of armed conflict and complex emergencies. Its staff of some 800 in Geneva, plus another 1,200 or so in the field (including those seconded from national Red Cross/Red Crescent societies but not counting those hired locally), is extremely hesitant to comment unless its delegates in the field can directly verify what has transpired. This author could find few examples, in the ICRC's long history,

---

[17] AI has manifested internal debate about its proper focus. Traditionalists want it to concentrate on a narrow range of civil rights, while others want it to broaden its focus and activities. The basic identity of the organization has been the subject of disagreement. See especially Stephen Hopgood, *Keepers of the Flame: Understanding Amnesty International* (Ithaca: Cornell University Press, 2006).

[18] For details about AI, see its News Service Release 108/99, March 1999.

[19] James Ron, et al., "Transnational Information Politics: NGO Human Rights Reporting, 1986–2000," *International Studies Quarterly*, 49, 3 (September 2005), 557–588. Some of the findings pertain to HRW as well as to AI.

of false public statements about factual conditions. When they occurred, they arose from repeating information that had been obtained from other organizations but without sufficient verification. There seemed to be no examples in contemporary international relations of ICRC delegates misrepresenting what they had directly observed in conflict situations.[20]

While various actors may disagree with some of the policies that human rights NGOs advocate, very few scholars and responsible public officials challenge the record of accurate reporting over time by the most salient NGOs. The actors that do attack their veracity usually have something to hide. This was true of the Reagan Administration in the 1980s, which supported gross violations of human rights by its clients in Central America while trying to roll back what it saw as communism in especially El Salvador and Nicaragua. Reagan officials therefore attacked the veracity of AI, when it reported on brutal US clients, precisely because they found its reports – which were eventually proved accurate – irritating and embarrassing.[21] The George W. Bush Administration attacked the veracity and impartiality of AI when the latter criticized US politics toward enemy detainees after 9/11, but at the same time used AI reports to try to highlight the brutality of Saddam Hussein in Iraq. Israel has at times charged AI and Human Rights Watch with being biased against the Jewish state. So even democracies will at times seek to try to discredit the human rights organizations presenting critical reports.

Second, the human rights advocacy NGOs, on the basis of their analysis and dissemination of information, try to persuade public authorities to adopt new human rights standards or apply those already adopted. This activity can fairly be termed lobbying, but in order to preserve their non-political and tax-free status in most western societies, the groups tend to refer to this action as education.[22] The techniques are well known

---

[20] See further David P. Forsythe, *The Humanitarians: The International Committee of the Red Cross* (Cambridge: Cambridge University Press, 2005); and Forsythe and Barbara Ann J. Rieffer-Flanagan, *The International Committee of the Red Cross* (London and New York: Routledge, 2008). This is not to say that the ICRC was never involved in controversy about public statements, only that its public statements were almost never shown to be at variance with facts "on the ground." If one goes back in history, however, say to the ICRC's involvement in the Italian invasion of what is now Ethiopia, the record may be otherwise. See Ranier Baudendistel, *Between Bombs and Good Intentions: The International Committee of the Red Cross and the Italo-Ethiopian War, 1935–1936* (New York and Oxford: Berghahn Books, 2005).

[21] See further David P. Forsythe, "Human Rights and US Foreign Policy: Two Levels, Two Worlds," in David Beetham, ed., *Politics and Human Rights* (Oxford: Blackwell, 1995), 111–130, especially 120.

[22] Claude E. Welch, Jr., makes the argument that human rights NGOs are not interest groups because they are altruistic rather than self-centered actors seeking interests for themselves. This is not persuasive. There are public interest groups, like Common

to students of politics. One can organize letter-writing campaigns, meet face-to-face with officials, arrange briefing sessions for staff assistants, submit editorials or "op ed" pieces to the print media, become a "talking head" on television, and so forth. A mass organization like AI will frequently combine a letter-writing campaign with elite contact. An organization like Human Rights Watch or the International Commission of Jurists, lacking a mass membership, eschews grassroots letter writing and other grassroots lobbying and concentrates on contact by the professional staff with public officials. The point is to press one's point of view, and of course its reasonableness under law, until it becomes controlling policy.

In this process prominent NGOs such as AI and HRW can be considered part of the "gatekeepers" who determine what claims are to be considered human rights claims, and with what prominence.[23] The HIV/AIDS pandemic was once considered strictly a public health issue. Water was once considered an economic or geographical issue. Both, among other issues, were transformed into human rights issues, at least partially, by the decisions and actions of various agencies and personalities – including human rights NGOs.

According to one study that focused on basic civil rights called rights to personal integrity (made up of the right to life, to freedom from forced disappearances and summary execution, and freedom from torture and inhumane treatment), international NGOs worked with domestic groups both to protect the space for action of the domestic groups and to bring about change in the policy of the target government.[24]

A danger for human rights NGOs is that in their single-minded pursuit of the issue of human rights, and with a concern for moral consistency, they may come across to public officials as moralistic, rigid, and politically naive.[25] Top foreign policy officials are challenged to manage the

---

Cause in the USA, that are similar to the international human rights NGOs. They lobby in traditional ways for values that benefit society in general, and particular persons or groups of persons along the way. Common Cause is a public interest group, and so is Amnesty International. They are both interest groups. Compare Welch, *Protecting Human Rights in Africa: Strategies and Roles of Non Governmental Organizations* (Philadelphia: University of Pennsylvania Press, 1995), 44 and *passim*.

[23] See Clifford Bob, ed., *The International Struggle for New Human Rights* (Philadelphia: University of Pennsylvania Press, 2008).

[24] Thomas Risse, et al., *The Power of Human Rights* (Cambridge: Cambridge University Press, 1999).

[25] See the debate in *Foreign Policy*, 105 (Winter 1996–1997), 91–106, between Aryeh Neier, formerly of Human Rights Watch, who stresses the importance of moral consistency for human rights NGOs ("The New Double Standard"), and Jeffrey Garten, a former US official, who stresses the many roads to progress and the necessity for flexible judgment in context – and by implication the tolerance of inconsistency ("Comment: The Need for Pragmatism"). This debate was covered in detail in Chapter 4.

contradictions inherent in the effort to blend security, economic, ecological, and human rights concerns into one overall policy.[26] I noted in Chapter 6 how difficult it was for any state with multiple goals and interests, which means all of them, to present a consistent record on human rights issues. An NGO quest for perfect moral consistency may strike many foreign policy professionals as utopian. Only 11 percent of surveyed NGOs reported success in achieving policy change in favor of the human rights positions they advocated.[27]

The other side of the coin, however, is that many movements that seemed moralistic and utopian at the outset achieved changed policies and situations over time. Slavery, jousting, foot-binding, denial of the vote to women, and many other ideas were firmly institutionalized in many societies in the past. Being ideas, they were all subject to change, and all did change under relentless pressure over time.[28] What was utopian became practical. What was firmly entrenched, even central, became anachronistic. In the 1980s there were not many foreign policy officials, or human rights advocates for that matter, who thought a standing international criminal court was likely. By 1998–2002, it became a reality, although its future was uncertain.

Even agreement between governments and NGOs on general or long-term goals may lead to disputes about immediate tactics. In the 1990s, many human rights NGOs pressed for immediate action to arrest those indicted for gross violations of human rights in former Yugoslavia. Many US officials, supportive of international criminal prosecution in principle, but concerned about neo-isolationistic impulses within the public and Congress should there be US casualties, chose a policy on arrest that was more cautious than most human rights NGOs desired. Likewise during the 1990s, many human rights NGOs pressed for immediate sanctions on China in the context of continued systematic repression. Many US officials, desiring China's cooperation on a range of security, economic, and ecological issues, chose a policy on human rights in China that was more cautious and long term than many human rights NGOs desired. The broad responsibilities of top state officials even in liberal democracies guaranteed that from time to time their views of the "right" course of action would differ from those of human rights NGOs.

---

[26] On foreign policy as the inherent management of contradictions, see Stanley Hoffmann, "The Hell of Good Intentions," *Foreign Policy*, 29 (Winter 1977–1978), 3–26.

[27] Smith, et al., "Globalizing Human Rights," 392.

[28] On the role of ideas in international relations, see especially John Mueller, *Quiet Cataclysm: Reflections on the Recent Transformation of World Politics* (New York: Basic Books, 1995); and Judith Goldstein and Robert O. Keohane, eds., *Ideas and Foreign Policy: Beliefs, Institutions, and Political Change* (Ithaca: Cornell University Press, 1993).

During 1999 AI bitterly denounced the brief and *pro forma* meeting that had been called to discuss the application of the Fourth Geneva Convention of 1949 to the territories occupied through war by Israel in the Middle East.[29] AI wanted a longer and more substantive meeting to deal with such questions as interrogation methods used by Israel on Palestinian detainees. But the Palestinian Authority, the United States, Israel, and finally most other participants decided that after the election of the Barak government in Israel, restarting a general peace process took precedence over criticizing Israel about issues in the territories. AI emphasized human rights issues in Israeli-controlled areas, whereas the key public authorities thought that peace and stable relations between the Israelis and Palestinians constituted the top priority, after which one could make better progress on other issues.

In Syria in 2011, as the Arab Spring spread street protests demanding more democracy and attention to human rights in a state dictatorially ruled by the same family for some four decades, the US government deplored the killing of protestors. But, despite ample NGO and media reports about the extent of repression, it did not move decisively and quickly against the Assad regime. The Obama team worried about what governing arrangements might follow the fall of Assad and the implications particularly for Turkey, its NATO ally (which, like Syria, had an important Kurdish minority), and Israel (Assad in fact had not made much direct trouble for Israel for quite some time). So as deaths mounted at the hands of the government's security forces, the Obama team did not intervene militarily or push NATO to do so, as had been the case in Libya where the US complicating concerns were fewer. It was also the case that, by the time of increasing street protests and fatalities in Syria, the USA was militarily bogged down in Libya whether acting unilaterally or via NATO under UN general mandate. Human rights NGOs maintained their singular focus on human rights in Syria, but as usual various governments including Israel looked at the situation with much concern for their version of national interests. (The Netanyahu government in Israel was not, in general, a strong advocate for more democracy and human rights in the Arab world. It knew that some of the dictators, such as Mubarak in Egypt, had been a quiet friend, and that more genuinely democratic governments in the Arab world might result in more sympathy, at a minimum, for the plight of Palestinians in the West Bank and Gaza, and thus more difficulties for the Jewish state.)

Traditional human rights NGOs cannot utilize two basic resources of many successful interest groups when dealing with public officials,

[29] News Service Release 135/99, July 15, 1999.

because human rights NGOs possess neither the large or concentrated membership to threaten electoral punishment, nor the budgets to threaten the withholding of significant financial contributions. In the absence of these two resources, these NGOs fall back on accurate information and energetic lobbying by whatever name. These are combined with knowledge of the timing of key public policy decisions (easier in the legislative rather than the executive process of decision making), and the development of access to key policy makers and media outlets.

Third, traditional human rights NGOs publish information in the hopes of long-term education. This blends with the objective of influencing policy in the short term through dissemination. Today's education may become the context for tomorrow's policy making. Those educated today may be the policy makers of tomorrow. Virtually all of the traditional human rights NGOs manifest an active and extensive publishing program. Human Rights Watch has a publishing agreement with Yale University Press. Most of the human rights NGOs have a line in their budget for publishing books, brochures, reports, etc. They all make use of the internet to disseminate their information. They wish to raise the consciousness of both policy makers and the attentive public, so as to provide a better environment for their lobbying efforts.

The issue of publication to create and maintain a supportive political environment for human rights policy is crucial, whether one pictures it as part of grassroots lobbying or long-term education. We know that in the USA in the 1990s, American public opinion in general tended to support pragmatic internationalism but not so much moral internationalism.[30] That is to say, American public opinion was supportive of an active foreign policy on trade and other issues such as interdicting illegal drugs from abroad, as long as some direct connection could be shown to the betterment of American society. But where projected foreign policies seemed to be based on morality divorced from self-interest, as was the case with ending starvation in Somalia, American public opinion was not so supportive if perceived national interests had to be sacrificed – e.g., the deaths of American soldiers. In this type of political environment, private human rights groups regularly bemoaned their lack of ability to significantly and consistently influence foreign policy and international

---

[30] Ole Holsti, "Public Opinion and Human Rights in American Foreign Policy," in David P. Forsythe, ed., *The United States and Human Rights: Looking Inward and Outward* (Lincoln: University of Nebraska Press, 1999), ch. 7. This point was covered in Chapter 6 of the present volume.

relations.[31] This type of pragmatic environment worked to the advantage of those business and labor organizations that advocated business as usual and the downgrading of human rights concerns to the extent that they interfered with international trade. Self-interest being the strong factor that it was, the Executive Director of AI-USA wrote a book about why American citizens should be concerned about human rights in other countries. He based his arguments on American self-interest, not transnational morality.[32]

Symptomatic of the situation in the USA, the one remaining superpower, was a growing consensus in both the executive and legislative branches that general and unilateral economic sanctions interfered with trade objectives, caused friction with allies, and were not very effective.[33] General economic sanctions in support of human rights goals were not very popular. Policy makers in Washington knew that they would not be subjected to mass public pressure in support of most human rights situations abroad. They knew that if foreign policy exceeded a certain permissive range and began to incur costs divorced from evident self-interest, that policy would be in trouble – as in Somalia from late fall 1993. This attitudinal environment helps explain the NATO policy of relatively high-altitude air strikes on Yugoslavia in 1999 and the reluctance to commit ground troops in Kosovo. It also partially explains the reluctance of most western states to put troops on the ground in the Libyan civil war of 2011. This general political environment, in which many citizens in many countries were unwilling to sacrifice for the rights of others, undercut much effort by private human rights groups. Samantha Power has shown that the American public has never generated strong pressure on any American president to respond decisively to even genocide abroad, or punished a president for having failed to do so.[34] All of this did not rule out, however, "smart" sanctions against particular repressive rulers, allowing trade and assistance to continue to the nation while targeting the ruling elites' travel and banking.

---

[31] In addition to Neier, "The New Double Standard," see Ellen Dorsey, "US Foreign Policy and the Human Rights Movement: New Strategies for a Global Era," in Forsythe, ed., *The United States and Human Rights*, ch. 8.

[32] William F. Schulz, *In Our Own Best Interest: How Defending Human Rights Benefits Us All* (Boston: Beacon Press, 2001).

[33] Eric Schmitt, "US Backs Off Sanctions, Seeing Poor Effect Abroad," *New York Times*, July 31, 1998, 1. But in 1999 the Clinton Administration announced unilateral economic sanctions against the Taliban government in Afghanistan, primarily in reaction to alleged state-supported terrorism, but also because of discrimination against women. Congress and the American public quietly deferred.

[34] Samantha Power, *"A Problem from Hell": America and the Age of Genocide* (New York: Perennial, 2002).

A pragmatic rather than moralistic political culture, as a general political environment, did not mean that no advances could be made on behalf of internationally recognized human rights. Some private human rights groups teamed up with the Black Caucus in Congress to successfully direct attention to the situation in repressive Haiti in the mid-1990s. The Clinton Administration, which had from its beginnings manifested some officials also interested in doing something about repressive rule in Haiti, was able to undertake a military operation in support of democracy there and essentially end Haitian illegal emigration to the USA – but only as long as "significant" amounts of American blood and treasure were not sacrificed. Had Clinton's Haitian policy incurred the same costs as that in Somalia, namely the combat deaths of a dozen or so soldiers, it is highly likely the Haitian policy would have resulted in the same fate as the US's Somali policy – the withdrawal of congressional and public support. The same analysis could be applied to the deployment of US troops in Bosnia and their arrest of indicted war criminals. The Executive could advance human rights abroad as long as no costs arose that important political circles might deem "significant." But if perceived major costs arose, especially human costs, the public would expect the Executive to show a direct connection to expediential US concerns. (All of the examples noted above involve congressional influence, as much as NGO influence, along with the influence of the media.) Whether NGO human rights education could make transnational political culture more sensitive to, and supportive of, human rights concerns was an important question.[35]

At least in the USA after the terrorist attacks of September 11, 2001, if one wanted to do something about violations of human rights and lack of democracy in a failed state such as Somalia, one was more likely to get a sympathetic hearing in Congress and the public if one stressed US self-interests in closing down a safe haven for terrorists, rather than stressing the need for better rights for foreigners. Even so, in that situation the USA worked very hard to involve Kenya, Ethiopia, the African Union, and the United Nations, so as to reduce the need for direct US intervention.

Fourth and finally, some human rights advocacy groups also provide direct services to those victimized by human rights violations. They may engage in "judicial lobbying" or legal advocacy by participating in court

---

[35] NGO human rights education was joined by formal human rights education at all levels of learning, and by human rights education in professional associations. See further George J. Andreopoulos and Richard Pierre Claude, eds., *Human Rights Education for the Twenty-First Century* (Philadelphia: University of Pennsylvania Press, 1997); and Sia Spiliopoulou Akermark, *Human Rights Education: Achievements and Challenges* (Turku/Abo, Finland: Institute for Human Rights, Abo Akademi University, 1998).

cases. They may advise litigants or submit friendly briefs (*amicus curiae* briefs) in an effort to get courts to make rulings favorable to human rights standards. They may advise asylum seekers about how to present their claims to refugee status under international law. They may observe trials in the hopes of deterring a miscarriage of justice. A unique (*sui generis*) organization like the ICRC engages both in detention visits to help ensure humanitarian conditions of detention (and sometimes the release of the detainee on humanitarian grounds), and in multifaceted relief efforts for both prisoners and other victims of war and political conflict.

In sum to this point, the number of advocacy groups for various human rights causes grew dramatically in the last quarter of the twentieth century, even if the core group with a global focus and a link strictly to the international law of human rights and humanitarian affairs has remained relatively small. At the 1993 UN Conference on Human Rights at Vienna, the UN officially reported that 841 NGOs attended.[36] Particularly remarkable has been the number of groups advocating greater attention to women's rights as human rights. Their presence was felt both at Vienna and at the 1991 UN Conference on Women at Beijing. These and other UN conferences were sometimes criticized as nothing more than talking shops or debating societies. Hardly ever did states drastically change their policies immediately after these meetings. But the conferences provided focal points for NGO organizing and networking. And at least for a time they raised the world's consciousness about human rights in general or particular rights questions.[37] In the early twenty-first century there were more private reports being issued on more human rights topics than ever before in world history. Women's rights, children's rights, prisoner's rights, etc. all drew extensive NGO attention. True, biases continued. Social and economic rights continued to be the step-children or illegitimate offspring of the human rights movement, especially on the part of NGOs based in the West. Nevertheless, an international civic society was emerging in which human rights advocacy groups and their shifting partners were highly active.

Influence?

The most important question was not so much what the human rights groups did, and how; that was reasonably clear to close observers. Rather,

---

[36] UN Doc.: A/conf.157/24 (Report of the World Conference on Human Rights), October 13, 1993, Part I, 9.
[37] In general see Michael Schechter, *UN Global Conferences* (London and New York: Routledge, 2005).

the challenging question was how to specify, then generalize about, their influence.[38] It had long proved difficult to precisely analyze the influence of any interest group or coalition in any political system over time.[39] Why was it that in the USA the "tobacco lobby" seemed so powerful, only to suddenly be placed on the defensive in the 1990s and lose a series of votes in the US Congress that produced tougher laws on tobacco advertising and use? Why was it that the "Israeli lobby," generally thought to be one of the more powerful in American politics, seemed to weaken in the 1990s and was certainly unable to block a whole series of arms sales to Arab states? Why was the "China lobby," presumably strong in Washington during the Cold War, unable to block a rapprochement between Washington and Beijing? These and other questions about the influence of lobbies in general, or in relation to foreign policy, are not easy to answer. It was often said that "special interests" dominated modern politics, but proving the precise influence of these "special interests" became more difficult the more one probed into specifics.

A pervasive difficulty in analyzing NGO influence centered around the concept of success. If one or more NGOs succeeded in helping a UN Security Council resolution creating a criminal court for Rwanda to be adopted, but the *ad hoc* court turned out to have little impact on the Great Lakes region of Africa, could that be considered a success for NGO influence? But if later the *ad hoc* court contributed to the creation of a standing international criminal court at the UN, would the criteria for success change? If Amnesty International or the International Committee of the Red Cross prevented some instances of torture, how would one prove that success since the violation of human rights never occurred? If in Bosnia in the 1990s actors such as the ICRC and UNHCR helped reduce political rape and murder, but in so doing, by moving vulnerable civilians out of the path of enemy forces, they thereby contributed to ethnic cleansing and the basic political objective of a fighting party, was that a success?

In dealing with the sometimes elusive notion of success or achievement, sometimes it helped to distinguish among the following: success in getting an item or subject on the agenda for discussion, success in

---

[38] See further Don Hubert, "Inferring Influence: Gauging the Impact of NGOs," in Charlotte Ku and Thomas G. Weiss, eds., *Toward Understanding Global Governance: The International Law and International Relations Toolbox* (Providence, RI: ACUNS Reports and Papers, No. 2, 1998), 27–54.

[39] Bernard C. Cohen, *The Public's Impact on Foreign Policy* (Boston: Little, Brown, 1973). In general see David P. Forsythe, *Human Rights and World Politics*, 2nd edn. (Lincoln: University of Nebraska Press, 1989), ch. 6.

achieving serious discussion, success in getting procedural or institutional change, and finally success in achieving substantive policy change that clearly ameliorated or eliminated the problem. In the early stages of campaigns against slavery or female genital mutilation, it could be considered remarkable success just to get high state officials to think about the subject as an important problem.[40] In addressing gay rights in Muslim nations, it might be a mark of success just to get reasonable public debate.

Relatedly, one of the most helpful contributions that a human rights NGO or movement could obtain was the supportive finding of an epistemic community. Epistemic communities are networks of scientists or "thinkers" who deal in "truth" as demonstrated by cause and effect. To the extent that there is widespread agreement on scientific truth, public policy tends to follow accordingly – albeit with a time lag during which advocacy or lobbying comes into play. If the scientific evidence of the harmful effects of "second-hand smoke" had been stronger sooner, those campaigning against smoking in public and indoor places would have had an easier time of it. When medical personnel can show conclusively that female genital mutilation presents clear risks to those undergoing this ritual cutting in much of Africa and other places, the reporting and dissemination of this scientific truth aids those human rights groups trying to eliminate the practice.[41] If the science of global warming led to clearer conclusions now, effectuating policy change would be easier. Unfortunately, most decisions in support of international human rights involved political and moral choice rather than scientific truth.

The greatest obstacle to proving the influence of human rights NGOs was that in most situations their influence was merged with the influence of public officials in the context of other factors such as media coverage. In social science jargon, this is the agent–structure problem: agents, or actors, operate in a particular context (structure). Even using the same tactics, sometimes an agent is successful and sometimes not, as with the London-based Anti-Slavery Society in the anti-slave trade and the anti-slavery movement. What made the crucial difference was "structure" in Europe or the Caribbean – namely, e.g., whether the British government was under serious pressure from France.[42]

---

[40] Keck and Sikkink, *Activists Beyond Borders*.

[41] See further Ernst Haas, *When Knowledge Is Power: Three Models of Change in International Organizations* (Berkeley: University of California Press, 1990); and Peter Haas, "Introduction: Epistemic Communities and International Policy Coordination," *International Organization*, 46, 3 (Winter 1992), 1–36.

[42] Adam Hochschild, *Bury the Chains: Prophets and Rebels in the Fight to Free an Empire's Slaves* (Boston and New York: Houghton Mifflin, 2005, 2006).

Private human rights groups had long urged the creation of a United Nations High Commissioner for Human Rights, and the post was voted into being in 1993. This was two years after the implosion of the Soviet Union and the discrediting of European communism. Many private groups wanted to claim credit, but many governments had also been active in support of this cause. Salient personalities like former President Carter had campaigned vigorously for the creation of the post. And much media coverage was at work as well. Given that it was governments representing states that voted to create the office, it was difficult if not impossible to specify the exact influence of human rights advocacy groups.

Likewise human rights NGOs like Helsinki Watch (which evolved into Human Rights Watch) certainly pressured the European communists during the Cold War, acting in tandem with private individuals and groups inside those communist states. But western states were also active on human rights issues through the CSCE process. When European communism fell, it was impossible to say scientifically what was the exact impact of the human rights NGOs compared with state pressures, or for that matter compared with the economic difficulties of the European communists themselves (as noted in Chapter 4).

Most events have multiple causes, and it is often impossible to factor out in a precise way the exact impact of a human rights NGO or even a movement or coalition. In 1975 a relatively unknown member of the lower house of the US Congress, Donald Fraser, decided to hold hearings on human rights in US foreign policy. As chair of a sub-committee in the House of Representatives, Fraser had the authority to take such a decision by himself.[43] The Fraser hearings led to the reintroduction of the issue of human rights into US foreign policy after an absence of some two decades. But NGOs had some impact on these events in three ways.

Various anti-war NGOs and movements, which were the forerunners of several human rights NGOs in the USA, helped set the stage for the Fraser hearings.[44] It was growing domestic opposition to US policies in Vietnam, and a growing sense that US foreign policy had become amoral if not immoral, that contributed to the political climate in the USA in which Fraser acted. NGOs and social movements helped create that climate of opinion. Second, once scheduled, the Fraser hearings were

---

[43] See further Donald M. Fraser, "Freedom and Foreign Policy," *Foreign Policy*, 26 (Spring 1977), 140–156; and John Salzburg, "A View from the Hill: US Legislation and Human Rights," in David D. Newsom, ed., *The Diplomacy of Human Rights* (Lanham: University Press of America, 1986), 13–20.

[44] Lowell W. Livezey, *Non Governmental Organizations and the Idea of Human Rights* (Princeton: Princeton University Center for International Studies, 1988).

the scene of testimony on human rights issues by AI-USA and other human rights NGOs. Third, Fraser's principal staff person on foreign policy, John Salzburg, had worked for an NGO and still shared the values of a number of those in the NGO community in Washington. So although there is no clear evidence that NGOs pressed Fraser to take the momentous course of action he did, NGOs did have some influence, probably of rather high significance, in combining with Fraser and other public officials to emphasize human rights in US foreign policy.

Nial McDermot, an experienced staff member of the International Commission of Jurists, wrote accurately: "NGOs create the conditions in which governmental pressure can be effective."[45] It is in the synergy or interplay of public and private action that one normally understands the full role of human rights NGOs and their coalitions. Thus influence by private human rights groups is normally exercised in a quasi-private, quasi-public way. Just as much policy making is now transnational or interdomestic, involving both international and domestic players, so that policy making is also both public and private at one and the same time. Public officials may join with NGOs and the media, etc. to effectuate change. This is precisely why a focus on movements or coalitions or networks has come into vogue, although it is still challenging to try to determine which actor in the movement exercised crucial influence at crucial times.

In some situations it is relatively clear that human rights NGOs, or a coalition of them and their allies, have had direct impact on what might be termed a human rights decision. Several authors have shown that one can trace the release of one or more prisoners of conscience to action by AI.[46] One can also show that NGOs made significant contributions to the negotiation of human rights standards in certain treaties.[47] A strong case can be made that human rights NGOs, in combination with other actors such as media representatives, *inter alia*, have helped transform the

---

[45] N. McDermot, "The Role of NGOs in the Promotion and Protection of Human Rights," in *The Role of Non Governmental Organizations*, 45–52.

[46] Jonathan Power, *Amnesty International: The Human Rights Story* (New York: McGraw-Hill, 1981); Egon Larsen, *A Flame in Barbed Wire: The Story of Amnesty International* (London: F. Muller, 1978). See also Jane Connors, "Amnesty International at the United Nations," in Peter Willetts, ed., *"The Conscience of the World": The Influence of Non-Governmental Organizations in the UN System* (Washington: Brookings, 1996).

[47] Peter R. Baehr, "The General Assembly: Negotiating the Convention on Torture," in David P. Forsythe, ed., *The United Nations in the World Political Economy* (London: Macmillan, 1989), 36–53; Lawrence J. LeBlanc, *The Convention on the Rights of the Child: United Nations Lawmaking on Human Rights* (Lincoln: University of Nebraska Press, 1995), ch. 2.

political culture of Mexico, Argentina, and other states in the Western Hemisphere which now show more sensitivity to human rights issues.[48] Many if not most of the UN monitoring mechanisms, from review committees to Special Rapporteurs, rely on NGO information in conducting their activities. When critical questions are raised, or critical conclusions reached, it is frequently on the basis, at least in part, of NGO information. The reduction of state funding for certain UN activities has increased the impact of NGOs in the human rights domain; the UN offices lack the resources to conduct their own extensive inquiries, and thus fall back on information from the human rights NGOs.[49]

From time to time certain states have tried to block some human rights NGOs from receiving or renewing their consultative status with the UN system. This is a status that allows NGOs to circulate documents and speak in certain UN meetings. If NGOs had no influence, and never proved irritating to states, the latter would not be so interested in blocking the activities of the former. State opposition to, and criticism of, NGOs is a reasonably clear indication that states, meaning the governments that speak for them, pay some attention to human rights NGOs and worry about what they say. It is obvious that most states care about their reputations in international relations, and go to great efforts to try to counter critical commentary.[50]

During 1999, the UN Committee on Non-Governmental Organizations, which reports to ECOSOC, withdrew consultative status for Christian Solidarity International, based in Zurich. That controversial NGO had antagonized the government of Sudan in several ways. Likewise the committee refused to approve the credentials of Human Rights in China, based in New York, which had offended the government in Beijing.[51] So even after the Cold War, and despite the immense influence of western states in the UN system, mainly the states of the global south continued to try to limit the role of some human rights advocacy groups in UN proceedings.

---

[48] Keck and Sikkink, *Activists Beyond Borders*, 3.

[49] P. H. Kooijmans, "The Non Governmental Organizations and the Monitoring Activities of the United Nations in the Field of Human Rights," in *The Role of Non Governmental Organizations*, 15–22; Peter R. Baehr and Leon Gordenker, *United Nations University Public Forum on Human Rights and Non Governmental Organizations* (Tokyo: United Nations University Lectures, September 14, 15, 18, 1996).

[50] A classic case in point is the effort by the Argentine junta in the 1980s to try to block criticism of its human rights record in the UN Human Rights Commission, as recorded by Iain Guest in *Behind the Disappearances: Argentina's Dirty War Against Human Rights and the United Nations* (Philadelphia: University of Pennsylvania Press, 1990).

[51] Paul Lewis, "UN Committee, Under Pressure, Limits Rights Groups," *New York Times*, June 22, 1999, A3.

It cannot be scientifically proved, but a null hypothesis is certainly interesting: if human rights NGOs had not existed during the past thirty-five years, human rights would have a much less salient position in international relations. Serious, even grave, human rights violations in Cambodia in the 1970s and Mexico in the late 1960s did not lead to international attention and pressure because local and international NGOs were not in place to report on and act against those violations.[52] More positively, what began as action by the Anti-Slavery Society in London in the early nineteenth century triggered a successful movement against slavery and the slave trade over about a century. It is quite clear as well that since 1863, what is now called the International Committee of the Red Cross has advanced the cause of international humanitarian law, or the law of human rights in armed conflict. These are clear examples of NGOs that have had a broad impact on international relations, even if they frequently acted, or act today, in conjunction with public authorities. Public officials may take the decision to adopt human rights standards or seek certain forms of implementation. But they may act in an environment ("structure") created to a considerable extent by human rights NGOs or human rights coalitions. Much of this influence is amorphous and remains difficult to specify. In the future it might prove possible to further elaborate the conditions under which a human rights NGO or movement might expect to be successful – e.g., where leaders of a state targeted for pressure are on record as favoring human rights in principle, where such leaders do not regard the human rights violation as crucial to their hold on power or to the security of their state, where a target state is not a pivotal or vital state to others in strategic or economic terms, etc.

In the meantime, human rights NGOs have helped create a climate of opinion in international relations generally sympathetic to human rights. In this regard these NGOs have helped restrict and thus transform the idea of state sovereignty. It can be stated in general that the responsible exercise of state sovereignty entails respect for at least certain internationally recognized human rights. Recall the norm of R2P, approved in 2005 at the UN: when a state is unwilling or unable to protect against genocide, crimes against humanity, major war crimes, and/or ethnic cleansing, outside parties have a duty to become involved. States, like Saddam Hussein's Iraq, that engage in gross and systematic violation of the most elemental human rights are not afforded the normal prerogatives that stem from the principle of state sovereignty. During the 1990s Iraq was

---

[52] On Mexico, see Keck and Sikkink, *Activists Beyond Borders*. On Cambodia, I refer to genocide on a massive scale after most foreign observers had been kicked out by the Khmer Rouge.

put into *de facto* receivership under United Nations supervision. This was because of the misuse of sovereignty via violations of human rights in Iraq and Kuwait, combined with aggression against Kuwait. A similar analysis could be made about Milosevic in Yugoslavia or Kaddafi in Libya. It is still valid to say, as Francis Fukuyama wrote, that in dominant international political theory, the most fully legitimate state is the liberal democratic state that respects civil and political rights.[53] Advocacy groups for human rights play the basic role of reminding everyone of human rights performance, and particularly when gross and systematic violations occur that call into existence the basic legitimacy of a government to act for the state. This is why governments pay human rights NGOs so much attention, including sometimes trying to undermine and restrict what they do.

Private action for relief and development

As we have seen, the International Bill of Rights contains economic and social rights such as the rights to adequate food, clothing, shelter, and medical care in peacetime. International humanitarian law contains non-combatant rights to emergency assistance – referring to similar food, clothing, shelter, and medical care – in armed conflict.[54] United Nations resolutions have extended these same rights to "complex emergencies," an imprecise term meant to cover situations in which the relevant authority denies that there is an armed conflict covered by international humanitarian law, but in which civilians are in need and public order disrupted. In a tradition that defies legal logic, private groups working to implement these socioeconomic rights in peace and war are not normally referred to as human rights groups but as relief (or humanitarian) and development agencies. This semantic tradition may exist because many agencies were working for relief and development before the discourse on human rights became so salient.

---

[53] Francis Fukuyama, *The End of History and the Last Man* (New York: Free Press, 1992). Of course there is a gap between the political theory of legitimate states and the practice of international relations. In practice, persons and public authorities may grant legitimacy, meaning a sense of correct rule, on the basis of tradition, alliances, and/or effective exercise of power, and not just human rights performance. See David P. Forsythe, *Human Rights and Peace: International and National Views* (Lincoln: University of Nebraska Press, 1993), ch. 3. Compare Jack Donnelly, "Human Rights: A New Standard of Civilization?," *International Affairs*, 74, 1 (1998), 1–24.

[54] Legal obligations in this regard under the 1949 Geneva Conventions, and 1977 Additional Protocols, for victims of armed conflicts have been analyzed by numerous commentators, including Monika Sandvik-Nylund, *Caught in Conflicts: Civilian Victims, Humanitarian Assistance and International Law* (Turku/Abo, Finland: Institute for Human Rights of Abo Akademi University, 1998).

Whatever the semantic traditions, there are complicated international systems for both relief and development, and neither would function without private agencies. At the same time, the private groups are frequently supported by state donations of one type or another, and frequently act in conjunction with intergovernmental organizations. As with advocacy groups, so with relief and development agencies, the resulting process is both private and public at the same time. In both relief and development, the United States and the states of the European Union provide most of the resources.[55] In both, UN agencies are heavily involved – UNICEF, the WHO, the World Food Program, the UN Development Program, etc. But in both, private grassroots action is, to a very great extent, essential to whether persons on the ground get the food, clothing, shelter, and medical care which international law guarantees on paper. It is the private groups that turn the law on the books into the law in action. It is the private groups that condition and sometimes transform the operation of state sovereignty.

Relief

Because of international humanitarian law, the relief system in armed conflict and complex emergencies is somewhat different from that in peacetime. The norms supposedly guiding action are different, and some of the actors are different. For reasons of space, only relief in wars and complex emergencies is covered here.[56]

In so-called man-made disasters, the private International Committee of the Red Cross usually plays a central role because of its long association with victims of war and international humanitarian law. It was ultimately, for example, the best-positioned relief actor in Somalia in the early 1990s, and remained so even after the arrival of tens of thousands of US military personnel. The ICRC does not monopolize relief in these situations, however. In Bosnia in the first half of the 1990s, it was the Office of the UN High Commissioner for Refugees that ran the largest civilian relief program, followed by the ICRC. In Cambodia in the late 1980s, the UNHCR and the ICRC were essentially co-lead agencies for international relief. In Sudan during the 1970s and 1980s, UNICEF and the

---

[55] See further Alexander Natsios, *US Foreign Policy and the Four Horsemen of the Apocalypse: Humanitarian Relief in Complex Emergencies* (Westport: Praeger, 1997).

[56] Relief in natural disasters such as floods, earthquakes, typhoons, volcanic eruptions, etc. is analyzed in many sources, including by the late expert Frederick Cuny in *Disasters and Development* (New York: Oxford University Press, 1983). See also Peter Walker and Daniel G. Maxwell, *Shaping the Humanitarian World* (New York and London: Routledge, 2009).

ICRC carried out important roles. But in these and similar situations, numerous private agencies are active in relief: World Vision, Church World Service, Caritas, Oxfam, Save the Children, Doctors Without Borders, etc. It was not unusual to find several hundred private relief agencies active in a conflict situation like Rwanda and its environs in the mid-1990s.

Relief: process

One can summarize the challenges facing all these private relief agencies (aka socioeconomic human rights groups).[57]

(1) *They must negotiate access to those in need.* One may speak of guaranteed rights, even a right to assistance. And in the 1990s there was much discussion about a right to humanitarian intervention. But as a practical matter, one must reach agreement with those who have the guns on the ground in order to provide relief/assistance in armed conflict and complex emergencies. Even if there is some general agreement between public authorities (*de jure* and *de facto*) and relief agencies on providing relief, specifics have to be agreed upon for particular times and places. Negotiating conditions of access can be a tricky business, as fighting parties may seek to divert relief for military and political objectives, even as relief agencies may insist on impartiality and neutrality. With numerous relief agencies vying for a piece of the action, Machiavellian political actors may play one off against another. Some of the smaller, less-experienced agencies have proved themselves subject to political manipulation.

(2) *Relief agencies must provide an accurate assessment of need.* Relief must be tailored to local conditions, and there should be control for redundant or unneeded goods and services. The use of systematic rape as a weapon of war, terror, and ethnic cleansing has meant the need for gynecological and psychiatric services for many women.

(3) *The private groups must mobilize relief in a timely and effective way.* Here the ICRC has certain advantages, as it is well known and respected by most western states, and has links to national Red Cross or Red Crescent societies in over 185 states. But other private agencies have their own means of mobilization, being able to tap into well-established religious or secular networks.

(4) *Of obvious importance is the ability of a private group to actually deliver the assistance in a timely and cost-effective way.* Here again the ICRC

---

[57] The following is drawn from David P. Forsythe, "The International Committee of the Red Cross and Humanitarian Assistance: A Policy Analysis," *International Review of the Red Cross*, 314 (September–October 1996), 512–531.

presents certain advantages, as it is smaller and less bureaucratic than some UN bodies; has regional, country, and intra-country offices in many places around the world (in addition to the national Red Cross/Red Crescent societies); and since the 1970s has built up experience in the delivery of relief in ongoing conflicts and occupied territory. Its reputation for effectiveness on the ground was particularly outstanding in Somalia in the early 1990s. But other agencies, particularly the UNHCR, have been accumulating experience as well. And often the sheer size of a relief problem can be too great for the ICRC. In Rwanda in 1994 and thereafter, where as many as two million persons fled genocidal ethnic conflict and civil war, the ICRC concentrated its activities inside Rwanda and left to other actors the matter of relief in neighboring countries.

(5) *All relief agencies have to engage in evaluation of past action and planning for the future.* All of the major relief players do this, but some of the smaller, less-experienced, and more *ad hoc* groups do not.

The international system, movement, or coalition for relief in man-made disasters faces no shortage of pressing issues.

(1) *Should there be more coordination?* There has been much talk about more coordination, but none of the major players wants to be dominated by any other actor. Legally speaking, the ICRC is a Swiss private agency whose statutes give policy-making authority to an all-Swiss assembly that co-opts members from Swiss society only. It resists control by any United Nations body, any other Red Cross agency, or any state. Also, the UNHCR, UNICEF, the WHO, and the WFP all have independent budgets, executive heads, governing bodies, and mandates. Each resists control by any UN principal organ or by the UN Emergency Relief Coordinator (now the Under Secretary-General for Humanitarian Assistance) who reports to the Secretary-General. The latter UN office lacked the legal, political, and budgetary clout to bring the other actors under its control. Politically speaking, the major donors, the USA and the EU, have not insisted on more formal coordination. There are advantages to the present system. The UNHCR may be best positioned in one conflict, UNICEF or the ICRC in another. And there was *de facto* cooperation among many of the relief actors much of the time, with processes for voluntary coordination both in New York and Geneva. More importantly, there was considerable cooperation among agencies in the field. Yet duplication and conflicts occurred with regularity; there was certainly room for improvement.

(2) *Should one try to separate politics from humanitarian action?* Particularly the ICRC argued in favor of strict adherence to the

principles of impartiality and neutrality, and preferred to keep its distance from "political" decisions which involved coercion or any official preference for one side over another in armed conflict and complex emergencies. But even the ICRC had to operate under military protection in Somalia to deliver relief effectively (and had to accept military protection for released prisoners on occasion in Bosnia). In Bosnia, much of the fighting was about civilians – their location and sustenance. The UNHCR's relief program became "politicized" in the sense of intertwined with carrots and sticks provided in relation to diplomacy and peacemaking. There was disagreement about the wisdom of this course of action. But it was clear that once the UN authorized use of force in places like Bosnia to coerce a change in Serbian policy, then UN civilian (and military) personnel on the ground became subject to hostage-taking by antagonized Serb combatants. It was clear that the idea of a neutral Red Cross or UN presence for relief purposes was not widely respected in almost all of the armed conflicts and complex emergencies after the Cold War. Relief workers from various organizations were killed in places like Chechnya, Bosnia, Rwanda, Burundi, Liberia, Somalia, Afghanistan, etc. Other relief workers were taken hostage for ransom. Sometimes armed relief, even "humanitarian war," seemed the only feasible option, but others disagreed.[58]

(3) *Could one change the situation through new legislation and/or better dissemination of norms?* It was evident from the Soviet Union to communist Yugoslavia, to take just two clear examples, that former states had not taken fully seriously their obligation to teach international humanitarian law to military personnel, despite the strictures of especially the 1949 Geneva Conventions and additional 1977 Protocols for the protection of victims of war. After especially the French failed to have codified new laws on humanitarian intervention in the 1990s, action turned to international criminal justice and the creation of international tribunals to try those individuals accused of war crimes, genocide, and crimes against humanity. NGOs lobbied vigorously for these new norms and agencies to enforce them, as I have already noted in Chapter 4. But much violence was carried out by private armies such as rebel or secessionist groups, clans, and organized mobs. Relief workers more than once faced child soldiers on drugs

---

[58] Adam Roberts, "Humanitarian War: Military Intervention and Human Rights," *International Affairs*, 69, 3 (July, 1993), 429f. See further Jonathan Moore, ed., *Hard Choices: Moral Dilemmas in Humanitarian Intervention* (Lanham: Rowman & Littlefield, 1998); and Thomas G. Weiss, "The Humanitarian Identity Crisis," in *Ethics & International Affairs*, 13 (1999), 1–22, with associated commentary.

armed with automatic weapons. How to make international norms, whether new or old, effective on such combatants was a tough nut to crack. It was said of Somalia, only in slight exaggeration, that no one with a weapon had ever heard of the Geneva Conventions.[59] At least many of the relief agencies agreed on a code of conduct for themselves, which approximated but did not exactly replicate the core principles of the Geneva Conventions.

Relief: influence?

There is no question but that private actors have considerable if amorphous influence or impact in the matter of international relief in "man-made" conflicts. The ICRC was a major player in Somalia 1991–1995, the UNHCR and its private partners were a major player in Bosnia 1992–1995. The UNHCR does not so much deliver relief itself as contract with private agencies for that task. The UNHCR manages, supervises, and coordinates, but private actors like Doctors Without Borders do much of the grassroots relief. To use a negative example of influence, if several private groups disagree with a policy decision taken by the UNHCR and decide to operate differently, the UNHCR is constrained in what it can do. The same is even more true for the World Food Program, which has a very limited capacity to operate in the field by itself. The ICRC, as should be clear by now, is a private actor whose norms and accomplishments often affect the other players, directly or indirectly.

Having noted this NGO independent position, one must still recognize that states and intergovernmental organizations are the major sources for material resources directed to humanitarian assistance in wars and complex emergencies. It is states, directly or through IGOs, that provide the physical security that relief NGOs need for their grassroots operations – at least in territory that these states control. (These NGOs may prefer to rely on their own reputation for security of operations, but if that fails, they have to rely on the hard power of states.) Influence is a complex two-way street. Public authorities need the NGOs, which opens up possibilities for subtle influence on the part of the latter. But the NGOs need the support and cooperation of the public authorities. If NGOs pull out of a relief operation and develop the image of unreasonable non-cooperation, they will: (1) cut themselves out of operations that constitute their reason for being, (2) perhaps get bad publicity, and (3) make it more difficult to

---

[59] Jennifer Learning, "When the System Doesn't Work: Somalia, 1992," in Kevin M. Cahill, ed., *Framework for Survival: Health, Human Rights, and Humanitarian Assistance in Conflicts and Disasters* (New York: Basic Books, for the Council on Foreign Relations, 1993), 112.

raise money. Once again, as with traditional advocacy for human rights, we find that the movement to provide relief is both private and public at the same time, and that influence among the disparate elements is difficult to pinpoint in general.

The challenge facing relief/humanitarian agencies is probably even greater than that facing more traditional human rights advocacy groups. The former are dealing with states and other primary protagonists that have resorted to violence in pursuit of their goals. The issues at stake have already been deemed worth fighting over. In this context of armed conflict or complex emergency, it is exceedingly difficult to get the protagonists to elevate assistance to civilians to a rank of the first order. Moreover, in all too many conflicts, especially after the Cold War, intentional attacks on civilians, and their brutal manipulation otherwise, became part of the grand strategy of one or more of the fighting parties. It was therefore difficult if not impossible to fully neutralize and humanize civilian relief.[60]

Development: process

As in relief, the development process on an international scale presents a mixture of public and private actors. If we focus just on the PVOs based in the North Atlantic area we find they are exceedingly numerous – perhaps now up to about 5,000 in number – and quite varied in their orientations.[61] While some of these PVOs or VOLAGs reject state funding to protect their independence, and consequently wind up frequently on the margins of the development process, most act otherwise and serve as conduits for public monies and public policies. PVOs themselves provide only about 10 percent of development assistance in a typical year.

Private development agencies, like Oxfam, that cooperate with public authorities and operate consistently across international borders are a crucial part of the public–private development process. These development NGOs provide values and services often lacking in the public sector: "smallness, good contacts at the local level, freedom from political manipulation, a labor (rather than capital) intensive orientation, innovativeness, and flexibility in administration."[62]

---

[60] See further Michael Barnett and Thomas G. Weiss, eds., *Humanitarianism in Question: Politics, Power, Ethics* (Ithaca and London: Cornell University Press, 2008); and Richard A. Wilson and Richard D. Brown, *Humanitarianism and Suffering: The Mobilization of Empathy* (Cambridge and New York: Cambridge University Press, 2009).

[61] *Directory of Non-Governmental Organisations Active in Sustainable Development* (Paris: OECD, 1996).

[62] Brian H. Smith, *More than Altruism: The Politics of Private Foreign Aid* (Princeton: Princeton University Press, 1990), 6.

The OECD states find "mainstream" NGOs useful in implementing their goals while reducing suspicions of neo-imperialism or other unwanted intrusions in the affairs of developing states. Other public authorities seem to be coming around to this same view. Major intergovernmental actors are the World Bank (officially the International Bank for Reconstruction and Development), other development banks on a regional basis, and the United Nations Development Program (UNDP). The International Monetary Fund (IMF) is not, strictly speaking, a development institution. It frequently functions, however, in conjunction with the World Bank in making loans (affording drawing rights) to stabilize currency transactions or correct balance of payments problems.

Increasingly the World Bank officially endorses the participation of NGOs and community-based organizations (CBOs) in establishing development programs.[63] Theory and practice are not always the same, and historically relations between the Bank and development NGOs have been less than perfectly smooth. Many development NGOs have criticized the Bank for being insensitive to the needs of especially the rural poor, and within that group especially indigenous peoples, who did not benefit so clearly from the past industrial schemes of the Bank, and who may have been forced out of their traditional homes by development projects funded by the Bank.

The UNDP also officially endorses the bringing together of NGOs and CBOs to provide grassroots participation in development projects. If practiced seriously, this type of micro- or economic democracy would combine *de facto* attention to civil and political rights, as the rights of participation, with social and economic rights. Endorsement of NGO and CBO participation in the development process by the Bank, UNDP, and OECD states comprised part of the mantra of "sustainable human development" at the turn of the century. As theory, it was an improvement over the top-down massive infrastructure projects devised in Washington and New York in the 1960s and 1970s.

Development: influence?

Private development agencies faced no lack of problems in trying to help achieve sustainable human development in keeping with internationally recognized human rights. A new barrier in the 1990s was that the prevalence of ethnic conflict and other forms of internal armed conflict and political instability caused public authorities to channel vast amounts of

---

[63] See further David P. Forsythe, "The United Nations, Human Rights, and Development," *Human Rights Quarterly*, 19, 2 (May 1997), 334–349.

resources into relief. Consequently, fewer funds and less attention went to development. Moreover, from about 1980 and especially after 1990, western donor governments put great emphasis on "market solutions" and the role of direct foreign investment by transnational corporations, rather than official development assistance (ODA) by governments.

A historical problem was that PVOs and VOLAGs did not always think of development in relation to human rights,[64] although with time there was a shift toward focusing on empowerment – which was a synonym for participatory rights.[65] This shift was certainly welcomed by those development NGOs that had long expressed concern about authoritarian rather than democratic development.[66] I noted above how the theory of the World Bank, UNDP, and OECD states all accepted participation in decision making by NGOs and CBOs. There was also a considerable shift toward integrating women's rights with development strategies.[67] Much less pronounced historically was any shift toward emphasizing socioeconomic rights in the development process. But since at the UN, in the era of Boutros Boutros-Ghali and Kofi Annan, there was an effort to "mainstream human rights" in the development process, this approach affected the private development agencies. This rights-based approach (RBA) to development certainly affected the rhetoric and semantics of both public and private development agencies, and maybe even some of the substance.[68]

Development NGOs, much like traditional advocacy NGOs for human rights, had trouble in precisely specifying their influence in the development process *vis-à-vis* other actors.[69] As with the advocacy groups, many leaders of development NGOs were active out of moral commitment and would continue with their ideas and objectives whether or not they were able to change public programs to their liking. As with advocacy groups, the real influence of development NGOs was to be found in

[64] Theo van Boven, "Human Rights and Development: The UN Experience," in David P. Forsythe, ed., *Human Rights and Development: International Views* (London: Macmillan, 1989), 121–135.

[65] Julie Fisher, *Non-Governments: NGOs and the Political Development of the Third World* (West Hartford: Kumarian Press, 1998).

[66] Smith, *More than Altruism*, 72.

[67] See, for example, Sue Ellen M. Charlton and Jana Everett, eds., *NGOs and Grassroots in Development Work in South India: Elizabeth Moen Mathiot* (Lanham: University Press of America, 1998).

[68] See further Joel Oestreich, *Power and Principle: Human Rights Programming in International Organizations* (Washington: Georgetown University Press, 2007).

[69] Michael Edwards and David Hulme, eds., *Beyond the Magic Bullet: NGO Performance and Accountability in the Post-Cold War World* (West Hartford: Kumarian Press, in cooperation with Save the Children Fund, 1996).

their amorphous contribution to a wider movement, network, or coalition interested in sustainable *human* development. While true that public authorities provide most of the capital for development projects, some influence flows from the NGOs back toward public authorities – especially through the give and take over different approaches to development. Public authorities have no monopoly over ideas related to development, and some of the ideas that prove controlling over time originate with NGOs. If the point of the human rights discourse was to allow human beings to maximize their full potential as rational and autonomous beings worthy of dignity, this was essentially compatible with the notion of sustainable human development.

Conclusion

NGOs that advocate for human rights ideas, that implement the right to humanitarian assistance for those in dire straits, and that contribute to the human rights inherent in sustainable human development have impacted both public authorities and private individuals in numerous ways. They have advanced some form of liberalism in international relations through their emphasis on individuals and law, as compared with state interests and power. Advocacy groups provide much of the information that allows the rights agencies of international organizations to function, while challenging or validating the facts and policies put forward by states. It is difficult to believe the making and implementing of human rights standards would operate in the same way without these advocacy groups. The international relief system would simply not be able to get humanitarian assistance to those in need in most situations without the private relief agencies. The development process would be seriously hampered without the private development organizations to serve as intermediaries between the public authorities that provide most of the resources and the individuals and indigenous groups that implement, and benefit from, the development programs at the grassroots level.

States and their intergovernmental organizations are thus dependent on these NGOs. States share the stage of international relations with these NGOs, which is to say that state sovereignty is at times restricted by the activity of these NGOs that work for civil and political, social and economic rights. A restricted sovereignty is a transformed sovereignty, no longer absolute.

As much as NGOs need states – to arrest war criminals, to provide food and tents and sometimes physical protection for relief, to provide capital and guidelines for development – states need NGOs for a variety of ideas and services. Thus the stage is set for the subtle interplay of influence between the two types of actors on behalf of human rights, relief, and sustainable *human* development.

Case study: women's NGOs and mobilizing women voters in Ghana

In sub-Saharan Africa, decolonization and national independence produced much autocracy of a patriarchal nature in the 1960s and 1970s.[70] This was true in Ghana, which until 1957 was a British colony manifesting at times elections to a restricted local parliament. During the Nkrumah era (1957–1966), politics evolved into one party rule. He gave some attention to women's concerns and even instituted some gender quotas in certain offices. But over time many women's interests were often excluded from public policy matters, and women's civic society organizations of various sorts were mostly underdeveloped.

After much political instability, a coup in 1981 by Flight Lt. Jerry Rawlings proved to be a major event as he retained power for nineteen years until 2000: first as strong man, then as winner of clearly flawed elections, and finally as winner of elections generally judged to be reasonably fair and free. He oversaw a peaceful transition to a genuinely elected successor in 2001. The latter part of his rule can thus be considered a transition to genuine democracy, and during this time of political opening women's civic society organizations became more active – with some demonstrable impact on women's participation in the political process. This exercise of their civil and political rights is our focus here.

A combination of international and internal pressures led Rawlings to try to legitimize his power via elections in 1992. Not only foreign governments providing foreign assistance and western-based NGOs interested in democracy and human rights pushed in this direction, but also so did a wide variety of Ghanaian civic society organizations such as trade unions, student groups, and lawyers' associations. While autocratic, the Ghanaian state was not totalitarian.

For women's groups seeking influence in public affairs, a particular problem was that Rawlings had created the 31st December Women's Movement (later headed by his wife). This GONGO (governmentally organized non-governmental organization) existed primarily to enlist women's support for the regime. With governmental support and

---

[70] Author's adaption from Kathleen M. Fallon, "Getting Out the Vote: Women's Democratic Political Mobilization in Ghana," *Mobilization: An International Journal*, 8, 3 (2003), 273–296.

resources, the 31st Movement constricted the political space for genuinely independent groups to mobilize and have effect.

Research that was focused on groups such as the Christian Council Women's and Children's Desk, Christian Mothers Association, CUSAASA, Ghana Association of Women Entrepreneurs, the International Association for the Advancement of Women in Africa, International Association for Women Lawyers, the United Women's Front, Women in Law and Development in Africa, and the Young Women's Christian Association indicated that these organizations had an impact on women's political thinking and action. Members of these groups, and other women having some contact with these groups, were more likely to vote in the 1996 elections than other women. (Other factors also correlated with voting, such as living with a husband and having a larger number of children, but not as strongly as membership in these civic society organizations.) Shortly after the 1996 elections women took to the streets to demonstrate for more governmental attention to their concerns, and in the context of physical attacks on women, sometimes fatal, they formed Sisters' Keepers which had demonstrable effect in replacing certain officials and improving female physical security – certainly in the capital city of Accra. By 2010, Ghana scored better than the average for sub-Saharan Africa on the Human Development Index as adjusted for gender issues.[71]

This brief study does not directly emphasize the international norms codifying the right to participate in the public policy process, nor the states and human rights advocacy groups that made reference to those norms in trying to push the Ghanaian government to respect those standards. No doubt this combined public and private human rights pressure helped set the stage for the political opening or liberalization in Ghana in the 1990s during the Rawlings regime. It was true that some who were politically active in Ghana saw this foreign commentary (pressure?) as a neo-colonial or neo-imperial intrusion into domestic affairs. Nevertheless, Rawlings did progressively move toward genuine multiparty elections.

What this study does emphasize, during the transition to genuine democracy, is the effect of a wide variety of grassroots civic society

---

[71] See hdrstats.undp.org/en/countries/profiles/GHA.html. The UN Human Development Index (HDI), compiled by UNDP, the UN Development Program, is based on three core factors: literacy rates as a reflection of education; longevity as a reflection of nutrition and health care; and per capita GDP as a reflection of income or economic well-being. It also produces a gendered HDI paying special attention to factors affecting women.

organizations. The latter did indeed mobilize women to greater political participation. This reflects commitment not just to the political right to vote, but also to the necessary civil rights inherent in that process such as freedom of thought, speech, and association. The women in Ghana then used their newly found political awareness to advance various public policies of interest to them.

The exercise of women's civil and political rights in Ghana, and in sub-Saharan Africa more generally, can be compared to women's political participation in Latin America (and elsewhere, of course). There are variations in patterns and sequences. Women's civic action groups do not always operate according to the same dynamic or metric in every country and region. But Ghana shows that women's grassroots organizations, sometimes called community-based organizations (CBOs), can be a potent force to advance women's interests starting with political participation. A key structural factor is that the electoral regime must be relatively free and fair, and the political contestants have to abide by its outcome, which is often encouraged by international pressure – both public and private.

Discussion questions

- Is it more helpful for understanding to focus on separate or distinct private human rights organizations, or to focus on networks or movements? Can one understand a movement without understanding the precise actors that make up that movement? Can public officials be part of a human rights or humanitarian movement?
- Are western-based private human rights organizations part of western cultural imperialism? To what extent does an organization like Amnesty International have broad support in the non-western world?
- Are the better-known private human rights organizations moralistic and legalistic, in that they fail to consistently understand and appreciate the political context within which governments take decisions that impact human rights? Do they unreasonably discount other values and policies that governments and their publics consider legitimate – such as peace, security, economic growth? Or are the private groups absolutely vital to shaking governments and mass public opinion out of their set ways regarding the death penalty, gay rights, the continuing prevalence of torture, excessive spending on the military compared with basic human needs, etc.?
- What practical steps can be taken to improve the delivery of food, clothing, shelter, and medical care to civilians in armed conflicts and complex emergencies? Do these steps involve private actors such as the

International Committee of the Red Cross, Doctors Without Borders, etc.? Given that a number of fighting parties *intentionally* attack and abuse civilians, should humanitarian action be left to NATO or the US Department of Defense in place of private relief organizations? After all, national military establishments (at least the major ones) have tremendous logistical capacity. Paradoxes aside, should humanitarian action be nationalized and militarized?

- Is the global pursuit of "development" sufficiently attentive to "sustainable *human* development" and human rights? How important is the role of private actors like Oxfam in this development process? Do public authorities like the World Bank, the UN Development Program, and the US Agency for International Development approve of a large role for private organizations and human-oriented development? Is this orientation perhaps theory and not practice? How would practical policies change if human rights were genuinely incorporated into the "development" process?

SUGGESTIONS FOR FURTHER READING

Bob, Clifford, ed., *The International Struggle for New Human Rights*, Pennsylvania Studies in Human Rights Series (Philadelphia: University of Pennsylvania Press, 2008). A study of how NGOs and other actors serve as "gatekeepers," endorsing some claims as new human rights while failing to endorse others and thus denying prominence.

Cahill, Kevin M., ed., *Framework for Survival: Health, Human Rights, and Humanitarian Assistance in Conflicts and Disasters* (New York: Basic Books, for the Council on Foreign Relations, 1993). A good stock-taking of problems early in the post-Cold War period. Much attention to private actors.

Edwards, Michael, and David Hulme, eds., *Beyond the Magic Bullet: NGO Performance and Accountability in the Post-Cold War World* (West Hartford: Kumarian Press, in cooperation with Save the Children Fund, 1996). Deals with the central question of how democratic, accountable, and open NGOs really are, even though they claim to represent "the people."

Fisher, Julie, *Non-Governments: NGOs and the Political Development of the Third World* (West Hartford: Kumarian Press, 1998). A critical look at the impact of human rights and development NGOs in the global south.

Florini, A., *The Third Force: The Rise of Transnational Civil Society* (Washington: Carnegie Endowment, 2000). An excellent overview of the global spread of NGOs in all their variety.

Haas, Ernst, *When Knowledge Is Power: Three Models of Change in International Organizations* (Berkeley: University of California Press, 1990). A complicated model of why international organizations develop the policies that they do, stressing the role of private scientific communities in that process. Considerable attention to human rights.

Hochschild, Adam, *Bury the Chains: Prophets and Rebels in the Fight to Free an Empire's Slaves* (Boston and New York: Houghton Mifflin, 2005, 2006). A very readable study of the organizations and personalities active in the anti-slave trade and anti-slavery movements in the nineteenth century.

Hopgood, Stephen, *Keepers of the Flame: Understanding Amnesty International* (Ithaca: Cornell University Press, 2006). A creative study of the internal dynamics of AI and concentrating on a clash over the organization's proper mandate and programs.

Keck, Margaret E., and Kathryn Sikkink, *Activists Beyond Borders: Advocacy Networks in International Politics* (Ithaca: Cornell University Press, 1998). An outstanding example of using the concept of "movement" to try to analyze essentially private action for human rights, although the authors conceive of certain public officials as part of a movement.

Korey, William, *NGOs and the Universal Declaration of Human Rights: "A Curious Grapevine"* (New York: St. Martin's Press, 1998). A personalized and disjointed account, but containing much useful information for introductory purposes. Places great weight on NGO action, especially by Jewish groups, in the evolution of modern human rights.

Livezey, Lowell W., *Non Governmental Organizations and the Idea of Human Rights* (Princeton: Princeton Center for International Studies, 1988). A thoughtful if somewhat dated overview.

Mathews, Jessica Tuchman, "Power Shift," *Foreign Affairs*, 76, 1 (January–February 1997), 50–66. A sweeping argument and highly optimistic view about the growing influence of all sorts of NGOs in international relations. The other side of her coin is the declining influence of the territorial state.

Moore, Jonathan, ed., *Hard Choices: Moral Dilemmas in Humanitarian Intervention* (Lanham: Rowman & Littlefield, 1998). A good collection by practitioners and theorists about different views toward, and experiences with, humanitarian assistance.

Natsios, Alexander, *US Foreign Policy and the Four Horsemen of the Apocalypse: Humanitarian Relief in Complex Emergencies* (Westport: Praeger, 1997). The author, who was at different times both a US official and a key player for World Vision, a church-related private relief organization, focuses on the USA but stresses the interactions of governments, international organizations, and private actors like the ICRC.

Power, Jonathan, *Amnesty International: The Human Rights Story* (New York: McGraw-Hill, 1981). A solid if somewhat dated overview.

Smith, Brian H., *More than Altruism: The Politics of Private Foreign Aid* (Princeton: Princeton University Press, 1990). A sharp look at private development and relief organizations.

Smith, Jackie, Charles Chatfield, and Ron Pagnucco, eds., *Transnational Social Movements and Global Politics: Solidarity Beyond the State* (Syracuse: Syracuse University Press, 1997). A good collection of case studies featuring private networks and their impact on human rights.

Smith, Jackie, and Ron Pagnucco, with George A. Lopez, "Globalizing Human Rights: The Work of Transnational Human Rights NGOs in the 1990s,"

Human Rights Quarterly, 20, 2 (May 1998), 379–412. An essential if largely descriptive overview.

Steiner, Henry J., *Diverse Partners: Non Governmental Organizations and the Human Rights Movement* (Cambridge, MA: Harvard Law College, 1991, for the Harvard Law School Human Rights Program and the Human Rights Internet). A short analysis of the different types of private actors working on human rights issues.

Tolley, Howard J., Jr., *The International Commission of Jurists: Global Advocates for Human Rights* (Philadelphia: University of Pennsylvania Press, 1994). A careful look at a well-known, Geneva-based human rights NGO with a legal focus. Also an attempt to blend political history with social science theory.

Weiss, Thomas G., "The Humanitarian Identity Crisis," *Ethics & International Affairs*, 13 (1999), 1–22. A leading scholar of humanitarian affairs nicely summarizes much debate, while advocating major changes in international action. Accompanied by other views on the same topic in the same journal.

Weiss, Thomas G., and Leon Gordenker, eds., *NGOs, the UN, and Global Governance* (Boulder: Lynne Rienner, 1996). An examination of how private actors intersect with UN bodies, with attention to human rights, humanitarian affairs, and women's rights.

Welch, Claude E., *Protecting Human Rights in Africa: Strategies and Roles of Non Governmental Organizations* (Philadelphia: University of Pennsylvania Press, 1995). A good overview of this subject, with a generally favorable view of African NGOs and their impact over time, despite a hostile environment.

NGOs and Human Rights: Promise and Performance (Philadelphia: University of Pennsylvania Press, 2001). A solid overview.

Willetts, Peter, ed., *"The Conscience of the World": The Influence of Non-Governmental Organizations in the UN System* (Washington: Brookings, 1996). An excellent collection with a very good chapter on Amnesty International and human rights by Jane Connors.

8   Transnational corporations
       and human rights

We saw in Chapter 7 that the international law of human rights was directed mainly to public authorities like states and their governments, but that private non-profit actors like human rights advocacy groups helped shape the rights discourse and action. In this chapter I will show that for-profit private actors like transnational corporations have a tremendous effect on persons in the modern world, for good or ill. For the first fifty years after the adoption of the United Nations Charter and Universal Declaration of Human Rights, these business enterprises mostly fell outside the mainstream debate about the promotion and protection of internationally recognized human rights. This was so despite the fact that the leaders of the German firm I. G. Farben had faced legal justice at the Nuremberg Trials for their role in the Holocaust. This general situation was changing in the early twenty-first century. Attention to transnational corporations and human rights constitutes an important dimension in the international discourse on human rights.[1] Non-profit human rights groups, along with the media and particularly consumer organizations and movements, are targeting the corporations. The result is renewed pressure on public authorities, especially states, to adopt norms and policies ensuring that business practices contribute to, rather than contradict, internationally recognized human rights. The corporations themselves are under considerable pressure to pay attention to human rights, although there remain formidable structural obstacles to a broad corporate social responsibility that includes human rights.[2]

---

[1] Jedrzej George Frynas and Scott Pegg, eds., *Transnational Corporations and Human Rights* (London: Palgrave Macmillan, 2003); Michael K. Addo, *Human Rights Standards and the Responsibility of Transnational Corporations* (The Hague: Kluwer Law International, 1999); S. Rees, ed., *Human Rights, Corporate Responsibility: A Dialogue* (Sydney: Allen and Unwin, 2000).

[2] See Mahmood Monshipouri, Claude E. Welch, Jr., and Evan T. Kennedy, "Multinational Corporations and the Ethics of Global Responsibility: Problems and Possibilities," *Human Rights Quarterly*, 25, 4 (November 2004), 965–989. They argue against MNC self-policing and for some combination of external pressures.

Enormous impact

It has been long recognized that business enterprises that operate across national boundaries have an enormous impact on the modern world. If we compare the revenues of the twenty-five largest transnational corporations (TNCs) with revenues of states, as in Table 8.1, we see that economic significance.

The world's 200 largest TNCs are incorporated in just ten states, as shown in Table 8.2, above all in the United States and Japan. This means, of course, that if one could affect the national policies of these TNCs in this small number of states, one could greatly affect TNCs' global impact.

Beyond macro-statistics, it is clear that with regard to the internationally recognized right to health, and if we take the case of the HIV/AIDS pandemic in Africa and other places, the role of drug companies (often claiming intellectual property rights) is central. The willingness of these companies, under pressure of course, to contribute to managing the crisis through such policies as helping with lower-priced generic drugs is highly important.[3]

Debate continues as to whether TNCs, because of their enormous economic power, which can sometimes be translated into political power, are beyond the effective control of national governments. A classic study concluded that TNCs were not, in general, beyond the reach of the "sovereign" state.[4] At the same time, however, most observers today agree that it is difficult for a given state to effectively regulate "its" corporations abroad for a variety of reasons. Business enterprises move resources, especially capital, rapidly around the globe, and it is only with some difficulty and a time lag that national governments know what TNCs are doing. Also, TNCs normally have considerable influence in national political systems, especially through pro-business political parties and personalities. This, of course, makes regulation of business difficult to achieve.

Moreover, it is difficult for one state to act alone in this regard. International law has not historically encouraged states to try to project extraterritorial jurisdiction in economic matters.[5] And if the state did so, it might restrict "its" corporations in global competition so that the state

---

[3] See, for example, Nana K. Polu and Alan Whiteside, eds., *Political Economy of AIDS in Africa* (Aldershot: Ashgate, 2004).

[4] Raymond Vernon, *Sovereignty at Bay: The Multinational Spread of US Enterprises* (New York: Basic Books, 1971).

[5] But see Mark Gibney and David R. Emerick, "The Extraterritorial Application of United States Law and the Protection of Human Rights: Holding Multinational Corporations to Domestic and International Standards," *Temple International and Comparative Law Journal*, 10, 1 (Spring 1996), 123–145.

Table 8.1 *States and TNCs compared*

Rank	Country/corporation	GDP/revenue $ millions
1	United States	11,667,515
2	Japan	4,623,398
3	Germany	2,714,418
4	United Kingdom	2,140,898
5	France	2,002,582
6	Italy	1,672,302
7	China	1,649,329
8	Spain	991,442
9	Canada	979,764
10	India	691,876
11	Korea, Rep.	679,674
12	Mexico	676,497
13	Australia	631,256
14	Brazil	604,855
15	Russian Federation	582,395
16	Netherlands	577,260
17	Switzerland	359,465
18	Belgium	349,830
19	Sweden	346,404
20	Turkey	301,950
21	Austria	290,109
22	Wal-Mart Stores	287,989
23	BP	285,059
24	Exxon Mobil	270,772
25	Royal Dutch Shell Group	268,690
26	Indonesia	257,641
27	Saudi Arabia	250,557
28	Norway	250,168
29	Denmark	243,043
30	Poland	241,833
31	South Africa	212,777
32	Greece	203,401
33	General Motors	193,517
34	Finland	186,597
35	Ireland	183,560
36	DaimlerChrysler	176,688
37	Toyota Motor	172,616
38	Ford Motor	172,233
39	Portugal	168,281
40	Thailand	163,491
41	Hong Kong, China	163,005
42	Iran, Islamic Rep.	162,709
43	General Electric	152,866

(*cont.*)

Table 8.1 (*cont.*)

Rank	Country/corporation	GDP/revenue $ millions
44	Total	152,610
45	Argentina	151,501
46	Chevron	147,967
47	ConocoPhillips	121,663
48	AXA	121,606
49	Allianz	118,937
50	Malaysia	117,776
51	Israel	117,548
52	Volkswagen	110,649
53	Venezuela, RB	109,322
54	Citigroup	108,276
55	Czech Republic	107,047
56	Singapore	106,818
57	ING Group	105,886
58	Nippon Telegraph & Telephone	100,545
59	Hungary	99,712
60	New Zealand	99,687

Source: news.mongabay.com/2005/0718-worlds_largest.html.

received fewer economic benefits and competitors more. When in 1977 the USA passed anti-corruption legislation (the Foreign Corrupt Practices Act) making it illegal for corporations registered in the country to pay bribes to get contracts from foreign parties, this put those firms at a competitive disadvantage in global competition. It was only in 1998 that the USA could persuade its partners in the Organization for Economic Cooperation and Development to level the playing field by adopting a multilateral convention, implemented through national legislation, on the subject.[6] The logic of cooperation under conditions of anarchy, or in this case relatively unregulated market competition, is an important subject. Particularly social regulation is weak – viz., regulation for social rather than economic purposes.

The central question is not so much the power of TNCs, or the difficulty of their regulation. Both points are readily agreed to. The more complex question is what, on balance, the impact of TNCs is on persons and their human rights in the modern world. On this there is considerable debate. It follows that there is also a lively exchange on whether

[6] AP, "Congress Passes Bill to Curb International Business Bribery," *New York Times*, October 22, 1998, A5.

Table 8.2 *Top world companies 2008: most profitable*

		Profits: return on revenues		
Rank	Company	Global 500 rank	2008 profits ($ millions)	Profits % change from 2007
1	Exxon Mobil	2	45,220.0	11.4
2	Gazprom	22	29,864.1	16.1
3	Royal Dutch Shell	1	26,277.0	−16.1
4	Chevron	5	23,931.0	28.1
5	BP	4	21,157.0	1.5
6	Petrobras	34	18,879.0	43.7
7	Microsoft	117	17,681.0	25.7
8	General Electric	12	17,410.0	−21.6
9	Nestlé	48	16,669.6	87.8
10	Industrial & Commercial Bank of China	92	15,948.5	48.8
11	Total	6	15,500.4	−14.1
12	BHP Billiton	120	15,390.0	14.7
13	Petronas	80	15,308.9	−15.5
14	Wal-Mart Stores	3	13,400.0	5.3
15	China Construction Bank	125	13,323.7	46.8
16	CVRD	205	13,218.0	11.8
17	Banco Santander	35	12,992.3	4.8
18	Johnson & Johnson	103	12,949.0	22.4
19	ENI	17	12,917.0	−5.7
20	AT&T	29	12,867.0	7.7
21	International Business Machines	45	12,334.0	18.4
22	Procter & Gamble	68	12,075.0	16.8
23	China Mobile Communications	99	11,442.0	35.8
24	Rosneft Oil	158	11,120.0	−13.5
25	Telefónica	66	11,112.3	−8.8
26	China National Petroleum	13	10,270.8	−31.2
27	ArcelorMittal	28	9,399.0	−9.3
28	Bank of China	145	9,260.5	25.2
29	Lukoil	65	9,144.0	−3.9
30	Siemens	30	8,595.1	69.8
31	GlaxoSmithKline	168	8,438.6	−19.1
32	Hewlett-Packard	32	8,329.0	14.7
33	Roche Group	171	8,288.1	1.9
34	Novartis	183	8,195.0	−31.4
35	Pfizer	152	8,104.0	−0.5
36	Cisco Systems	191	8,052.0	9.8
37	Barclays	83	8,035.2	−9.1

(*cont.*)

Table 8.2 (*cont.*)

		Profits: return on revenues		
Rank	Company	Global 500 rank	2008 profits ($ millions)	Profits % change from 2007
38	Merck	378	7,808.4	138.4
39	Enel	62	7,747.3	42.3
40	Statoil Hydro	36	7,664.2	1.8
41	PDVSA	27	7,451.0	38.7
42	Agricultural Bank of China	155	7,406.4	28.7
43	Unilever	121	7,357.9	38.3
44	Banco Bilbao Vizcaya Argentaria	113	7,347.7	−12.4
45	GDF Suez	53	7,109.3	110.1
46	Volkswagen	14	6,956.9	23.4
47	Philip Morris International	345	6,890.0	N.A.
48	Occidental Petroleum	365	6,857.0	27.0
49	Verizon Communications	55	6,428.0	16.4
50	TNK-BP Holding	234	6,384.0	11.4

Source: money.cnn.com/magazines/fortune/global500/ . . . /profits/.
Note: Rankings of corporations in Tables 8.1 and 8.2 vary slightly because data are for different years.

there should be more public regulation of TNCs in the name of human rights. On the one hand are the traditional economists who argue that the business of business is business, and human rights have no place in this paradigm. On the other hand are those who believe that TNCs are really quasi-governmental organizations who should not only do no harm but also actively advance internationally recognized rights.[7]

A critical view

Few persons other than Social Darwinists look with favor on the early stages of the capitalist industrial revolution. There was a certain national economic advance that was achieved via basically unregulated capitalism, and certainly the property owners benefited. But now there is almost universal rejection of the human conditions (not to mention environmental

[7] See Florian Wettstein, *Multinational Corporations and Global Justice: Human Rights Obligations of a Quasi-Governmental Institution* (Stanford: Stanford Business Books, 2009). He addresses the traditional view while advocating active human rights policies by TNCs.

damage) of that early industrial capitalism, illustrated by the novels of Charles Dickens. No western market democracy, and no capitalist state in any developed country, now endorses pure *laissez-faire* economics.

A first basic point is that a sophisticated view of modern markets recognizes they are a social construct, with deep governmental intrusion.[8] Markets are actually created by governments, and extensively regulated by them, for reasons of economic effectiveness. Markets have rules and supervisors to promote investor confidence and minimize inhibiting factors like corruption, fraud, and theft. Modern national markets do not exist in nature, as it were, but as the result of governmental action. Even so-called *laissez-faire* economics results from governmental action, not a state of nature.

A second basic point is that in contemporary market democracies, even so-called political conservatives such as Ronald Reagan and Margaret Thatcher endorsed certain aspects of regulated and welfare state capitalism (Thatcher was a strong defender, for example, of the British National Health Service). Socially responsible pro-business persons recognize that capitalism is a harsh system, that not all persons benefit, that some persons require the protection of the state for a life with dignity under an economic system based on the right to private property.[9] It has never proved persuasive to argue that both the poor and the rich have the same freedom to sleep under the bridges as they wish.[10] And so all modern market democracies regulate national markets for social as well as economic reasons. All use tax and other policies to limit the harshness of crude capitalism. At the national level, all western democratic politics try in different ways to create capitalism with a human face.[11]

---

[8] See especially Cass Sunstein, *The Second Bill of Rights: FDR's Unfinished Revolution and Why We Need It More than Ever* (New York: Basic Books, 2004), especially ch. 2.

[9] See Michael Novak and Leslie Lenkowsky, "Economic Growth Won't End Poverty," *New York Times*, July 24, 1985, A19. The authors were associated with the American Enterprise Institute, a conservative, pro-business think tank in Washington.

[10] See further Rhoda Howard-Hassmann and Claude E. Welch, Jr., eds., *Economic Rights in Canada and the United States* (Philadelphia: University of Pennsylvania Press, 2006).

[11] Those unfamiliar with the history of the Cold War may not fully appreciate this irony of semantics. In events leading up to 1968, particularly reform communists in what was then Czechoslovakia tried to create what was called communism with a human face. The attempt was to create a communism that was less harsh and repressive, that blended a new socialism with certain civil and political rights. This move was endorsed by western market democracies, even as it was crushed by a pre-Gorbachev Soviet Union. In the early twenty-first century it was the western-led economic globalization that was often said to be in need of a human face.

This brief reference to historical patterns and basic realities is an important critique of unregulated business. If left to itself, even in western countries that manifested so much concern for the individual that they evolved into liberal and/or social democracies, unregulated business has often exploited, crushed, de-humanized, and affronted human dignity. Once the bonds of community, found in rural and agricultural settings, were replaced by the urban and more impersonal conditions of industrial capitalism, the have-nots were clearly in need of protection from the power of the haves. Whatever the difficulties of the political process, relatively humane national regulation of the for-profit system was achieved (at least relative to Dickens' England). The intervention of the state was used to limit the enormous power of the Henry Fords and Andrew Carnegies and the other "robber barons" of early industrial capitalism.[12] One of the great problems immediately after the Cold War in places like Russia and Albania, *inter alia*, was that this regulation of the robber barons had yet to be made effective. This is why the successful financier, investor, and philanthropist George Soros wrote that the greatest threat to democracy in the former communist lands of the Soviet Union and Eastern Europe is precisely capitalism.[13] As one who understands capitalism well, Soros knows that crude capitalism is so harsh and unfair that it is not sustainable when citizens have the freedom to accept or reject it.

What has not been tolerated in the national political economies of the West for about a century, namely unregulated capitalism, has been allowed to proceed in international relations – at least until recently. And while one can chart growing international law in the domain of economics, most of that regulation is designed to encourage free trade and commercial activity, certainly not to restrict it in the name of human rights. That regulation is for economic, not social, reasons. The General Agreement on Tariffs and Trade (GATT) and the World Trade Organization (WTO) are primarily designed to encourage international capitalism, not regulate it according to social values. This was also the main thrust of NAFTA (North American Free Trade Agreement), with provisions on ecology and labor rights added only as afterthoughts when demanded by American unions and others. There is a disconnect between much of the normative framework for *national* capitalism (to prevent gross exploitation) and the main concern of regulation of *international* capitalism (to stabilize capitalism regardless of exploitation).

---

[12] On the political system as a counterweight to business power in the West, see especially E. E. Schattschneider, *The Semi-Sovereign People: A Realist's View of Democracy in America* (New York: Holt, Rinehart and Winston, 1960).

[13] George Soros, "The Capitalist Threat," *Atlantic Monthly*, 279, 2 (February 1997), 45 and *passim*.

Thus one of the central questions about the future of global capitalism is whether leading states, who make the rules, can come together in the WTO and other forums and agree on international capitalism with a human face – as they have done, after much political struggle, in their national political economies.[14] In other words, will economic globalization be accompanied by progressive social and political globalization?

In the national political economy, at least from the view of nationality and with class considerations aside, we are all "us." In the international political economy, there is an "in" group – us – and an "out" group – them. Nationalism being what it is, as long as the benefits flow to "us," as a political fact the moral imperative to show concern for "them" is reduced. The World Development Report, produced by the United Nations Development Program, regularly chronicles the large and growing gap between the wealthy global north and the impoverished global south. As one would expect in a situation of mostly unregulated international economics where a sense of global community is weak, the elites with property rights and capital prosper, and many of the have-nots live a life on the margins of human dignity. Dickens would not be surprised.

Against this background, one can easily find horror stories of unprincipled TNCs making handsome profits at the expense of clearly exploited employees and bystanders. Authors from Stephen Hymer to David Korten have chronicled the record.[15] Economic globalization is partly the story of sweatshops, child labor, dangerous work, low pay, forced and slave labor, opposition to unions, and in extreme cases crimes against humanity and genocide. IBM and other outside companies were complicit in the German Holocaust.[16] As early as 1938, before Nazi Germany had invaded Poland and before Swiss leaders had reasonable concern about a Nazi invasion of Switzerland, some Swiss banks were stealing the

---

[14] See Rhoda Howard-Hassmann, *Can Globalization Promote Human Rights?* (University Park, PA: Penn State University Press, 2010). See also Jorge Heine and Ramesh Thakur, eds., *The Dark Side of Globalization* (Tokyo: United Nations University Press, 2011), for the same point in different terms. See further David Kinley, *Civilising Globalisation: Human Rights and the Global Economy* (Cambridge: Cambridge University Press, 2009), who argues for combining notions of social justice with pursuit of economic growth.

[15] Stephen Hymer, "The Multinational Corporation and the Law of Uneven Development," in J. W. Bhagwati, ed., *Economics and World Order* (New York: Macmillan, 1971), 113–140; David Korten, *When Corporations Rule the World* (West Hartford: Kumarian Press, 1995). See also Richard J. Barnet and John Cavanagh, *Global Dreams: Imperial Corporations and the New World Order* (New York: Simon & Schuster, 1994).

[16] See further Edwin Black, *IBM and the Holocaust: The Strategic Alliance Between Nazi Germany and America's Most Powerful Corporation* (New York: Random House, Crown, 2001). In general, however, on the role of business in the German Holocaust, see the scholarship of Peter Hayes, including a critical book review of Black's *IBM and the Holocaust*.

property of Austrian Jews and turning it over to well-paying Germans.[17] More recently, Union Carbide has been less than exemplary in ensuring that those killed and hurt by the poisonous gas leak at its plant in Bhopal, India in 1984 have had their minimal rights to fair compensation respected.[18] The dark underside of globalized business is represented by trafficking in human beings, driven by the profit motive.[19]

Debora L. Spar of the Harvard Business School believes that the social record of TNCs engaged in the extraction of natural resources in foreign countries has been especially poor.[20] On the one hand, the TNC must have cozy relations with the (all-too-often reactionary or at least insensitive) government that controls access to the resource. The TNC and local government share an interest in a docile and compliant labor force. On the other hand, the TNC often shows little interest in other aspects of the local population. The resource is mostly sold abroad, with a certain amount of the profits going to the governmental elite. If that elite does not act progressively to reinvest the profit into infrastructures that improve the lot of the local population, such as education, health care, and ecological protection, the TNC has often seen little short-term economic interest in the situation.

It is reasonably clear that Royal Dutch Shell in Nigeria cooperated closely with military governments in suppressing local resistance to prevailing policies centering on extraction of oil in Ogoniland. Not only did Shell make it possible, at company expense, for the Abacha government to violently suppress those objecting to environmental degradation by Shell in Ogoniland. But also Shell refused to intercede with the government to object to the execution of Ken Saro-Wiwa, one of the most outspoken leaders of the Ogoni people in Nigeria. In reaction to considerable criticism, Shell took a number of steps to elevate the discourse about human rights as related to its business operations. But on balance the facts to date indicate that Shell has been less than fully socially responsible in its operations in Nigeria.[21]

---

[17] William Glaberson, "Huge Award Details How Bank Aided Nazis," *International Herald Tribune*, April 14, 2005, www.iht.com/articles/2005/04/13/news/austria.html.

[18] Saritha Rai, "Bhopal Victims Not Fully Paid, Rights Group Says," *New York Times*, November 30, 2004, W3.

[19] See especially Siddharth Kara, *Sex Trafficking: Inside the Business of Modern Slavery* (New York: Columbia University Press, 2009).

[20] Debora L. Spar, "Multinationals and Human Rights: A Case of Strange Bedfellows," *Human Rights Interest Group Newsletter*, American Society of International Law, 8, 1 (Winter 1998), 13–16.

[21] For one overview out of a vast literature see Kenneth Omeje, *High Stakes and Stakeholders: Oil Conflict and Security in Nigeria* (Aldershot: Ashgate, 2006).

The most fundamental *raison d'être* of the TNC is precisely economic self-interest, not to be a human rights actor. At least that has been the historical situation. "Investors and executives tended to see human rights as a matter for government officials and diplomats to implement, and resisted pressures to have their businesses used as tools for political reform... The globalization of the economy and the globalization of human rights concerns, both important phenomena in the second half of this century, developed separately from each other."[22]

Some TNCs went beyond cooperation with, and active support for, a reactionary elite. United Fruit in Guatemala (1954) and ITT in Chile (1973) actively cooperated with the US government in helping to overthrow politicians (Arbenz in Guatemala and Allende in Chile) who were champions especially of labor rights for their nationals.[23] Various TNCs, from United Fruit to Coca-Cola, actively opposed progressive governments and laws designed to advance labor rights and other human rights.

There are powerful economic and political forces pushing corporations into exploitative and otherwise abusive policies. Economically there is the bottom line: companies must make a profit to stay in business. If the competition uses cheap labor, then it is difficult if not impossible for a company to use unionized, well-paid labor. The history of Levi Strauss demonstrates this clearly.[24] This San Francisco based company, with a reputation for treating its labor force properly, has basically stopped manufacturing in the USA, and has felt compelled to outsource its production to foreign countries like China with poor human rights records, all because of pursuit of the bottom line. Within countries like the USA, when labor organized in northern cities like Detroit, management moved production to places like South Carolina and Alabama where labor was cheap and unions weak. The same process now characterizes business on a transnational or global scale. In this sense economic globalization does reflect a race to the bottom.[25]

Politically, when corporations deal with repressive governments and/or those known to violate international standards on human rights and

---

[22] Lance Compa and Tashia Hinchliffe-Darricarrere, "Enforcing International Rights Through Corporate Codes of Conduct," *Columbia Journal of Transnational Law*, 33 (1995), 665.

[23] On Arbenz and Guatemala, see especially Piero Gleijeses, *Shattered Hope: The Guatemalan Revolution and the United States 1944–1954* (Princeton: Princeton University Press, 1991). On Allende and Chile, see especially Richard Z. Israel, *Politics and Ideology in Allende's Chile* (Tempe: Arizona State University Press, 1989).

[24] See Karl Schoenberger, *Levi's Children: Coming to Terms with Human Rights in the Global Marketplace* (New York: Atlantic Monthly Press, 2000).

[25] See further Kimberly Ann Elliott and Richard B. Freeman, *Can Labor Standards Improve Under Globalization?* (Washington: Institute of International Economics, 2003).

humanitarian affairs, to get the business, companies tend to defer to governmental policies. This is true not just of IBM in Nazi Germany. The Caterpillar Company, when urged by certain human rights groups to not allow its bulldozers to be used by Israel in ways that violated international humanitarian law in the West Bank (collective punishments through destruction of houses alleged to be linked to "terrorists"), said it was a matter for the Israeli government.[26] Had Caterpillar withdrawn, it is likely that Israel would have continued the policy through a different company. When the USA prohibited its oil companies from doing business in Sudan, because of major human rights violations principally in the Darfur region, other oil companies took the business, especially those from China.

The economic "laws" of competition, of supply and demand, tend to produce major human rights violations when markets are unregulated for social reasons.

A more positive view

At the same time that Professor Spar, as noted above, believes that extractive TNCs in particular have a poor social record, she observes that there are other types of TNCs: consumer products firms, manufacturing firms, service and information firms. Some of these, she argues, are engaged in business that is compatible with several human rights. She goes so far as to argue that TNCs sometimes export human rights values.[27] According to her research, some TNCs are interested in not just cheap labor but a good labor force that is highly educated and exists in the context of stable democracy. Thus Intel chose Costa Rica for one of its foreign plants. Firms intending to sell in foreign markets have an interest in a well-paid labor force with disposable income to buy their products.

Above all, Spar argues, all firms have an economic interest in avoiding negative publicity that might damage their sales. Thus TNCs do not want to face consumer boycotts and negative publicity because of the harsh, exploitative conditions in their foreign plants, or cooperation with pariah regimes. She cites a number of firms that have altered their policies, especially to establish codes of conduct for business practices

---

[26] See Human Rights Watch, "Israel: Caterpillar Should Suspend Bulldozer Sales," www. hrw.org/English/docs/2004/11/22/isrlpa9711_txt.htm.

[27] In addition to her views already noted, see her article "The Spotlight and the Bottom Line: How Multinationals Export Human Rights," *Foreign Affairs*, 77, 2 (March–April 1998), 7–12. See further Kenneth A. Rodman, "Think Globally, Punish Locally: Non-State Actors, Multinational Corporations, and Human Rights Sanctions," *Ethics & International Affairs*, 12 (1998), 19–42.

and to allow independent monitoring of labor conditions, in relation to widespread criticism: Starbucks Coffee, the Gap clothiers, Nike, Reebok, Toys R Us, Avon, etc. She notes that a number of firms have pulled out of Burma, where a highly repressive military government has been internationally condemned: Levi Strauss, Macy's, Liz Claiborne, Eddie Bauer, Heineken, etc. She cites as especially effective the international campaign against child labor in the making of soccer balls, which led major TNC sporting firms to certify that no child or slave labor was used in the making of the balls. After all, one might add, if it is common practice to certify that tuna are not caught with nets that endanger dolphins, why not certify that consumer products are not made with processes that violate human rights?

Moreover, beyond reacting to negative publicity that might hurt the firms' bottom line on their economic books, some observers note that TNCs export standard operating procedures that are sometimes an improvement over those previously existing in a developing country. TNC plants in the global south may provide infirmaries for health care, or improved safety conditions. TNCs, even while paying wages below standards in the global north, may pay wages in developing countries that permit growth, savings, and investment over time.

After all, the Asian Tigers such as Taiwan made remarkable economic progress from the mid-1950s to the mid-1990s on the basis of an economy open to TNCs. Countries like South Korea and Taiwan not only became more prosperous over time, with a skilled work force, but also became liberal and social democracies, at least relative to their past. Thus, it is argued, there is nothing inherent in the operations of TNCs that requires that they block beneficial change in host countries or that they oppose human rights standards. While they have certainly done so in the past on occasion, an emerging world of liberal market democracies, or even social democracies, would be perfectly compatible with a bottom line in the black for TNCs.

Also relevant is the fact that the major trading partners of the USA are other market democracies such as Canada and the states of the European Union. These states vigorously protect a wide range of human rights, including a right to health care and extensive unemployment and social security entitlements, while maintaining an economy that does very well over time. Clearly many states that recognize socioeconomic rights and manifest a relatively large social safety net score very well on indexes purporting to measure economic competitiveness. There is nothing inconsistent about being a competitive capitalist society and also providing for the socioeconomic needs of citizens and legal residents.

Table 8.3 *Most competitive world economies 2010*

Singapore	1	Iceland	30
Hong Kong	2	India	31
USA	3	Poland	32
Switzerland	4	Kazakhstan	33
Australia	5	Estonia	34
Sweden	6	Indonesia	35
Canada	7	Spain	36
Taiwan	8	Portugal	37
Norway	9	Brazil	38
Malaysia	10	Philippines	39
Luxemburg	11	Italy	40
Netherlands	12	Peru	41
Denmark	13	Hungary	42
Austria	14	Lithuania	43
Qatar	15	South Africa	44
Germany	16	Colombia	45
Israel	17	Greece	46
China (mainland)	18	Mexico	47
Finland	19	Turkey	48
New Zealand	20	Slovak Republic	49
Ireland	21	Jordan	50
United Kingdom	22	Russia	51
Korea	23	Slovenia	52
France	24	Bulgaria	53
Belgium	25	Romania	54
Thailand	26	Argentina	55
Japan	27	Croatia	56
Chile	28	Ukraine	57
Czech Republic	29	Venezuela	58

Source: www.imd.org/research/publications/wcy/upload/scoreboard.pdf.
Note: The World Competitiveness Scoreboard presents the 2010 overall rankings for fifty-eight economies. The economies are ranked from the most to the least competitive

Some social science research finds a positive correlation between foreign economic penetration, or direct foreign investment, and the respect for a wide range of human rights.[28] Another study has found similarly that the presence of TNCs and direct foreign investment is positively correlated with the practice of civil and political rights in developing

[28] David L. Richards, et al., "Money with a Mean Streak?: Foreign Economic Penetration and Government Respect for Human Rights in Developing Countries," *International Studies Quarterly*, 45, 2 (June 2001), 219–240.

countries. Those same civil and political rights were also positively correlated with higher GNP, US foreign assistance, and higher debt. Direct foreign investment was also positively correlated with the Physical Quality of Life Index, measuring longevity, nutrition, and education. Hence the author of this study concluded that in the modern world TNCs were engines of progressive development, associated with both improved civil-political and socioeconomic rights.[29] There are other optimistic accounts of the social and political workings of capitalism over time.[30] A 2009 study found that human rights clauses in trade agreements among governments had a positive effect on the practice of human rights, as these trade agreements set ground rules affecting corporate behavior.[31]

One does not need gross exploitation to make capitalism work, Marxist analysis notwithstanding. But one may need global social regulation to level the playing field, so that corporations are not tempted to move from rights-protective polities to oppressive ones.

A balance sheet

Two overviews of the effects of economic globalization on individuals and their human rights point in the same direction. Rhoda Howard-Hassmann concludes that global capitalism will be good for many individuals in the grand scheme of things over time, but that there will be the danger of many human rights abuses along the way.[32] The challenge is to leap over the human rights abuses that characterized the development of national capitalism, so that the workings of global capitalism are more humane. Pietra Rivoli concludes likewise that capitalism works to the benefit of many, but that there are usually large numbers of individuals who are negatively affected either through exploitation or loss of jobs. She too sees an important role for public authorities in constructing a global capitalism with a more human face.[33]

---

[29] William H. Meyer, "Human Rights and Multi-National Corporations: Theory v. Quantitative Analysis," *Human Rights Quarterly*, 18, 2 (Spring 1996), 368–397; and his book making the same points, *Human Rights and International Political Economy in Third World Nations: Multinational Corporations, Foreign Aid, and Repression* (Westport: Praeger, 1998). There followed a debate about his methods and conclusions.

[30] Max Singer and Aaron Wildavsky, *The Real World Order: Zones of Peace, Zones of Turmoil*, rev. edn. (Chatham, NJ: Chatham House Publishers, 1996).

[31] Emilie Hafner-Burton, *Forced to Be Good: Why Trade Agreements Boost Human Rights* (Ithaca: Cornell University Press, 2009).

[32] "The Second Great Transformation: Human Rights Leapfrogging in the Era of Globalization," *Human Rights Quarterly*, 27, 1 (February 2005), 1–40. See also her book, *Can Globalization Promote Human Rights?*, on human rights and economic globalization.

[33] Pietra Rivoli, *The Travels of a T-Shirt in the Global Economy: An Economist Examines the Markets, Power, and Politics of World Trade* (New York: Wiley, 2005).

It follows that if left unregulated, many TNCs will opt for short-term profits at the expense of human dignity for many persons affected directly and indirectly by their practices. It seems there must be countervailing power, either from public authorities, or from human rights organizations and movements, if TNC practices are to be made basically compatible with the International Bill of Rights (IBR). Given what I have noted before, namely that many parties are not enthusiastic about the IBR, effective human rights are usually wrestled from below in a tough struggle.[34] The clear experience of the global north is that unregulated capitalism is injurious to human dignity and social justice. Just as limitations on crude capitalism were achieved in western market democracies through tough struggle, sometimes bloody, so globalized economics is likely to be changed only in a similar process. Protests against the WTO in particular and economic globalization in general reflect this historical pattern.

Events in Indonesia during 1998 fit this larger pattern. The authoritarian Suharto government, with the support of many TNCs, clung to the *status quo* under the general banner of "Asian values" – meaning for present purposes that authoritarian Asian states had found a model of successful economics that did not require broad political participation, independent labor unions, and other manifestations of internationally recognized human rights. There was a pattern of impressive economic growth, but the continuation of much poverty – exactly as predicted by Novak and Lenkowsky.[35] But the "Asian flu" of economic recession caused a re-evaluation of "crony capitalism," led by students, labor groups, and others demanding more attention to human rights. Suharto stepped down, the succeeding government ceased to be a champion of "Asian values," and numerous changes occurred. Parts of the elite took reform measures, under popular pressures, which was precisely the pattern that had obtained in the West during earlier periods.

Relevant also was the history of Nike and Reebok in Asia. Both companies had sub-contracted the production of athletic shoes and soccer balls, *inter alia*, to firms that operated sweatshops, employed child labor, and otherwise violated internationally recognized labor rights. Negative publicity caused both companies to alter certain policies, and at one point Nike hired a prominent American public figure, Andrew Young, to examine some of its Asian operations. But a debate continued over whether the companies were engaged primarily in public relations and

---

[34] See further, for example, Rhoda Howard, *Human Rights in Commonwealth Africa* (Totowa, NJ: Rowman & Littlefield, 1986).

[35] Cf. Novak and Lenkowsky, "Economic Growth."

damage control, or in substantive change in keeping with human rights standards. (As noted in Chapter 3, certain labor rights such as freedom from slavery, freedom to bargain collectively, freedom of association, etc. are considered to be part of basic human rights.) The controversy was especially troubling to Reebok, which had pioneered certain policies related to human rights such as sponsoring rock concerts to benefit Amnesty International and making an annual human rights award. These two companies and others did participate in a program designed to guarantee that child labor was not used in the manufacture of soccer balls carrying their brand name (small fingers had proved useful in sewing).[36] By 2005 Nike, under considerable pressure, had promised to disclose the location of all of its manufacturing, presumably to enhance transparency and convince consumers and others that it was not operating sweatshops.

Regulation for human rights?

Three points are noteworthy about TNCs and international regulation in the name of human rights:

(1) the weakness of current international law, especially as developed through the United Nations system, in regulating the social effects of international business;

(2) the growing importance of private activism, including law suits and consumer and other social movements, plus the communications media, in providing critiques of for-profit behavior; and

(3) the facilitative actions of some states, especially the USA during the Clinton Administration, but not Japan in general or the George W. Bush Administration, in trying to close the gap between much TNC practice and human rights standards.

Weakness of international law

As noted earlier in this chapter, international law has had little to say about the social effects of TNC action. International law is directed mostly to states. States are held responsible for human rights conditions within their jurisdiction. The basic rule of international law is that TNCs are not subjects of that law, but only objects through the intermediary role of the state where they are incorporated.[37] Thus, TNCs are not directly responsible to international law, and TNCs – outside the EU

---

[36] As with Shell in Nigeria, so with particularly Nike in Asia, there is a small library on the subject. See further, for example, Philip Segal, "Nike Hones Its Image on Rights in Asia," *New York Times*, June 26, 1998, 1. In 1998 alone, the *New York Times* and other members of the global media carried numerous stories on this subject.

[37] See further the Barcelona Traction case, *International Court of Justice Reports*, 1970, 3.

framework – have mostly escaped direct regulation under international law.

The example of the Convention on the Rights of All Migrant Workers and Members of their Families was instructive. Those bound by this multilateral treaty were states. The twenty-one ratifying states needed to bring the treaty into legal force was achieved in 2003. But no industrialized country ratified, and it is these countries that serve as hosts to most migrant workers. It was the sending states that tended to ratify (e.g., Bosnia, Mexico, the Philippines, Uganda, etc.). So despite the treaty, most migrant workers and the companies that employed them remained outside the legal protections of the treaty, because the industrialized states refused to obligate their corporations under this part of international law.[38]

UN narrowly defined

During the 1970s when the United Nations was the scene of debates about a New International Economic Order (NIEO), there were demands from the global south, supported by the communist East, for a binding code of conduct on TNCs. Like the NIEO itself, this binding code for TNCs never came to fruition, due to blocking action by the capital exporting states whose primary concern was to protect the freedom of "their" corporations to make profits. (The OECD, made up of the westernized democracies, approved a non-binding code, but it has generated little influence.) A code of conduct for TNCs was negotiated in UNCTAD (UN Conference on Trade and Development) but never formally approved. A series of statements from UNCTAD, controlled by the developing countries, has been generally critical of the TNC record, but these statements were muted during the 1980s and thereafter. Attracting direct foreign investment via TNCs, not scaring it away, became the name of the game, especially after the demise of European communism.

For a time one could find a series of critical statements about TNCs from the former UN Human Rights Sub-Commission. A typical statement was issued by a Special Rapporteur in August 1998. El Hadji Guisse of Senegal called for criminal penalties in the national law of home states to regulate TNC actions that violated internationally recognized social and economic rights.[39] By 2003 the Sub-Commission, comprising

---

[38] See Human Rights Watch, "Migrant Workers Need Protection," July 1, 2003, www. hrw.org.press/2003/06/mwc063003.htm.

[39] Inter Press Service, "Human Rights: Holding Transnationals in Check," Global Policy Forum, www.igc.apc.org/globalpolicy/socecon/tncs/humrig.htm.

independent experts rather than state representatives, had adopted a set of "Norms on the Responsibilities of Transnational Corporations and Other Business Enterprises with Regard to Human Rights."[40] Arguing that all corporations and business have an "obligation" (moral?, legal?) to protect the human rights recognized in national and international law, this UN document then goes on to elaborate such basic principles as equality and non-discrimination, personal security, labor rights, and so on.

In 2005, the UN Human Rights Commission, before it was sidelined in favor of the new UN Human Rights Council, itself appointed an individual to make a study of business and human rights. This move was opposed by the governments of Australia and the USA.

All of this effort directed to non-binding codes and further studies at the UN fit with the creation of the Global Compact, an initiative of Secretary-General Kofi Annan to get TNCs to endorse a set of nine principles dealing mainly with human rights but also with ecological protection. The approach was positive in the sense of asking business to police itself and accept certain standards of social responsibility. Whether all of this standard setting and "social pressure light" would prove more effective than the various non-binding codes of conduct in the past remained to be seen.[41] It is possible that assertive pressure from civil society might cause corporations to take these UN norms at least somewhat seriously.[42] One study published in 2010 concluded that those TNCs that became parties to the UN Global Compact were more likely to adopt corporate statements on human rights and more likely to receive positive outside assessment of their human rights performance.[43]

UN broadly defined

The International Labour Organization has not played a highly effective role in efforts after the Cold War to target abusive practices by TNCs. In part this was because national business associations made up one-third of the membership of the ILO. Another reason was that some western states, chiefly the USA, did not favor channeling their major

---

[40] UN Doc: E/CN.4/Sub.2/2003/12/Rev.2 (2003).

[41] See further Andreas Rasche and Georg Kell, eds., *The UN Global Compact: Achievements, Trends, and Challenges* (Cambridge: Cambridge University Press, 2010).

[42] See further Sean D. Murphy, "Taking Multinational Corporate Codes of Conduct to the Next Level," *Columbia Journal of Transnational Law Association*, 43 (2005), starting at 389.

[43] Patrick Bernhagen and Neil J. Mitchell, "The Private Provision of Public Goods: Corporate Commitments and the United Nations Global Compact," *International Studies Quarterly*, 54, 4 (December 2010), 1175–1187.

concerns through the ILO. During the Cold War the ILO had fallen out of favor with Washington due to various political battles. By the turn of the century the ILO had not recovered from these bruising struggles and had not proved to be a dynamic organization capable of achieving striking developments in defense of labor rights. The ILO had a role to play in long-term socialization. Its basic standards fed into other developments at the UN Human Rights Commission and the Global Compact. But its record of decisive, short-run improvements was not striking.

The ILO was old and distinguished, and it has long manifested a human rights program in relation to labor rights. As I noted in Chapter 3, since 1919 it had developed a series of reasonable – if sometimes vague – standards about international labor rights pertaining to a safe and healthy work environment, non-discrimination, fair wages, working hours, child labor, convict or forced labor, freedom of association, the right to organize, and the right to collective bargaining. But despite an elaborate system for reviewing and supervising its conventions, the ILO was unable to achieve very much "support in international practice – at least in the sense of universal compliance by multinational corporations with these standards."[44] The ILO Tripartite Declaration of Principles Concerning Multinational Enterprises and Social Policy (1977) also failed to affect the practice of TNCs. In theory during the Cold War, labor rights should have been an area for cooperation between East and West, if not north and south. But the ILO was able to produce little progressive change during the Cold War,[45] as after. The abstract norms might remain valid. The principles underlying the basic conventions might have entered into customary law and become binding even on non-parties that were members of the ILO. The question was how to develop a political process that paid them some concrete attention.

A bright spot in the global picture after the Cold War was the growing attention to child labor.[46] The International Convention on the Rights of the Child was almost universally accepted – only the USA and Somalia

---

[44] Diane F. Orentlicher and Timothy A. Gelatt, "Public Law, Private Actors: The Impact of Human Rights on Business Investors in China," *Northwestern Journal of International Law and Business*, 14 (1993), 116 and *passim*.

[45] Ernst A. Haas, *Human Rights and International Action* (Stanford: Stanford University Press, 1970).

[46] See Samantha Besson and Joanna Bourke-Martignoni, "Children's Convention (Convention on the Rights of the Child)," in David P. Forsythe, ed., *Encyclopedia of Human Rights* (New York: Oxford University Press, 2009), vol. I, 300–308. See further Burns H. Weston, ed., *Child Labor and Human Rights: Making Children Matter* (Boulder: Lynne Rienner, 2005).

refused to ratify, the latter state often lacking effective government.[47] This law obligated states to protect child workers against forced and unsafe labor, *inter alia*.[48] UNICEF, the UN's premier agency dealing with children, was increasingly linking itself to this treaty and was seeing itself as much an actor for human rights as for relief and development. At a global conference in 1997 UNICEF expressed some optimism that the worst forms of exploitation of the 250 million working children could be successfully challenged, as had proved true with regard to much child labor in the garment industry.[49]

One needed to be careful, however, about a negative approach to the subject that insisted on a simple ban on child labor. This approach alone condemned children and their families to continued poverty and a denial of the recognized right to an adequate standard of living. What was required was a ban combined with positive developments. The source of child labor was underdevelopment. Small steps like providing the funds for better meals in schools could get children out of the fields and sweatshops. Overall development would have the same effect. Just removing children from the production of soccer balls in Pakistan did little but to guarantee continued grinding poverty for them and their families, plus a boost for machine-made soccer balls in the sweatshops of China.[50]

Trade law

On the other side of the coin, embryonic trade law might not prove so supportive of growing attention to human rights. As noted earlier in this book, there was some fear that dispute panels under the new World Trade Organization would strike down national and sub-national legislation designed to curtail TNC activity in repressive states like Burma.

---

[47] Important circles in the USA championed parental and privacy rights and were skeptical of the intrusion of public authority into this domain, whether national or international. While some of the American opposition to this convention was irrational, it remained strong. Fears about the introduction of abortion rights or the undermining of parental authority in matters of religion might be misguided, but they were held intensely by some.

[48] Especially Article 32.

[49] Reuters, "Child Labor Conference Ends on Hopeful Note," www.yahoo.com/headlines/970227/international/stories/children_1.html.

[50] See further Mahmood Monshipoori, "Human Rights and Child Labor in South Asia," in David P. Forsythe and Patrice C. McMahon, eds., *Human Rights and Diversity: Area Studies Revisited* (Lincoln: University of Nebraska Press, 2003). See also a series of articles on this subject in the *New York Times* by Nicholas D. Kristof, as in "The Fuss over Child Labor Is Misguided," April 6, 2004.

Observers had been fearful that human rights legislation, such as from the state of Massachusetts, would be struck down in the WTO as an impermissible restraint on free trade. But the US Supreme Court made this particular point moot. Massachusetts had adopted a state law specifying that any company doing business in repressive Burma/Myanmar could not contract for services with Massachusetts. But the highest US court ruled unanimously that such internal state legislation was unconstitutional, as the US federal government had preempted legislation pertaining to Burma. Thus the Court held that Massachusetts was unconstitutionally interfering with the foreign policy power of the federal government.[51] (In the past, other internal legislation on human rights in foreign states, as in the Republic of South Africa under white minority rule, had been allowed, as the federal government had not tried to preempt internal state and local action.)

At the time of writing, efforts to interject stronger provisions into the WTO regarding human rights, and especially labor rights, had not been successful.[52]

In fact, the WTO continued to strongly endorse business prerogatives especially when buttressed by TRIPS – the agreement linked to the WTO protecting trade-related intellectual property rights. Among other issues, TRIPS protected the right of transnational drug companies under patent law to ensure the sale of their higher priced drugs, and to block the sale of cheaper generic drugs that might impinge on those patents. But in places like sub-Saharan Africa, where HIV/AIDS was rampant, many human rights organizations pressured the drug companies to put people ahead of profits, to cooperate with the use of the cheaper generic drugs despite intellectual property rights. After much controversy the TNC pharmaceuticals did yield on a number of points, while making their own point that protection of patents was necessary to ensure some profitable return on investments, it being those investments in costly research that led to new drugs. There were several barriers to an adequate response to the African HIV/AIDS pandemic, a situation that might repeat itself in parts of Asia as well. The arrangements for Africa showed both the clash of different human rights – to private property and to adequate health – as well as the prevalence of negotiated arrangements rather than

---

[51] For an analysis of *National Foreign Trade Council v. Crosby*, see Peter J. Spiro, "US Supreme Court Knocks Down State Burma Law," *ASIL Insights*, American Society of International Law, June 2000, www.asil.org/insights/insigh46.htm.

[52] See further Daniel B. Braaten, "World Trade Organization," in *Encyclopedia of Human Rights*, vol. V, 395–398; and Susan Ariel Aaronson and Jamie M. Zimmerman, *Trade Imbalance: The Struggle to Weigh Human Rights Concerns in Trade Policymaking* (New York: Cambridge University Press, 2007).

legal solutions.[53] The pharmaceuticals were concerned about damage to their brand names by a full and absolute insistence on their recognized property rights.

There is also regional trade law. In the North American Free Trade Agreement (NAFTA), unlike the WTO, there is a "side agreement" on labor rights (as well as on ecological protection). This reference to labor is relatively weak, at least in the view of Human Rights Watch and many other unions and human rights NGOs.[54] But one labor expert took a more positive view, arguing that NAFTA's labor provisions had legitimized the linkage between trade and human rights, while advancing a number of important principles as well as some regional cooperation on labor rights.[55] The same general situation characterizes the Central American Free Trade Agreement (CAFTA): there is some mention of labor rights, but the supervising and adjudicatory measures are weak. Given the influence of the Republican Party, the party of big business in US politics, it was difficult to get strong labor provisions in these regional arrangements in the Western Hemisphere. Even in the USA, a member of both CAFTA and NAFTA, and with its own federal and internal state legislation, there were significant labor abuses. In the state of Florida, for example, a number of agricultural workers existed in conditions of virtual forced labor and slavery, not to mention poor working conditions, lack of health care, and low wages.[56]

The only relatively strong protections for labor rights at the regional level are to be found in the European Union (EU).[57] Within the EU, treaty law and the case law of the European Court of Justice (ECJ) protect the free movement of workers within the EU without discrimination on grounds of nationality. ECJ cases also stipulate equal pay for men and women, and that such standards are directed not just to the goal of economic prosperity but to advancing the rights of individuals as part of

---

[53] For one view see Susan K. Sell and Aseem Prakash, "Using Ideas Strategically: The Contest Between Business and NGO Networks in Intellectual Property Rights," *International Studies Quarterly*, 48, 1 (March 2004), 143–175.

[54] Human Rights Watch, "Nafta Labor Accord Ineffective," April 16, 2001, www.hrw.org/English/docs/2001/04/16/global179.htm. See also the criticism in David Bacon, *The Children of NAFTA: Labor Wars on the US/Mexico Border* (Berkeley: University of California Press, 2004).

[55] Lance Compa, "A Glass Half Full: The NAFTA Labor Agreement and Cross-Border Labor Action," in George J. Andreopoulos, ed., *Concepts and Strategies in International Human Rights* (New York: Peter Lang, 2003).

[56] See further Human Rights Watch, "Human Rights of Florida's Farm Workers Are Under Serious Threat," March 2, 2005, www.hrw.org/english/docs/2005/03/02/usdom10284_txt.htm.

[57] See further Paul Craig and Grainne de Burca, *EU Law: Text Cases and Materials*, 3rd edn. (Oxford: Oxford University Presss, 2003), chs. 17 and 20.

the pursuit of social progress. Directives by the EU Council of Ministers endorse not only equal pay for equal work, but also equality in pension benefits and equal parental leave. Not just state members of the EU but corporations operating within the EU are obligated to follow these standards.

An ICC role?

The first prosecutor of the International Criminal Court suggested in several venues that he might be inclined to bring indictments against business leaders who are complicit in genocide, or crimes against human-ity, or major war crimes.[58] There has been considerable discussion of the relevance of this possibility in situations like the Democratic Republic of the Congo. There, where public authority is weak and in some areas virtually non-existent, as in the Ituri district, a number of corporations are involved in extracting the abundant and valuable natural resources of the country – such as diamonds, gold, coltan (used in cell phones), and timber. The industries involved hire security firms to protect their oper-ations, and allegedly these militia are some of the actors engaging in the atrocities often reported in various sources.[59] The longrunning conflict in the DRC is the most disruptive and deadly in any country since World War II. The size and complexity of the problem makes it very difficult to find outside parties that want to seriously engage in order to manage the situation. There is little prospect of "humanitarian intervention" by states, and the IGOs controlled by states, like the UN or African Union, are only engaged in marginal ways. In this situation, where one finds "resource wars" and "blood diamonds," prosecution of corporate lead-ers under international criminal law might be one of the few promising avenues for doing something about systematic abuse, including murder, rape, persecution, and forced displacement.

Indictment of business leaders in the ICC, however, is not likely to encourage the USA to support or tolerate the Court, at least as long as the Republican Party, with its reluctance to link business and human rights, controls or substantially influences US foreign policy. On the other hand, some corporations are supportive of international action against those benefiting from these resource wars. The De Beers diamond company wants to shut off the flow of black market diamonds from places

---

[58] James Podgers, "Corporations in the Line of Fire," *ABA Journal*, January 2004, 13.
[59] See, for example, Julia Graff, "Corporate War Criminals and the International Criminal Court: Blood and Profits in the Democratic Republic of Congo," *Human Rights Brief*, 11, 2 (Winter 2004), 23–26.

like Angola and Sierra Leone, in order to protect its market share. De Beers, with the support of Belgium, a traditional center for the diamond trade, would be only too happy to see the curtailment of black market diamonds.[60]

To date, none of the ICC investigations or cases has focused on corporations or corporate leaders, as previously discussed in Chapter 4.

Non-profit dynamism

Chapter 7 charted the growth of an international civic society in which various non-profit organizations and movements, including human rights groups, were increasingly active on public policy issues. This chapter follows up by showing that numerous organizations and movements have begun to focus on TNC practices in the light of human rights standards. One may use the broad phrase "social responsibility" in reference to TNCs, but human rights values are part of that concern (which also includes anti-bribery and anti-corruption measures, along with ecological matters).[61] As far back as 1972 the International Chamber of Commerce adopted a non-binding code of conduct for TNCs. Some business executives formed the Caux Round Table, which promotes TNC social responsibility, including "a commitment to human dignity, [and] political and economic freedoms."[62] Standard human rights organizations like Human Rights Watch and Amnesty International began to pay more attention to TNCs.[63] Groups that had long tracked business practices in the interests of consumers, such as Ralph Nader's Global Trade Watch in Washington, began to focus more on human rights issues. Labor unions like the AFL-CIO were highly active on transnational labor issues. An important internet site was the Business and Human Rights Resource Center, created by AI and a number of other private groups, that provided broad monitoring of business and human rights issues (www.businesshumanrights.org). There were other important websites

[60] Alan Cowell, "De Beers Plans Guarantee: Diamonds Not from Rebels," *International Herald Tribune*, March 1, 2000, 15.

[61] See further Lance A. Compa and Stephen F. Diamond, eds., *Human Rights, Labor Rights, and International Trade* (Philadelphia: University of Pennsylvania Press, 1996); John W. Houck and Oliver F. Williams, *Is the Good Corporation Dead?: Social Responsibility in a Global Economy* (Lanham: Rowman & Littlefield, 1996); and Lee Tavis, *Power and Responsibility* (Notre Dame: Notre Dame Press, 1997).

[62] See www.cauxroundtable.org/.

[63] On this point see especially the chapter by David P. Forsythe and Eric Heinze, "On the Margins of the Human Rights Discourse: Foreign Policy and International Welfare Rights," in Howard-Hassmann and Welch, *Economic Rights in Canada and the United States*, 55–70. One has only to observe the websites or publication lists of these NGOs. See, for example, www.hrw.org/about/initiatives/corp.html.

run by NGOs as well, such as by Social Accountability International (www.cepaa.org).

In some cases of private pressure there has been undeniable success. In response to a citizen boycott of its operations in south Florida over the treatment of immigrant workers picking tomatoes, Taco Bell agreed in 2005 to raise the wages of affected workers and imposed a tough code of conduct pertaining to its suppliers.[64] The "Sullivan Principles" at least directed attention to the effects of apartheid on working conditions in the Republic of South Africa under white minority rule, even if Reverend Sullivan of Philadelphia eventually concluded that his code – intended to affect investments – was inadequate for achieving major improvements in an integrated work force in South Africa during apartheid. The "McBride Principles" directed attention to sectarian discrimination in employment practices in Northern Ireland, as any number of investors in that British province tied their investments to these principles designed to reduce prejudice against Catholics or Protestants. As noted, other firms have been shamed into altering their policies in the light of human rights values. Starbucks Coffee opened its foreign operations to human rights monitors, Heineken withdrew from doing business in Burma, and Levi Strauss withdrew from manufacturing in China for a time.

In the fall of 1998, a group of companies in the apparel and footwear industries, including Liz Claiborne, Nike, Reebok, and others, agreed to open their overseas operations to independent human rights monitors under formal agreement. The "Apparel Industry Partnership" or "Fair Labor Association" provided for periodic inspection by the Lawyer's Committee for Human Rights, now renamed Human Rights First, based in New York, and other respected human rights NGOs under detailed provisions.[65] The deal was brokered by the Clinton Administration, which had worked for over two years to get such an agreement. While arrangements were criticized by various American labor groups, some American university students, and others as not going far enough, this development was hailed by its supporters as a major advance in providing specific attention to labor rights on a transnational basis.[66] About twenty major American universities with well-known sports programs and popular sports apparel, like Michigan, Notre Dame, and Nebraska, among others, joined this arrangement.[67]

---

[64] Eric Schlosser, "A Side Order of Human Rights," *New York Times*, April 6, 2005, A29.

[65] For one summary see www.lchr.org/sweatshop.summary.htm.

[66] Steven Greenhouse, "Groups Reach Agreement for Curtailing Sweatshops," *New York Times*, November 5, 1998, A18.

[67] Steven Greenhouse, "17 Top Colleges Enter Alliance on Sweatshops," *New York Times*, March 16, 1999, A15.

When, for example, the University of Nebraska in 2005 concluded a new contract with Adidas for the provision of sports apparel, the contract contained a human rights clause that required the company and its sub-contractors to meet certain standards pertaining to freedom of association and collective bargaining, limitations on working hours, women's equality, prohibition of discrimination and harassment, etc. – a clause that would be independently supervised. The wording, however, did not address explicitly and specifically a fair or living wage.

Under the AIP/FLA, reports on companies are made public, allowing consumers to take whatever action they want on the basis of the reports. The reports focus on a workplace code, detailed in the agreement, and are based on a selected percentage of the companies' operating facilities. Analysis of wages are pegged to a US Department of Labor study regarding employee basic needs in the country at issue. There is also a procedure for filing complaints against the company. A "no sweat" label can be added to products made in compliance with this agreement.

Also in 1998, a number of companies including Toys R Us and Avon created the Council on Economic Priorities (CEP). This CEP deals with the usual labor rights in foreign subsidiaries or sub-contractors, but also with what constitutes a "living wage" in different countries. On this latter point, according to a specific formula, one calculates the cost of basic human need in caloric terms. This is done in a way that allows specific numbers to be provided country by country. The formula has been generally regarded as appropriate. But the CEP terms were sufficiently demanding for some business groups and commentators to endorse the AIP/FLA as indicated above, on the grounds that a specific "living wage" standard would curtail some foreign investment leading to loss of jobs in the global south.[68] After all, certain governments as in Malaysia have been very explicit about low wages constituting one of their important comparative advantages in global markets.

Still other companies created the American Apparel Manufacturers Association. While this arrangement provided monitoring of labor rights, the standards were so low that it was generally discredited by most human rights groups, unions, attentive university students, and other observers outside the apparel industry.

Still further, some students and union leaders created the Worker Rights Consortium (WRC). This movement, excluding business leaders in the formulation of its plans, pushed for unannounced inspections of plants and factories as well as for a tough "living wage" for workers. Its

---

[68] Aaron Bernstein, "Sweatshop Reform: How to Solve the Standoff," *Business Week*, May 3, 1999, 186–190.

approach was abrasive enough for Nike to break off arrangements with several major American universities, like Michigan, when they accepted WRC terms.[69] Later, however, Nike, while still not agreeing to WRC terms, did promise to open all of its foreign operations to public disclosure and did admit that a certain number of labor problems existed in its various facilities.[70]

A summary analysis of private action intended to make TNCs more sensitive to human rights standards is elusive. As noted already, Shell Oil was not forced out of Nigeria, nor into providing clearly different policies in Ogoniland where Shell operations had allegedly damaged the environment, nor into saving the life of Ken Saro-Wiwa and his Ogoni compatriots who had protested against Shell policies. At best Shell was forced into paying more attention to public relations and fending off calls for major boycotts and sanctions. Yet the story about Shell and Nigeria is not over, and it remains to be seen whether relations between this TNC and post-Abacha governments in Lagos remain the same as in the past. Private advocacy for better TNC policies may yet prove at least somewhat influential in this case. In Chapter 7 I noted the elusive nature of "success" for human rights groups and movements, as well as noting the importance of long-term, informal education in changing views over time.

Finally in this section I should note that some private actors have brought law suits in national courts against TNCs and their global operations. For example, in the USA, the Alien Tort Statute of 1789 allows civil suits against private parties where a violation of the law of nations is involved, regardless of the nationality of the parties. Most of the case law under this statute has concerned torture.[71] But in the 1990s certain individuals sought to sue the Unocal oil firm, based in California, for engaging in – or allowing sub-contractors to engage in – forced labor and other human rights violations in its operations in Burma. The US district court in question, in a jurisdictional ruling of considerable importance, allowed the case to proceed. In the merits phase, however, the court held that plaintiffs had not proven legal culpability by Unocal. Despite this ruling, while the case was still under appeal, Unocal agreed to settle with the plaintiffs, thus giving the impression that litigation in US courts

---

[69] Mark Asher and Josh Barr, "Nike Pulls Funds from Campus Critics," *International Herald Tribune*, May 6–7, 2000, 9.

[70] Rukmini Callimachi, "Nike Reveals Overseas Factories," AP report, carried in *Lincoln Journal Star*, April 14, 2005, C1.

[71] Beth Stevens and Steven R. Ratner, *International Human Rights Litigation in US Courts* (Irvington-on-Hudson, NY: Transnational Publishers, 1996).

against TNCs for human rights violations might be effective in producing progressive settlements.[72]

Complicating matters, however, was the fact that as private citizens, human rights groups, and their lawyers sought to use the Alien Tort Statute to go after businesses for violating international human rights standards, the George W. Bush Administration tried to get US courts to narrow the scope of application of that statute.[73] The Bush Administration, reflecting the pro-business and free-enterprise philosophy of the Republican Party, was not happy when businesses were made defendants in US courts regarding international human rights issues. And in March 2004, the US Supreme Court did try to narrow the application of the Alien Tort Statute.[74] Thereafter, in November 2004, a federal district court in New York threw out a suit against several major American corporations (e.g., General Electric, General Motors, etc.) for being complicit in the human rights violations in South Africa during the apartheid era.[75]

Unfortunately for human rights advocates, the US Appellate Court for the 2nd Circuit held by a 2–1 margin that a business corporation was not a legal person in the sense that it could be held responsible for human rights violations under the Alien Tort Statute (Kiobel v. Royal Dutch Shell, 2010).[76] If one looked at the history of US case law under ATS even prior to the Kiobel case, plaintiffs were likely to lose when corporations were defendants and the Executive expressed interest in the case.[77]

The US Supreme Court had previously held that corporations were legal persons with a right of free speech, and that political donations were

---

[72] For a good review of this general subject, see Beth Stephens, "Upsetting Checks and Balances," *Harvard Human Rights Journal*, 17 (Spring 2004), 169–205. See also her essay, "National Courts," in *Encyclopedia of Human Rights*, vol. IV, 41–49.

[73] See Daphne Eviatar, "A Big Win for Human Rights," *The Nation*, May 9, 2005, www.thenation.com/20050509&s=eviatar . But see also Human Rights Watch, "US: Ashcroft Attacks Human Rights Law," May 15, 2003, www.hrw.org/press/2003/05/us051503.htm.

[74] For a readable analysis of the Alvarez-Machain case, see Warren Richey, "Ruling Makes It Harder for Foreigners to Sue in US Courts," *Christian Science Monitor*, June 30, 2004, http://0-web.lexis-nexis.com.library.unl.edu/universe/document?_m=77a8f707d45981ecda.

[75] For a readable analysis of the South African case, see Julia Preston, "Judge Dismisses Big Rights Suit on Apartheid," *New York Times*, November 30, 2004, A6.

[76] The judges in their concurring and dissenting opinions engaged in a spirited debate about such non-technical matters as the likelihood of corporations violating human rights and the wisdom of US courts adjudicating matters vital to the economies of foreign nations: *Kiobel v. Royal Dutch Petroleum Co.*, 621 F.3d 111 (2d Cir. 2010), *rhrg. denied*, ___ F.3d ___ (2d Cir. Feb. 4, 2011).

[77] Jeffrey Davis, *Justice Across Borders: The Struggle for Human Rights in US Courts* (Cambridge: Cambridge University Press, 2008).

an expression of free speech that could not be regulated (Citizens United, 2009). In still another case, the US Supreme Court held that corporations were not legal persons in the sense of possessing a constitutionally protected right of privacy in the face of a request under the US Freedom of Information Act as related to a charge of violation of personal privacy (Federal Communications Commission v. AT&T, 2011). So in the USA on the matter of rights and duties of US corporations where they were seen as legal persons, courts seemed to engage in judicial legislation without a great deal of consistency. On balance, courts seemed to favor corporate freedom from legal control in matters of violation of human rights abroad and political activity at home.

It bears noting that it was the threat (promise?) of judicial action that caused Swiss banks to reach an out of court settlement about claims pertaining primarily to Jewish account holders arising from the Holocaust era.[78] Likewise it was the prospect of similar judicial action that caused Volkswagen and other German corporations also to reach an out of court settlement that provided a fund to compensate slave laborers whose rights were violated in that same era.[79]

Nation-state action

In the 1970s, as already noted, western or home state governments tried to fend off demands for new international law to regulate TNCs as part of the NIEO. By the 1990s this situation had partially changed, as a number of governments – including some that were pro-business and right of center – in westernized democracies advocated at least codes of conduct and other non-binding measures designed to advance social responsibility, including attention to human rights, in the activities of TNCs. The German government of Helmut Kohl underwrote the "Rugmark campaign," designed to ensure that Asian rugs were not made with child labor. The Chretian government in Canada also began to address the issue of child labor abroad. The Clinton Administration brokered the AIP/FLA arrangement discussed above, while trying to pressure Shell because of its policies in Nigeria. European governments, through the European Parliament, tried to embarrass British Petroleum over its policies in Colombia which allegedly led to the repression of labor rights through brutal actions by the army in constructing a BP pipeline. On the

---

[78] See Stuart E. Eizenstat, *Imperfect Justice: Looted Assets, Slave Labor, and the Unfinished Business of World War II* (New York, Public Affairs, 2003).
[79] "Volkswagen Joins Holocaust Fund," www.news.bbc.co.uk/2/hi/europe/279070.stm.

other hand I have noted the opposition of the George W. Bush Administration to linking TNCs to international human rights standards, an opposition which included voting against a measure which passed in the UN Human Rights Commission in the spring of 2005 calling for further attention to this subject.

In general it can still be said that home state governments remain reluctant to firmly and effectively use public law to regulate TNCs in the name of international human rights. The real shift that is under way is for national governments to prod "their" corporations to regulate themselves, under non-binding codes and now increasingly NGO monitoring. The sanction at work is that of negative publicity and consumer sanctions. This has proved somewhat effective for those companies that sell directly to individual consumers, as Heineken and Nike, *inter alia*, will attest.

A review of US foreign policy and TNC action for human rights, however, is an example that indicates more vague rhetoric than concrete examples of effective action – certainly beyond the AIP/FLA agreement.[80] The United States, especially under Republican administrations, is still wary of "statism" that would intrude deeply into the marketplace.

In 1996 the US Department of Commerce advanced a code called the Model Business Principles linked to universal human rights. The code referred to a safe and healthy workplace, fair employment practices, and free expression and opposition to political coercion in the workplace, along with environmental and anti-corruption concerns. But aside from the AIP/FLA agreement, it seems that nothing much has come about in the wake of this code. The Department of Commerce is normally pro-business, and was notably so in the Clinton Administration by comparison with the Labor Department under Robert Reich. As in most governments, there was tension between competing elements.

It is said that the State Department, the Office of the US Trade Representative, and other US bodies take up labor concerns in foreign countries. It is true that the Annual Country Human Rights Reports, compiled by the State Department's Bureau of Democracy, Human Rights, and Labor, consider labor issues. But it is well known that there has been a persistent gap between the recording of violations of internationally recognized human rights in these reports, which has been done fairly conscientiously since 1976, and any effective follow-up steps by the USA. Washington's trade statutes include language that allows trade to

---

[80] See www.state.gov/www/global/human_rights/business_principles.html.

be made conditional on human rights behavior.[81] But as in EU relations with non-European trade partners, this conditionality is rarely if ever invoked in practice.

It is also true that US foreign policy officials make speeches on behalf of labor rights and corporate social responsibility, but concrete action by the USA in opposing certain TNC practices is not always easy to demonstrate. The United States has been more active, for a longer period of time, in opposing TNC bribery than in opposing child labor and other violations of labor rights.

It can be noted, however, that the USA joined a number of other actors like UNICEF in providing funds to allow underage children to return to school rather than work in Asian sweatshops. The Departments of Commerce and Labor do publish information on child labor abroad, and provide a list of codes of conduct and possible monitoring organizations for TNC use if they so choose. And the United States continues to support certain ILO programs, even if these have not always proved very effective.

Conclusions

Whereas not so long ago TNCs were urged not to get involved in the domestic affairs of host states, now there has been a considerable shift in expectations; TNCs are frequently urged by citizens and their governments to undertake a more active commitment to international human rights.[82] As a *New York Times* editorial noted: "A quarter-century ago, business argued that protecting the environment was not their job. Few American companies would say so today. A similar change may be developing in corporate attitudes about human rights. Companies are increasingly recognizing that their actions can affect human rights, and that respecting rights can be in their business interest."[83]

Despite the fact that most public international law, and so far contemporary international criminal law, does not apply thus far to TNCs, there are ways to reorient private corporations to public standards of human rights. Non-binding codes of conduct, devoid of monitoring mechanisms,

---

[81] Compa and Hinchliffe-Darricarrere, "Enforcing International Rights," 667.

[82] The Dutch Sections of Amnesty International and Pax Christi International, *Multinational Enterprises and Human Rights* (n.p.: AI and PCI, n.d.), 22–23. See further Thomas Donaldson, "Moral Minimums for Multinationals," in Joel H. Rosenthal, ed., *Ethics and International Affairs: A Reader*, 2nd edn. (Washington: Georgetown University Press, 1999), 455–480.

[83] Quoted in "Human Rights and Business: Profiting from Observing Human Rights," *Ethics in Economics*, 1998 (nos. 1 & 2), 2, 125 E. Broad St., Columbus, Ohio, www.businessethics.org.

have proved uniformly weak in the 1970s and 1980s, whether originating from the International Chamber of Commerce, the OECD, the ILO, the US government, or in draft form from UNCTAD. But private codes, in the form of negotiated agreements, accompanied by independent monitoring and public reporting, hold some promise for changing corporate behavior. This is especially so when such agreements have the backing of governments which can be expected to assist in implementation. Recall that the AIP/FLA is underwritten by the US government, whose Department of Labor carries out studies, *inter alia*, to promote compliance. Recall that the Rugmark campaign was underwritten by the German government. Recall that the UN Global Compact can claim some modest successes.

It is in this a-legal gray area of public and private action that one is most likely to see progress in the near future in getting TNCs to pay more attention to human rights standards. The pressure will come mostly from the non-profit side, in the context of media exposure, with the threat of consumer or citizen action that endangers the corporation's profit margin. But socially responsible partners will exist within some corporations and governments. The process is likely to remain quasi-legal and extra-judicial, although national court cases making TNCs liable for civil penalties for human rights violations could be a factor of great significance. Most states, however, do not manifest their equivalent of the US Alien Tort Statute which opens up national courts to petitions about corporate violations of human rights globally. And even the USA has recently seen a reluctance of judges to hold corporations liable for human rights violations abroad.

Despite US judicial backsliding, globally speaking there is a new psychological environment in which TNCs are expected by many to engage in socially responsible policies. Many of these policies center on international standards of human rights. It was in this context that the JPMorgan Bank apologized for its role in supporting slavery in the past in the USA, and then set up a five million dollar program in Louisiana (where several of its acquired banks had operated) for African-American students to pursue higher education.[84]

Case study: Chinese oil companies and corporate social responsibility

There are three major Chinese oil companies that have become important international actors especially in African countries: China National

---

[84] Associated Press, "JPMorgan: Banks Had Links to Slavery," *Lincoln Journal Star,* January 21, 2005, A9.

Petroleum Corporation (CNPC), China Petroleum and Chemical Corporation (Sinopec), and China Offshore Oil Corporation (CNOOC).[85] They all profess commitment to the idea of corporate social responsibility (CSR), a composite non-binding or voluntary code of conduct consisting of segments on human rights, ecological protection, and good business practices including financial transparency. The central question here is the impact of CSR on these three Chinese oil firms and whether their relevant records are very different from western oil firms.

All three Chinese firms are members of the UN Global Compact and make voluntary public reports under this and other relevant international standards. They all profess allegiance to either the 1948 Universal Declaration of Human Rights or unspecified human rights values, to ecological protection, and to proper business practices. Information about these companies is available from the 2005–2006 era when the firms became important if relatively small players on the international oil scene.

In general the evidence shows that these Chinese oil companies seek the extraction of oil from countries such as Sudan, Nigeria, Equatorial Guinea, Angola, and elsewhere for international sale with the least degree of difficulty possible. They do not exist to advance democracy or promote human rights in any country, which of course one would not expect from firms based in authoritarian China. They do on occasion plow some of their profits back into the local communities through building schools or distributing water during the dry season. Their overall record on CSR is not significantly different from western-based oil companies over a longer time span.

To the extent that Nigeria, for example, has mismanaged its oil resources and in the process contributed to the violation of various human rights especially in the delta region of Ogoniland, the responsibility resides primarily with the Nigerian government as reinforced by western oil companies such as Royal Dutch Shell. The Chinese firms played no role. To the extent that oil resources in Angola prolonged the civil war there, feeding the conflict on both sides, the primary responsibility rested with the contesting factions as reinforced by the western oil companies that extracted the resources. The Chinese firms played no role, appearing on the scene after the conflict. To the extent that the Chinese firms moved into Sudan when western firms were compelled to withdraw because of human rights violations in Darfur, over time the record of China's oil firms has become more nuanced and is not radically different from the stated objectives of western governments.

---

[85] Adapted from Scott Pegg, "Social Responsibility and Resource Extraction: Are Chinese Oil Companies Different?," *Resources Policy*, in press.

It is true that the presence of these Chinese corporations gives contracting governments some leverage in bargaining with western entities as well as with the World Bank and IMF. But an African backlash against some early Chinese practices has caused the overall Chinese record especially in Africa to be similar to their western counterparts. Attacks on Chinese workers in Nigeria, much criticism of early Chinese policy in Sudan, and similar events have caused Chinese authorities to be more careful about local impact against the background of international scrutiny of international standards. For example, they changed course with regard to some dealings with the much criticized Mugabe government in Zimbabwe.

One might keep in mind that, according to some analysts, the western-based oil firms do not have an outstanding record under CSR to begin with. So if we say that the Chinese oil firms have a record that is no worse, that is not holding those Chinese corporations to a very high standard. Nevertheless, the fear that the Chinese oil firms would greatly undermine democracy and human rights in Africa is, so far, much overstated. CSR is not a very powerful tool for promoting democracy and human rights to begin with; it cannot compel corporations interested in production and sales to become agents for progressive public policy. Primary responsibility for democracy and human rights in oil-producing states still rests with national governments. To the extent that an "oil curse" has led to negative human rights conditions in sub-Saharan Africa, one cannot look primarily to these Chinese firms.

Discussion questions

- Are transnational corporations too large and powerful for control by public authorities? To what extent are international authorities, compared with national authorities, important for the regulation of TNCs?
- What is the experience in OECD countries with regard to private, for-profit corporations and their impact on labor at home? Has the lesson of this experience been properly applied to international relations?
- Are human rights considerations, when applied to TNCs, actually a form of western imperialism in that the application of human rights standards to protect workers actually impedes economic growth and prosperity in the global south?
- If you are a stockholder in a TNC, do you really want "your" company to pay attention to human rights as labor rights if it reduces the return on your investment? What if you are both an owner and a consumer at the same time: does this change any important equation in your thinking? Why should we expect American and European owners or

consumers to be concerned about Asian, African, or Latin American workers?

- Are companies like Nike and Reebok engaged in public relations maneuvers by joining a-legal codes of conduct like AIP/FLA, or do they show a real commitment to the human dignity of the workers in their Asian sub-contractors? Is there any real difference between Nike and Royal Dutch Shell when it comes to social issues in foreign countries?
- Can TNCs be effectively counterbalanced on sweatshop issues by a movement featuring primarily university students, unions, human rights groups, and the media? Is it necessary for governments to lend their support to such a movement? Can private a-legal codes of conduct be effective on TNC policies?
- Given that the ILO has been around since about 1920, why does so much action on labor rights take place outside the procedures of this organization? Can one make more progress on labor rights by circumventing international law and organization? Conversely, should we make TNCs directly accountable under international law, instead of indirectly accountable through nation-states? Is politics more important than law?
- Was the George W. Bush Administration correct in arguing that the Alien Tort Statute of 1789 was not intended to cover civil suits for violations of international human rights in the twenty-first century? Regardless of the original intent of those who drafted and passed that statute, was it proper policy for that administration to try to narrow the application of that law so as to exclude attempts to protect against corporate abuses?

SUGGESTIONS FOR FURTHER READING

Barnet, Richard J., and John Cavanagh, *Global Dreams: Imperial Corporations and the New World Order* (New York: Simon & Schuster, 1994). A hard look at TNCs and public policy from left of center.

Compa, Lance A., and Stephen F. Diamond, eds., *Human Rights, Labor Rights, and International Trade* (Philadelphia: University of Pennsylvania Press, 1996). A good collection that provides a solid overview.

Donaldson, Thomas, "Moral Minimums for Multinationals," in Joel H. Rosenthal, ed., *Ethics and International Affairs: A Reader*, 2nd edn. (Washington: Georgetown University Press, 1999), 455–480. A good, short treatment of ethical conduct in the world of TNCs.

Frynas, Jedrzeg George, and Scott Pegg, eds., *Transnational Corporations and Human Rights* (London: Palgrave Macmillan, 2004). Useful short studies of private activism, codes of conduct, conflict situations, oil companies in

Nigeria, mining in Papua New Guinea, the coffee industry, labor in South East Asia, community–corporate partnerships in Canada.

Gilpin, Robert, *The Political Economy of International Relations* (Princeton: Princeton University Press, 1987). A classic study. Chapter 6 deals with TNCs. Not much explicitly on human rights, but lots on TNC behavior in broad political perspective.

Haas, Ernst A., *Human Rights and International Action* (Stanford: Stanford University Press, 1970). Concludes that the ILO during the Cold War was not able to improve labor rights in the communist bloc.

Houck, John W., and Oliver F. Williams, *Is the Good Corporation Dead: Social Responsibility in a Global Economy* (Lanham: Rowman & Littlefield, 1996). A thorough examination of the concept of social responsibility in relation to corporate behavior.

Howard-Hassmann, Rhoda, "The Second Great Transformation: Leapfrogging in the Era of Globalization," *Human Rights Quarterly*, 27, 1 (February 2005), 1–40. A broad argument about the place of human rights in the transformation from national industrial capitalism to global technocratic capitalism.

Can Globalization Promote Human Rights (University Park, PA: Penn State University Press, 2010). In this expansion of a 2005 article, she discusses the interplay of political, social, and economic globalization. She holds that global capitalism can contribute to the protection of human rights if social and political developments keep pace with international economics.

Hymer, Stephen, "Multinational Corporations and the Law of Uneven Development," in J. W. Bhagwati, ed., *Economics and World Order* (New York: Macmillan, 1971), 113–140. A classic study of the evils TNCs can do.

Korten, David, *When Corporations Rule the World* (West Hartford: Kumarian Press, 1995). Another critical look, some would say hypercritical, at TNCs and the damage they can do.

Meyer, William H., *Human Rights and International Political Economy in Third World Nations: Multinational Corporations, Foreign Aid, and Repression* (Westport: Praeger, 1998). A quantitative study finding positive correlations, in general, between the presence of TNCs in the global south and lots of good things. The author's methodology has been questioned by other scholars.

Omeie, Kenneth, *High Stakes and Stakeholders: Oil Conflict and Security in Nigeria* (Aldershot: Ashgate, 2006). A balanced treatment.

Rasche, Andreas, and Georg Kell, eds., *The UN Global Compact: Achievements, Trends, and Challenges* (Cambridge: Cambridge University Press, 2010). Multiple authors provide an informed overview of the subject.

Rivoli, Pietra, *The Travels of a T-Shirt in the Global Economy: An Economist Examines the Markets, Power, and Politics of World Trade* (New York: Wiley, 2005). A broad and readable view of how global economics works, with attention to both benefits and problems – including why certain individuals will not benefit under free trade and the WTO.

Rodman, Kenneth A., "Think Globally, Punish Locally: Non-State Actors, Multinational Corporations, and Human Rights," *Ethics & International Affairs*, 12 (1998), 19–42. Notes the growing pressure on corporations to better respect labor rights, principally from human rights organizations and consumer movements.

Schlesinger, Stephen C., and Stephen Kinzer, *Bitter Fruit: The Untold Story of the American Coup in Guatemala* (Garden City, NY: Doubleday, 1982). American corporations team with the US government to overthrow the Arbenz government in Guatemala, ushering in several decades of brutal repression.

Soros, George, "The Capitalist Threat," *Atlantic Monthly*, 279, 2 (February 1997). The successful Hungarian financier and philanthropist warns of the dangers of unregulated capitalism in Eastern Europe and the former Soviet Union.

Spar, Deborah, "The Spotlight and the Bottom Line: How Multinationals Export Human Rights," *Foreign Affairs*, 77, 2 (March–April 1998), 7–12. A short essay that is basically positive about the role of regulated or pressured corporations. The author notes that some corporations have a very poor record on human rights.

Tavis, Lee, *Power and Responsibility* (Notre Dame: Notre Dame Press, 1997). Another useful look at social responsibility and corporate behavior.

Vernon, Raymond, *Sovereignty at Bay: The Multinational Spread of US Enterprises* (New York: Basic Books, 1971). A classic study arguing that TNCs have not escaped control by the modern state.

Part III

Conclusion

This book has clearly shown the extent to which human rights has become a routine part of international relations. Michael Ignatieff has captured the trend succinctly but brilliantly: "We are scarcely aware of the extent to which our moral imagination has been transformed since 1945 by the growth of a language and practice of moral universalism, expressed above all in a shared human rights culture."[1] The language and practice of universal human rights, and of its first cousin, regional human rights, has been a redeeming feature of a very bloody and harsh twentieth century.

But the journalist David Rieff reminds us of a more skeptical interpretation of universal human rights. "The universalizing impulse is an old tradition in the West, and, for all the condemnations that it routinely incurs today, particularly in the universities, it has probably done at least as much good as harm. But universalism easily declines into sentimentalism, into a tortured but useless distance from the particulars of human affairs."[2] Or, to drive the same point home with a more concrete example, whereas virtually all states formally endorse the abstract principles of human rights in peace and war, "Combatants are as likely to know as much about the laws of war as they do about quantum mechanics."[3]

The international law of human rights is based on liberalism, but the practice of human rights all too often reflects a realist world. A classical example was provided by the situation in Syria in the first half of 2011: the Assad security forces killed and otherwise repressed those demanding more human rights and democracy; and various states such as Israel, Turkey, and the United States were reluctant to endorse regime change preferring the devil they knew (Assad) to unforeseen events that might lead to regional instability. (In the midst of its repression, Syria was at least blocked from sitting on the UN Human Rights Council.) State interests

---

[1] Michael Ignatieff, *The Warrior's Honor: Ethnic War and the Modern Conscience* (New York: Metropolitan, 1997), 8.
[2] David Rieff, "The Humanitarian Illusion," *New Republic*, March 16, 1998, 28.
[3] David Scheffer, "The Clear and Present Danger of War Crimes," Address, University of Oklahoma College of Law, February 24, 1998, unpublished.

rather than personal rights often prevail, interpersonal equality often gives way to disrespect for – if not hatred of – "others," violent conflict is persistent, and weak international institutions are easily demonstrated.[4]

It is a type of liberal progress in keeping with Ignatieff's view that we now recognize the enslavement and other exploitation of the persons in the Congo river basin between about 1460 and 1960 as a violation of their human rights.[5] It is a testament to the continuing explanatory power of David Rieff's realism that we note the lack of effective or decisive international response to the massacres and other gross violations of human rights in the Congo river basin after 1998, whether one speaks of Zaire or Democratic Republic of Congo. Approximately five million persons died from that conflict and its effects, and the rapes were perhaps too numerous to count precisely. (The DRC was the worst place in the world to be female, with on average over 1,000 raped *every day*.)[6] Yet the conflict continued at the time of writing.

We recognize rights, but often we do not act to protect them. This provides one general answer to the frequently heard lament: "How could the rhetoric of human rights be so globally pervasive while the politics of human rights is so utterly weak?"[7]

Evidence suggests that the idea of human rights still resonates well with publics, but whether governmental elites will follow that opinion is another question. In 2008, sixty years after the UN General Assembly adopted the Universal Declaration of Human Rights, a sample of 15,000 people in sixteen countries which reflected 59 percent of the world's population believed that there had been progress concerning sexism and racism. They believed that there was more equality in the world since 1948. Of this sample, 71 percent thought women had made progress in matters of equality. In fifteen of the sixteen countries large majorities indicated that governments should act to block discrimination against ethnic and racial minorities. In the same year large majorities in twenty-one countries believed that governments were responsible for seeing that persons could achieve their basic needs in food, health care, and education. Even in the USA, which does not accept socioeconomic rights such

---

[4] To expand on notions of realism discussed in Chapter 1, see further among many sources Jack Donnelly, *Realism in International Relations* (Cambridge: Cambridge University Press, 2000). On the difference between human and national interests in international relations, see especially Robert C. Johansen, *The National Interest and the Human Interest: An Analysis of US Foreign Policy* (Princeton: Princeton University Press, 1980).

[5] Adam Hochschild, *King Leopold's Ghost: A Story of Greed, Terror, and Heroism in Colonial Africa* (Boston: Houghton Mifflin, 1998).

[6] See www.abc.net.au/pm/content/2011/s3215390.htm.

[7] Kenneth Cmiel, "The Recent History of Human Rights," *American Historical Review*, 109, 1 (February 2004), 118.

as a human right to adequate health care, in 2008 even a small majority of John McCain supporters, not to mention an overwhelming majority of Barack Obama supporters believed government should ensure adequate health care for all. In 2006 a poll of 27,000 people across twenty-five countries found 60 percent opposed to torture even if it were considered to protect innocent civilian lives from a terrorist attack. In the same year in the USA, a poll found that between 57 and 73 percent of those sampled were in favor of due process rights for terror suspects, ranging from freedom from threats of torture to rights of habeas corpus (right to challenge the reason for detention).[8]

As for governmental policies, a careful study of the fate of thirteen human rights during 1981–2006, broken down into two segments, during and after the Cold War, mostly but not entirely focused on civil and political rights, found mixed results. This study attempted an objective measurement of the practice of rights, whatever publics might think. Most rights associated with democratic governance showed improvement. As for what the authors term physical integrity rights, freedom from arbitrary arrest and forced disappearance showed improvement. On the other hand, freedom from torture and extra-judicial killing did not. According to them, the decline in protection against torture started *before* 9/11 and the follow-on abusive counterterrorism policies. Women's political rights showed marked improvement; their economic and social rights did not.[9]

To review

Given the ground covered in this work thus far, a brief review of main points is in order. Dichotomies and paradoxes characterize the turbulent international relations of the turn of the century in 2000, as noted in Chapter 1. International human rights are here to stay, but so is state sovereignty in some form. The latter notion is being transformed by the actions, *inter alia*, of intergovernmental and transnational nongovernmental organizations. But state consent still usually matters legally, and state policy and power still count for much in human affairs. One

---

[8] See the data compiled and analyzed at worldpublicopinion.org run by the University of Maryland's Program on International Public Attitudes.

[9] David L. Cingranelli and David L. Richards. "The Cingranelli and Richards (CIRI) Human Rights Data Project," *Human Rights Quarterly*, 32, 2 (May, 2010), 401–424. Compare Todd Landman, *Protecting Human Rights: A Comparative Study* (Washington: Georgetown University Press, 2005). On women's rights see further International Center for Research on Women, "Recognizing Rights, Promoting Progress," 2010, www.icrw.org/publications/recognizing-rights-promoting-progress. This is a CEDAW impact report.

historian – tongue in cheek – quotes a British diplomat to the effect that we need an additional article in the UN Charter: "Nothing in the present Charter should be allowed to foster the illusion that [state] power is no longer of any consequence."[10] This remains relevant despite the rise of armed non-state actors. Our moral imagination has been expanded by the language of universal rights, but we live in a world in which nationalism and the nation-state and national interests are frequently powerful barriers to effective action in the name of international human rights. Trade-offs and compromises between liberal and realist principles are legion, as human rights values are contextualized in a modified nation-state system of international relations.[11]

As covered in Chapter 2, the International Bill of Rights and supplemental standards give us the modern international law of global human rights. For all of its defects, noted in various critiques covered below, it is far more developed (meaning specified and structured) than some other parts of international law pertaining to such subject matter as ecology.

Like all law it is the result of a political process, frequently contentious. Surely it comes as no surprise that transnational standards pertaining to the right to life or to the right of freedom of religion or to freedom from discrimination, *inter alia*, should prove controversial. The existence of international human rights law owes much to the western-style democracies – their liberal values and their hard power (the liberal values themselves can be a type of soft power). Still, internationally recognized human rights were also affected by the old communist coalition, and certainly by the newly independent states of the global south after about 1960.

It cannot be stressed too much that whereas certainly the practice of politics on the basis of respect for the notion of human rights was extensively developed in certain western states, the idea of human rights is a defense against abuse of power everywhere.[12] Wherever the bicycle was invented, its utility is not limited to that historical and geographical situation. So it is also with the idea and practice of human rights.

The human dignity of especially those without great power and wealth normally benefits from the barriers to injurious acts of commission and omission provided by human rights standards. Intentional mass murder and neglectful mass misery are equal affronts to any conception of human dignity. Mass misery no less than mass murder can be changed by human endeavor, and is thus grist for the mill of human rights discourse. As often

---

[10] Geoffrey Best, Book Review, *Los Angeles Times*, August 16, 1998, 8.
[11] See further Rein Mullerson, *Human Rights Diplomacy* (London: Routledge, 1997).
[12] See further Thomas M. Franck, "Is Personal Freedom a Western Value?," *American Journal of International Law*, 91, 4 (October 1997), 593–627.

noted, there is no material or moral reason for world hunger, save for the way we choose to organize ourselves as inhabitants of the planet earth.[13] We create territorial states whose governments are sometimes said to have responsibility only to their citizens; foster a type of nationalism that tends to restrict morality to within national borders; and internationally endorse a harsh form of *laissez-faire* economics despite its rejection on moral grounds at home. The idea of universal human rights seeks to change those mind sets.

But human dignity itself, and human rights as a means to that end, are contested constructs whose meaning must be established in a never-ceasing process of moral, political, and legal debate and review. Beyond mass murder and mass misery, the dividing line between fundamental personal rights and myriad optional legal rights is a matter of considerable controversy.

In Chapter 3 we saw that the UN has moved beyond the setting of human rights standards toward the systematic supervision of state behavior. This is a very broad and accelerating development, unfortunately partially undermined not only by a paucity of resources that states allow the overall UN human rights program, but also by the disjointed nature of the beast. The sum total of the diplomacy of shaming, or the politics of embarrassment, certainly has had an educative effect over time, even if the calculated violation continued in the short term.

At least at first glance it was encouraging that the United Nations Security Council after the Cold War should pay so much attention to human rights issues in the guise of threats to international peace and security. The Council's deployment of field missions under the idea of second-generation or complex peacekeeping, mostly directed to producing a liberal democratic order out of failed states, showed a willingness to deal with many of the root causes of human rights violations – as long as the principal parties gave their consent to the UN presence. Such missions clearly were on the progressive side of history in places like El Salvador, Namibia, and Mozambique. The trend continued in places like Bosnia, Kosovo, East Timor, and Cambodia.

It was also noteworthy that the Council should authorize enforcement actions on behalf of democratic governance and other humane values in places such as Haiti, Somalia, and Libya, even if the job had to be contracted out to one or more member states, and even if the follow-up left something to be desired. Unfortunately the Council was heavily dependent on the one remaining superpower, the United States, to make

---

[13] Thomas Pogge, *World Poverty and Human Rights: Cosmopolitan Responsibilities and Reforms* (Cambridge: Polity, 2002).

its enforcement actions effective. The result was a very spotty record of UN accomplishments, especially where the USA saw few traditional national interests to sustain a complicated involvement. In the Kosovo crisis of 1999 the United States tried to enforce human rights protections via NATO, but without Security Council authorization and through a highly controversial military strategy.

On balance the UN was paying more attention to human rights, not less. It was being creative in the interpretation of Chapters VI and VII of the Charter, in calling emergency sessions of the Human Rights Council (as had the Commission), in expanding the authority of its monitoring mechanisms, in creating the office of the High Commissioner for Human Rights, in utilizing NGO information, and in other ways.

Some of this UN creativity had to do with the establishment of various *ad hoc* international or mixed criminal courts by the Security Council, as we saw in Chapter 4. The standing international criminal court, whose statute was overwhelmingly approved in 1998, and which began to function during 2002–2003, was loosely associated with the UN. This renewed foray into international criminal justice was a noteworthy development after a hiatus of some fifty years. It triggered a new round of debate about peace v. justice, and about what was central to peace as compared with a moral sideshow. Ignatieff is again brilliantly concise when he writes, "Justice in itself is not a problematic objective, but whether the attainment of [criminal] justice always contributes to reconciliation is anything but evident."[14] New efforts at international criminal justice also caused national policy makers to calculate carefully about how vigorously to go after those indicted for war crimes, crimes against humanity, and genocide, for fear of undermining larger objectives or incurring human costs difficult to justify according to traditional notions of national interest.

What started out in 1993 as mostly a public relations ploy, namely to create an *ad hoc* tribunal to appear to be doing something about human rights violations in Bosnia without major risk to outsiders, by 2005 had become an important global movement for international criminal justice formally accepted by more than 110 states. Such were the unexpected outcomes of a series of "accidental" or *ad hoc* decisions, as states muddled their way through complex calculations of media coverage, popular pressure, traditional national interests, and state power. Private armies might commit many of the violations of human rights, and private human rights groups might be players in the legislative process, but ultimately it was states that decided.

---

[14] Ignatieff, *The Warrior's Honor*, 170.

Broad European support for the ICC was partly because, as we saw in Chapter 5, most European states had become accustomed to having supranational courts make judgments on human rights in both the Council of Europe and the European Union. French policy in particular had undergone a considerable change. Like the USA, France long considered its record on human rights beyond the need for the type of international review provided by individual petitions and a supranational regional court. But France – and Turkey – shifted over time, providing at least a glimmer of hope that eventually US nationalism might prove more accommodating to multilateral human rights developments.[15]

Be that latter point as it may, European regional protections of civil and political rights remained relatively strong. The Council of Europe and the European Union proved that liberal principles of human rights could often be effectively combined with realist principles of the state system. Of course European developments transformed the regional state system in important ways, as states used their sovereignty to restrict their independence of policy making. Yet states continued to exist in meaningful ways, as did their views of their national interests. States such as Russia and Turkey remained difficult to regulate through regional human rights regimes. At the same time, an international view on protecting human rights also mattered in very important ways, mostly through the judgments of the supranational courts existing in Strasburg (and Luxemburg for EU members).

In less striking, more diplomatic (as compared with legal) ways the Organization for Security and Co-operation in Europe mattered regarding especially the diplomatic protection of national minorities. That NATO should be used to try to protect Albanian Kosovar rights in 1999 was indicative not only of the importance of regional organizations, but also of the importance of international action for human rights in Europe. It was not hyperbole to say that commitment to human rights was the touchstone of being European. Beyond Europe, the human rights agencies associated with the Organization of American States, especially the InterAmerican Commission on Human Rights, at least generated some impact sometimes on some issues. While the short-term view regarding African regional developments for human rights was even less encouraging, it was at least possible that the Banjul Charter and the African Commission on Human Rights were laying the foundations for long-term progress. After all, both the European Commission and Court

---

[15] In *Of Paradise and Power: America and Europe in the New World Order* (New York: Vintage, 2003, 2004), Robert Kagan argues that European states are much more committed to international law and organization as essential public goods than is the USA.

had mostly undistinguished records during their first decade of operation, although both operated in an environment more conducive to real regional protection compared with Africa (and historically the Western Hemisphere). At least for Latin American states (but not so much the English-speaking states of the Western Hemisphere), there were more states (not less) accepting the jurisdiction of the InterAmerican Court of Human Rights, and that court was handing down more (not fewer) judgments. Last but not least, NATO was an important actor in avoiding a humanitarian disaster in Libya in 2011.

Permeating all these international developments on human rights was state foreign policy, as we saw in Chapter 6. It is states that take the most important decisions in most intergovernmental organizations, and it is states that are the primary targets of lobbying activities by traditional advocacy groups. State sovereignty is being transformed by transnational interests and movements, but states and their conceptions of sovereignty remain an important – indeed essential – aspect of world affairs at the turn of the century.

Contrary to some realist principles, rational states do not always adopt similar foreign policies despite their existing in anarchic international relations. Because of history, culture, ideology, and self-image, some states do strongly identify with international human rights – at least sometimes. They may take diffcrent slants and emphases when incorporating human rights into their foreign policies. But increasingly many states wish to stand for something besides independent existence and power. States certainly have not abandoned self-interest and pursuit of advantage, but more so than in the past they often seek to combine these traditional expediential concerns with concern for the human rights of others. The liberal framework of international relations, embedded in international law and organization, pushes them in that direction. Inconsistencies are legion, but some progress over time is demonstrable.

To be sure the result is usually inconsistent foreign policies that fall short of the goals demanded by the human rights advocacy groups. But in empirical and relative terms, there is now more attention to human rights in foreign policy than was the case in the League of Nations era. In a shrinking world, states that profess humane values at home find it difficult to completely ignore questions of human rights and dignity beyond their borders. Their self-image, their political culture, mandates that linkage. States that initially seek to bypass issues of individual human rights, like China and Iran, find themselves drawn into a process in which they at least endorse, perhaps in initially vague ways, human rights standards.

Traditional human rights advocacy groups have been active concerning both legislation and implementation of norms, as we traced in Chapter 7.

Basing their actions mostly on accurate information, they have followed a self-defined moral imperative to try to "educate" public authorities into elevating their concerns for internationally recognized human rights. Frequently coalescing into movements or networks entailing diverse partners, they have engaged in soft lobbying (viz., lobbying that bypasses electoral and financial threat). Mostly relying on the politics of embarrassment or shaming, they have sought to use reason and publicity to bring about progressive change.

It has usually been difficult to factor out the general but singular influence of this or that human rights NGO, or even this or that movement. Nevertheless, given the flood of information they produce and the persistent dynamism the major groups such as Amnesty International or Human Rights Watch exhibit, it is difficult to believe that the same evolution concerning international human rights would have occurred over the past thirty years without their efforts. In some cases and situations NGO influence can indeed be documented. It is certainly true that the international system for provision of emergency relief in armed conflict and complex emergencies would not be the same without private groups such as the International Committee of the Red Cross. Likewise, there are numerous groups active for "development," or social and economic rights, like Oxfam, Save the Children, etc., and they often provide an important link between the donor agencies and the persons who presumably benefit from "development."

Increasingly it is necessary to look beyond not only states and their intergovernmental organizations, but also beyond the private groups active for human rights, relief, and development for an understanding of the fate of human rights in the modern world. We especially need to look at transnational corporations, as we did in Chapter 8. Given their enormous and growing power in international economics, and given the dynamics of capitalism, it is small wonder that their labor practices have come under closer scrutiny. It may be states that formally make and mostly enforce human rights norms. But it is private corporations, frequently acting under pressure from private groups and movements, that can have a great impact on the reality of human rights – especially in the workplace. Sometimes states are rather like mediators or facilitators, channeling concern from private advocacy groups and movements into arrangements that corporations come to accept.[16] Such was the case with the US government concerning labor standards in the apparel industry,

---

[16] See further B. Hocking, *Catalytic Diplomacy* (Leicester: Centre for Diplomatic Studies, 1996).

and with the German government concerning child labor in the international rug industry.

One of the more interesting developments concerning international human rights at the close of the twentieth century was the linkage between student activism and labor standards at many universities in the global north. This merger resulted in growing pressure on particularly the apparel industry to end the use of not only child labor but sweatshops by their foreign sub-contractors. But progressive developments were not limited to that one industry, as corporations selling coffee and other products felt the need to protect their brand name and bottom line by opening their foreign facilities to international inspection under international labor standards. It was not so much muscular international law and established intergovernmental relations that brought about new developments. Rather it was a movement made up of consumer groups, unions, the communications media, student movements, churches, and traditional advocacy groups that brought about codes of conduct with inspections and public reports.[17] Much has been written about the social media and grassroots networking that drove the Arab Spring of 2011 in places such as Tunisia and Egypt and the resulting demand for improved democracy and human rights.

Still, one should not be Pollyannaish. Many of the corporations dealing in extraction of natural resources had compiled a record quite different from at least some TNCs in the American-based apparel industry. And many companies seemed more interested in public relations than in genuine commitment to either human rights or other means to human dignity. The corporate push to minimize expenses and maximize profits remained strong.

Toward the future

The future of international human rights is not easy to predict with any specificity. One might agree with the statement attributed to the Danish philosopher Kierkegaard: life is lived forward but understood backward. Or one might agree with a statement from Vaclav Havel, first President of the Czech Republic: "That life is unfathomable is part of its dramatic beauty and its charm."[18] Nevertheless, one point is clear about human rights in international relations. We will not lack for controversy.

---

[17] For example, the Presbyterian Church USA considered divesting from certain corporations providing military equipment to Israel, such was that church's concern about Israeli policies in the occupied territories. See Laurie Goodstein, "Threat to Divest is Church Tool in Israeli Fight," *New York Times*, August 6, 2005, A1.

[18] Vaclav Havel, *Summer Meditations* (New York: Vintage, 1993), 102. See further James F. Pontuso, "Vaclav Havel," in David P. Forsythe, ed., *Encyclopedia of Human Rights* (New York: Oxford University Press, 2009), vol. II, 361–364.

Human rights has indeed been institutionalized in international relations, but that discourse will remain controversial. This is paradoxical but true. Debate is inherent in the concept of human rights. I do not refer now to the effort by philosophers to find an ultimate metaphysical source of, or justification for, the notion of human rights. Rather I refer to debates by policy makers and others interested in practical action in interpersonal relations. There is debate both by liberals of various sorts who believe in the positive contributions of human rights, and by non-liberals such as realists and Marxists.

Controversies in liberalism

Enduring questions

Even for those who believe that international human rights constitute on balance a good thing, there are no clear and fixed, much less scientific, answers to a series of questions. What defines universal human dignity? What are the proper moral human rights that constitute the means to that dignity? Which are truly fundamental, and which are optional? Which are so fundamental as to be absolutely non-violable, even in war and other situations threatening national security or the life of the nation, and thus constituting part of *jus cogens* in international law (legal rules from which no conflicting rules or derogation is permitted)? What crimes are so heinous that the notion of universal jurisdiction attaches to them? When moral rights are translated into legal rights, and when there is conflict among legal rights, who resolves the conflicts, and on what principle? Which violations of internationally recognized human rights justify forceful intervention?

Traditional principles

If we focus on particular principles that are said to be human rights principles in contemporary international law, derived from liberalism, we still cannot avoid debate. Revisit, if you will, the principle discussed in Chapter 2 and codified in Article 1 of the two International Covenants in the International Bill of Rights: the collective right of the self-determination of peoples. How do we define a people with such a right – the Kosovars, the Quebecois, the Basques, the Ibos, the Kurds, the Slovaks, the Chechens, the Ossetians? Who is authorized to pronounce on such definitional issues? If we could define such a people, what form or forms can self-determination take? And why have states in contemporary international relations been unable to specify authoritative rules under this general principle that would prove relevant and helpful to conflicts over self-determination? Why is the evidence so overwhelming that most of these disputes are settled by politics, and frequently on the basis of superior coercive power, rather than on the basis of legal rules about collective rights?

Even if we take the widely shared principle of freedom from torture, we cannot avoid controversy. The classic counterexample involves the hypothetical prisoner who has knowledge of a "dirty bomb" that is about to explode. Is it moral to observe the no-torture principle if it results in death or serious injury and sickness to millions? As I noted especially in Chapter 6, the USA from 2002 (with much support from allies) employed some coercive interrogation in its military detention centers, ran a secret detention system in which abusive interrogation was probably the norm (why else keep it secret?), and "rendered" persons to other states where mistreatment and even torture were widely regarded as prevalent. Was all of this truly necessary for US homeland security? Could the same information have been extracted by more humane methods? If one did obtain some "actionable intelligence," but in the process engaged in a widely known abusive process that produced even more "terrorists" because of their outrage, how should one evaluate the overall costs and benefits? How should one evaluate the experience of other countries that had employed mistreatment or torture, like France in the Algerian war, Britain in Northern Ireland, and Israel, say between 1967 and 1999?

Even if we take the widely shared principle about a right to religious freedom, we cannot escape controversy.[19] This is so even in countries that recognize the principle (and thus I exclude for the moment various controversies about Saudi Arabia and other states that reject the basic principle). What is a religion? The US government says that scientology is a religion, whereas the German government says it is a dangerous, perhaps neo-fascist cult. Do certain Native Americans in prison have a right to use marijuana as part of their claimed religious practices? Is religious belief a valid basis for refusal to serve in the military? Should religious freedom be elevated to those basic rights of the first order, as demanded at one point by the Republican-controlled Congress in the 1990s, and be made the object of special US concern? Or should religious freedom be considered one of many rights, and deserving of no automatic priority over other rights in state foreign policy? The latter was the position of the Clinton Administration, although as noted it did

[19] See further Kevin Boyle and Juliet Sheen, eds., *Freedom of Religion and Belief: A World Report* (London: Routledge, 1997).

respond to congressional pressures by creating a special office in the State Department to deal with religious freedom.

Even if we note the central position in human rights discourse of the principle of non-discrimination, does the quest for personal equality extend to acceptance of sexual and gender diversity? The answer in much of the West tends toward the affirmative, as views have shifted over time. But tolerance for gay and lesbian persons and acceptance of gay rights are markedly different in some other parts of the world.[20]

New claims

Certainly if we observe the demands for acknowledgment of a new, third generation of human rights in international relations, we cannot escape the reality of continuing controversy. Should the principle be recognized of a human right to a safe environment?[21] If so, would the enumeration of specific rules under this principle provide anything new, as compared with a repetition of already recognized civil rights about freedom of information, speech, association, and non-discrimination? On the other hand, is it not wise to draw further attention to ecological dangers by recasting norms as human rights norms, even at the price of some redundancy? Then again, given that many states of the global north already have extensive legal regulations to protect the environment, why is it necessary to apply the concept of human rights to environmental law?[22] Do we not have a proliferation of human rights claims already?[23] Do we not need a moratorium on new claims about human rights, perhaps until those rights already recognized can be better enforced?[24]

---

[20] See further Douglas Sanders, "Sexual and Gender Diversity," in *Encyclopedia of Human Rights*, vol. IV, 433–445.

[21] For starting points see Svitlana Kravchenko, "Environment," ibid., vol. II, 139–149; and Richard P. Hiskes, *The Human Rights to a Green Future: Environmental Rights and Intergenerational Justice* (Cambridge and New York: Cambridge University Press, 2008).

[22] See further W. Paul Gormley, *Human Rights and the Environment: The Need for International Co-operation* (Leiden: W. W. Sijthoff, 1976); and Human Rights Watch, *Defending the Earth: Abuses of Human Rights and the Environment* (New York: Human Rights Watch, 1992). See also Alan Boyle and Michael Anderson, eds., *Human Rights Approaches to Environmental Protection* (New York: Oxford University Press, 1996); Barbara Rose Johnston, ed., *Life and Death Matters: Human Rights and the Environment at the End of the Millennium* (Walnut Creek, CA: AltaMira Press, 1997).

[23] See further Carl Wellman, *The Proliferation of Rights: Moral Progress or Empty Rhetoric?* (Boulder: Westview, 1999).

[24] See Philip Alston, who opposes the development of most new categories of human rights when the older categories are not well enforced, in "Conjuring Up New Human Rights: A Proposal for Quality Control," *American Journal of International Law*, 78, 3 (July 1984), 607–621.

Process priorities

As should be clear by now, classical and pragmatic liberals do not always agree on how to direct attention to human rights, how much emphasis to give, and what priorities to establish when desired goals do not mesh easily. The classical liberal places great faith in persistent emphasis on law, criminal justice, and other punishments for violation of the law. The pragmatic liberal argues for many avenues to the advancement of personal dignity and social justice, of which attention to legal rights, adjudication, and sanctions is only one. Classical liberals emphasize the hard law of adjudication. Pragmatic liberals aspire to that hard law on human rights but accept much soft law through diplomatic process – and even accept turning a blind eye to that law on occasion.

As a pragmatic liberal, I see no alternative to a case-by-case evaluation of when to stress human rights law and adjudication, hard law, that is, and when to opt for the priority of other liberal values through diplomacy. I believe, for example, that it was correct to pursue the Dayton accord in 1995 for increased peace in Bosnia, even if it meant at that time not indicting and arresting Slobodan Milosevic for his support for and encouragement of heinous acts. The persons of that area benefited from increased peace, decline of atrocities, and the attempt to establish liberal democracies in the region. I believe it was correct to go slow in the arrest of indicted persons in the Balkans, lest the United States and other western states incur casualties, as in Somalia in 1993, that would have undermined other needed international involvement, as in Rwanda in 1994.

I believe it was correct to emphasize truth commissions rather than criminal proceedings in places such as El Salvador and South Africa, despite the gross violations of human rights under military rule in San Salvador and under apartheid in Pretoria. Long-term national reconciliation and stable liberal democracy are advancing in those two countries, whereas pursuit of criminal justice may have hardened animosities between the principal communities. On the other hand, I think it a good idea to try to hold Augusto Pinochet legally accountable for crimes against humanity, including torture and disappearances, when he ruled Chile. His extradition from Britain and prosecution in Spain, had that transpired, might have made other tyrants more cautious about violating human rights. At least the judgment remains that he was liable to prosecution.

Given the Chinese elite's preoccupation with national stability, in the light of their turbulent national history and the closely watched disintegration of the Soviet Union during Gorbachev's political reforms, I believe it is correct to take a long-term, diplomatic approach to the matter of improvement of human rights in China. I believe we should use the international law of human rights as a guide for diplomacy and a goal for China's evolution. But in the absence of another massacre as in Tiananmen Square in 1989, or some comparable gross violation of human rights, I believe that constructive engagement is the right general orientation.

None of these policy positions is offered as doctrinal truth. Many of them depend on the evolution of future events which are unknowable. All are offered as examples of policy choices that the typical pragmatic liberal might make, that are based on liberal commitment to the welfare of individuals over time regardless of nationality or gender or other distinguishing feature, and that sometimes avoid an emphasis on criminal justice and other forms of punishment in the immediate future.

The pragmatic liberal approach allows for a great deal of flexibility and guarantees a certain amount of inconsistency. The pragmatic liberal may support criminal justice for human rights violations in one situation, e.g., Spain regarding Chile (the Pinochet case), but not in another, e.g., Cambodia regarding the Khmer Rouge. The pragmatic liberal might well regard major sanctions as mostly inadvisable for Chinese violations of human rights, but find them useful in dealing with Iraq, or Afghanistan, or Burma, or Yugoslavia – or maybe not.

Characteristic of controversy about proper human rights policy was the western response to the Arab Spring of 2011 and the grassroots demand for human rights and genuine democracy across the region. There was military intervention in Libya and a *de facto* policy of regime change for Kaddafi, but a much weaker response in Syria that sought to leave the repressive Assad regime in charge while hoping (improbably?) for moderation in the future. Was an uncertain future any more threatening in Syria than in Libya? And whose interests were threatened by the departure of Assad, such that protesting Syrians were left to pay the price for lack of regime change?

What we are certainly going to continue to see, even among liberals, is considerable debate about policy choice.

Feminist perspectives

Given that half of the planet's population is female, if we could continue to make major strides in better protecting women's rights, that would lead to a quantum leap in human rights protection overall.[25] And given the

---

[25] On the progress that has been made since about 1970, in addition to Cingranelli and Richards, "The Cingranelli and Richards (CIRI) Human Rights Data Project," see

reality of "missing girls," namely that particularly in Asia there continues to be preference for male children, resulting in abortion of female fetuses and even infanticide of female babies, there is a pressing need to focus on women's rights. The great imbalance between males and females in the global population tells the distressing story, with perhaps 60–100 million "missing girls" overall.[26] Moreover we can note or already have noted various issues of women's rights requiring more attention: coercive sex trafficking (largely but not entirely pertaining to girls and women); rape as a political strategy (again largely but not entirely pertaining to girls and women); discrimination against women regarding compensation in the workplace; female cutting or mutilation; etc.[27]

Even the most radical feminists do not reject the international law of human rights, in the last analysis,[28] and thus I list feminist perspectives as part of liberalism despite great variety among feminist publicists. Much of the feminist critique of extant human rights actually turns out to be gendered liberalism or pragmatic liberalism.[29]

Rhoda Howard-Hassmann, "Universal Women's Rights Since 1970: The Centrality of Autonomy and Agency," paper presented at ISA-Montreal, spring 2011, forthcoming in *Journal of Human Rights*; read by permission. She notes the negotiation of CEDAW in 1981 (Convention on the Elimination of Discrimination against Women) and argues that three major issues were omitted: violence against women, abortion rights, and lesbian rights. See further Ann E. Towns, *Women and States: Norms and Hierarchies in International Society* (Cambridge: Cambridge University Press, 2010), who links the domestic status of women to foreign policy and global governance; and Niamh Reilly, *Women's Human Rights* (Cambridge: Polity, 2008), who links human rights to feminist perspectives. For a strong feminist approach to human rights, see Brooke Ackerly, *Universal Human Rights in a World of Differences* (Cambridge: Cambridge University Press, 2008).

26 Compare Niall Ferguson, "Men Without Women: The Ominous Rise of Asia's Bachelor Generation," *Newsweek*, March 6, 2011, www.newsweek.com/2011/03/06/men-without-women.html; and Aarti Dhar, "'Missing Girls' Increasing in Asia: UNDP," *The Hindu*, March 9, 2010, www.hindu.com/2010/03/09/stories/2010030962351200.htm.

27 See Barbara Stark, "Women's Rights," in *Encyclopedia of Human Rights*, vol. V, 341–351. See further Howard B. Tolley, Jr., "Human Trafficking," ibid., vol. II, 494–502. See also Hope Lewis, "Female Genital Mutilation and Female Genital Cutting," ibid., vol. II, 200–213.

28 Eva Brems, "Enemies or Allies?: Feminism and Cultural Relativism as Dissident Voices in the Human Rights Discourse," *Human Rights Quarterly*, 19, 1 (February 1997), 140–141.

29 It can be noted in passing that one strand of feminism reflects a "post-modern" or "critical" or "essentialist" approach in that it argues that, unless one is female, one cannot understand female human dignity and the rights (and perhaps other institutions) needed to protect it. Male observers and scholars, as well as policy makers, are simply incapable of comprehending either the problem or its solution. I myself would not consider this approach part of the liberal tradition, for liberalism stresses a common rationality and scientific method available to all without regard to gender. See further Christine Sylvester, "The Contributions of Feminist Theory to International Relations,"

The traditional feminist critique of human rights centers on the argument that those norms, being produced in a male-dominated legislative process, focus on the public rather than private domain.[30] The public arena is the man's world, while women have been confined to the home as sexual object, mother, unpaid domestic worker, etc. Thus it is said that international human rights fail to deal adequately with domestic abuse and oppression of women. International human rights have supposedly been gendered to the detriment of women, despite an active role for some women in the drafting of the Universal Declaration of Human Rights (as noted in Chapter 3).

One feminist critique attacks one half of the International Bill of Rights as it exists today, preferring to emphasize supposedly feminist values like caring and responsibility.[31] Here the argument is that a rights-based approach can only lead to negative rights of the civil and political variety. If one wishes to move beyond them to adequate food, clothing, shelter, and health care, one needs a feminist ethics of care that stresses not rights but the morality of attentiveness, trust, and respect.

Parts of international human rights law are being revised to respond to the first critique. International and more specifically comparative refugee law now stipulates that private abuse can constitute persecution and that women can constitute a social group subject to persecution. Thus a woman, crossing an international border to flee such behavior as female genital mutilation, or a well-founded fear of such behavior, particularly when the home government does not exercise proper protection, is to be provided asylum and is not to be returned to such a situation. Canada and the United States have led the way in reading this new interpretation into refugee law, acting under advisory guidelines established by the Office of the UN High Commissioner for Refugees.[32]

As for the second critique, it should be repeated that the discourse on human rights does not capture the totality of ethics pertaining to

in Steve Smith, Ken Booth, and Marysia Zalewski, eds., *International Theory: Positivism and Beyond* (Cambridge: Cambridge University Press, 1996), 254–278.

[30] See further, from a growing literature, Rebecca J. Cook, ed., *Human Rights of Women: National and International Perspectives* (Philadelphia: University of Pennsylvania Press, 1994). See the extensive literature cited regarding women's rights on the internet at www.law-lib.utoronto.ca/diana. See further the extensive citations to women's issues in international relations at www.umn.edu/humanrts/links/women/html.

[31] Fiona Robinson, "The Limits of a Rights Based Approach to International Ethics," in Tony Evans, ed., *Human Rights Fifty Years On: A Reappraisal* (Manchester: Manchester University Press, 1998), 58–76.

[32] In general, see Stephen H. Legomsky, *Immigration and Refugee Law and Policy*, 2nd edn. (New York: Foundation Press, 1997). See also Connie M. Ericson, "In Re Kasinga: An Expansion of the Grounds for Asylum for Women," *Houston Journal of International Law*, 20, 3 (1998), 671–694.

interpersonal relations. No doubt an ethics of care and responsibility has its place. Whether such an ethics in international relations is particularly feminine, and whether it can be specified and encouraged to better effect than the human rights discourse, are interesting questions. It is by no means certain that a rights approach must be limited to negative rights, and cannot adequately lead to minimal floors for nutrition, clothing, shelter, and health care.[33]

The second feminist critique overlaps with parts of the pragmatic liberal argument in arguing the merits of at least supplementing legal rights with action not based on rights but still oriented to the welfare of individuals. Once again we find that much of the feminist critique of human rights reflects some form of liberalism, mostly gendered pragmatic liberalism. One needs the concept of human rights, if perhaps revised to take further account of special problems of dignity and justice that pertain to women, but one may also need to go beyond rights to extra-legal or a-legal programs that do not center on adjudication of rights.

Still, a reason for legal rights is the reliability and efficacy of thinking in terms of entitlements that public authority must respect. That is precisely why Henry Dunant and then the ICRC started with the notion of charity toward those wounded in war, but quickly moved to trying to make medical assistance to the wounded a legal obligation in international law.

Controversies beyond liberalism

When considering the future of human rights, I have tried to indicate the tip of the iceberg of controversy even when one accepts the concept of human rights as a beneficial part of international relations. But there is controversy of a different order, based on a more profound critique of human rights as that notion has evolved in international relations. This second type of controversy, which takes different forms or schools of thought, is based on the shared view that individual human rights based on liberal philosophy is misguided as a means to human dignity. The dominant critique, at least for western liberals, has been by realists. But we should also note, at least in passing, the views of Marxists.[34]

---

[33] Paul Hunt, *Reclaiming Social Rights: International and Comparative Perspectives* (Aldershot: Dartmouth, 1996).

[34] It should be stressed that there are numerous approaches to understanding international relations and the place of human rights therein. A short introductory overview such as this one cannot be expected to be comprehensive. See further Scott Burchill and Andrew Linklater, eds., *Theories of International Relations* (New York: St. Martin's Press, 1996). As noted in Chapter 1, Michael Doyle has shown that one can gain many insights by concentrating on liberalism, realism, and Marxism/socialism. The present

Realism

Realism in its various versions has historically captured some prevalent features of traditional international relations. Its strong point has been its emphasis on collective egoism, as numerous political leaders, claiming to speak for a nation, have indeed acted frequently on the basis of their view of narrow self-interest. It has also been accurate in emphasizing calculations of power and balance – or more precisely distribution – of power, however elusive the objective perception of power and its distribution might prove. Such calculations have indeed been a prevalent feature of international relations. In being state-centric, realism captures much of the real strength of nationalism and national identity.

The central weakness of realism has always been its inability to specify what comprises the objective national interest, and therefore its inability to say what is the rational pursuit of that interest based on power calculations. Realism assumes the permanence of a certain nineteenth-century view of international relations in which the dominant principles are state sovereignty understood to mean independence, non-intervention in the domestic affairs of states, and the inevitability of interstate power struggles culminating in war.

Most versions of realism discount the possibility that states would see their real security and other national interests advanced by *losing* considerable independence – e.g., by joining supranational organizations. Realism discounts the possibility of the rise of important transnational interests so that the distinction between domestic structure and issues and international relations loses much of its meaning. Realism discounts the possibility of a decline if not elimination of hegemonic global war among the great powers, and thus does not contemplate the irrationality of saving one's major preoccupations for a war that will not occur – perhaps at all and certainly without great frequency.

Realism discounts the emergence of values such as real commitment to universal human rights and instead posits, in the face of considerable contradictory evidence, that states will always prefer separateness and independent policy making over advancement of human rights (or for that matter over quest for greater wealth through regulated trade or better environmental protection). Realists are prepared to look away when gross violations of human rights are committed inside states; morality and state

book follows that approach. Some authors stress not liberalism versus realism but liberalism versus communitarianism – the idea that the community, not the individual, is the proper dominant concern. All liberal orders have to deal with individual rights and autonomy versus the rights and needs of the larger community. I have covered part of this controversy when discussing "Asian values."

obligation tend to stop at national frontiers – and anyway the game of correction is not worth the candle. To realists, international liberalism, and the international human rights to which it gives rise, is a utopian snare left over from the European enlightenment with its excessive belief in human rationality, common standards, and capacity for progress.

In situations *not* characterized by intense fear, suspicion, and the classic security dilemma, however, realism misses much of the real stuff of international politics. Where states and governments do not perceive threats to the life of the nation as they have known it, they behave in ways that realism cannot anticipate or explain. Realism is largely irrelevant to international integration in Europe through the Council of Europe and European Union. After all, French fears of German power led to integration between the two, not to French marshaling of separate military power. Realism has no explanation for NATO's unified commitment to a democratic Europe, and hence to its intervention in federal Yugoslavia to protect Kosovars, save for the argument that the entire policy of intervention was to demonstrate NATO's dominance (an argument much too simple). Realism cannot explain international human rights developments over the past fifty years, except to suggest that most of the states of the world have been either hypocritical or sentimental in approving human rights norms and creating extensive diplomatic machinery for their supervision. Realists like Kissinger were out of touch with important developments in international relations when he opposed the human rights and humanitarian aspects of the 1975 Helsinki Accord, and when he came to accept those principles only as a useful bargaining tool with, and weapon against, the European communists. Even then, he was more comfortable with traditional security matters as Metternich and other nineteenth-century diplomats would have understood them.

In some types of international politics realists are relevant, but in other types they are anachronistic.[35] Realists well understand the prevalent negative correlation between war and protection of most human rights. Insecurity does indeed breed human rights violations. On the other hand, much of international relations cannot be properly understood by simple reference to "prisoner's dilemma," in which fear of insecurity is the only attitude, explaining all policies. Some states will pursue human rights abroad only when such action can be made to fit with traditional national interests. But some states in some situations will pursue human rights through international action even at the expense of certain traditional

---

[35] See further Robert O. Keohane and Joseph H. Nye, *Power and Interdependence: World Politics in Transition* (Boston: Little, Brown, 1977). In their view, realism is not very relevant to that type of international relations called complex interdependence.

interests, such as independence in policy making, hence the Council of Europe and European Union. At least sometimes they will incur some costs for the rights of others, as NATO did over Kosovo and Libya, as the British did in Sierra Leone, etc. Realists do not understand that some states, like some natural persons, wish to stand for something besides independent power, obtained and used in other than a Machiavellian process.

Marxists

The Marxist and various neo-Marxist critiques of international human rights merit a separate book. But it is accurate to say here, albeit briefly, that classical Marxists consider individual legal rights a sham in the context of economic forces and structures that prevent the effective exercise of human rights. Legal human rights on paper are supposedly negated by exploitative capitalism that leads to the accumulation of profit rather than the betterment of human beings. When large parts of the world manifest persons earning less than one dollar per day, extensive human rights in legal form are meaningless. In this view international human rights have been used more since 1945 to legitimate international capitalism than to protect human beings from predatory capitalistic states which empower their corporations.[36] There is also the view, not based on strictly economic factors, arguing that the modern push for human rights, dominated as it has been by western states, is a new form of neo-colonialism.[37]

For a classical Marxist, "the contradictions that characterize human rights reflect the conflicts inherent in capitalist society, lead to pervasive violations of those rights, and make respect for them impossible, particularly in this era of global capitalism."[38] Thus, material conditions control, exercising rights depends on having wealth, corporate for-profit rights trump individual fundamental rights, and the Universal Declaration of Rights cannot be realized as long as international relations reflects global capitalism.

There is some overlap between Marxists and certain pragmatic liberals. Both would agree that the international financial institutions such as the World Bank and the International Monetary Fund need to consider

---

[36] See, for example, Norman Lewis, "Human Rights, Law, and Democracy in an Unfree World," in Evans, ed., *Human Rights Fifty Years On*, 77–104.

[37] Makau Mutua, *Human Rights: A Political and Cultural Critique* (Philadelphia: University of Pennsylvania Press, 2002).

[38] Gary Teeple, *The Riddle of Human Rights* (Amherst, NY: Humanity Books, 2005). See also his "Karl Marx," in *Encyclopedia of Human Rights*, vol. III, 466–476.

further the human hardship caused by their structural adjustment programs. Both argue the futility of seeing and dealing with human rights apart from their socioeconomic context. Pragmatic liberals differ from Marxists in believing that regulated capitalism, and its primary global agent the transnational corporation, can be a force for progress and is not irredeemably exploitative. Pragmatic liberals also differ from Marxists in seeing in western history an effort to combine political freedom, economic freedom, and checks on gross abuses of human dignity, and not a record of unrelenting economic exploitation.

In summary of these two illiberal critiques, one can say that first of all realism has been the most important historically. Realism (meaning the varieties thereof) has been the dominant prism in the powerful western world for understanding international relations. Some realists have argued that national liberals, if rational, would not be liberal in anarchical international relations, or if they understood the evil "nature of man." Christian realists have argued, in effect, for realism with a human face (spiritually guided, of course) but that this quest leads to a perpetually unsatisfying compromise between power and morality. Second one can say that nowhere has the *practice* of Marxism led to an attractive model of human development entailing an acceptable degree of personal freedom.[39] Marxism, perhaps in the form of democratic socialism, however, would seem to have continuing relevance by reminding us of the exploitative tendencies of unregulated capitalism, and of the weakness of legal rights when divorced from certain social and economic facts – e.g., minimal achievements in education and income.

In the final analysis even most of the critics of what I have termed classical political liberalism at the close of the twentieth century do not reject entirely the concept of universal human rights. They argue for its validity, but stress various cautions, reforms, and refinements. Even Kissinger and most other realists tolerate international human rights as a necessary if unwise addition to power calculations, although they do not give personal rights high priority and they are unwilling to greatly complicate traditional diplomacy with much attention to them.[40]

Francis Fukuyama, as discussed in Chapter 1, may yet be proved correct, however, in that no theory save some type of liberalism offers much prospect of a better world in the twenty-first century. The Arab Spring

---

[39] See further Zbigniew Brzezinski, *The Grand Failure: The Birth and Death of Communism in the Twentieth Century* (New York: Scribner, 1989).

[40] In his book *Diplomacy* (New York: Simon & Schuster, 1994), Kissinger writes that pure realism is unsustainable at least in US foreign policy.

of 2011 would seem to support his view that political liberalism based on human rights is the most appealing model for organizing national societies. A caution bears repeating. If Fukuyama is read to mean support for libertarianism and minimal governance, instability is the likely result. Libertarian liberalism wants to emphasize private property as a civil right, and to elevate it to a central and absolute position in its view of the good life. But the result of this view is Dickens' England, or the USA in the era of Henry Ford. There are definitely liberal interpretations that are injurious to human dignity, as recalled particularly in Chapter 8 where the misdeeds of certain private corporations were reviewed. It is no small task to combine property rights featuring "economic freedom" with other rights and freedoms so as to produce a widely shared view of social justice or human dignity.

The big picture

Are there important and enduring patterns and correlations on the subject of human rights in international relations? The answer is yes, with awareness of limitations and constant modification through new research.[41] If we focus on rights of personal integrity such as freedom from torture, forced disappearances, summary execution, and the like, we find that the protection of these rights is positively correlated with: democracy, economic development, peace, former status as British colony, and small population size. In other words, individuals are most at risk for torture and other violations of personal integrity in populous, authoritarian, poor states, facing international or internal armed conflict, and without the restraining traditions of British heritage.

If we inquire more carefully into why democracy seems to generally reduce violations of personal integrity, research by Bruce Bueno De Mesquita and others suggests that: full democracy through the form of multiparty competitive elections is necessary to get this effect; more limited forms of democracy short of multiparty elections do not produce the same effect; and the notion of real accountability to the electorate seems to be the key to the process.[42]

Such general trends are then crosscut by others. For example, economic development in Arab-Islamic states does not have a positive

---

[41] For an overview, see David P. Forsythe and Patrice C. McMahon, eds., *Human Rights and Diversity: Area Studies Revisited* (Lincoln: University of Nebraska Press, 2003), especially chs. 1 and 2, and the conclusion.

[42] Bruce Bueno De Mesquita, "Thinking Inside the Box: A Closer Look at Democracy and Human Rights," *International Studies Quarterly*, 49, 3 (September 2005), from 439.

correlation with protection of women's rights. Particular cultural factors intervene to block the normally beneficial impact of economic development.

Can we say for sure what produces democracy, with its civil and political rights? No, but there are some correlations between economic wealth and sustaining democracy. According to Adam Przeworski and Fernando Limongi, democracy does not last very long in the face of economic adversity.[43] During the Cold War more or less, a democratic polity with a per capita income of $1,500 lasted eight years or less; a per capita income up to $3,000 increased the longevity of a democratic state to an average of 18 years; above a per capita income of $6,000, democratic sustainability was largely assured. Against this background, it made complete sense that in 2004 citizens in relatively poor states like Russia or several states in the Western Hemisphere expressed considerable sympathy for a return to authoritarian government, given that existing democratic (or partially democratic) governments had compiled a poor record on increasing per capita income.[44]

One could group states in different ways, and inquire into correlations about different rights and types of rights, but it was clear that some insights into the fate of rights could be obtained through careful research.[45] One of the most persistent conclusions out of this type of research was that it was futile to focus on civil and political rights without regard to their socioeconomic and cultural context. From the time of Weimar Germany in the 1920s and 1930s to Afghanistan after the Taliban, holding elections would only mean so much over time. Without attention to economic development and equitable distribution of the fruits of that development, and without attention to cultural factors impeding equity if not equality, elections would not necessarily contribute to sustained human dignity.

One might recall at this point that the UN General Assembly has repeatedly endorsed the notion that civil, political, economic, social, and cultural rights are interdependent and equally important. (At the same time, I noted that the same body had given priority to certain rights in the construction of international criminal courts and in endorsing the

[43] Adam Przeworski and Fernando Limongi, "Modernization: Theories and Facts," *World Politics*, 49, 2 (January 1997), 155–183.

[44] Warren Hoge, "Latin Americans Are Nostalgic for Strongman Rule," *International Herald Tribune*, April 21, 2004.

[45] See Forsythe and McMahon, eds., *Human Rights and Diversity*, especially the chapter by David L. Richards. And recall his work with David Cingranelli, "The Cingranelli and Richards (CIRI) Human Rights Data Project," regarding the practice of rights during 1981–2006.

notion of R2P – namely genocide, crimes against humanity, and major war crimes, and in the case of R2P ethnic cleansing.)

Final thoughts

In the early 1980s the conclusion to one overview of human rights in international relations started with a discussion of Stalinism in the Soviet Union and finished with a discussion of apartheid in South Africa.[46] In the late 1990s neither the Soviet Union nor legally segregated South Africa existed. Things do change, and sometimes in mostly progressive fashion.[47] That is one reason for a guarded optimism about the future of human rights.

Both European Stalinism and white racism in southern Africa are spent forces. Each yielded to persistent criticism and concerted opposition over many decades. Along the way elites in Moscow and Pretoria were staunchly committed to gross violations of human rights, albeit rationalized in the name of some "higher good." In the case of communism it was the quest for a classless utopia. In the case of apartheid it was betterment through separate development. Prospects for radical change often seemed bleak. And yet a historical perspective shows a certain progress.

To be sure, human rights violations remain both in former European communist states and in South Africa. Far too many in both areas lack adequate food, clothing, shelter, and health care mandated by internationally recognized human rights. Corrupt judges and police officers make a mockery of many civil rights, as does rampant crime – much of it organized transnationally. In some areas free and fair elections are not secure. Nor are minorities. The plain fact is that in Europe, for example, the political changes of 1989–1991 proved generally progressive but led to semi-autocracy in Russia and a bloodbath in former Yugoslavia. The unpleasant fact is that even progressive revolutions that improve the general condition of human rights leave us with new human rights problems to confront. To paraphrase an old saying, the price of sustained human dignity is eternal vigilance about protecting human rights.

Certainly from the perspective of NATO states, the end of European communism was replaced in short order by the threat of militant Islamists. If anything, restrictions on civil human rights increased after

---

[46] David P. Forsythe, *Human Rights and World Politics* (Lincoln: University of Nebraska Press, 1983), ch. 6.

[47] See further especially Paul Gordon Lauren, *The Evolution of International Human Rights: Visions Seen* (Philadelphia: University of Pennsylvania Press, 1998).

the Al Qaeda attacks on the USA in 2001 – and related terrorist attacks in Spain, the United Kingdom, and elsewhere. Not just the USA but many NATO states responded to the new security threats with policies of enforced disappearances and mistreatment of security prisoners on a scale unknown during the Cold War.

From the perspective of most developing countries, the end of the Cold War and even the rise of militant Islamists did not change the challenges of achieving sustainable human development and the protection of the human rights entailed in that concept.

And so the quest for better protection of individual and collective human rights continues. All human rights victories are partial, since the perfectly rights-protective society has yet to appear. The end of Stalinism in the Czech Republic seems to have done little to change discrimination against the Roma in that country. Some human rights victories are pyrrhic, since the *ancien régime* can look relatively good in historical perspective. Tito's Yugoslavia did not implement anything close to the full range of internationally recognized civil and political rights. But it did not engage in mass murder, mass misery, ethnic cleansing, and systematic rape as a weapon of war. These things did appear, however, in both Bosnia and Kosovo in the 1990s.

A balanced perspective would continue to note achievements, however partial, as well as challenges. The Arab Spring of 2011, in which significant parts of Middle Eastern societies demanded more democracy and human rights, was one such major development. In place of widespread assumptions about how liberalism continued to bypass much of the Arab world in particular, one saw broadly based demands for the same human rights as practiced in other parts of the world. In an era of real time communication through social and traditional media, one found pent-up demands for implementation of the same values that had characterized other rights-protective societies. The fact that progress was uneven – e.g., more in Egypt than in Syria – cannot detract from the ample evidence of the broad appeal of internationally recognized human rights in that part of the world. The profound assertion of demands was not for Islamist militancy but for polities compatible with the Universal Declaration of Human Rights.

The various levels of action for human rights – whether global, regional, national, or sub-national – were not likely to wither away because of lack of human rights violations with which to deal. Pursuing liberalism in a realist world is no simple task. And yet in broad historical perspective one could note some achievements. Even within the confining structures of a nation-state system of international relations prone to insistent insecurity and competition, there was evident room for agency on behalf of human rights.

Discussion questions

- Do the past fifty years show that serious concern for personal rights can indeed improve the human condition in the state system of international relations?
- If one compares the Congo during King Leopold's time with the Democratic Congo (formerly Zaire) today, has anything changed about the human condition?
- When is it appropriate, if ever, to grant immunity for past violations of human rights, and otherwise to avoid legal proceedings about human rights violations, for the sake of improving the human condition?
- Are the demands for a third generation of human rights to peace, development, and a healthy environment well considered?
- Do internationally recognized human rights require radical change so as to properly protect women's dignity?
- Even after the political demise of European Marxism, are Marxists correct that capitalism and the transnational corporation are inherently exploitative of labor? What social values can markets advance (e.g., efficiency?), and what social values can they not advance (e.g., equity?)?
- Should one be optimistic or pessimistic about the future of human rights in international relations?

SUGGESTIONS FOR FURTHER READING

Alston, Philip, "Conjuring Up New Human Rights: A Proposal for Quality Control," *American Journal of International Law*, 78, 3 (July 1984), 607–621. A plea for a moratorium on more human rights until protection improves for those already recognized.
Boyle, Kevin, and Juliet Sheen, eds., *Freedom of Religion and Belief: A World Report* (London: Routledge, 1997). An encyclopedia on the subject.
Brzezinski, Zbigniew, *The Grand Failure: The Birth and Death of Communism in the Twentieth Century* (New York: Scribner, 1989). An overview of what went wrong particularly with European communism, written in engaging style by the National Security Advisor to President Carter.
Cook, Rebecca J., ed., *Human Rights of Women: National and International Perspectives* (Philadelphia: University of Pennsylvania Press, 1994). A good and broad coverage of feminist perspectives on human rights.
Forsythe, David P., and Patrice C. McMahon, *Human Rights and Diversity: Area Studies Revisited* (Lincoln: University of Nebraska Press, 2003). A collection

of essays studying the interplay of universal rights and global trends with factors particular to certain areas and regions.

Franck, Thomas M., "Is Personal Freedom a Western Value?," *American Journal of International Law*, 91, 4 (October 1997), 593–627. Suggests that the West has no monopoly on the desire for personal freedom.

Gormley, W. Paul, *Human Rights and the Environment: The Need for International Co-operation* (Leiden: W. W. Sijthoff, 1976). An early study based on the premise that we need a third-generation human right to a healthy environment.

Hiskes, Richard P., *The Human Right to a Green Future: Environmental Rights and Intergenerational Justice* (Cambridge and New York: Cambridge University Press, 2008). An argument for more attention to ecology based on the human rights of unborn generations.

Hochschild, Adam, *King Leopold's Ghost: A Story of Greed, Terror, and Heroism in Colonial Africa* (Boston: Houghton Mifflin, 1998). A gripping history of the lack of human rights in Central Africa when the Congo was the personal fiefdom of the King of Belgium.

Hocking, B., *Catalytic Diplomacy* (Leicester: Centre for Diplomatic Studies, 1996). Argues that in the modern world what governments frequently do is organize others for agreement and action, rather than establish a foreign policy completely independent from other actors.

Ignatieff, Michael, *The Warrior's Honor: Ethnic War and the Modern Conscience* (New York: Metropolitan, 1997). A cosmopolitan and Renaissance man reflects on whether humane limits can be applied to ethnic war, arguing for the importance of traditional conceptions such as military honor.

Johansen, Robert C., *The National Interest and the Human Interest: An Analysis of US Foreign Policy* (Princeton: Princeton University Press, 1980). Shows clearly that if one starts with realist principles of state interest, one winds up with different policies than if one starts with liberal principles of human interest.

Kagan, Robert, *Of Paradise and Power: America and Europe in the New World Order* (New York: Vintage, 2004). Supposedly the Europeans are interested in human rights and international law and organization, while the USA is interested in the use of power to protect national security in a hostile world.

Keohane, Robert O., and Joseph H. Nye, *Power and Interdependence: World Politics in Transition* (Boston: Little, Brown, 1977). A major study arguing that there are different types of international relations. Realism may be appropriate to some, liberalism or pragmatic liberalism to others. Argues that realism is less and less appropriate to contemporary international relations.

Pogge, Thomas, *World Poverty and Human Rights: Cosmopolitan Responsibilities and Reforms* (Cambridge: Polity, 2002). A leading philosopher reflects on, and provides data about, poverty, hunger, and human rights.

Slaughter, Anne-Marie, *A New World Order* (Princeton: Princeton University Press, 2005). The former Dean of the Princeton Woodrow Wilson School and former State Department official in the Obama Administration argues that national authorities are cooperating with international courts in a way that is already producing considerable transnational protection of certain human rights.

Teeple, Gary, *The Riddle of Human Rights* (Amherst, NY: Humanity Books, 2005). A clearly argued Marxist analysis.

Towns, Anne E., *Women and States: Norms and Hierarchies in International Society* (Cambridge: Cambridge University Press, 2010). A transnational analysis linking the position of women inside states to various issues in foreign policy and international relations.

Index

Page numbers followed by t indicate tables; those followed by n indicate footnotes.